AFRICAN WOMEN

AFRICAN WOMEN

Early History to the 21st Century

Kathleen Sheldon

Indiana University Press

This book is a publication of

Indiana University Press
Office of Scholarly Publishing
Herman B Wells Library 350
1320 East 10th Street
Bloomington, Indiana 47405 USA

iupress.indiana.edu

Manufactured in the United States of America

Cataloging information is available from the Library of Congress.

ISBN 978-0-253-02716-0 (cloth)
ISBN 978-0-253-02722-1 (paperback)
ISBN 978-0-253-02731-3 (ebook)

1 2 3 4 5 22 21 20 19 18 17

Contents

Acknowledgments

As with any big project, this book has been years in the making and has accumulated huge debts to many colleagues and friends. In 1975, as I began my graduate study in African history, I enrolled in one of the first courses offered in the United States on African women, a seminar on African women and social change taught by Margaret Strobel. We were barely able to find ten weeks' worth of readings, but nonetheless, we held informative and lively discussions. By the time I was teaching similar courses in the 1980s and 1990s, the field had grown enormously, and there was an abundance of new articles, books, and collections to assign to students.

This textbook is completely dependent on the multitude of scholars who completed significant research and publications on African women's history. The wider cohort of feminist historians has been my community for decades, with too many friends in the Women's Caucus of the African Studies Association and elsewhere to name individually. African women scholars in particular brought new rigor and insight to African women's history, and I treasure their research and their friendship. Those who are directly cited are included in the bibliography, but they represent only a fraction of the books and articles I have been reading, enjoying, and debating for forty years. Writing this text would have been an impossible task without such a wealth of work to draw on.

Those who read and critiqued various early drafts saved me from embarrassing errors and contributed substantially to helping me focus and organize the masses of stories from across time and place. My husband, Steve Tarzynski, has lived with every step of my writing, and he was the first to read the entire manuscript when it was a messy draft. My son, Ben Tarzynski, had some helpful comments when he critiqued one chapter as I was making final revisions. Margot Lovett read an early chapter and later the entire text; Edna Bay also read the entire manuscript, and they both had many critical but helpful comments and insightful suggestions. I have gained so much from ongoing conversations about African history with Margot, Eddy, and Laura Mitchell as we have shared meals and book discussions over several years; their support and friendship undergirds much of my writing. The two colleagues who read the manuscript for Indiana University Press (an anonymous reader and Judith Van Allen) had observations that were immensely valuable as I worked through the final revisions.

I offer special thanks to several individuals and organizations who shared their photographs gratis for publication in this book; they are credited in the captions. Dee Mortensen, the editor for African topics at Indiana University Press, has been both patient with my delays and endlessly encouraging. I also appreciated the collegiality of sister scholars at the Center for the Study of Women at the University of California, Los Angeles. For many years, the center has supported research by independent scholars, and I was pleased to receive a Tillie Olsen Research Affiliates Grant for 2015–2016, which helped with costs related to producing this textbook, including acquiring some of the images.

The women of Africa, especially in Mozambique, inspired me to write their history. The stories of their work, their political actions, and their commitment to their families and communities have too often been marginalized or ignored. This book is my effort to bring their histories to a wider audience, with gratitude for all they have done.

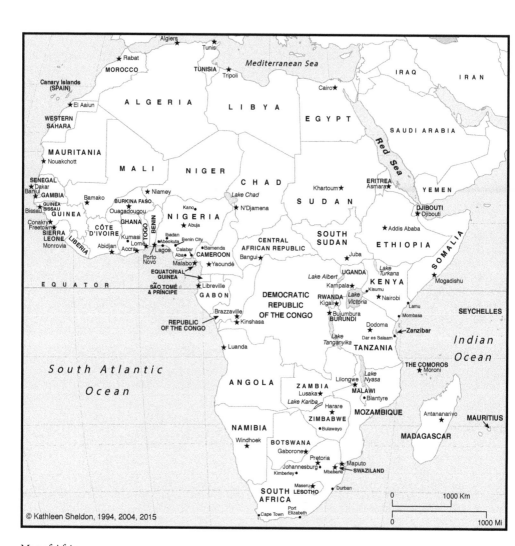

Map of Africa, 2015.

Introduction

AFRICAN WOMEN: EARLY History to the 21st Century presents a history of Africa with women as the starting point. The history of African women is a vital and successful field of study, growing from a small number of books and articles published in the 1960s and 1970s to the now thriving research that covers a huge range of places, times, and topics that has been achieved in the twenty-first century. In this book, coverage of important events and individuals documents women's involvement in critical episodes in African history, and it demonstrates how women have been central to well-known aspects of African history that are often seen solely from a male perspective. The inclusion of topics such as marriage, motherhood, women's work, and women as religious and political leaders, establishes the reality that knowledge of women's history is essential to making sense of African history more broadly.

Over many years of teaching and writing about African women's history, I encountered problems in two areas. Many textbooks on African history have neglected and marginalized women. Women are nearly absent in some books, and when they are included it is often in very limited and passive roles. At the same time, while the field of African women's history is strong, there has not been a textbook focused on African women that comprehensively covers the geographic, topical, and temporal breadth necessary to offer students and scholars a meaningful engagement with women's history. Many excellent books on African women's history are about a single country, a limited time period or topic, or are collections of articles that include a variety of approaches by different contributors. Two books that have been used widely in classrooms are now twenty years old, and they do not include the important new publications that have expanded and given nuance to research on African women. Given those issues and limitations in available African history texts, *African Women: Early History to the 21st Century* is designed to accomplish two goals.

My first objective was to write a comprehensive narrative of African women's history by bringing together information that is usually scattered and narrowly focused. Naturally, it is not possible to be completely inclusive because there is far too much research and information to easily compress into one book. African women's history is a vast topic that embraces a wide variety of societies in over fifty countries with different geographies, social customs, religions, and historical situations. Women enter the story with differences in their ages, marital statuses, education, work experiences, ethnicities, and rural or urban backgrounds.

I have sought to include stories and histories that address the breadth of women's experiences, with sections on all regions of the continent and representing the variety of women's circumstances. I also approached the material as a historian and therefore, as much as possible, followed a chronological format while demonstrating how social and political change progressed over the centuries.

My second aim was to show that fully understanding the history of the continent requires knowledge of women's contributions to their communities and their accomplishments in their families. As scholars of women's history have argued for other world areas, it is not enough to prove that women were present and were agents in their own lives. Women's presence and agency have profound implications for the ways in which history is interpreted and understood. Historical experience is not only found with political rulers and conflict, but includes families, household work, and women's involvement in their societies. Women were, of course, engaged in politics and conflict, and knowing about their participation in those areas alters how those topics are understood. The historical narrative is completely changed when women's religious roles, labor, options for marriage and childbearing, and access to political authority are the beginning point for that history. This book tells the story of women and advances African history more broadly by demonstrating the central place women have occupied in making that history.

Knowing women's history will make it possible to better understand where African women stand today. Women once had greater power in many African societies where they were able to wield both individual and collective authority, sometimes with greater success than others. As this book shows, women still draw on older forms of exercising female collective power, often developing innovative approaches out of their historical experiences in order to deal with new situations. Some patterns in the division of labor, marital options, and other gendered relations were more fluid in the past, and they may still be more fluid than is usually recognized. While those social structures have changed, some aspects have also persisted, such as women's focus on farming as the basis of their economic contributions, as well as their expectation that motherhood is a source of power.

Book Organization

This book begins with early history, an era which yields few or no written records, though other sources are employed to discover new information about peoples' lives in the eras before human events were documented. Drawing on some innovative recent research, the first chapter introduces material about how women in early societies in Africa worked, organized their families, and developed communities. Archeology has helped us grasp the roles of women in hunter-gatherer societies. Historical linguistics has brought insight to notions of motherhood and family, as well as to more concrete topics such as agricultural cultivation and iron smelting, in pre-literate eras. Concepts such as matrilineal descent, bridewealth, and polygyny are introduced in chapter 1 as well, along with an overview of African religious practices, including the early history of women-centered initiation rites. Due to the nature of available sources, we often know about individual elite women and women who were rulers, such as Amina, who governed a wide region of West Africa in the sixteenth century, and Nzinga, who resisted seventeenth-century Portuguese incursions in the area that became Angola. Despite the scarce and scattered sources for early African history, historians are able to determine many aspects of women's everyday lives and elite politics for the centuries before European colonialism.

Chapter 2 moves forward to the seventeenth and eighteenth centuries, and it investigates women's roles as European contact began to have an impact on African societies. Women traders were essential to the expansion of West African trading networks, and they often acted as intermediaries between European merchants and African communities. Slavery and international commerce rose in prominence, and the wide variations of women's experience of slavery are examined in both the development of the international slave trade, and in local institutions such as the enslaved women who were soldiers for the king of Dahomey in West Africa. Chapter 2 also examines women's involvement in international trade in Mozambique and women's resistance to Portuguese attempts to convert them to Catholicism in Ethiopia. Finally, building on the section on initiation rites in chapter 1, this chapter introduces further information about women's societies, organizations that offered a parallel political and religious structure to men's groups for women in some communities.

Chapter 3 returns to the theme of religion, moving into the nineteenth century with analyses of local beliefs among the Igbo in West Africa and the Luba in Central Africa. Those beliefs placed women at the center of a society's spirituality, with attention to the complementary female and male components in local religions. The nineteenth-century expansion of both Islam and Christianity had important effects on women's lives. This chapter introduces female Islamic leaders, including Nana Asma'u in West Africa and Mwana Kupona in East Africa, whose adherence to Islam and activities in spreading the Muslim faith were key factors in nineteenth-century African history. Their stories also provide an important counter-narrative to common Western misunderstandings of Muslim women as oppressed and secluded. The arrival of Christian missionaries had an impact on women in the realms of Western-style education and new ideas about family formation. Case studies of girls' schooling in nineteenth-century Sierra Leone and South Africa emphasize the long history of educated African women and indicate how missionaries were able to exert their influence.

Chapter 3 then continues the history of African women in the nineteenth century with a further investigation of slavery and what it meant for women across the continent, with attention to the work that enslaved women performed and the particular vulnerability of women to capture and enslavement. The notorious life story of Sara Baartman (also known as the Hottentot Venus), who was taken from South Africa to be placed on display in England and France, exemplifies an extreme case of that vulnerability. Finally, this chapter looks at southern Africa in the 1800s, with sections on some women leaders who emerged during difficult times.

Chapter 4 introduces the period of intense colonialism, assessing the century between 1850 and 1945. This period offers a much greater availability of documentation and historical analysis than during earlier history. Colonialism changed women's work and family lives, with results that were often negative as women found their precolonial status eroded. A variety of case studies of women's work under colonialism assesses cocoa production in Ghana, changes in access to land for agricultural cultivation in Kenya, the development of mining compounds in southern Africa, changes in the long-standing market trade of West African women, and the introduction of African forms of prostitution.

Still in chapter 4, the next section discusses changes in religious practice as European missions became established in Tanzania, the Congo, and southern Africa. Transformations in marital expectations and customs were seen in Lagos, Nigeria, while independent churches, often led by women, grew out of the intersection of African beliefs and European proselytizing. Finally, this chapter investigates some important aspects of women's health and sexuality as Europeans began to try to control women through new laws about female genital mutilation, motherhood, and health education more generally.

Chapter 5 turns to the resistance and protests that involved women in the first half of the twentieth century, as they reacted to the losses and change that they faced. That story is illustrated with brief profiles of women who rose to prominence in the struggle to end colonialism and reclaim women's rights. In an array of actions led by women, the chapter presents female leaders in eastern and southern Africa. Some were spiritual leaders, such as Nyabingi in Uganda and Nehanda/Charwe in Zimbabwe, who drew on their roles as mediums and healers to struggle against European colonialism. Others, including Mary Nyanjiru in Kenya, turned to more modern forms of resistance, rejecting new taxation and forced labor. In the Maji Maji rebellion in Tanzania, women were not the leaders, but research has shown how the seeds of the revolt were found in women's agricultural practices. Across the continent, women demonstrated against unwanted Western intrusions, using forms of protest that had long been invoked to protect women's rights. South African women demonstrated as early as 1913 against the expansion of pass laws to women, while women in Aba, Nigeria, staged an anti-tax protest in 1929 that came to be known as the Women's War. While chapter 4 showed how women experienced increased oppression under colonialism, chapter 5 supplies extensive evidence of their refusal to accept such new limitations.

Chapter 6 carries that story forward to the years of committed nationalism that marked politics across the continent in the 1950s and 1960s. In West Africa in the years after World War II, women engaged again in anti-tax protests, and joined nationalist parties where they fought for both African independence and women's rights. East African women were likewise members and activists in nationalist parties in Tanzania and Kenya. The Kenyan Mau Mau insurgency involved women in a variety of activities, and it is also noted for the imprisonment of thousands of women in deplorable conditions. Women leaders, such as Bibi Titi Mohammed in Tanzania, Hannah Kudjoe in Ghana, and Funmilayo Ransome-Kuti in Nigeria, influenced women and their various nationalist organizations. By the 1960s, most African nations were independent, though the Portuguese colonies, including Mozambique and Angola, continued to fight for majority rule until the 1970s, and Zimbabwe only became independent in 1980. The campaign to end apartheid in South Africa continued until the 1990s. Women were centrally involved in all of those liberation struggles.

The final chapters focus on women in independent Africa. Chapter 7 considers women's work and international development projects, as women continued to struggle to regain and retain their historic roles in managing their own lives and communities. Women's daily lives were affected by increased urbanization, the spread of HIV/AIDS and other issues concerning their health and sexuality, and the introduction of World Bank structural adjustment policies. The years following independence also were a time of increased cultural activity in literature, music, art, and sport, as women's artistic and leisure production expanded.

Women's involvement in modern political structures, as well as their participation in conflicts that occurred in too many places, are the topics covered in chapter 8. Beginning with the influence of the United Nations Decade for Women, especially a significant 1985 meeting in Nairobi, the chapter examines how women participated in the spread of democratization, with case studies of Ghana, South Africa, and Kenya. Women suffered in several conflicts, while also actively working for peace, in Sierra Leone, Liberia, Rwanda, and the Democratic Republic of the Congo. Women moved into new leadership roles, whether as first ladies, prime ministers, or presidents, and women's organizations tackled such issues as citizenship, women and media, and trade unions.

Chapter 9 brings the history of African women into the twenty-first century, with attention to current events and women's ongoing resistance to threats to their well-being. Women reacted to new topics such as human rights, land grabbing, and lesbianism, and they protested events that impinged on their lives, including rigged elections in Côte d'Ivoire and oil companies' environmental damage in the Niger Delta.

The book is organized along clear chronological lines, which should facilitate using it in a wide variety of classes. Either the entire text or selected chapters can be assigned in traditional African history courses, as well as in comparative women's studies classrooms. The book could form the core reading for a course on women or gender in Africa, with additional selected readings assigned to expand on specific topics. Any single section within a chapter would work as a prompt for research papers and classroom essays, along with the sources that are listed as footnotes for each chapter and cited in full in the bibliography at the back of the book. At certain points in the narrative, I have indicated when a topic is discussed elsewhere in the text, to assist in connecting the discussion between different time periods. Many issues such as religion, slavery, women's work, marriage and family, health, and political leadership, among others, recur as changes in African experiences shifted over time. While it may not be necessary to read the chapters in order, it would be helpful for readers to understand women's earlier roles in order to more fully appreciate how those roles changed over time.

Throughout the book women from a variety of backgrounds are profiled as individuals and are seen working together in organizations and communities. With a wealth of women to choose from, I have included those whose accomplishments had an impact on their societies and whose stories illuminate different aspects of African history.

For students seeking other sources, I recommend my own reference work, *Historical Dictionary of Women in Sub-Saharan Africa*, available in a second edition (2016), which includes an extensive bibliography organized by topic.[1] The online subscription reference source, *Oxford Bibliographies in African Studies*, includes many articles on women in an annotated bibliographic format.[2] Many documents and sources written or composed by African women can be found in the *Women Writing Africa* collections, published by the Feminist Press.[3]

Women flourished and were able to become accomplished leaders and wealthy businesswomen, while at the same time others suffered and lived in poverty. Issues that caused rifts in society, such as class differences, religious affiliation, and language and ethnic variations, also applied to women. Women were slaves and slave owners; they actively participated in marriage negotiations and they were forced into arranged marriages while still girls; they barely provided for themselves by selling peanuts along the roadside and they managed international trading networks; they cultivated food in small rural garden plots, and they sold imported cloth in urban markets; they were required to serve at religious shrines, and they founded influential independent churches; they were kept out of formal schooling, and they earned doctorates.

While women as a group were oppressed by patriarchal traditions and structures, many individuals were able to find the space to develop their own interests. In various African communities, women's and men's roles were recognized as complementary. The gender division of labor might assign different tasks to men and to women, but both women and men were viewed as essential to the completion of those tasks, and their cooperation was required in order to support family and community well-being. Those factors were present in African women's history, and they have continued to inform their presence in the modern world.

African Women: Early History to the 21st Century provides an up-to-date and comprehensive guide to major issues in African women's history. While African women are often only viewed as oppressed and immobilized by poverty, this book tells a more expansive and more accurate narrative of initiative, resilience, and success. Readers will find stories about historic women and their contributions, evidence for the central role women played in African history, and a greater understanding of the course of African history across the continent and across centuries.

Notes

1. Sheldon, *Historical Dictionary of Women in Sub-Saharan Africa*.

2. Spear, ed., *Oxford Bibliographies in African Studies*. This source includes several articles specifically on women, is regularly updated, and continues to expand with new entries.

3. Daymond, Driver, and Meintjes, eds. *Women Writing Africa: The Southern Region*; Lihamba, et al., eds. *Women Writing Africa: The Eastern Region*; Sutherland-Addy and Diaw, eds. *Women Writing Africa: West Africa and the Sahel*.

AFRICAN WOMEN

1 Women and Gender in Africa before 1700

THE EARLY CENTURIES of African civilization and community are the most difficult to study, and it is complicated and frustrating at times to find information about women in early African history. Yet recent advances in historical research, involving the expanded use of historical linguistics and new approaches in archaeology and art history, have brought greater insight into gender and women during a time when there was little to no European contact. While some documents exist, they are scarce, and the earliest written sources from European visitors tend to focus on unusual elite women, with the day-to-day activities of the vast majority of African women remaining obscured.

Nonetheless, the evidence points toward women's central role in their societies and their leadership potential, especially in communities that followed matrilineal lines of succession. Sources also detail the impact of female decision-making regarding agriculture, family configuration, and religious beliefs. Women were involved in the economy from the earliest times, particularly through their work cultivating crops and participating in local and long-distance trade networks. They were also likely responsible for items essential to community well-being, such as making cooking pots and introducing food preparation methods. Despite the crucial nature of women's contributions, notably as mothers to future generations, they were rarely recognized with a public form of authority. Though African settlements were more often led by men, women frequently played an essential advisory role, and at times they were recognized as chiefs.

The significant role of women in organizing their communities and ensuring the continuity of their families and societies is a critical point of departure for understanding African history. Women's choices and activities shaped the ways in which African societies developed over the following centuries.

Women in Early African History

Research into early African history, referring to the centuries prior to 1500, has uncovered some information about African societies, though frequently such material is not specifically gendered.[1] Using innovative methods such as historical linguistics and archaeology, scholars can discover specifics about early African communities. Historical linguistics is a research method that traces the development of language and the introduction of terminology to analyze the presence of certain material goods and particular social practices. Generally, however, while such studies demonstrate that early peoples in the Great Lakes Region of central Africa grew millet, yams, and bananas, they cannot prove that agriculture or food preparation was specifically women's work or men's work. A close investigation of language and ethnicity from the perspective of women's roles in families and as religious leaders illuminates our understanding of social relationships more generally. For instance, describing the linguistic history of terms referring to mothers helps historians understand early family formations. Researchers combine insights from historical linguistics and archaeology to develop ideas about motherhood, early cultivation, and religious beliefs that present some sense of what women's lives might have been like.

Archaeologists have studied housing, farming techniques, and tool and equipment manufacturing based in part on remnants of settlements and artifacts, but again, they cannot always state whether such tasks were the responsibility of men or women. Historical evidence reveals how people in the northeastern regions of the continent developed pottery as early as 9000 to 8000 BCE and how that technological innovation allowed them to use local grains such as sorghum and pearl millet to make porridge, a food that became a staple that was supplemented with vegetables and meat. The difficulty is that the evidence can show how bananas, for instance, became an important crop in the area now part of Uganda, but it cannot definitively demonstrate the gender division of labor.[2] Nevertheless, it is quite plausible that women prepared and cultivated food, along with making pots and other tools needed for that work in the early eras of human activity.

The earliest millennia brought some key developments in human society, including the domestication of cattle, sheep, and goats in northern regions of the continent. Although many communities pursued a nomadic life, for others, caring for livestock on a regular basis required digging wells and building more permanent settlements. That in turn affected the housing style, which by 7000 BCE was typically a family compound of multiple structures surrounded by thorn-bush fencing. Along rivers, lakes, and seacoasts, other communities were becoming expert at fishing as the basis for their livelihoods. People were also making progress in the domestication of plants for consumption and other uses. Spindles for spinning cultivated cotton into thread dating back to 5000 BCE have been found.

In West Africa the earliest agricultural communities relied on tubers such as yams, which were grown by planting a section of the yam itself, rather than propagating seeds. They also nurtured tree crops, notably oil palm and raffia palm. The latter was used to make palm wine and as a fiber to make clothing and other household supplies. The main domesticated animal was the guinea fowl.

Southern Africa supported nomadic groups of hunters and gatherers, with settled agricultural communities developing slowly over millennia as northern cultivators expanded into forested areas and planted crops in savannas, gradually moving south across the continent. Africa remained the least densely populated region in the world. While there were a few areas of concentrated populations in towns and cities, most Africans lived in widely dispersed villages and small-scale settlements that supported localized, nonhierarchical political and social structures.

Using the study of historical linguistics, researchers have found that terms related to life cycle events have origins as early as 3000 to 1000 BCE. It appears that boys were circumcised as part of initiation rites, while girls were not. Girls participated in ceremonies marking the onset of puberty when they became "young women," and following the birth of their first child, which brought them into the status of adult women. The absence of linguistic evidence for marriage as a key event in women's lives suggested that marital bonds may have been weak. However, the ability to become pregnant, which was signaled by the beginning of menstruation, and pregnancy itself resulting in the birth of new members of the clan were significant since those changes in biological status marked the continuity and possible expansion of the community.[3]

Rock art paintings found in the Western Cape region of southern Africa frequently included human figures. The paintings are ancient, predating the earliest settled communities that appeared at the beginning of the Common Era. The artists in many cases were careful to distinguish men from women by showing exaggerated sexual characteristics (penises on men, breasts and large buttocks on women). The paintings show men with their hunting bows and quivers and a few women with the digging sticks they used to gather roots and other foods, though the most common images are of groups or lines of people, possibly involved in ritual dancing or other community activities.[4]

Hunting and Gathering

The earliest human societies were most likely based on gathering foods that grew in the wild and on hunting animals, with more settled agriculture and herding activities developing gradually over many centuries. There was no sharp division between settled agriculturalists and nomadic societies based on gathering. The boundary that divided hunting and gathering groups from nomadic pastoralists was also fluid, as both groups moved around on a seasonal basis to find food and water, and gatherers at times kept small numbers of cattle, goats, or sheep.

The conventional discussion of such groups described men as hunters and women as gatherers, a depiction that positioned men as more important in such societies, based on an assumption that the meat caught by male hunters was the primary food source. While it is likely that there was a gender division of labor, based in part on the need for women to bear children and care for them during the earliest months of breastfeeding, research does not support such a strict division between women's and men's work. Studies focused on women found that men also gathered and women sometimes hunted, particularly for smaller animals and birds. Women's hunting activities included traveling to seek animals, as well as setting traps and attracting desired animals and birds so that they could be caught through more passive methods. In addition to understanding that hunting was not only a male activity, analysis has shown that daily meals and the bulk of the diet in the family and community relied on women's foraging and food preparation of grains, nuts, fruits, eggs, and other foods, with meat supplying an occasional source of protein rather than daily sustenance.

Many societies changed over time, but such change was not necessarily perceived as a positive development or as steady progress to a more "civilized" social order. Hunting and gathering communities were particularly suited to their environments, especially as seen in their use of more simple technologies. Societies based on hunting and gathering that continue to exist have usually been found in some of the most difficult climates on earth, in areas where settled agriculture was difficult to sustain. In Africa, such regions included the desert areas of southern Africa, as well as the densely wooded rain forests of central Africa. At the same time, those societies were not static.

Twentieth-century examples of such societies may provide clues to the past but should not be considered exactly the same as societies from past millennia. A more variable division of labor was often related to less complex social and political structures. Hunters and gatherers typically had very small-scale, egalitarian and flexible formations, with few tasks being considered only men's or only women's responsibility. Where there was little stratification along political or economic lines, gender constructions were also less hierarchical.

These basic factors persisted among the Aka peoples of the forests of the Central African Republic in the early twenty-first century. Women were sometimes seen hunting with a knife or spear, with a baby in a sling at their sides. The Aka practiced net hunting, and that was often a task done by the whole family. Men joined their wives in collecting mushrooms, wild nuts, and forest tubers. One woman told how her husband and family would praise her for her bravery when she went alone to dig for yams in the forest, where she risked encountering dangerous wild animals. Fathers spent much of their time caring for their children, more than was found in any other human society that has been studied. The near absence of a gendered division of labor was reflected in an extremely nonhierarchical social order.[5]

In addition to comparisons with modern hunting and gathering groups such as the Aka or the San in southwestern Africa, studies of early hunting and gathering groups have drawn information from archaeology. Evidence found at sites

Fig. 1.1 South African rock painting showing women with bored stones weighting their digging sticks; the original art was painted directly onto rock face circa 1000 BCE. Source: Patricia Vinnicombe, *People of the Eland: Rock Paintings of the Drakensberg Bushmen as a Reflection of Their Life and Thought* (University of Natal Press, 1976), 276.

where people lived in the distant past is highly scientific, relying on using isotopes to date particular findings and microscopically studying tools, human remains, animal bones, and food refuse such as seeds and shells. The interpretation of that evidence is often contested among archaeologists, and it rarely provides an exact portrait of how early peoples organized their societies and lived from day to day.

For instance, studies revealed that stones shaped into smooth ovals with a hole bored through the center were often made by women for use in their gathering activities. A digging stick could be fitted into the center hole of the stone, which would then give weight to the stick and facilitate women's work of digging for roots, water sources, and other requirements for the desert-dwelling San. Bored stones found in the region have been dated as twenty thousand years old, though San women were still observed making and using such stones in the twentieth century. While bored stones may also have been used as weapons and as a hunting tool by men, they were certainly among the earliest known tools used by women in collecting food.[6] They might also have been used in ceremonies in which women beat on the ground with the stone in order to communicate with spiritual leaders and ancestors.

Among the Namaqua, a Khoekhoe group in southern Africa, women performed most of the domestic labor, including collecting water and firewood,
milking the stock, and preparing food. Women owned the huts and the cooking implements and pots. Many women also had their own cattle or goats that
they inherited from their parents, and they controlled the distribution of milk
products. Close family relationships meant that men had deep concern for their
own sisters, which informed their attitude to other women in the group. While
there was certainly competition over access to resources, and men were recognized as community leaders, women were not completely subordinate. They were
respected as a result of their central contributions to the well-being of the community and were able to play an influential role in the day-to-day activities and
long-term decisions of the group.[7]

Increased knowledge and understanding of how ancient hunters and gatherers functioned has indicated the central roles of women both materially and
politically, as they contributed to the physical survival of their societies and participated in the daily decisions and seasonal rituals that insured the continuation
of the group as a cohesive whole.

Early Women Rulers in Ethiopia

Some of the earliest information on individual African women comes from
Ethiopia, which was the center of a long-standing Coptic Christian community.
People followed a strong set of beliefs drawn from the Bible and their relationship
with King David, his son King Solomon, and the Queen of Sheba, also known
as Makeda. Makeda was acknowledged as the founding ruler of Ethiopia in
the tenth century BCE. As the story was told in the *Kebre Negest*, an important
source for Ethiopian history, she traveled to Jerusalem to learn from Solomon
and returned to Ethiopia to have his child, Menelik I. She abdicated in Menelik's
favor when he was twenty-two years old, and that dynasty continued into the
twentieth century. In Arabic legends she was known as Bilkis.

Some sources refer to another early ruler as "Candace," suggesting that Candace was a proper name, but it was a title equivalent to queen (alternately, Kan-
dake) in the ancient Kushite kingdom of Meroë, which flourished for 1,250 years
until 350 CE. The title appeared to last for five hundred years (from the third
century BCE until the second century CE). There were four women most often
cited as Candace: Amanerinas, Amanishakhete, Nawidemak, and Maleqereabar,
each of them powerful rulers in a kingdom known for strong female leaders. One
converted to Christianity after she was influenced by a slave in her entourage who
was baptized by St. Philip (Acts of the Apostles 8:28–39, KJV). Another, probably
Amanerinas (and perhaps the same Candace as the convert), fought the Romans.
After suffering a damaging attack on her capital at Napata by Petronius in 22 BCE,

she attacked the retreating Romans and succeeded in having a boundary estab-lished between Roman and Kushite lands. Although the stories are ancient and have entered into legend, the reality of influential queens in Ethiopian history cannot be ignored. Despite the unusual prominence of these royal women, their activities and authority suggest the ways that women in ancient African societies could wield real political power.

Iron Smelting, Pottery, and Agricultural Expansion

One key development in Africa was the invention of iron smelting, giving com-munities the ability to forge their own usable iron. Archaeological evidence indi-cated that iron metallurgy was developed independently in Africa, and perhaps in more than one location in sub-Saharan Africa before 1000 BCE. Control over making iron was generally in the hands of men, though women were known to participate in various stages of the smelting process. As iron was smelted in many different African societies, there was a range of actual practice. In some areas female sexuality was considered to be threatening, and male iron smelters remained sexually abstinent throughout the process of building the ovens and producing the iron. Women who were menstruating were believed to be particu-larly harmful, as were pregnant women in some cultures, and they might have been forbidden from approaching the forge. In other areas, associating ironmak-ing with female fertility meant that women could play a ritual role in ensuring a successful smelting procedure. They were almost never directly involved in the actual smelting and forging of iron, which was controlled and performed by men. The entire iron-making enterprise was commonly associated with spiritual forces, and it has been considered a magical process that required ritual to pro-tect those involved.[8]

The development of iron smelting and subsequently iron tools and weapons brought about some significant changes in African daily life. Africans used iron tools to make household items such as carved wooden three-legged stools, and to make agricultural hoes and other implements that allowed them to greatly expand their cultivation of food crops.

In order to cultivate food crops, land had to be cleared of the existing for-ests. In central Africa, linguistic evidence points to women as the primary farm-ers, while men were more often responsible for clearing the land. Clearing could involve cutting down trees and, in some areas, burning the debris, which accom-plished two goals: removing the brush and adding ash that helped fertilize the soil. Once the plots had been prepared for cultivation, women performed most of the daily tasks of planting, hoeing, and weeding. Children also assisted in chas-ing away birds and other small predators. Women were major contributors to the increasingly sedentary and stable life of agricultural communities.

Fig. 1.2 Nok terracotta figure of woman grinding grain or spices, created circa 100 BCE. Source: Gert Chesi and Gerhard Merzeder, eds, *The Nok Culture: Art in Nigeria: 2,500 Years Ago* (Munich: Prestel, 2006), 24, courtesy of Gerhard Merzeder.

Eastern Africa, after approximately 300 BCE, was marked by the relatively rapid expansion of cultures and communities that shared a number of characteristics, from their polyrhythmic music dependent on drumming to a focus on ancestor veneration as the basis of religious belief. Another shared practice was the central role of women in agriculture. Women were recognized as the primary labor in cultivating fields and as innovators who introduced improved methods of growing food for their families.

The development of tools and other items, such as baskets and pots, was essential to the expansion of settled agricultural communities. While earlier evidence was not conclusive about women making pottery, by the beginning of the Common Era and perhaps earlier, linguistic evidence connects pottery making to women. Clay pots were a requirement for regular daily tasks such as collecting water and preparing and cooking food, as well as for important ritual needs. Women were potters in all regions of the continent, with men constituting as few as 5 percent of potters. Female control over the critical provision of pots in assorted sizes and shapes for all the daily and ritual needs of a community was a further indication of the centrality of women to society. The connection of pots to other concepts of creation including female fertility and the creator god(s) signified the intensity of value ascribed to pots and to the women who formed them.[9]

Given African women's responsibility for making all types of pottery, it is quite possible that women had a role in making the well-known two-thousand-year-old Nok ceramic heads from what is now Nigeria, as well as other figures from Chad. Researchers once assumed those well-known ancient pottery statues were made by men because the statues were considered "art" rather than "craft" and because they were believed to have a spiritual component, qualities that generally were associated with men by many Western observers.

Historically, patterns used in working with clay were repeated in tattoo designs on women's bodies, and those designs reflected social ideas about womanhood and femininity. Such patterns recognized natural elements such as rain and plants, and they reminded viewers of the importance of agriculture to social relations. If women made some of these items and designed the emblems decorating the pottery, then it is apparent that "women, through what they make, contribute to the construction of symbolic systems," and thus to the development of culture.[10]

Pastoral Societies

Particularly in southern and eastern Africa, communities relied on herding as a source of food and livelihood, and in many places people combined their prior practice of hunting and gathering with herding. Societies that focused on herding cattle or other animals, such as sheep, goats, or camels, sometimes involving lengthy migration in search of good pasture, were called pastoral. From available evidence for southern Africa, it appeared that as herding communities increased in size, they were less able to rely on kin relationships to govern their society. Among the herders, a patrilineal form of kinship and descent became the norm, primarily based on lineage chiefs who were leaders and spokespersons for kinship groups.

Recent scholarship has investigated women's roles in pastoral societies that ranged from the well-known Maasai of Kenya and Tanzania, Somali people in the Horn of Africa, and western Saharan groups including the Tuareg and Fulani, to lesser known and smaller groups, such as the Turkana, Nuer, Okiek, and Samburu (all in East Africa), and the Damara and Khoekhoe in southern Africa. New analyses and greater appreciation of women's involvement demonstrated that women played a central role in both caring for animals and governing their communities. These findings have undercut conventional ethnographies of pastoral communities, where men were described as owners of the animals and kinship and descent were characterized as exceptionally patriarchal in their organization. Where men dominated in positions of authority, women were often depicted as marginal, and their subordinate position was considered to be related to male ownership of cattle and other animals. Women's positions have changed over time, and individual women experienced shifts in their social and productive roles as they married, had children, grew older, and gained or lost wealth and status.

Nineteenth-century descriptions of the Maasai detailed the age and gender lines of distribution of work and authority, which shifted for women as they aged from girlhood to married women to mothers, and finally to elders with years of experience. Tasks were divided between men and women, but women were not excluded from caring for livestock. In general, though men were the primary political leaders in their communities, women's religious leadership gave them moral authority, and the "responsibilities and interactions of men and women were complementary and interdependent." The Masaai mode of social organization was drastically interrupted by the advent of colonialism in the early twentieth century.[11] That evidence both demonstrates the problem with using modern observations to describe social organization in earlier times and illustrates the fluidity and change experienced by societies over the centuries. It also emphasizes the centrality of women's work to the success and continuity of their societies.

Similar information was found among the nomadic Tuareg (Twareg) of Niger in West Africa.[12] It was common for women to control livestock and to hold positions of authority, practices that the people traced back to pre-Islamic times. When research was conducted in the mid-twentieth century, people commonly accepted that women held spiritual power and were responsible for organizing community rituals. The Tuareg regularly arranged for their daughters to inherit herds of cattle. The daughters also controlled the drums that signified political leadership. Women had a great deal of control in their marriages as well, and, as they owned the tents, they could move away if their husbands were mistreating them. In a conclusion similar to what is known about the Maasai, "in the case of the Twareg, we have women who think of themselves as qualitatively different from men, who engage in traditional female activities such as bearing children and regularly cooking family meals, and whose social role is very different from men's. Yet it is widely acknowledged . . . that, in nearly all aspects of women's status among the Twareg, women enjoy an assertiveness, independence, prestige and respect that is about equal to that of men."[13]

Certainly, Western observers viewed other societies through the lens of their own experiences. As will be seen in many different societies in Africa, the assumption that African women were oppressed and subservient to men has obscured the realities of women's active participation in their families and communities, where they worked and contributed economically and culturally through numerous activities that shaped African history.

Trade and Political Centralization

After iron smelting and agricultural expansion, the second occurrence that had an impact on communities at the beginning of the Common Era was the development of trade networks and commercial activity in general. The new organization of trade brought about the rise of a merchant class who began to control market routes, displacing the political rulers who previously had that authority. Long-distance trade generally spread from the Mediterranean area south, with African raw materials exported in exchange for imported processed supplies. Long-distance trade brought more than goods, however, as the opening of these new connections between cultures also brought new ideas and practices.

After 300 CE and for the next millennium, African history was marked by the growth in size of political entities and by increasing evidence of the development of social hierarchies. In some areas military groups emerged and elite or noble classes began to appear. With increased hierarchies, enslaved populations also spread in some areas of the continent. Most Africans, however, continued as small-scale farmers or herders. In southern Africa the gendered division of labor became more pronounced and entrenched, as women continued the cultivation of food crops while men took control of cattle herding. As the ownership of livestock increasingly became a measure of social status, women consequently faced restrictions, and their access to power and authority in their communities declined. The intersection of increased community scale and of stratification in society led to the common practice of accepting men as chiefs. Those men began to contract marriages with women from different parts of their chiefdoms, making alliances, and reinforcing allegiance from their followers. After the tenth century, this form of political organization began to spread outward from communities in the Transvaal region of southern Africa, reaching into what is today Zimbabwe by about 1300 CE. Although most of the evidence demonstrated that chiefs were nearly always men, it was likely that there were women chiefs in Central African communities where there were strong matrilineal kinship ties that were centered on the mother and other female kin.

One important example of an urban settlement was Great Zimbabwe in southern Africa, which thrived in the twelfth to fifteenth centuries. It then declined for reasons that are not well understood, though a major factor may have been ecological, including climate change and a resultant lack of resources. That change could have made nearby firewood for cooking scarce. When women refused to walk great distances to gather wood, the people dispersed into smaller, less urban settlements. Debates about the development and decay of Great Zimbabwe rely heavily on interpretations of archaeological evidence concerning royal wives, their housing, female initiation rites, and male and female images. The great enclosure near the center of the ruins, which researchers originally thought belonged to the king, was more likely a place where girls were initiated into adulthood. That initiation site was adjacent to the king's sister's household because she was responsible for organizing the annual rites, while the royal household was in a different location. The girls' schools served several functions, including providing agricultural labor for the royal household and controlling marriage as a factor in developing political alliances.[14]

During the millennium of development after 300 BCE, West Africa also saw the beginnings of urban cultures related to the increase in long-distance trade, perhaps also a result of the local production of cotton cloth and the exploitation of gold fields. Especially in the area that is now southern Nigeria, a number of urban areas marked by population density became prominent. Islam also was a factor, first arriving in Africa in the ninth century. Muslim merchants settled along the East African coast and also moved along trans-Saharan trade routes into West Africa. There were wide variations in the history and practice of Islam between and within regions, since early converts were more often of noble origin and ordinary Africans continued to practice local religions.

By the 1200s, a tendency for strong political hierarchies was in place, with successful kingdoms rising in several different areas. Further to the west, in areas populated by Yoruba societies, they formed city-states rather than kingdoms, and the royal genealogies show that while most rulers were men, women were also considered leaders. Women participated with men in trading activities, and they maintained some personal independence after marriage, rather than being considered the property or wards of their husbands, as was common in other world areas.

Early Women Rulers in West Africa

One of the earliest women named in West African historical traditions was Yennenga. Though her story has entered into legend, it may have a core of truth. According to the enduring accounts, Yennenga was a princess in the twelfth century CE in the Dagomba Empire of the Mossi people in a region that much later became part of northern Ghana. She was renowned for her beauty and her skill as a horsewoman, and she participated with her father's soldiers in defending their lands against attack. Her father forbade her to marry and locked her up to prevent her acting against his will. She escaped, fought heroically in a battle, and rode north until she met a famous elephant hunter named Riale. They fell in love, married, and had a son they named Ouedraogo, meaning "male horse," and it is now a common family name in Burkina Faso.

Women seemed to be absent from many traditional West African epics, which tended to focus on male warriors. Upon closer reading, however, the active presence of women was revealed, especially women who were kin to the male heroes. Women had ambiguous roles in many West African histories, appearing as seductive and dangerous while their trickery was a pivotal factor in the victory of their heroic male family member. They were repeatedly described as untrustworthy and considered to be sorcerers who knew occult methods of bringing about victory. But men in the stories were reckless, and they required a woman, usually their mother or sister, to provide guidance. Women were also described as baring their buttocks or displaying their menstrual cloths to influence men and armies. Women called on the power of their female bodies throughout history, though the appearance of these actions in the early epics provide a sense of the longevity of this powerful action. Many of the foundational stories included women who not only gave birth to heroes, but were themselves heroic.[15]

The thirteenth-century West African epic of Sunjata, whose story was well known in Mali and is a classic of world literature, described how women's actions affected the course of history as they influenced the founding of the Mande Empire. The Sunjata epic included at least two notable women: Sogolon, the mother, and Do Kamissa, known as the Buffalo Woman. Even the name Sunjata (sometimes written *Sundiata* or seen in other forms such as *Son-Jara*) was a reference to the warrior leader known as Sogolon's Jara, referring to a warrior named Jara, being the son of Sogolon, his mother. In Mande history, every male leader who was described as capable of conquest and destruction was paired with a woman whose skills and knowledge provided support that was essential to his success. Do Kamissa represented all older women who had participated in the marriage negotiations of their descendents and thus helped shape the ongoing renewal and formation of their communities. In the Sunjata epic, Do Kamissa sacrificed herself by allowing hunters to kill her; her death initiated a series of events that resulted in Sogolon giving birth to Sunjata, who was the founder of the Mande Empire. Sogolon was portrayed as a distraught bride in some versions of the epic, but her character was more ambiguous. She was a well-known sorcerer, a factor that was signaled by her often-described ugly and misshapen features. In some versions of the epic, her masculine qualities were extolled.

Aspects of the story revealed familiar themes related to the quest of the mythical hero seen in many cultures and were not necessarily explicitly describing historical events. However, the expectation of female strength as a source of male leadership appeared in Mande histories and demonstrated how Mande women should conduct themselves and how they were viewed by both men and women.[16]

Another West African ruler whose story has entered into legend was Amina, a queen in the northern Nigerian Hausa state of Zaria (alternatively known as Zazzua). Born around the year 1533 as one of two daughters of a female ruler named Bakwa Turunku, Amina was a warrior. She married Chief Karama, and after his death in 1576, she took the throne and ruled for thirty years. She was renowned for her efforts in expanding the boundaries of her state and for building the earthworks that surrounded many Hausa city-states, including a well-known wall around Katsina. She was also responsible for expanding Hausa trade along east-west trade routes. Although there was some debate about when she actually ruled, with some sources proposing that she was active in the fifteenth century rather than the sixteenth, she was a celebrated woman whose state-building contributions were notable.[17]

Several societies in West Africa recognized royal women as having a great deal of influence and authority as queen mothers and queen sisters, although men held most ruling positions. Seventeenth-century European travelers who visited Benin commented on the queen mother's court, which was established on the outer edge of the capital. In her court she was surrounded by many women and girls, and "her advice was sought on all the affairs of the land."[18] West African women were considered important councilors to the kings, and they had unusual access to power. The political authority of royal women in West Africa is covered in chapter 2, and Ghanaian queen mothers are discussed in greater detail in chapter 5.

Kinship and Descent Systems

The centrality of agriculture to African societies was connected to control over access to land and labor by kin groups and clans. In most of Africa, land was not owned by individuals but by a social group that held the rights of access to particular fields. The use of specific plots of land was decided by leaders of the group, who were usually but not always elder men of status. Control of labor, and especially of female agricultural labor, was a key element in developing and administering the land. Thus, leadership was intertwined with control over women's labor, and the arrangement of families through marriage was a matter of significant interest to the clan leaders. One of the central markers of different ethnicities was the method of descent, a factor that was directly related to women through social ideas about marriage and kinship.

Not all communities reckoned descent through the male line. Africa was the world region that was most noted for a high incidence of matrilineal descent systems, found in an extensive belt across the center of the continent, and including peoples in parts of West Africa, central Africa, and extending into southern Africa. Linguistic evidence shows that matrilineal descent was common in Africa from around 3500 BCE, initially seen in local matrilineal settlements, and by 1000 BCE the practice expanded into larger groups of clans centered on women (called matriclans), found in groups of several smaller related villages. In that same period, some groups in southern Africa developed systems of matrilineal and patrilineal dual descent, in which communities recognized ancestors and authority from both the mothers' and the fathers' families of origin.

Matrilineal descent systems privileged the mother's family, with the mother's brother playing an important role in the lives of his sister's children. Matrilineal societies embodied an idea of community organization that "favours the personal and social power of women."[19] The kinship network focused on the relationship between sisters and between siblings more generally, giving a place of honor to mothers and their children rather than fathers and their children. Mothers were often revered, and frequently all senior female kin were considered to be "mothers" to the kin group. The role of a woman's brother commonly was of greater importance to her children than her husband (their father). All known matrilineal societies were based on agricultural production and tended to have small-scale political systems.

Also integral to the society were assumptions about an abundance of resources and the ability to share communally, which was very different from ideas of scarcity and control over the distribution of resources. When cash crops were introduced, or in other ways the society allowed some members to become wealthier than others, there was a tendency for men who controlled the new resources to leave their property to their sons rather than their nephews, rupturing the basic structure of matrilineal kin relations. Men who desired greater control over their own production wanted to pass their goods on to their own children, not to the uncontrollable children of their sisters.

Patrilineal kin systems represented a reverse image to matrilineality. The primary connection was between fathers and their children. The women who married in were seen as strangers who had less authority than the women of the father's kin group. Thus a man's mother and sisters played important roles in raising his children, as they emphasized the integration of children into the patrilineal clan. While wives could appear to be powerless, women did have important social roles as sisters; in matrilineal societies the opposite was the case, where children were seen as part of their mother's ancestral group with those kin and clan connections having primacy.[20]

There were complex issues involved in understanding when a society was matrilineal or patrilineal. Although these were often used as descriptive terms, their application to a society did not always indicate the many varieties of matrilineality, or how a society might have included some practices considered matrilineal and others considered patrilineal. Reckoning descent through mothers and aunts, making the mother-child bond the central one, and emphasizing matrilocal residence (where a man typically would move into his wife's village and home) all indicated what has been considered "matrilineality." In peoples' actual lives, there was much greater flexibility in their kin relationships than such a strict description implied.

In the Great Lakes region of east central Africa, as in patrilineal societies elsewhere in Africa, people maintained strong ties among kin in a mother's family. A woman's father and brother had important rights and responsibilities for the children of their daughter or sister, and they worked to show their interest in those children despite the understanding that the children's primary connection was with their father's clan. Those cross-cutting ties were centered on motherhood, and the expanded kin networks between the extended families of fathers and mothers were an essential component in the continued prosperity and survival of the community.[21]

Thus motherhood was a key institution in all societies. While women became mothers mainly by giving birth to children, the social role of mothers went beyond the biological event of childbirth. Once a woman had children, most frequently within a marriage, she gained improved access to land and political authority. Having many children could enhance a woman's status, but successfully raising a child to be a leader was also a route to recognized social standing. Though the important influence of the mother's family within a patrilineal community was noted in the areas that later became Uganda, similar complex patterns of kinship and descent were found in other regions of Africa.

The term "matriarchy" was sometimes used to describe societies where women had the kind of authority found in matrilineal societies. The use of that word was confusing, as it was often understood to mean that women ruled over men, in an obverse form of organization to patriarchy. Early African societies were not matriarchal in that sense; women were not the overarching authority figures, simply because the communities were so small and decentralized that neither men nor women held that kind of role. The authority of the matrilineal kin group allowed women and men to share power in their society in a kind of gender parity.

In both matrilineal and patrilineal systems, women played a central role in agricultural production, food preparation, and child care. In most pastoral societies livestock was controlled by men, and the amount of cattle a man accumulated reflected the social standing and strength of his household. Even in societies that were heavily dependent on cattle, women's agricultural labor was a key factor since grains and other agricultural crops were the mainstay of people's daily diet. Women also made a less recognized contribution to sustaining their society's cultural history through their activities in ceremonies devoted to maintaining ties with the ancestors and helping group members through important life stages. Their commitment was essential to the history and development of their societies, and it helped configure the daily lives and spiritual beliefs of all members of the community.

Marriage

Many African societies have long practiced polygamy—or, more accurately, polygyny. Polygamy meant that a person may have multiple spouses, while polygyny more specifically referred to men having multiple wives. Many societies from across the continent allowed and sometimes encouraged men to marry more than one wife. The actual practice and extent varied greatly, with wealthier men and men in leadership positions being more likely to marry many women, while it was more common for most men to marry two or three wives. A common element was also that older men married young women, as those men had the financial means to acquire multiple wives, and in some instances the woman's family arranged such unions. As mentioned, the development of agriculture relied on female labor and contributed to the desire of men to have more than one wife and therefore a larger household supply of labor.[22] Islam restricted men to four wives and required that they be able to equally support each wife.

Travelers' reports from West Africa in 1668 suggested that the king of Benin had over one thousand wives, as he had inherited those wives that his father had not slept with at the time of his death.[23] Other reports in the early eighteenth century numbered the Benin king's wives at three hundred or more. Those wives likely represented political alliances, and some may have been slaves. As in other similar cases, such large numbers of wives were reserved to royalty and did not reflect the family life of ordinary people.

There were examples of families where the cowives viewed each other as rivals, and any perceived inequality of treatment lead to jealous outbursts. And there were counterexamples of families where the first wife assisted in finding a suitable second wife and appreciated having someone to share in the burdens of farm work and child-raising. In some areas, women welcomed sisters or cousins as cowives, thus bringing compatible women into their household. Allowing only men to have access to multiple spouses was inherently unequal, but the practice of polygyny by itself was not always a source of friction and discontent.

The practice of polyandry, in which a woman may have multiple husbands, has been little documented in the world, and Africa was no exception. A study of the Birom people in northern Nigeria suggested that their practice of *njem*, an unusual system where married women had open, recognized relationships with men other than their husbands, indicated a form of polyandry. The relationship was not considered marriage, but it was seen by the Birom as "good, appropriate, and even necessary."[24] Women were free to choose the man to whom they wished to be connected, and the relationship was formalized by the presentation of a goat from the outside man to the woman and her husband. There was an expectation that *njem* partners would help each other with farming, and there was an ongoing exchange of gifts and services throughout the relationship, which in many cases lasted for years.

BRIDEWEALTH AND BRIDE SERVICE

A common method of formalizing marriages throughout Africa involved the exchange of bridewealth. Typically, a man who planned to marry would begin giving gifts to the family of his intended wife. In the nineteenth century and earlier, such gifts in southern Africa were often cattle and hoes. As the economy changed and men began working for wages, cash payments and other valuable items began to enter into the exchange. In West Africa, cowrie shells, a form of local currency, were often involved. For example, among the Bamana people of Mali in the early twentieth century, a standard payment was thirty thousand cowries.

Although "brideprice" was sometimes used as a synonym for bridewealth, it was considered a less accurate term because of the implication that women were sold for a price. It misrepresented the actual transaction and, because it implied that women were a marketable commodity, "it is difficult to exaggerate the harm done to Africans by this ignorance."[25] Other terms such as dowry, earnest, indemnity, or settlement were also considered inaccurate, and anthropologists advocated substituting the term "bridewealth."

Although Western observers sometimes interpreted such exchanges as signifying the sale of the woman by her family, Africans valued bridewealth for venerating the relationship and for tying families together in an economic and social community. It was rare that there was a one-time payment, as the exchange often continued over a period of time with certain specified gifts given to mark the stages of the relationship such as courtship, moving into the same residence, and the birth of the first child. Families sometimes used the bridewealth that came into the family through a daughter's marriage in order to send bridewealth to the bride of their son, thus circulating the wealth among several families. In some societies it was a reciprocal arrangement, and the bride's family also contributed substantially to the marital expenses and sometimes gave a dowry as well to their daughter, the newly married woman. It was expected that the bridewealth would be returned if a marriage ended with a divorce or separation.

Societies in eastern and southern Africa, especially groups that depended to a greater extent on cattle or other livestock husbandry, often were patrilineal. It was common in many of those societies for cattle to be an integral part of marriage, as families exchanged bridewealth, including cattle, as part of the marital process. The usual form was for the family of the husband-to-be to make an arrangement with the family of the woman he planned to marry regarding the number of cattle and other goods that would be given to her family. For African communities, the exchange of bridewealth established a tangible economic connection between clans that strengthened both the marital relationship and the bond between families that were becoming kin. In southern Africa, no new homestead could be established without at least the promise of cattle, and cattle ownership was the basis of wealth and well-being.

In some areas, particularly matrilineal communities in Central Africa, a new husband or husband-to-be would make much smaller gifts. His primary payment was his labor. A man joined his wife's family and worked on their fields for a period of time as part of the process of formalizing the new marital relationship, an activity that was sometimes called "bride service." It was related to bridewealth as an obligation from a man to the family of his new wife. The institution of bride service illustrated the key role of female authority in Central African societies. In groups across the middle of the African continent, women made their relationships with their sisters and their mothers a priority, sometimes extending the network to their mother's sisters and adult daughters (their matrilineal cousins).

These women acted together and supported each other in determining the allocation of male agricultural labor, requiring certain tasks and deciding how long such labor would continue. In some instances, a man continued working for his wife's mother and extended clan for many years. Women, through their female kin group, controlled crucial activities related to food cultivation and, therefore, to the viability of the community as a whole.

Bride service was observed into the mid-twentieth century in Zambia, but the practice had roots in antiquity. Historical linguistic evidence demonstrated that the central role of female kin in controlling agricultural labor can be traced back to the earliest farming settlements prior to 600 CE. Similar data from the area that now constitutes Tanzania suggested that the primacy of female kin relations dates back to the second millennium BCE. Early human settlements relied on women's authority, where women made decisions about the agricultural calendar, about which lands were to be used for cultivation, and about who had access to the land and to the produce that resulted from cultivating that land. Women's authority was also closely linked to spiritual beliefs and rituals, which were intertwined with the annual cycle of the seasons and agricultural production.

WOMAN-WOMAN MARRIAGE AND LEVIRATE

African societies sometimes included a practice referred to as "woman-woman marriage," in which a woman could "marry" another woman by offering bridewealth to her family. In many cases the new wife had a conjugal relationship with a man chosen by her "female husband." Any children born to the wife would be affiliated with the woman who had paid bridewealth. By making such a payment, a woman was recognized as having political and economic power, as she was able to gain control of female labor, a domain that was more often reserved for men. It was sometimes an option for women who had been unable to have children of their own and had been rejected by their (male) husbands when they seemed to be barren. The "female husband" usually had authority over property rights and inheritance as related to the offspring, authority which otherwise devolved to a male husband, but they were not considered to be male themselves. Little is known about the emotional and social bonds shared by women in such relationships. Observers continue to debate the degree of intimacy experienced between women who married other women, though it seems that these relationships did not parallel Western lesbian interactions.

The custom of levirate was prevalent in the past in many patrilineal African cultures, though the extent was difficult to ascertain. Levirate was the marital practice in which a widow was expected to remarry a member of her husband's clan, most often her deceased husband's brother. In some instances the family of the deceased father claimed any children from the marriage as part of their clan and encouraged the mother of those children to remarry within the clan as a strategy to maintain that link. Widows in that situation sometimes preferred to remarry within their deceased husband's family in order to keep contact with their children as well as to retain access to land they had cultivated. The particular experience of remarriage within the family was at times harsh and oppressive, but it also possibly offered a flexible and practical way for a family to support a woman as she aged.

Religious Beliefs

Many societies in Africa have followed religious beliefs based on revering the wisdom of the ancestors and respecting the natural environment. Women played important roles in the rites associated with such beliefs, as healers, as teachers for girls in their initiation rites, and as practitioners knowledgeable about rituals related to marriage, birth, and death.[26] The existence of male gods was not the norm. Based on linguistic evidence, societies in central Africa shared a belief in a creator god, sometimes called Leza. The word *leza*, or *leesa*, was derived from early terms that denoted nurturing, specifically a mother caring for her child. Later names that developed for the creator also often referred explicitly to "the mother of all beasts," "the one from who all things come," or "the mother of water." In nearly every case, the creator was clearly gendered as female, was considered both male and female, or was perceived as beyond gendered. Such beliefs were deeply imbedded in peoples' spiritual systems, and they further indicated the importance of matrilineal social structures. Women's contributions as spiritual healers, mediums, and leaders were most often related to fertility and reproduction.[27] With the intricate interconnection between marriage, family, children, and agricultural production, it was evident that women were at the center of local politics and economics, and they were not relegated to marginal positions outside of public activity. Their religious responsibilities were central to family health and the continuation of their communities.

Origin Stories and Goddesses

As with all societies, Africans had creation myths that accounted for the origins of their communities, and those tales often had a gender component that explained why women and men had particular roles. Among the Gikuyu (also spelled Kikuyu) in Kenya, for example, the myth of origin told how Gikuyu (the male progenitor) and Mumbi (the female) had nine daughters who married men from outside, and the families of those women were the core of the clans that eventually developed in Gikuyu society. Women were the center of authority for many years, but according to the story, they became domineering and brutal, punishing men for adulterous behavior while they took multiple husbands. The men conspired to seduce the leading women simultaneously; the women were portrayed as weak in their acquiescence to the men, and when they were immobilized at the end of their pregnancies the men staged a coup and Gikuyu society became patriarchal. As beliefs changed over the centuries, the terms used for the creator god came to include the skies, containing clouds, stars, and phenomenon such as lightning. The crucial role of rain in agricultural success was also tied to the religious beliefs and rituals that emerged in a wide variety of communities.

Other myths from eastern Africa illustrated the separate but complementary spheres that men and women inhabited. In the origin story of the Nata in Tanzania, a farming woman and hunting man met and found that they could help each other. They married, and their children were the beginning of Nata society. The Korekore people in what is today Zimbabwe recognized a powerful goddess called Dzivaguru. She was said to be the original great deity, the earth goddess who was the oldest of the Korekore deities. She had been a goddess of great wealth and magical power, but she was driven away by Nosenga, the son of the sky god, Chikara.

Some of the stories indicated that while the societies followed matrilineal descent systems in earlier eras, they shifted at some indeterminate time to a patrilineal system. Although the mechanism or motivation for such a shift was not fully understood, one part of the evidence for matrilineal descent was the continued knowledge of stories of origin, in which women were often present as founders of clans although the clan had switched to patrilineal descent.

An example of such a creation story was told by the patrilineal Kran of Liberia. Their origin myth began with an all-powerful woman, Gonzuole. Gonzuole had many lovely daughters, though she never had a husband or any long-term relationship with a man. Men who saw the daughters conspired to trap them with special mushrooms; when the girls stopped to taste the treat, the men surrounded them and made a bargain with Gonzuole that resulted in marriages between the men and her daughters. The girls were not happy in their new situation, and their actions led to factions and warfare.

In many African local religions, goddesses were a common presence in the pantheon of ancestors and spirits from whom people sought support. Goddesses were considered patrons of the earth or water, and their role in supplying regular rainfall gave them special powers over human and agricultural fertility. People left offerings at local shrines built to honor goddesses who had a history of helping believers.

Osun was a prominent goddess in the Yoruba pantheon of *orisha* (or *orisa*), a system of spiritual beliefs expressed through multiple representations of the deity. Osun had devoted followers in Nigeria, particularly in her home area of Osogbo, which sponsored an annual festival in her name. Her followers carried their beliefs to Brazil, Cuba, and elsewhere in the African diaspora. Her name, Osun, meant "the source," and she was commonly associated with water, which was necessary for life itself. Though Osun was sometimes called a river goddess, that name did not reflect the breadth of her authority. Women appealed to Osun for assistance with fertility issues, and she was recognized for her role in matters concerning maternity and health, though she was not limited to those areas. She was generally paired with Ogun, who can be characterized as a male warrior god associated with iron, while she was associated with cowrie shells (both iron and cowries being sources of wealth in Yoruba society).

Yemoja was another goddess associated with water; she was especially worshiped by the Yoruba of Abeokuta, who recognized her as the mother of all rivers, particularly the Ogun River. Women who were barren or facing fertility problems believed she had special value, and they would keep a jar of Ogun water close by to encourage fertility. Cowries symbolized her wealth, and women brought her offerings of yams, goats, maize, and other foods.

Some goddesses were believed to have special authority as a source of justice, such as Akonadi, a goddess associated with the area around Accra, Ghana. A story was told that illustrated her role as a goddess of justice and one who protected women and children. Three brothers came to a shrine of Akonadi and asked for advice because there had been several deaths in their family. She told them to go to their grandmother's home, where they would find stolen items, as the grandmother was working with a group of thieves. The brothers went to the home where they found a metal box with precious items under their grandmother's bed. They brought the box to the goddess, with the understanding that if the stolen items were no longer in their family's household, there would be no more deaths. Soon after that two men came to the goddess and announced that a box of valuables had been stolen from their mother's estate, and they asked if the goddess knew who the thieves were. Her priestess gave her answer, that the box was in the shrine, and though they were welcome to take it, they were advised to leave it so that it could be used for charity for poor women and children. Knowing how much suffering the box of treasure had caused, the men chose to leave it with the goddess for distribution to the needy.

People maintained shrines to goddesses and revered ancestors, calling on them for assistance and advice. Most of these were flexible and changed over time, with some rising in importance while others were forgotten or declined in influence.

Initiation Rites

Most African societies held ceremonies for both girls and boys that marked their entry into puberty as the first step toward adulthood. Such rites were central to forming girls into women who could participate in their communities as adults, eventually marrying and bearing children. The specific elements of such rites varied from one society to another, but most often girls began the procedures at menarche, when they had their first menstruation. They could be physically separated from the rest of the community, sometimes with other girls of their age cohort, for periods of up to three months. In central and eastern Africa, evidence from past centuries suggested that girls were more often initiated as individuals, based on each girl's biological changes and a desire to initiate a girl before she became pregnant. It was considered to be courting danger to postpone her initiation for too long in order to accommodate a group initiation, though an additional impact might have been a lesser sense of female group solidarity.

In the ritual itself, girls were taught adult behavior and responsibilities by mature women who were ritual specialists, respected elders, and sometimes midwives and herbalists. Lessons could include imparting sexual information, in which girls were taught how to please their husbands while celebrating the joys of adult female sexuality, often through song and dance. Instruction also focused on other aspects of women's work, such as their responsibility for agriculture and food preparation. In some societies, it was important that the girls undergo a painful ritual, ranging from burning the inner thigh to various forms of female genital cutting. Among many southern African societies, girls lengthened their labia by repeatedly pulling on them, contributing to the transformation of their bodies into adult females. The ritual itself, with the isolation from daily life and taboos about eating certain foods or behaving in particular ways, was considered a transitional phase. Following the end of the rites, the girls reentered their societies as young women rather than children, in a ritual rebirth that affirmed their place in their local community and in the world at large as life-giving human beings.

Women used items such as figurines in the process of teaching girls. Though sometimes called "dolls," such figures were not playthings, as they had specific meanings that facilitated teaching important concepts concerning women's duties and female knowledge. Women also painted symbols, which in central Africa were commonly made using a thick white pigment that was applied to walls in hidden or secret locations. The symbols were restricted to mature women, and young girls and all men and boys were prevented from viewing any image that signified women's power.

In central Africa, women in some societies held a second ritual when a young woman first became pregnant. The ritual particularly signified a young woman's incorporation into the matrilineal kin group, and it included the pregnant woman being carried to her mother's house by a woman who had already had a successful pregnancy. The newly pregnant woman then was allotted her own cooking fire and she was permitted to thresh her own grain, both crucial aspects of female responsibility and authority.

In a sense, the ceremony at the time of menarche marked a girl's ability to become a woman, while pregnancy and imminent motherhood indicated full adulthood. In terms of life cycle events, the biological changes in a woman's body were worthy of note and ceremony, while marriage was not regarded in the same way. Though rites that have been observed in more recent years cannot be extrapolated back into ancient times, linguistic evidence has demonstrated the early existence of these ceremonies in forms that are still recognizable as performing a similar role in educating girls as they become women and take on adult obligations.[28]

Another type of initiation rite occurred when a person accepted their calling to be a spirit medium. Women and men who underwent this process often began with an illness; they would suffer an incident that they experienced as a kind of death from which they were reborn into a more spiritual existence. They would wear particular clothing, carry implements that marked them as seers, and be trained to communicate with ancestors and the supernatural world. In some societies, spirit mediums were considered to have entered into a "marriage" with their avatar or deity. Women who felt they had undergone such a possession would sometimes display an alternate personality, dressing in male clothing, following food taboos that usually were not followed by ordinary people, and sometimes being exempt from other social restrictions. At times they acted as prophets, guiding their community through their special knowledge and analysis of events that threatened the society. These attributes raised those women from the social subordination they might experience otherwise. They were widely revered as leaders who had esoteric knowledge and abilities related to the communities' spiritual beliefs and to the material needs related to reproduction and production, that were essential for survival.[29]

Case Study: Buganda (Uganda)

Examining a single society will allow for a more coherent understanding of the interconnection of various factors that have been discussed as separate aspects of African societies—kinship, marriage, religious beliefs, political organization, ethnicity, and work are intimately intertwined. Buganda was a strong kingdom in the past, and it eventually was incorporated into the modern nation of Uganda. Research into early settlements in that region showed that in the eleventh through the thirteenth centuries, people lived in dispersed agricultural settlements that gradually coalesced into five distinctive political entities under male chiefs or elders.[30]

During the fourteenth and fifteenth centuries, those polities faced the arrival of peoples from the northeast, led by the legendary historical figure, Kintu. The new arrivals, according to tradition, brought the technology of iron smelting with them, as well as crops such as plantain and bottle gourd, techniques for growing and making bark-cloth, and increased reliance on domesticated cattle and poultry. Those changes and improvements allowed for a noticeable growth in population, which in turn brought more pressure on access to land, and increased the authority of village leaders to allocate land. People were organized by clans, which were collections of kinship groups, and more clans were recognized as communal entities in order to cope with the population growth. The primary labor was cultivating food crops, work that was done by women. Leadership of the extended family and of the clans was men's work. By the early sixteenth century, evidence from historical linguistic research demonstrates that the clans were closely associated with ownership of particular parcels of land, and clans were charged with protecting land assigned to them. Politically, the clan leaders took on more tasks such as judging disagreements, assigning fines for misdeeds, assessing taxes, and exacting revenge on clans that infringed on their rights. Land and cattle were not owned by individuals, but they were held by the clan, whose leaders had final say over who was a legitimate member of the lineage and therefore had a right of access to land for cultivation, housing, grazing, and gathering wild crops.

For women, the increased centralization of authority was associated with increased patriarchy, as it was expected that they would live with their husbands' clan and only gain access to the land required for cultivation through the male leaders of their husbands' kin group. The impact on marriage was also noticeable, as the emphasis on descent and, in particular, descent through the male line governed who was accepted as a clan member. Sisters were members of the patrilineal clan by birth, while wives were vulnerable as perpetual outsiders. The practice of polygyny became an important route for a clan to increase its members, as male clan insiders could improve their own standing by marrying more wives and producing more children, all of whom became dependent followers.

People in the Buganda ancestral areas recognized the connections between their land and trees, people of their kin group, and the fertility of people and territory. Local shrines were common, where people paid homage to their ancestors and to their land. In one area, a large tree was seen to have special influence over fertility, and two large roots that resembled a woman's outspread legs were a site of reflection and ritual. The tree had grown out of the grave of a respected woman, and it represented the value of childbirth. Local women would bring offerings and request support for successful pregnancies. The tree held significance in other areas as well, demonstrating the interconnected nature of peoples' daily lives and spiritual beliefs.

Kintu, recognized as the founder of the larger political entity of Buganda, held spiritual and ritual importance as well as political authority. He and his wife, Nambi, are considered the first couple who represent the origins of the people of

Buganda. His multiple roles as a healer, spirit medium, and political authority further reflected the way that peoples' family lives, daily agricultural work, and religious beliefs were interconnected and mutually supportive. Growing food to sustain the family depended on labor; having people to provide agricultural labor relied on marriage and childbirth; marriage practices were part of beliefs about the centrality of clan and lineage; and clans were connected by history and by blood via the shared ancestors, who continued to play a part in the decisions made by clan elders.

In addition, while both men and women could be healers, they were commonly considered to be the "wives" of the spirit that they served, or who possessed them. Thus spirit mediums and healers were defined as part of a marital household. Mediums who were "wives" could eventually become "mothers," and they would have particular influence over fertility and women who had difficulty conceiving or completing a successful pregnancy.[31]

With the introduction of bananas and plantains around the fourteenth century, people in Buganda gradually began more intensive cultivation practices and became more settled. Women probably began tending wild banana trees during the slower seasons of their bean and vegetable crops. Over time, the banana plants became permanent groves and women continued to be the primary banana cultivators. People no longer needed to move to find new fertile land for their crops, as had been required for beans and grains; instead, they became tied to the land where their banana plants were thriving. Bananas required much less work than many other crops because they produced fruit all year and perennially, reducing the need to clear new fields and rotate through the seasons of planting, weeding, and harvesting. The bananas needed care, but it was less seasonal and less intensive. Problems of food storage and seasonal hunger were reduced as well. This shift in the primary crop had a major impact on women's daily round of work.[32]

As the communities relied more on bananas as their food staple, the banana fields became more valuable and represented not only the food that was produced, but the generations of labor that had developed the land and the productive plants. People wanted to maintain control over the land on which they worked, and while land was still held by the clans rather than by individuals, issues of lineage and inheritance became more important. The male clan leaders enforced the claims of their own offspring to particular growing areas, which exacerbated male interest in controlling women's labor and reproduction.

The clans were not only focused on the material needs of their members as related to agriculture. They were the repository of accumulated knowledge about farming and ancestors, which were tied up with beliefs about healing and the role of clan leaders as spiritual managers who were responsible for the health of the group. The shrines and the spirit mediums likewise became less mobile. When people had shifted their agricultural fields from time to time, they had taken religious materials with them. As they settled to cultivate bananas, their shrines became more permanent, and the ancestors became more important as a source of health and well-being in a broad sense.

As the population grew, however, it required that new generations would establish their own settlements while maintaining their lineage connections and association with the founding clan. The developing hierarchy led to the rise of particularly successful families that were regarded as royalty. Patrilineal descent and patrilocal practice, where women moved to their husbands' home, became more common. Men were thus the center of the clans while women who married in were viewed as perpetual outsiders, while retaining membership in their birth clans. The legendary history of Kintu and his marriage to Nambi placed their monogamous patrilocal marriage as the model for Buganda society and marital customs.

In the late fourteenth century, Buganda was invaded by a neighbor, Kimera of Bunyoro, and seven more clans were incorporated into the Buganda community. Kimera was recognized as the leader responsible for introducing what has been called "elite polygyny," as male leaders began to marry more than one wife. While ordinary men were not prohibited from marrying more than one wife, the expense of bridewealth was so high that most men could not afford to marry multiple wives.[33]

Kimera strengthened the role of the king, bringing the clans under his authority and marrying women from the various clans in order to make alliances with them. As more and more women were brought into the royal household, they were given titles that reflected their rank, and they were housed in special compounds under the control of senior wives. As in many other societies, however, women in the royal family enjoyed prerogatives that ordinary women did not. The women who were ranked as princesses were able to behave in ways similar to men in Buganda society.

The new political and economic configurations put most women in Buganda at a disadvantage since they were restricted from holding political power or owning land. But elite women had land in their names throughout Buganda, and they were in charge of local governance in those areas where they had economic interests. They were allowed to move about freely and use obscene language that other women could not use. All people in Buganda, including clan chiefs, were required to bow down to the princesses and show them respect. The royal women also engaged in sexual activity with men of their own choice, although as daughters of the king they were not allowed to marry. They also were not supposed to have children, though they avoided aborting their pregnancies and had children in secret who were passed off as someone else's child. The princesses also were important in mediating between chiefs and the king, and they were influential as potential king makers as well.

In many ways, the construction of the princesses' gender as masculine was similar to the way that spirit mediums were perceived. The parallels could be related to the princesses' position as spiritual healers as well as royal family representatives, making the interconnections even stronger between political and religious authority and reinforcing beliefs about fertility and political power.[34] Thus, when the organization of power in Buganda began to shift at the end of the eighteenth century, the position of the royal women was changed in important ways. By the nineteenth century the Buganda princesses no longer had their sexual freedom or their political and economic authority.

A pattern of potential conflict between women who wielded authority as spiritual advisors and healers and men who generally held more overt political power and controlled aspects of the economy could be seen in many Central African societies. Both healers and chiefs "compete[d] for followers within social and economic systems," where they each had ritual responsibilities and control over the distribution of certain resources. Eventually, they could form alliances and work together or experience friction and cause social disruptions.[35] The gender aspect of these interactions can be seen in the history of Buganda, but it was not limited to that kingdom.

Labor, Pawnship, and Slavery

Many African communities developed systems of control over labor in response to the abundance of land, an abundance that was useful only if there was sufficient labor to cultivate it. In all regions of Africa there were examples of systems of forced labor, ownership of people by others, and what was often referred to as "pawnship," in which debts and fines could be paid by giving up control over oneself or a family member to the person who was owed goods or money.

Slavery can be a difficult term to define, and it can take many forms, though most basically it referred to one person owning or controlling another who was involuntarily servile. Slaves were usually individuals who were marginal to the society; their identity as members of a servile class could linger into subsequent generations, although African slavery was more usually attached to individuals rather than to a race or other larger cohort.

African slavery can be described as a continuum of control over people. Many societies accepted pawning as a way of repaying debts or acknowledging an affiliation or dependent relationship. Pawning could offer more opportunities for slaves to move out of their enslaved situation than was common in the North and South American slave systems, though it shared some attributes with indentured servitude. But the complicated issues of male control over women's labor meant that women were more vulnerable to capture, pawning, and enslavement, especially in areas where they were already dependent on men for access to land.

It also meant that in some communities those who had been pawned were considered marginal and were therefore liable to be traded to Europeans and drawn into the international slave trade.

Evidence concerning internal slavery in Africa is scanty for earlier centuries. When Portuguese explorers first arrived on the West African coast in the fifteenth century, they encountered societies that incorporated captives and pawned individuals in servile situations, though in general the practices were on a small scale. By the middle of the 1400s, political and economic changes were beginning to occur in the interior that allowed for the expansion of slavery in the regions where the Malian empire was declining. By 1550, the demand for labor in the Americas coincided with increased numbers of available captives in West Africa, both feeding the nascent slave trade. From an initial volume of around six hundred individuals entering the international slave market before 1500, the numbers rose to four thousand slaves purchased in West Africa by European traders in 1650. After another century passed, the trans-Atlantic trade of West African slaves had grown to fifty thousand in 1780. These numbers reflected the increase in plantation production of crops such as sugar in the Caribbean and Brazil, cotton in the southern regions of North America, and labor demands including domestic work and mining in Peru and Mexico. There was also some specialization based on the region; Brazil relied on slave imports from areas now part of Angola and the Congo, while slaves from the West African coastal areas of Senegal, Guinea, and elsewhere most often ended up in North America and the Caribbean. There was also an active slave trade on Africa's east coast, with some of those people being shipped to the Americas, and many others sent to the Arabian Peninsula.

The history of slavery in Africa was deeply gendered. Most slaves in Africa were female. The reasons for this pattern included the valuable agricultural labor women could provide, as well as their ability to bear and raise children. A related factor was the greater demand for male slaves in the international market, as the European slave traders bought twice as many men as women. Male slaves captured during warfare in Africa were more likely to be killed, while women were integrated into the society; sometimes wars were waged so that men could have access to a new set of women as potential wives. In matrilineal societies, this method of acquiring wives could circumvent the influence of a man's mother and sisters over his choice of wife, and captive women were vulnerable because they remained outside of the existing female-centered kin relations. The children of enslaved women would have a primary loyalty to their father because they would not be part of the matriclan. In some areas of east Africa it appeared that the practice of men marrying slave women and gaining control over their offspring was a way to mitigate the female focus of matrilineal descent. By developing their own kin group with an outsider wife and their clan-less children, men could avoid some of the strictures of the matrilineal clan over men who married into that community.

In patrilineal societies, men were able to increase their authority by marrying enslaved women who lacked the support of their own kin groups. Because men already had a stronger position of control in such communities, slave women were seen as more appropriate as wives or "concubines" for marginal men who were either transient or of low status themselves.

Though there was some evidence of infertility or low fertility among enslaved women, they still presented the potential of adding members to the lineage that claimed them. Some historians have argued that because of the uncertainty of slave women's fertility, they were more valued for the physical labor they could contribute to cultivating food crops and performing such essential domestic chores as collecting water and firewood and contributing to the arduous labor of preparing food for consumption.

Hausa City-States

Slave women in Islamic Hausa city-states such as Kano, located in the region that later became northern Nigeria, were usually attached to the royal family. They lived in the palace and they played key roles in the management of the royal estates. Though they also provided sexual services and are usually referred to as concubines, their work covered a much wider assortment of responsibilities. The royal palace at Kano in the sixteenth century included hundreds of enslaved women who performed a range of work related to the agricultural calendar. Archaeological evidence shows that the royal granary was controlled by women who were enslaved. Their fertility and reproductive abilities, along with their agrarian knowledge, placed them in the center of royal decision-making, especially concerning the distribution of food.[36]

An important aspect of concubines' experience was the legal position of their children, who took on the status of their free father. As the royal father had not married the concubine, he could not divorce her, but he was obligated to provide for her and for their children, giving her a more stable connection to the royal family than a wife who did not bear a child. Though most concubines joined the royal household as a result of being captured during a war, as a group they were able to develop a nexus of power within the palace. Subsequent generations remained aware of their ancestors' origins, but their compromised status did not descend through the generations. In addition, because these women came from polities outside the royal group, they offered the chance to develop alliances between the Hausa leadership and other communities. The captive women were allowed to maintain contact with the communities of their birth, and at times they acted as emissaries to their home districts. They were thus an important link in regional politics, as well as contributing to the growth of the royal family and the success of state agriculture.

The concubines' era of greatest influence did not last, however, as male power increased and women's roles, especially those of the concubines, declined throughout the eighteenth century. By the nineteenth century when British colonizers arrived, concubines apparently were no longer at the center of royal administration. The British gradually introduced laws that eroded the legal existence of slavery and concubinage, until they conquered Kano in 1903. Along with other political changes in the region the institution declined.

Nonetheless, the long time period when enslaved women had control of the distribution of grain and sometimes acted as royal emissaries to outlying regions illustrates how women's work was at the center of the daily functioning of an African society. The women, as captured slaves, might have appeared to be marginal, yet they worked together to dominate a key sector of Kano royal life and used their knowledge of agriculture to improve their social position and the status of their children.

Female Leaders in Eastern and Southern Africa

East Africa: Daca and Fatuma

The importance of women in eastern Africa was seen with Daca, who was a powerful ruler in the sixteenth century in the Lwo area of the East African Lake Region also known as Bunyoro-Kitara. It was common in Bunyoro to include women in the administration, especially as regional officers in the non-Bunyoro dependent states. Daca was named by her husband, the Mukama of Bunyoro, as a regional governor in the Madi government, and under her rule it became a substantial and successful state. She maneuvered her kin, marriage, and political associations so that the region developed economically. She also became wealthy as a result of the tribute she collected in her position as governor, and she solidified Lwo power throughout the northern Lakes region. People's memory of her was so compelling that two centuries after her death, in the mid-eighteenth century, a new Acholi chiefdom adopted her name, the Koch Pa-Daca, meaning "The People of Daca."[37]

Another East African community that had some female rulers was Zanzibar, an island just off the coast of what is today Tanzania that was long the headquarters of Arab and Swahili trade and politics along the East African coast. Records list at least twenty-six female rulers along the coast during the seventeenth to nineteenth centuries. One of them was Fatuma, a member of the royal family of Zanzibar in the seventeenth century. Control of the east coast of Africa was then under dispute as the Portuguese claimed areas over which Arab rulers from Oman had previously held power. Fatuma came to the throne of Zanzibar during that time, and she married Abdullah, a ruler on the coast near Mombasa. When all the other Arab rulers along the coast united to oppose the Portuguese presence she arranged for food to be sent to the Portuguese, who were under siege at Fort Jesus near Mombasa. When the Arabs defeated the Portuguese in 1698, she was left on her own in Zanzibar, where she was captured by Arabs and exiled to Oman with her son. She returned to Zanzibar in 1709 and died there sometime in the early eighteenth century.

Angola: Nzinga and Beatriz Kimpa Vita

Along the southwestern coast of the continent, Nzinga a Mbandi (sometimes spelled Njinga) was a queen in seventeenth century Kongo, in what is now Angola. She was apparently born around 1582 to the Mbanda royal family of Ndongo, though some sources claimed she was of slave origin. When she was a young woman, the Portuguese began to make incursions into Ndongo and built some forts, though Ndongo remained independent. When her father died, her brother Ngola Mbandi took the throne; he faced increased military attacks by the Portuguese and was eventually exiled. Nzinga was first seen in historic documents in 1622, when she went to Luanda as an emissary to the Portuguese and participated in peace negotiations. She converted to Christianity and allied herself with the Portuguese. Though considered an early Christian in some sources, her adoption of the new religion is judged a strategic move by others. When her brother died in 1624 she came to the Ngola throne. There is further controversy about her rule, as some cite a tradition of female rulers while others claim she went against convention. She was forced by the Portuguese to flee Ndongo, and she continued to fight the expansion of Portuguese control. Around the year 1628, she moved north to Matamba and established herself as queen, drawing on the example of previous female rulers. She was a military leader as well, continuing to oppose Portuguese rule and battling their army after 1640. For some time, she also allied herself with the Dutch, who were enemies of the Portuguese. In 1656, she turned to Catholicism again and accepted a peace agreement. Matamba continued to have female leaders after her death of natural causes at age eighty in 1663. Nzinga was claimed by nationalist leaders in later anticolonial struggles as an antecedent and role model, and she was often portrayed as a heroine of the modern Angolan nation, though her own history was more contradictory and conflicted than the popular image would admit.[38]

Dona Beatriz Kimpa Vita, who was born around 1684 in what is today Angola, came from a noble Kongolese background.[39] She was a spiritual healer whose life was changed by the arrival of Italian and Portuguese missionaries, as the Europeans considered all local non-Christian practices to be witchcraft. She popularized a cult devoted to the Catholic Saint Anthony, claiming that she had died but was revived, and found she was possessed by Saint Anthony. With that persona she preached for reconciliation and the restoration of the Kongolese monarchy. In the aftermath of three decades of war and disruption, her peaceful message attracted many followers, who called themselves Antonians. She also drew the wrath of the local Angolan Catholic hierarchy with her calls for the recognition of black saints and her declaration that Jesus Christ was Kongolese. A coalition between two aristocratic households adhering to orthodox Catholic beliefs tried Beatriz for heresy, burning her at the stake in 1706. Her movement continued only until 1709, when her followers were decisively defeated by Portuguese King Pedro IV's army. Her vision and leadership, though short-lived, introduced intriguing ideas about African adaptations of Christian ideas to their own communities. As a woman she moved beyond the boundaries set by both the Kongolese society of her birth and by the increasingly influential European Catholic settlers.

Elite women in the Kongo did not always gain such a prominent leadership role. In many cases they would wield power through their husbands. In several documented examples, women played a pivotal role in clan politics. When men in power disputed royal claims, the women used their position in their natal and marital families to mediate or bridge factions. Some elder women were considered heads of their descent groups, and they used that authority to influence family members. As with royal families elsewhere in the world, marriage was often preferred within a close circle of cousins, so women would have noble background and have influence in both connected families. In the late sixteenth and early seventeenth centuries, Kongo experienced a series of contested claims to the throne, and women in the elite families were instrumental in putting forward their favored candidates, acting more openly than they had previously when their maneuvering was hidden within their immediate family.[40]

South Africa: Eva van Meerhoff

Eva van Meerhoff, born with the name Krotoa around 1642 in southern Africa and known popularly as Eva, was one of the first African women to marry a European. She encountered Dutch settlers in the 1650s at what became Cape Town, South Africa. She was of Khoena background, and initially she was employed from the age of twelve as a domestic worker by Jan Van Riebeeck, the commander of the Dutch. After learning Dutch and some Portuguese she worked as a translator. Her eventual husband, a Danish surgeon named Pieter van Meerhoff, arrived in 1659 and they were together soon after that date. In 1664, she converted to Christianity and they married later that year, eventually having three children and remaining together until Pieter's death in 1666. Her motivations are not known, but she then began drinking excessively and became promiscuous. Her unsavory behavior led the colonists to take custody of her children and discouraged other interracial marriages. She died in 1674. Although some aspects of her personal story may depict her as a victim, it can also be argued that she took the initiative in finding employment and gaining skills that allowed her to contribute to the new society forming on the Cape.

Eva has become a contradictory emblem of African women, seen alternatively as a victim and as positive force in South African history. She has been viewed as an exemplar of African female oppression by European men and as an example of African savagery that could not be civilized. Others have positioned her as an innovative synthesizer of African and Christian religious beliefs and as the mother of the first "Coloureds" (as mixed race people in South Africa are called).[41]

Conclusion

African women have always been present and active, yet they generally have remained invisible in published information, especially for earlier historical eras. As throughout history, women's contributions to family and community have helped shape the contours of marriage and motherhood, religious beliefs, agricultural production, artistic creations, and political authority. Though much of the detail of their efforts in the earlier historic periods is difficult to discover, we can draw from evidence found in linguistic and archaeological research that suggests what ordinary women's work involved. In most cases, we have more specific information about elite women and women who came into contact with Europeans. This chapter examined women's roles in early African societies, including the division of labor along gender lines, the broad themes of kinship and descent patterns, and gender aspects of religious beliefs; it also introduced some prominent women from centuries in the past. Those areas of contribution continued to develop while African women built on the foundation of early historical communities and continued to shape their societies and their future.

Notes

1. Ehret, *The Civilizations of Africa.*
2. Schoenbrun, *A Green Place, A Good Place.*
3. Ehret, *Civilizations of Africa*, 196.
4. Parkington, "Men, Women, and Eland."
5. Hewlett, *Listen, Here Is a Story*, 154–156, 161.
6. Ouzman, "Between Margin and Centre."
7. Smith and Webley, "Women and Men of the Khoekhoen of Southern Africa."
8. Herbert, *Iron, Gender, and Power.*
9. Saidi, *Women's Authority and Society in Early East-Central Africa.*
10. Berns, "Art, History, and Gender."
11. Hodgson, "Pastoralism, Patriarchy and History," 50.
12. Worley, "Property and Gender Relations among Twareg Nomads."

13. Worley, "Property and Gender Relations among Twareg Nomads," 34.

14. Beach, "Cognitive Archaeology," and Huffman, "Where You Are the Girls Gather to Play."

15. Conrad, "Mooning Armies."

16. Conrad, "Mooning Armies."

17. Abubakr, "Queen Amina of Zaria."

18. Dapper, *Olfert Dapper's Description of Benin (1668)*.

19. Poewe, *Matrilineal Ideology*, v.

20. Sacks, *Sisters and Wives*.

21. Stephens, *A History of African Motherhood*, 56–57.

22. Boserup, *Woman's Role in Economic Development*, chapter 2, "The Economics of Polygamy."

23. Dapper, *Olfert Dapper's Description of Benin (1668)*.

24. Smedley, *Women Creating Patrilyny*.

25. Evans-Pritchard, "An Alternate Term for Brideprice."

26. Hackett, "Women in African Religions."

27. Berger, "Fertility as Power."

28. Saidi, *Women's Authority and Society in Early East-Central Africa*.

29. Berger, "Fertility as Power."

30. Musisi, "Women, 'Elite Polygyny,' and Buganda State Formation."

31. Kodesh, *Beyond the Royal Gaze*.

32. Hanson, *Landed Obligation*, and Stephens, *A History of African Motherhood*.

33. Musisi, "Women, 'Elite Polygyny,' and Buganda State Formation."

34. Kodesh, *Beyond the Royal Gaze*.

35. Schoenbrun, *A Green Place, A Good Place*, 5.

36. Nast, *Concubines and Power*.

37. Sargent, "Found in the Fog of the Male Myths."

38. Thornton, "Elite Women in the Kingdom of Kongo," and Pantoja, "Nzinga a Mbandi."

39. Thornton, *The Kongolese Saint Anthony*.

40. Thornton, "Elite Women in the Kingdom of Kongo."

41. Wells, "Eva's Men."

2 Market Traders, Queens, and Slaves in the Seventeenth and Eighteenth Centuries

This CHAPTER ADDRESSES African women's experiences in the early colonial period. During a time when most African women continued to work in family agriculture in rural areas remote from European influence, the increasing presence of European merchants, missionaries, and explorers had an impact throughout the continent. This period is difficult to articulate by focusing on women because the evidence is inconsistent and sources often reflect the biases of observers. There was little, and in many areas nothing, that told the history as experienced by African women. Researchers have used some creative methods to learn more about their lives, but information and analysis remain overly dependent on observations made by European men who held gender and racial assumptions that have shaped the available records. Nonetheless, such sources also include specific information about individual women, women's involvement in trade, and the elite women who held important political and social positions.

European Contact

Europeans first arrived at coastal communities in Africa at the end of the fifteenth century. Their comments, found in published articles and archival collections, offer some of the earliest documentation concerning African women, although such sources must be used with care. Those documents are more likely to include information on elite women or on women who were in regular contact with the European settlers, such as market women on the West African coast. There are few or no written sources left by African women discussing those early contacts, so it is impossible to know with any certainty what women thought about their encounters. Nonetheless, the stories of the women who appear in the early documents demonstrate their resilience and the extent of their input into the history of African societies.

West African Trade Networks, Seventeenth Century

As European traders landed along the West African coast, Africans who lived in those areas began to form trading alliances with them. Beginning in the sixteenth century, many of the new arrivals were Portuguese, and their success and even their survival depended on how they arranged trading partners. There were important trading depots and market towns along the coastal areas of West Africa, where African women were among the most successful and experienced traders. They were well placed to play an important role as arbiters between local societies and European merchants.

The interactions between the European male traders and the African women who frequently controlled access to trade routes and markets make up a history of cultural contact. In many cases the women and men established personal relationships, and the European men were known to adopt African customs as they settled into the local communities. When the Portuguese arrived, they found women who were wealthy property owners as a result of local and long-distance trade. Those women held some power in their towns, and the Europeans were compelled to interact with them in order to advance their own commercial interests. European reports from the seventeenth century described women who owned houses, jewelry, and luxurious clothing. Those women were often referred to by the Portuguese term of respect for women, *senhora*, or by variants including *signare*, *nhara*, and the abbreviation *Ña*, all meaning "a woman of status."[1]

By the mid- to late-seventeenth century, women in communities along the West African coast had emerged as key figures in the growing international trade networks. All along the coast near Guinea Bissau, including the Cacheu region, women were actively exporting slaves and trade items such as ivory, beeswax, animal hides, and kola nuts. They were also importing commodities such as iron bars, firearms, gunpowder, brandy, and glass beads.

Information about these women traders can be found in court records related to the Inquisition, as with the example of Crispina Peres, who came to the unwanted attention of officials of the Catholic Church. Crispina Peres was a trader who was married to a Portuguese sailor. She called on local healers to sacrifice chickens and goats in order to ensure the health of her daughter and to secure the safe voyage of her seafaring husband. As a result, she was reported to Church officials for her involvement in what were considered pagan activities. As the trial transcript noted, she had a close relationship with local communities that were described as heathen, and she was recognized as someone who connected African producers with European merchants. Women in this region commonly visited local shrines and healers when seeking assistance with matters related to their families and their work, so the fact that she was brought to court for such conduct suggests that her success as a trader drew the attention of Church authorities.

The fact that her husband's family had fled Portugal because they were Jews who faced persecution during the Inquisition adds complexity to her story and complicates the picture of Cacheu. It was an African community that was home to residents who were developing global connections along both personal and commercial lines. Crispina was taken to Lisbon in the 1660s for a hearing before the inquisitors. After several years of prison and court appearances, she was released and returned to Cacheu. The key factor in her release was testimony from her husband and others that as a woman and an African, she was "badly converted" to Catholicism and therefore was not responsible for her continued adherence to local practices.

Another renowned woman trader from the Cacheu area was Bibiana Vaz, who was the daughter of an African woman and a European man. Her extensive trading networks and commercial activities were well known. She married into the locally prominent and well-to-do Gomes family. When she was widowed in 1679, her stepson challenged her when he tried to take control of his father's commercial interests, but she succeeded in protecting her assets. In the 1680s the mayor of Cacheu attempted to restrict local traders to dealing only with the Portuguese and not with other European merchants. Ña Bibiana, as she was known, joined with her brother and some male cousins to launch a protest because they were not willing to tolerate such a curtailment of their commerce and income. With the assistance of local people, they forced the mayor to allow a British merchant ship to enter the harbor. A few days later they took the mayor hostage, and he remained imprisoned in Ña Bibiana's residence for fourteen months.

When the Vaz family and their allies took over the municipal government, the baton that was a symbol of the governor's office was handed to Ña Bibiana in a public ceremony. The new leaders acted to keep the Portuguese out, and they relied on trade with British and French merchants. However, the governor escaped, leading to an inquiry that made it clear that Ña Bibiana was implicated in every action taken by her brother and other conspirators. In 1687, Ña Bibiana and her brother were arrested and sent to Santiago, Cape Verde. The authorities wished to bring them to Lisbon, but they protested their innocence, and observers noted that Ña Bibiana was elderly and ill and could not tolerate such an ocean voyage.

Ultimately, the official who captured Ña Bibiana by dragging her from the house of an African ruler was not able to gain control of any of her wealth. It was later learned that her cousin had taken her goods to Sierra Leone for safekeeping. The conspirators were given a royal pardon and paid only minimal fines, reflecting both Portuguese weakness in the region and the political and economic importance of Ña Bibiana and her family to stability in Cacheu and along the coast. She engineered her brother's release and was responsible for paying the fine imposed by the Portuguese. She apparently died around 1694, having acted to protect the interests of local merchants in opposition to imperial claims by the Portuguese in particular.

The primary sources of information for both Ña Crispina and Ña Bibiana were Portuguese reports and trial records, all written by European men. But even with that filter, which reflected a world view quite different from that of the African women under consideration, it was clear that those women had strong personalities, were active businesswomen, and were involved in the politics of the West African coast. They did not acquiesce to Portuguese expectations of sub-servient female behavior (not that all Portuguese women met such expectations themselves). They took advantage of their cross-cultural personal connections, probable multilingual abilities, acute commercial knowledge, and deep under-standing of local political alliances in their efforts to protect and advance their own positions, their families' wealth, and their political independence.

West African Trade Networks, Eighteenth Century

Women continued to play a visible role mediating trade between African and European merchants and communities in the eighteenth century. The historical records that provide clues about these women include official reports and legal proclamations. European men were restricted from cohabiting with local women, with the result that individual men frequently petitioned for exemptions from the law so that they could marry African women. Governor Dubellay, governor of St. Louis (in what is today Senegal) from 1722 to 1755, argued that if European men could establish households, they would become steadier employees of the local trading company. His proposal was rejected by the company directors, who expressly prohibited marriage between white men and women of color. Later gov-ernors tried repeatedly to allow such liaisons, suggesting that the prohibition of interracial marriage forced Christian men into illicit arrangements that were con-sidered sinful, and also maintaining they would have greater control over covert trading if the personal relationships were legalized. Women of mixed Portuguese or French and African backgrounds continued to appear in the reports throughout West Africa as people of great wealth, commercial ability, and political influence.

Marie Mar, who lived on the banks of the Gambia River, was noted for the assistance she gave to shipwrecked European sailors—her name, "Mar," perhaps referring to her affinity for the sea. She hosted French merchants in her large European-style house, and they reported on her wealth and the slaves who served them. In describing the race and nationality of Marie Mar and other African women intermediaries, the European men often seemed uncertain. Though Afri-can in appearance, the women were frequently fluent in French, Portuguese, and English, dressed in European clothing, and considered themselves to be Portu-guese or otherwise in a non-African category. Marie Mar was like many Afri-can women who married European men, and whose mixed-race offspring were prominent in the coastal trading towns; their very existence was evidence of the developing communities of people who maintained close ties with both the Afri-can kin of their mothers and the European networks of their fathers.[2]

European administrators were not successful in their attempts to restrict interracial unions, as many traders yielded to the attractions of marrying African women following local marriage customs. Descriptions of coastal communities in the mid-eighteenth century described a level of comfortable affluence that was in part a result of their trade in duty-free salt. The female merchants owned dozens of slaves who engaged in that trade. Their wealth allowed them to dress in fashionable clothing and sponsor dances and other entertainments. The European men who wrote about women presented a voyeuristic context that sometimes served to reduce the women in Senegal to sexual objects, with frequent references to their beauty and sometimes to nudity. Nonetheless, the Europeans' detailed catalogs of women's outfits provide evidence of female wealth and status.[3]

The marriages were usually contracted according to the *mode du pays*, the custom of the country, so African practices prevailed. Among the Wolof people in Senegambia, fathers arranged or approved the marriage of their daughters, and the groom, whether African or European, made a payment to the bride's family. The Europeans would sponsor a banquet for the wife's family. The women were acknowledged to be faithful, and they regarded themselves as legitimately wed. Any children were given the name of the father. As often occurred, when the father returned to Europe, the marriage ended and the wife was free to enter into a new marriage. As single women, whether widowed or abandoned, the women were able to protect their property and their financial interests despite potential claims from kin and local rulers. Their skills and wealth gave them an advantage in any negotiations and made them desirable partners for other Europeans.

By the early nineteenth century, men and women of mixed European and African descent were prominent in coastal politics and commerce. Marie Mar and other women like her were able to draw on their family connections within both European and local communities. They often enjoyed wealth that resulted from the successful trade of their parents and grandparents, who had collaborated in extending commerce throughout the region and between West Africa and Europe. They had been translators both in the literal sense of learning French or Portuguese, by interpreting conversations and facilitating commercial transactions, and in the broader sense as cultural ambassadors.

Markets in Sierra Leone

The coast of Sierra Leone was an integral part of the African and European regional trading networks that included Guinea and Senegal. In the 1700s there were trading systems that brought salt, fish, and rice from the coast to the interior in exchange for cattle, other livestock, and meat products. But a somewhat different history developed in Sierra Leone that did not solely involve local Africans and newly arrived Europeans. Beginning in the eighteenth century, the coast of Sierra Leone was known as a site for bringing Africans back to Africa from North America and Europe. Although there were indigenous people living in that region, in 1787 a group of British philanthropists interested in the abolition of slavery established a colony for black freedmen and women. The first group included only four hundred people, but they were soon joined by one thousand ex-slaves from Nova Scotia who had fought on the British side during the American Revolution. In 1800, another large group, known as Maroons, arrived from Jamaica, and the settlement began to develop its own cultural characteristics. By the end of the nineteenth century, the black people who colonized Sierra Leone became known as Krio (Creole); they viewed themselves as distinct from local groups and maintained a careful separation.

The Europeans and North Americans who funded and facilitated the colony were interested in gaining access to markets in the hinterland and in developing an alternative to the slave trade. Thus, women's work, especially as traders, was a key factor in the success of the settlement that later became the urban center of the colony, Freetown. As with urban areas in many parts of the world, it was possible for women to pursue a life of greater independence in town, and the settler women were particularly interested in finding such a life for themselves. Some of the women arrived with a strong sense of their own economic autonomy, and they fully expected to engage in trading and other activities in order to support themselves.

The settler women tended to have greater mobility than local women, as they did not have the same ties binding them to family and local land holdings that African inhabitants had. The Africans' interlude in Nova Scotia, for instance, introduced them to Christianity and reduced their expectations of following African marital customs such as the exchange of bridewealth and the practice of levirate marriage, in which a widow married a man from her deceased husband's clan. As a group, the immigrant women were more likely to be in monogamous marriages, but they were also more likely than local women to have access to divorce. In 1802, one-third of the households that originated in Nova Scotia were headed by women.[4]

The women were poised to get involved in trading, though at first they faced further obstacles since the European-managed Sierra Leone Company tried to control commercial and traveling traders. When the company allowed the settlers of African descent to apply for retail trading licenses in 1794, three of the first six applicants were women. One of those women, Mary Perth, demonstrated great initiative and skill. She had been a slave in Virginia and had sided with other slaves who supported the British in hopes of gaining their freedom if the British had succeeded in suppressing the colonial revolt. The British then helped her move with her three daughters to New York, where she married Cesar Perth.

The family went to Nova Scotia after the American Revolution, and in 1792 they traveled to Sierra Leone as part of the resettlement project. She had learned to read when she was younger and was active as a preacher. In Sierra Leone her abilities were recognized by the colonial governor who hired her to manage his household and teach the black children housed in his residence. She was noted for rescuing the children when Freetown was bombarded by the French in 1794. When the town was rebuilt following that attack, she established a boarding house and set up her trading enterprise. At one point she traveled to England with the governor, where she sought medical treatment for one of her children. She continued to be a Methodist religious leader throughout her life.[5] Sophie Smalls, also one of the initial three licensed women, was noted for building the first two-story house in Freetown in 1796, with her income reflecting her astute trading acumen.

The Nova Scotia settlers' success in trade was soon eclipsed by the arrival of Maroons from Jamaica and then larger numbers of Africans recaptured from slave ships and returned to Africa at Freetown by the British Royal Navy. Each of these groups brought very different ideas about family life, religion, and women's economic autonomy. The Africans from the recaptured ships were mainly of Yoruba background and originally from Nigeria. In Sierra Leone they became known as Aku, and archival records repeatedly comment on the trading abilities of Aku women. European visitors and settlers observed Aku success throughout the nineteenth century. As the governor wrote in 1879, "from babyhood the Aku girl is a trader, and as she grows up she carries her small wares wherever she can go with safety. The further she goes from the European trading depots the better is her market."[6] Aku women were involved in long distance trade of palm kernels and kola nuts, and the increased commercial interest encouraged an expansion in the cultivation of these items.

Though the social identities of the successful trading women shifted over time, they all played a role in the economic and cultural development of the resettled communities in Freetown. Their trading was at the basis of international commerce and stimulated local cultivation of cash crops. Certainly, Sierra Leone and other coastal settlements depended on the efforts of these women.

Angola

In the early Portuguese settlements in Benguela, Angola, many women moved between residence in rural African communities and work in the growing urban center of Benguela, and their status was noted sometimes clearly as free women and sometimes ambiguously as servile. Intimate relationships between Portuguese men and local women were common, though there was little detail concerning whether those unions were initiated by force or common interest. Relationships were sometimes between Portuguese men and elite African women, in which both individuals were able to improve their own positions in the newly developing urban trading society. In other cases, Portuguese slave owners had relations with enslaved women under their control. But as couples remained together and had children, they often sought to regularize their social status by church attendance and christening their offspring. Parish records provide some details about women in Benguela.

As in other coastal trading centers, indigenous women provided advantages to the European men in the form of familiarity with African languages, local produce and markets, and regional personnel. Some African women were certainly captured during the frequent raids and armed conflicts that occurred throughout the area, and many were sold into the international trade and sent to Brazil or other overseas sites. But for others, their enslavement could be mitigated by developing relationships with European men, gaining a foothold in local markets, and at times becoming slave owners themselves. Female slave owners were documented as relying on slave labor to tend crops on plots in Benguela, produce that was consumed by the household and sold in the local markets. The women also used their wealth to lend money to Portuguese men, as recorded in the will of one man that acknowledged his debt to Dona Joana Gomes Moutinho, an African female trader who had advanced slaves to him for sale overseas. Dona Joana lived in a two-story house, and her fifty slaves lived in housing in an adjacent yard.

Both African women and European men benefited from their interactions and relationships. The European men likely had a better chance of survival if they were able to live in a household that provided reliable meals, healthy accommodations, and companionship, as well as access to trade items and local markets that would have been off-limits without a personal connection. Their mixed-race children were considered to be Portuguese culturally, and they commonly played key roles in the Portuguese colonial bureaucracy and commercial efforts, as Portuguese settlers were insufficient in number and less competent in playing intermediary roles. The African women and their descendants were able to use their own local knowledge and skills to increase their wealth and the comfort of their living situations, gaining status in African societies and in the growing urban center.[7]

Slavery

The practice and experience of slavery varied widely from one place or region to another, was different in Muslim and non-Muslim societies, diverged for men and for women, and changed significantly over time. During the eighteenth century there was a notable increase in overseas slave trading, which built on the African practice of pawning individuals as payment for debts and on the incorporation of war captives into local societies. As the slave trade expanded, Western opinion in opposition to the trade also rose, with a strong movement for ending slavery and the slave trade rising in the late 1700s. In 1807, the United States and Great Britain were among the earliest nations to outlaw the slave trade, and other nations followed suit throughout the nineteenth century. In the United States, slavery ended in 1865 with a constitutional amendment outlawing it, and elsewhere it was made illegal over the ensuing decades. Legally ending the trade did not completely end slavery because there were delays in spreading the information, and for enslaved people it was often not a simple act to leave their conditions of forced servitude. Even into the twenty-first century, people in Africa and elsewhere in the world were still enduring forced labor, sexual trafficking, and other forms of slavery.

Although it was difficult if not impossible to accurately determine the number of slaves within Africa, it appeared that enslaved people were more likely to be women, a reflection of their productive and reproductive contributions to their communities. Female slaves also commanded higher prices than men in the internal African slave market. Of the estimated twelve million slaves taken from Africa to the Americas between the sixteenth and nineteenth centuries, about five million, or fewer than 40 percent, were women.[8] Africans were also shipped to the Arabian Peninsula and across the Sahara into Muslim markets, but the numbers are uncertain. Many women remained in African communities and households performing forced and unremunerated labor.

Women were also slave owners, as noted earlier in this chapter, especially in areas where they had the opportunity to accrue wealth through trading and market work. Female slave owners were particularly noted in West Africa, where some women gained wealth through their market trading and required labor to help them in that business.

The stigma of being enslaved varied from place to place. In some areas, people were clearly remembered as being slave descendants long after the slave trade and slavery officially ended. Simultaneously, however, slave men and women were often able to work in strikingly independent ways and to rise above their slave status through hard work. Specific histories of enslaved women in Africa will be told throughout this textbook, in order to suggest the range of experiences and to confirm the absence of a single story of slavery and women. The history of the enslaved women in the Fon royal palace in Dahomey provides a complicated and nuanced example.

Dahomey and Women in the Royal Household

Much remains obscure about the early organization of the Fon Kingdom of Dahomey, located in the modern nation of Benin. It was well established by the mid-eighteenth century, with an ethos of expansion and control over neighboring polities. Early European observers noted what caught their attention, which was a large number of women living in the royal household. Some of those women served as guards and soldiers, giving rise to the common but inaccurate idea that they were Amazons, a term that drew on Greek mythology to describe an unrelated African practice. For a time in the 1700s, Fon women appeared to have an unusual amount of power; by the nineteenth century, much of that had been eclipsed by changes in local economics and politics.[9]

African societies typically depended on controlling people, their labor, and reproductive capabilities, in order to develop. For the royal clan in a relatively new centralized state, control over dependent people was a key issue as they sought greater wealth and prestige. While the evidence is scanty, it appears that sometime during the seventeenth century, the king of Dahomey began capturing women to serve in his royal household as wives, often choosing women who facilitated forming alliances with neighboring chiefdoms. By 1724, a British visitor estimated that there were more than two thousand wives in the palace.

The women and other dependents in the palace were called *ahosi*. While there were enslaved women and others who were dependent on the royal family, many engaged in economic pursuits on their own account. Visitors described activities carried out by the royal women, including agricultural cultivation, making items for sale in the markets for their personal income, and, on occasion, involvement with palace and kingdom administration. While all women were farmers and market traders, only ahosi worked for the king as messengers, performers, spies, soldiers, and even ministers of state in the royal administration. The royal women were restricted from interacting with nonroyal community members. Entrance to the palace was strictly controlled, and when the royal women left the palace on business, other Fon were expected to step aside and allow them passage. The ahosi also carried out punishment on the orders of the king, destroying the property of an individual found guilty of crimes against the state, for instance. No one could stop the women, as they were agents of the king and it was forbidden to touch the wives of members of the royal clan.

Another category of women in the royal household were those born into the royal family, sometimes called princesses in historical literature. They married men from other clans, but their offspring were not considered members of that clan in the usual pattern of patrilineal societies. Rather, all of the children of princesses were incorporated into the royal clan. This practice added dependents to the royal household and also allowed a certain freedom to the women. Because the children did not become members of their fathers' clans, the identity of their fathers was of less importance, and those men, the husbands of the princesses, had a decreased interest in controlling their wives' sexual activities. The women recognized the leadership of one woman who was considered to be the oldest daughter. That woman could serve as regent, appoint new leaders to lineages, and was a pivotal person in all lineage decisions. Her responsibilities were much like queen mothers in other societies.

Though sources do not always agree about the details, there were royal women who assumed leadership. One of the best known was Hangbe, who became regent when her twin brother, the king, died unexpectedly around 1718 and her son was too young to assume the throne. Another brother contested her rule, and she assembled an army to protect the throne for herself and her own son. Little is known of her fate, as she lost the battle when her son was killed and she was forced to abdicate after three years of holding power at the center of government.

Although such examples of women who were rulers were rare, observers in the 1720s commented on the presence of women who surrounded the male king. It was women who received visitors and relayed messages directly to the king's ear; they attended the king with royal regalia such as gold, jewels, and umbrellas, a common marker of rank in West Africa. But what really caught the attention of the British visitors were the four armed women standing near the king who held muskets on their shoulders or pistols or sabers in their hands. Reports from other regions of West Africa included descriptions of women involved in combat, but there appears to be no similar situation where women were specifically armed with modern firearms and placed as royal guards.

Simultaneously with the introduction of armed female guards was the formalization of the institution of queen mother, known as *kpojito*, in Dahomey. The king always ruled with a reign-mate, a woman chosen from the ranks of the wives of the previous king. While that woman might not be the actual mother of the king, she was from the cohort of royal cowives and was considered to be the royal mother. The formal position was established by a royal woman named Adonon around 1720, building on existing positions of female authority in which women ruled in conjunction with male rulers. The mythic origins of the Dahomean state told of a leopard and a royal princess who mated and whose offspring were the beginning of the royal lineage. That princess and her son then ruled as a pair, and all kings thereafter also had a mother or mother figure as a coruler. While this practice had been followed for some time, and was similar to other West African royal procedures, only in the early eighteenth century was the kpojito established in a more formal way.

Kpojitos, who continued to use the term Adonon as a title to commemorate the first kpojito, were women of great wealth and influence. They owned plantations and slaves who cultivated their land. They were religious and ritual leaders of the local voudun religion (familiar in the Western hemisphere as "voodoo"). They had privileged access to the king. They were not necessarily born to the royal family, but in some cases were captured as part of the expansion of Dahomey in the region, and their incorporation into the monarchy represented the absorption of their homeland into the kingdom.

Later in the eighteenth century, the kpojito Hwanjile played a central role in organizing local groups of voudun followers in a way that complemented the

LES AMAZONES A L'EXERCICE.

Fig. 2.1 Women soldiers of Dahomey doing military exercises. Source: Edouard Foà, *Dahomey* (Paris: A. Hennuyer, 1895), facing p. 254, from the Bibliothèque nationale de France.

royal hierarchy and that lessened local conflict. While later kpojitos also assumed the name *Hwanjile* as a title, the first Hwanjile joined the royal household ranks of ahosi as an adult voudun leader who already had two children. Her skills and reputed beauty brought her to the attention of the royal family, who brought her into the palace to help organize and settle a volatile situation.

Dahomey's economy relied heavily on the export of Africans into the international slave trade during the 1700s. As part of a ritual of conspicuous consumption, the king controlled that trade and used his wealth to distribute women as wives to his followers, sometimes as outright gifts. European visitors regularly commented on the amount and quality of the food and beverages they were given, the cloth, silver, and other goods they received as gifts or in exchange for imports, and the level of luxury found in the royal palace. While there were plantations worked by slaves, the majority of royal income was not from crops but from the trade in people. Since slaves were collected as war captives, the slave trade in turn was built on conflict, and that conflict connected the territorial expansion of the Dahomean state, the wealth the royal family derived from selling those captives to slave traders, and the weapons they received in return, which then were used in the repetitive conflicts instigated by successive kings who sought to further expand the state. It was a grim cycle that was seen elsewhere in Africa during that century.

One result was that Dahomey had an army that was feared throughout the region. And the unusual aspect of that respected army was the inclusion of women, at least as armed royal guards. They were seen by Europeans marching in formation as part of parades to display royal wealth; "each [woman] well armed with a small musketoon and a small short sword for which the scabbard is ordinarily of crimson velvet; their only clothing is a little wrapper of silk around the hips, which comes down to their knees. Thus armed and with two or three flags of silk, these women with the commanders march slowly in rows of four each."[10] There were four or five companies, with as many as one hundred in each, amounting to a sizable force of powerful women.

Whether they were regularly used in combat was unclear; one example from 1729 had the women placed at the rear, so that they were removed from direct conflict while their presence served to frighten the enemy because their numbers suggested that the army was quite large. In 1781, there was a further report of the king leading eight hundred women to war upon learning that a military troop of his male soldiers had been defeated. The women went as replacements, and once again the sheer numbers of attackers compelled the enemy to flee. The evidence is slim, but it was probable that the Dahomean female soldiers were rarely used in actual combat outside the palace, while their role as armed guards within the royal household allowed more men to be actively involved in combat.

By the late eighteenth century, the palace was the site of a large population who provided links to their home villages and strengthened the networks connecting the kingdom. There were many slaves, both men and women, who resided in the palace, including war captives and women who were selected from Dahomean families that hoped to benefit from a direct relationship with the ruling dynasty. Nonetheless, it can be assumed that all of the ahosi were slaves who joined the royal household as a result of being captured during war, of being pawned by a family member to repay a debt, or by entering into an arranged marriage with the king. Dahomeans described the ahosi as being stolen or kidnapped. Since wives of the king were forbidden from divorcing him, unlike in ordinary marriages, they were not free to leave; and regardless of their route to the palace, they were unfree or enslaved to some degree.

The size and rate of growth of the royal household was indicated by observers who suggested first in 1724 that there were about two thousand women there, and then just fifty years later, they suggested that the palace housed three or four thousand women. Although polygyny was the norm in much of Africa, and high numbers of wives were not uncommon for royal men, the situation in Dahomey was unusual even by those standards. And despite their slave status, women who joined the palace hierarchy had an opportunity to enjoy great wealth and authority. Observers described a sense of community and even pride among the women who served the king and the royal family. As the slave trade grew and more adult men were shipped overseas, the numbers of available men declined, at times falling to only seventy men for every one hundred women. In a society where it was assumed that adult females would marry and have a family, the lack of potential husbands may have encouraged women to accept marriage to the king where they could enjoy a recognized status and personal stability.

Despite reports of luxury, it should not be assumed that life was comfortable in the palace. The work performed by the ahosi was similar to women's tasks in any household, with agriculture, food preparation, ritual duties, and sex all being expected of a wife. In the royal household, however, the extent of those domestic chores was much grander, as the number of people requiring food and housing was so large. The ahosi were also expected to provide sexual services, not only for their husband, the king, but certain women were placed in lodgings where they accepted all men who were willing to pay a pittance. Though the price the women could charge for each encounter rose over the decades, it remained a small fraction of the amount that people paid for a single chicken. Many of the women who were forced into prostitution for the king actually supported themselves by breeding chickens or brewing beer, not from their sexual availability.

The widespread references to female soldiers in Dahomey are not false claims, but they do not truly describe the complex situation in the palace during the eighteenth century. Though the situation shifted in the next century, at the end of the 1700s there were armed women who acted as guards; there were hundreds and even thousands of women slaves who comprised the royal household and served the king; and there were royal wives and sexual slaves. While women did hold important political positions, engage in the business of the kingdom, and occasionally rose to have wealth and status, they were also vulnerable and restricted to typical women's chores and limited options. As queen mothers, they could influence the royal succession. As enslaved prostitutes, they were forced into a life of pain and marginalization. As part of the majority of women in the household, they might be soldiers or farmers or ritual healers. Upon being recruited or dragooned into the palace, a woman's fate was largely in the hands of the king.

Varieties of Slavery in the Gold Coast

In Asante communities along the coast of what was later Ghana, European observers described a practice where young women were inducted into a status that had ritual importance, but that Europeans considered to be prostitution.[11]

The women were usually slaves who were expected to be sexually available for unmarried men; while they were not paid, the men offered them gifts following an encounter. Their role was to alleviate sexual tension and misbehavior by men; as was the case in many societies, the effort to control men's promiscuous behavior was achieved by restrictions on women's sexual conduct. Among the Asante, the ability of older wealthy men to acquire more than one wife contributed to a sexual imbalance, where there were too few young women for young men to marry. The women who were freely available were bought as slaves, introduced in a public ceremony, provided with an older woman who acted as a mentor, and settled in a small hut on the margins of the community. All adult Asante women were assumed to be married. In contrast, the slave women who lived in the communal building were considered "public women," whose role was to diminish cases of adultery and other sexual activity that might cause disruption and upheaval in society. The ritual for the public women paralleled Asante marriage ceremonies and the induction of priestesses, and it acknowledged them as adults with a specific place in the community.

Along the Gold Coast in Fante communities, enslaved women were sometimes employed in the merchant forts called "castles."[12] The male castle slaves worked in skilled jobs such as carpenters, porters, and translators, while women were responsible for domestic chores required by European traders. Though tied through bondage to the European merchants, they had freedom of movement in the community and were distinct from the many other Africans who were held at the castles in preparation for being shipped overseas as part of the international slave trade. Their numbers increased in the eighteenth century as the slave trade grew, though there were only a few hundred in the forts at any time. Nearly half were born in the fort, though others were there because they were captured for the international trade and then left behind; some were pawns who were left as collateral for a debt and then never redeemed or returned to their community of origin.

The presence of female slaves and the record of their work suggest some of the contradictions of the slave trade as well as the contributions of African women to the functioning of that trade. The enslaved women in the forts did the laundry and cooking, and they were recognized for their nursing skills in tending European merchants who became ill, as was often the case. It was likely that those skills were based on African knowledge of the healing properties of indigenous plants.

Although the available information is vague concerning relations between the women and European men, the women regularly worked in the domestic residences of the men, and it was likely that they were vulnerable to rape and sexual abuse. The growth of a mixed-race population certainly indicated that sexual relations occurred. Most of the female castle slaves were mothers, and log books from the forts list a high number of infants and small children among the residents. The 1764 records for Cape Coast Castle counted 112 castle slave women; 36 of them were raising a child or children. Those children, raised in the forts, often continued to work there and became the next generation of castle slaves.

As with other parts of the West African coast, at times such relations were mutually sought after and enjoyed, as indicated in the wills left by the men. In one example, a merchant named John William Mitchell left twenty pounds sterling and two gold rings to Nanie, "in consideration of her strict attention and attendance on me during the three years we have lived together."[13] Other wills mentioned the nursing care they received from the African woman who worked for them, and in some cases the European men left the women not only cash and gold, but slaves. Thus, as elsewhere, such relationships could result in notable wealth for the woman. Women's work in maintaining livable conditions for merchants along the coast has long been obscured, but it was essential to the success of that commerce and the development of a community.

West Africa: Women's Organizations

Women generally had only indirect access to power and authority in African societies. But there is evidence of a variety of routes to exercise authority, including through women's organizations. Women advanced to leadership positions through elaborate systems of rank and naming, and women's groups were viewed as complementary to men's groups within the community. In West Africa there were market women's groups that controlled marketplace activities. In many regions of Africa, women had important religious roles, especially as they aged and became senior members of their societies.

Nigeria: Dual-Sex Organizations

Among the Yoruba in what is today Nigeria, women's trading networks gained increasing importance in the fifteenth century. Existing markets in produce and crafts grew into long-distance systems of trade from their own coastal areas into the northern hinterlands. Men dominated the trade in luxury items, but women controlled trade in cloth, food, and locally produced crafts such as woven mats. And women organized their own local trading activities under a female authority known as the *iyalode*, meaning "mother in charge of external affairs," indicating her responsibilities for political affairs and especially for the concerns of market women. Considered the ruler of all women, the iyalode commanded her own entourage of servants, drummers, and bell ringers. Women did not inherit the iyalode position, but they earned it through a life of prosperous trade and virtuous behavior. An iyalode mediated conflicts and determined the location of new markets, and women relied on her to protect their commercial and personal interests.[14]

Among the Igbo, also in Nigeria, women participated in systems of political organization that have been termed "dual sex"; those systems granted equal and complementary roles to men and women.[15] Women usually had control over certain aspects of their communities, including marketing and the cultivation of particular crops, and they had authority over male behavior that infringed on women's domains. Both men and women had access to prestigious titles and positions within their respective societies, and men were not assumed to be above women in a hierarchical arrangement of power and authority. Under the flexibility of such systems, women held positions in royal councils, were associated with the establishment of towns and villages, at times were rulers and acted to defend their polities, held diplomatic positions, and were closely involved in the making and unmaking of male kings. Notably they exercised leadership in women's courts, as market authorities, and in female-specific secret societies and associations based on age-related or generational cohorts.

Women in dual-sex systems also had a judicial role, as they mediated in cases involving women or women's domains in society. Spiritually, the dual-sex societies recognized a parallel set of male and female deities, including Ala, an earth goddess who had a direct connection to people's daily lives and well-being. Many lesser goddesses were honored in shrines and ceremonies.

Sierra Leone: Girls' Initiation Societies

The origins of gender-connected secret societies were not recorded, but early European travelers in West Africa noted the presence of clandestine groups that sponsored rites of passage for young people. Many societies along what was called the upper Guinea coast, including what were later Sierra Leone, Liberia, Guinea, and Cape Verde, were organized into hierarchical age grades. Sande (sometimes called Bundu) was a women's secret society in Sierra Leone and Liberia among the Mende, Kpelle, and other related peoples. There was a parallel men's society called Poro, and Poro and Sande acted together to consolidate the larger community. The societies were a space where female leadership was able to develop, and older women who had matured and risen in status led Sande and at times became chiefs of the larger community beyond the women's societies.

A primary responsibility was to oversee girls' initiation rites and to enforce laws that female ancestors had handed down to regulate society. Girls (and boys) beginning puberty entered into a prolonged training program during which they were physically separated from the rest of their community. Often described as "secret societies" because of the degree of seclusion and the fact that men could not know about the women's rites and vice versa, the practice was central to teaching girls how to be contributing adult women in their community.

The female leaders determined the timing of initiation rites, the process of teaching, the practice of female circumcision or genital cutting, and the

Fig. 2.2 Women wearing Sande society masks during a ceremonial performance, Sierra Leone, 1970s. Photograph courtesy of Rebecca Busselle.

development of young girls into women ready for marriage, adult sexuality, and motherhood. During the initiation schools, women danced while wearing ritual masks that were well known as an art form. The masks, though fashioned by professional male woodcarvers, were only owned by women. A typical mask was shaped like a helmet and included a woman's face, an elaborate hairstyle, and additional pouches for holding medicines, although within those guidelines there was a great deal of variety. Relatively little is known about the function of the societies in earlier times, but many of the attributes observed by the early travelers were seen into the nineteenth and twentieth centuries. They were clearly parallel in structure and practice to the more deeply studied organizations of later eras.[16]

East and Central Africa

Although local organizations among women in various East African societies were generally less formalized than those in West Africa, they played a similar role in providing women the space to meet together and to act to protect women's interests within their communities. Examples in this section discuss women's groups of the Gikuyu in what is now Kenya, Ethiopian women's resistance to Portuguese religious propaganda, and women rulers in areas that are now part of Rwanda and Zambia.

Gikuyu

The Gikuyu in Kenya is one example of a society strongly organized along gender lines.[17] Men and women had different areas of responsibility, and generally men had a more public role of authority within the village and regional organizations. Women did much of the daily labor of collecting water and firewood, and weeding and other farming tasks, but these important contributions did not result in economic or political power. Men's work was more focused on livestock, and the ownership and exchange of cattle was also a source of political authority for men in a way that the production of food crops was not for women. While women were commonly consulted about issues such as the distribution of family resources and plans for agriculture and food production, they were not equal to men in the decision-making process. Men were able to rise through the ranks as warriors to become elders with real power in Gikuyu society. Women had women's councils, but these held less power and served a more advisory function. Their weaker position vis á vis men developed from legal concerns that placed all land-holding under male control; women could not own, transfer, or inherit land. Their agricultural work gave them managerial responsibility, but they continued to be dependent on their husbands or other male kin for access to that land. Men, especially elders, had political authority in part as a result of their land ownership.

Women did meet in women's councils, where they determined the timing of girls' initiation rites, disciplined girls and women for misbehavior, and had some control over other domestic and household concerns. Women's councils made collective decisions about agricultural work by organizing work parties, gathering thatch and other housing materials, and preparing food for ceremonial occasions. They also had some limited options for sanctioning men who transgressed the bounds of proper conduct. They were most visible in Gikuyu public life as participants, observers, and witnesses at ceremonial activities such as when new land was cleared or when a homestead had to be purified after a social rule had been contravened.

As was common in many African societies, and indeed societies around the world, women were restricted from a more central role by taboos designed to control their sexuality, fears about their reproductive activities including ideas about menstruation being unclean, and beliefs that women were responsible for bad events because they were practitioners of witchcraft or similar questionable endeavors. Despite the gender inequality, Gikuyu women's councils provided a basis for women's collective political action in later decades.

Ethiopian Women's Resistance

The story of European contact with the people and rulers of Ethiopia had a very different trajectory, which can be attributed at least in part to the key role of royal and religious women. After the mid-fifteenth century, some small king-doms arose in the Sudanic belt of northern Africa. In Sinnar, in eastern Sudan, governors of outlying areas were required to marry women from the royal family, who then acted as agents for the ruler in the far-flung regions under his control. The presence of women holding positions of authority over a long time period contributed to the suggestion that Meroë was a matrilineal society, though gener-ally matrilineal descent was not found in large centralized states.[18]

When Portuguese Roman Catholic priests began to arrive in the sixteenth century, they worked to convert the royal family, who were Coptic Christians, to Catholicism. The priests were able to convert male leaders in part because the men sought access to weapons provided by the Portuguese. But a key component of the eventual defeat of European Roman Catholic interests was the refusal of Ethiopian women to accept the new beliefs and reject their own historical reli-gious tenets.

Ethiopian royal women in the early modern era were powerful; they could act independently, were long-serving regents for young kings, and could not be deposed. Kinship rules insured that they married outside of the royal family, so they were usually more important socially and politically than the men they married. Surviving reports by Portuguese priests emphasized the political, sex-ual, and religious freedom of the royal women, though the priests framed that freedom in a negative way. Reading between the lines, it was clear that the Ethio-pian women had much to protect and certainly saw clearly what they might lose, when the Catholic priests tried to convert them.

In 1626, the arrival of a more aggressive Portuguese priest led to the conver-sion of Emperor Susenyos. But the emperor was opposed by the women in his own family, as his mother reproached him, his wife left, and his daughter took part in an armed insurrection. His daughter-in-law, Adero Maryam, refused to convert and led an armed revolt. Susenyos condemned her to death, an action that angered the other royal women who staged a nonviolent demonstration to show their opposition to his actions. Nonetheless, the emperor so feared Adero Maryam that he carried out the death sentence in 1628, commanding the other women to observe her hanging.

In 1632, Susenyos abandoned his own conversion and stopped his attempt to convert his people. He abdicated in favor of his son, who ended the Roman Catholic presence in Ethiopia. By 1645 all the European priests had been killed or exiled, and there was no longer any Portuguese presence in Ethiopia. This sin-gular victory over a European colonial incursion was in large part the result of the strong reaction of Ethiopian royal women who defended their own faith and rejected the foreign practices.

Of particular interest is the existence of early texts written by and about women, documenting their activities. The women spoke out publicly, preached against Catholic teachings, and in some cases fomented armed rebellion in order to protect their own culture and political arrangements. Both men and women who resisted Catholicism were the subject of hagiographies, and their stories were handed down as exemplars of religious and courageous people. At least a dozen of these texts recall the lives of heroic women.

One woman, Walatta Petros (1594–1643), was elevated to sainthood in the Coptic tradition in recognition of her actions. She came from a loving and prominent family, as was evident from some of the texts that have been discovered, carefully protected, and venerated in Ethiopian monasteries. Her father was governor of a province in Tigray. She later suffered the loss of all three of her children, and then left her marriage after her husband converted to Catholicism, and entered a convent planning to follow the celibate life of an Ethiopian nun. In his efforts to bring her back, her husband reportedly burned down the town that housed the monastery where she resided, only to have her leave again as she chose to live a religious life. Testimony provides further context for her actions; when closely questioned by Portuguese priests about her refusal to convert, she spoke out about preserving the faith of their ancestors and rejected the "filthy faith of the foreigners."[19] Walatta Petros was not the only woman to fight to retain her ancestral faith and refuse to submit. Powerful Ethiopian women were a key factor in the eventual defeat of an early Portuguese attempt to control this region of Africa.

Women continued to play leadership roles in Ethiopia in the eighteenth century. Menetewab ruled Ethiopia from around 1730 to 1769. Her name at birth was Walata Giorgis, and she was also known as Berhan Mogasa. A descendant on one side from Portuguese settlers, she married Emperor Bakaffa in the 1720s. On his death in 1730 she became regent on behalf of her infant son, Iyasu II, and continued to rule when it became clear that her son preferred to spend his time hunting and collecting rather than dealing with politics. Following his death in 1755, she continued to hold the throne in the name of her grandson, Iyoas, who died at an early age in 1769. Menetewab lost popularity among the nobility because she favored her relatives for powerful positions. After her candidate for succession in 1769 did not become emperor, she moved to Cusquam where she continued to maneuver to enthrone her own choices.

The actions of Ethiopian women were essential to the continuity of an independent Coptic Christian society. They held positions of authority and used those positions to maneuver their kin, to gather followers, and to oppose colonial incursions. Women's work shaped Ethiopia in crucial ways.

Royal Women of East Africa

AKECH

Other East African societies also recorded women in positions of power in the eighteenth century. Akech ruled from around 1760 until her death in 1787 in the

East African lake region chiefdom of Paroketu. She was the second wife of Rwoth (King) Nyabongo. Succession to the royal seat had been patrilineal, and in the customary order Nyabongo would have been succeeded by Jobi, the oldest son of Nyabongo's senior wife, Akura. But Akech rose to political prominence as a royal wife and ritual leader, and by 1760 she was able to move into a powerful position. After her son Roketu came to power, the people of the palace were known as the Pa-Akech, the people of Akech, and she was recognized as the founder of a ruling dynasty.[20]

NACHITUTI

A woman called Nachituti came to prominence among the people of the Luapula Valley in Central Africa in the eighteenth century. Although her story may be apocryphal, people in eastern Luapula in Zambia in the late twentieth century continued to care for her grave, which was located in the royal cemetery. That a social memory of her persisted suggests the importance of either a real woman or the centrality of the events that defined Luapula identity. Chiefs among the Luapula were male and patrilineal. They were known by the name Kazembe and were called Mwata (King) Kazembe, each new ruler taking on that name and rank. This practice of perpetuating names, ranks, and kin relations might also apply to Nachituti, suggesting that perhaps there was a series of women who carried the name.

The eighteenth century was a time of conflict and migration in Central Africa, with various groups invading and conquering their neighbors. A man considered to be the first Kazembe conquered groups in the Luapula River Valley in the middle of the century and settled there. According to accounts told by the people in the Luapula Valley, Mwata Kazembe III was the ruler in the late eighteenth century. At that time Nachituti lived with her brother Nkuba, who had many wives. When Nkuba discovered his favorite wife spending time with Nachituti's son, his nephew, he killed his nephew in a rage and then committed an atrocity. He reportedly skinned his nephew and after drying the skin, kept it hidden under his royal mat. Nachituti searched for her son, but could not locate him until one day a man told her where she would find her son's remains. After discovering the skin during a celebration when Nkuba was drunk and not sitting on his mat, Nachituti decided to report the murder to Mwata Kazembe III. After a series of raids, Mwata Kazembe's people found Nkuba and killed him. When Nachituti was certain her brother was dead, she filled a basket with soil and a pot with water. According to the tale, "She gave the basket to Mwata Kazembe and said, 'I give you the land'; and she gave the pot and said, 'I give you all the water, the rivers and lagoons this side and the other side of the Luapula are yours.'"[21] She then remained with Mwata Kazembe, and when she died she was buried in the royal cemetery in recognition of her leadership.

Her story was reminiscent of other narratives from central Africa because it provided a context for the origin of a community. It followed certain patterns, including the presence of a drunken king who was tricked, and an original female and male pair responsible for founding the group, in this case Nachituti and Kazembe. Other societies had similar accounts of an unmarried woman who gave the land away to a foreign conqueror. The tale might also have been related to tensions between matrilineality and patrilineality, with the conflicting interests of sisters as clan insiders and wives as outsiders. By reporting her brother for his crime, Nachituti opted to support a patrilineal leader rather than her brother who shared her matrilineal clan kinship. The factual basis of this narrative may not be very important, while more can be learned from the mythic elements that illuminated local understanding of historical change.

Southern Africa

Southern Mozambique

Southern Mozambique in the eighteenth century was part of a complex set of trade and political processes. People and communities were migrating from South Africa to neighboring regions. Portuguese and other Europeans were arriving at the port in Delagoa Bay in pursuit of trade. The local people were increasingly involved in regional and global transactions in ivory and other less valuable goods, and in the trade in slaves. Women were, as elsewhere, responsible for cultivating crops, preparing food, and making items such as pottery necessary for proper cooking and storage. By looking closely at women and food, it is possible to discern how women influenced wider issues related to trade and politics.[22]

Early European visitors regularly commented on the fertility of the soil, listing such staple crops as corn, rice, millet, and sweet potatoes; fruits including plantains and pineapple (newly introduced from Brazil); cabbage, onions, and other vegetables; and tobacco, indigo, sugar cane, and chili peppers, all grown by women. Their primary tool was a hoe, a valuable item that was exchanged as part of bridewealth upon marriage. Polygynous marriage was common, especially among wealthier families. Women recounted how they preferred having cowives to share the burden of cultivation and food preparation, which included pounding grain in a mortar each day and preparing alcoholic beverages that required several days of supervised processing to ensure a high quality drink. Women were also responsible for collecting water and firewood for the compound. The first wife was sometimes able to influence her husband to marry again, thereby enlarging the household so that women were able to share the labor. Often the senior wife could avoid the backbreaking work of hoeing once there were junior wives living in the compound. The complex system of trade, kinship, marriage, and women's labor can be seen in the brief outline that follows.

Women made pottery that was primarily used within their households for preparing food and drink and to collect water. By the late eighteenth century, traders mentioned that some pots were available for purchase, and at times they were exchanged as part of bartering for food and other items. Though pots for everyday use might sound mundane, skill and artistry were important factors in making pots that worked well and were also attractive. Knowledge of where to locate the proper clay, mold a useful shape, and fire the resulting vessel were skills that women learned from each other. The motifs and designs were geometric and sometimes were inspired by natural elements such as leaves and animals. Women used similar patterns for body ornamentation such as hair designs and tattoos or scarification. Such decorative work reflected important spiritual ideas, whether on a person or on pots and baskets.

Portuguese merchants who visited the Mozambican coast in the late eighteenth century commented on the hospitality they experienced. Local rulers, often called kings by the Europeans, invited the traders into their homes, where they were served a refreshing drink made from corn and sugar, and were fed and entertained while commercial discussion was carried out. The women of the household were described as friendly and welcoming in their appearance and bearing. The clothing and ornaments of the elite women were detailed by Portuguese men, as with the Tembe queen in 1757, who was said to be wearing a veil and "beautiful blue corals, several copper rings, [and] bracelets on the arms," clearly indicating her high rank.[23] Visitors would offer gifts of cloth, glass and iron beads, and other items to the king's first wife, recognizing that she would supervise their housing and food for the duration of their stay. When foreigners became ill, which was not an uncommon occurrence, they were cared for by local women.

Elephant hunters who collected ivory for export were expected to pay one tusk from each elephant to the local ruler; the gifts to the women were in addition to that required tribute. As the Portuguese gained control, they also saw great profit in their share of ivory. The entire regional trade was a complicated network of chiefdoms and tribute payments which the records of the time reported as occurring between men; however, without the participation of women, the system would not have run smoothly.

The involvement of African women was also seen when they accompanied their husbands onto the foreign ships and helped select the preferred gift items. Textiles were increasingly important as African women began to cover themselves; early visitors often mentioned that women went about naked or only partially clothed. Reports of woven grass mats being used to cover their bodies were common. Once cloth was available, African women came to prefer that material. The importance of cotton for clothing and beads for necklaces and ornamentation played a growing role in international trade, and women's interest in those products helped drive that aspect of commerce.

While many of the reports on society and trade in southern Mozambique were about elite women, there were also passing references to ordinary women's contributions to the development of commerce. Women were part of the large caravans that were necessary for carrying quantities of ivory from the interior to the coast. Some of the women were undoubtedly enslaved, as were the women reported as carrying soil for the construction of a Dutch fort in the 1720s. As women's domestic work included transporting heavy vessels of water and awkward bundles of firewood, their involvement in carrying heavy goods as part of a caravan or building construction was work that was expected of women. While the official registries of merchants included only male names, the work that women performed was vital to the commercial success of Africans and Europeans.

As societies faced drought and famine, as well as war and conflict, the contribution of women's work was crucial to survival. The crops they grew fed their families, and they entered into lucrative trade networks. Their innovations, persistence, and advanced planning allowed people to eat and to earn money or goods. At the same time, men controlled much of the trade and had oversight of marriage transactions and women's agricultural labor. The local hierarchy depended on paying tribute to chiefs who ruled over districts, and the tribute was in large part agricultural products that were the result of women's work. As the Portuguese arrived in greater numbers, they in effect became part of the centralized system of political rule as well. By the early nineteenth century, much of the rice that was grown was sold to Portuguese soldiers, with the quantities and prices set by an agreement between the Portuguese administrators and local chiefs, all men who did not do the work of growing rice and other crops. Despite women's daily efforts, for the most part they did not gain positions of public political authority or improve their own economic situation.

Conclusion

This chapter has described women's activities related to market trade, commercial activities with European merchants, the impact of the slave trade on women, and some of the ways in which women held political authority in the seventeenth and eighteenth centuries. Though the sources are scarce and sometimes difficult to analyze, women were centrally involved in the important political and economic decisions being made as African societies increasingly interacted with the wider world. The early years of what is now considered globalization were a showcase for African women's efforts to support themselves and their families when confronted with oppression and exploitation. As leaders in communities across the continent, they played key roles in early modern African history.

Notes

1. Havik, *Silences and Soundbytes*.
2. Ibid., 197.
3. Brooks, "The *Signares* of Saint-Louis and Gorée," and Brooks, *Eurafricans in Western Africa*.
4. White, *Sierra Leone's Settler Women Traders*, 20.
5. Pybus, "'One Militant Saint.'"
6. White, *Sierra Leone's Settler Women Traders*, 27.
7. Candido, "Concubinage and Slavery in Benguela" and Candido, *An African Slaving Port and the Atlantic World*.
8. Miller, "Introduction: Women as Slaves and Owners of Slaves."
9. Bay, *Wives of the Leopard*.
10. Ibid., 135, quoting Pommegorge, 1789.
11. Akyeampong, "Sexuality and Prostitution among the Akan of the Gold Coast c. 1650–1950."
12. Shumway, "Castle Slaves of the Eighteenth-Century Gold Coast," and Ipsen, *Daughters of the Trade*.
13. Quoted in Shumway, "Castle Slaves of the Eighteenth-Century Gold Coast," 93.
14. Awe, "The Iyalode in the Traditional Yoruba Political System."
15. Okonjo, "The Dual-Sex Political System in Operation."
16. Day, *Gender and Power in Sierra Leone*, 17–19.
17. Presley, *Kikuyu Women, the Mau Mau Rebellion, and Social Change in Kenya*, 13–33.
18. Ehret, "Matrilineal Descent and the Gendering of Authority."
19. Belcher, "Sisters Debating the Jesuits;" see also Belcher and Kleiner, *The Life and Struggles of Our Mother Walatta Petros*.
20. Sargent, "Found in the Fog of the Male Myth."
21. Gordon, *Nachituti's Gift*, 31–33.
22. Zimba, *Mulheres Invisíveis*, 45–82.
23. Jacob Francken in *Records of South-Eastern Africa*, 477–478, quoted in Zimba, *Mulheres Invisíveis*, 111.

3 Religion and Slavery in the Nineteenth Century

THE NINETEENTH CENTURY was a time of many changes in African women's lives. Although the majority of women continued their familiar rural agricultural work, international forces brought new religions, expanded commerce, and altered the practice of slavery. Beginning with some examples of African religious beliefs, this chapter then examines the expansion of Islam and the impact of Christian missionaries, especially in the field of girls' education. Another important topic addressed is women and slavery, including their role in the international trade, women's work as slaves in African communities, the continuum of control over people, including pawnship, women's experience as being more vulnerable to capture, and women as slave owners.

African Religious Beliefs

It can be difficult to separate religious beliefs in African societies from political practices and from family and kin relationships. In this section, some specific belief systems will be examined, demonstrating the variety of African experience. Though some of these beliefs undoubtedly were followed before the nineteenth century, they gained adherents and became more prominent during that time. They have been introduced here as a reminder that African societies were not spiritually empty sites, and those who proselytized for Islam or Christianity often confronted local beliefs with a long history and fervent devotees, especially when considering goddesses and beliefs that supported women's needs.

West Africa: Igbo Religious Beliefs

The Igbo of southern Nigeria believed in a pantheon of deities that had a role in governing their towns. In Igbo belief systems, water, usually viewed as female, was the necessary counterpart of earth, with specific deities representing different natural elements. Annual harvest celebrations recognized an ancestral mother related to the yearly flooding and receding waters that allowed the successful cultivation of yams. Though the particular rites varied by location, the centrality of a female ancestor and her connection to local waterways was seen across the region.

Many of the powerful deities were female, and the Adoro goddess was among the most potent. In the Nsukka area, Adoro was developed at the end of the nineteenth century as the slave trade was abolished and local rivalries increased. Initially, she was a remedial substance or medicine designed to heal rifts between and within towns. As the advent of peaceful relations demonstrated her success, she rose to a dominant position and was honored with shrines and followers who maintained her important status. In the early twentieth century, Adoro became a particular focus of Christian missionaries, who worked to demolish her shrines and end what they considered pagan worship.

Another important female deity was the water goddess, most familiar as Mami Wata or Mammy Water. She was clearly related to earlier manifestations of water goddesses and was also known as Nne Mmiri, or in some locations as Ugbuide.[1] She was commonly pictured as partially a sea creature such as a mermaid or a snake, and in some areas she was identified with crocodiles. A complex deity, the water goddess lived in lakes and rivers and was considered beautiful and benevolent and simultaneously as a dangerous source of turmoil and illness. Called the "mother of us all," her presence reflected the life-giving qualities of water more generally, but also the power of water to injure and kill. Mami Wata was linked with wealth, and ideas about reciprocity were central to her followers who believed there must be a balance between giving and receiving. Some also viewed her as a protector of pregnant women. In the twentieth century, an Indian image of an unrelated goddess gained popularity and influence, and it came to represent the older Mami Wata goddess. Many West African societies had similar water-related deities, including Faro among the Bambara, Tano in Ghana, and Bia in Côte d'Ivoire.

Reverence for this goddess was not marked by shrines and formal religious structures, but it was seen in the annual regeneration of secret societies of both men and women, as well as in the dances and masks that marked the changing seasons of planting and harvesting. Igbo spiritual practice was rooted in natural resources and the local landscape, and it was clearly reflected in the adherence to the female water goddess. Though observed and recorded in the twentieth century, such beliefs and practices had a history that began in the Igbo past.

Central Africa: Luba Religion and Politics

A study of carvings and wooden objects from the Central African kingdom of the Luba provides insight into political authority, women's roles, and beliefs about kinship and ancestral powers. Though these beliefs certainly existed in earlier periods, most of the objects that have been analyzed originated in the nineteenth century, and the social configurations they represent were most evident in that time period.

The Luba kingdom was not based on violent conquest, but it grew through intermarriage between allies, strategic gift giving, and spiritual empowerment.[2]

Fig. 3.1 Luba royal stool from the nineteenth century; this wooden carving depicts a serene woman with scarification supporting a major symbol of royal power in the Democratic Republic of Congo. Source: collection RMCA Tervuren; photograph by R. Asselberghs, EO.0.0.23137.

The kings came to the throne, an elaborately carved seat that was called a stool, through a ceremony that focused on regal responsibilities and community connections. Items that were used in addition to the stool could include cups, a staff, an ax, and a memory board called a *lukasa*. Although men carved these items and used them in ritual ways, many of the items depicted women. At first it might appear that a stool that showed a kneeling woman with downcast eyes holding up the royal seat was demonstrating women's oppression, but the reality was quite different. Such renditions indicated the central role of women in Luba society, where "women constituted the covert side of sacred authority and played critical roles in alliance-building, decision-making, succession disputes, and investiture rites."[3] Women were regarded as vessels of sacred authority, and cups, bowls, and headrests that included women with elaborate hairstyles and meticulous scarification on their bodies were a visible way of paying homage to women's place in society. In the case of the royal stool, the woman under the seat was considered to be holding up the realm. Many of the carvings of women showed them gesturing toward their breasts, which were believed to hold the secrets of power; likewise, images of women pointing toward their navels or bellies emphasized their female attributes as life-givers and mothers. Gender was often left ambiguous, with figures having both male and female sexual features, a reflection of the idea that kings transcended gender. As one Luba proverb claimed, "Men are chiefs in the daytime, but women are chiefs at night." Women were the basis for the king's power, because the king depended on his mother and other female elders to support him and his authority.

The Luba example suggests ways that women were a potent force in their societies, though a superficial look at hierarchy and politics would not reveal the extent of their authority. Women brought spiritual and religious strength to the Luba polity and Luba kings accepted the influence of their female ancestors and kin as a crucial element in their own ability to rule.

Islam in West Africa

Islam had been introduced into Africa by the ninth century, both along the east coast and in many areas in West Africa. Arab merchants introduced Muslim beliefs and practices as they traveled throughout the region, though the new religion spread slowly. Hausa people in what is today northern Nigeria had long considered themselves Muslims; they were influenced over the centuries by Fulani traders and travelers. People typically continued following local religious beliefs, and they added Islamic rituals. By the early nineteenth century, Fulani Muslims had become advisors to some Hausa rulers, and they were concerned about the unorthodox versions of Islam they observed. They pushed for greater orthodoxy and participated in jihads, or religious wars, across West Africa. The Hausa ruler Usman dan Fodio led the largest and most successful jihad, which brought Fulani rulers and orthodox Islam to a wide swath of the region in the early nineteenth century. While Islam had primarily been practiced by elites, after that jihad it became pervasive and was followed by people at all levels of society.

The spread of Islam in West Africa had contradictory effects on women. Following the jihad of Usman dan Fodio, many of his followers promoted a policy of keeping women out of public life. They advocated seclusion for women, and though women had earlier been observed in the markets and even as political leaders, they were restricted to their homes and required to wear clothing that covered them entirely when they went out. Selling goods and prepared foods became complicated, and children were recruited to sell items that were produced within the home. Strict interpretations of Islamic beliefs and practices encouraged greater limitations on women's public presence.

The impact of Islam was not uniform across West Africa. Women in Senegal were generally not subjected to seclusion and restrictions on their public activities in the same way as Hausa women in northern Nigeria.[4] For Wolof women in Senegal, Islam provided a set of legal rights that protected them from some aspects of overt subordination. For instance, as Muslim women they had the right to inherit property from their fathers; though the Qur'an stipulated that women would inherit half the amount of their brothers, previously they had not been able to inherit at all. They were able to keep money they earned and to keep money and goods that had been part of the bridewealth paid upon their marriage. Even Islamic rules about men marrying four wives gave women some protections they previously did not have, since the Qur'an limited the number of wives to four and stipulated that the man had to be able to provide equally for all of his wives. Women also preserved rights to their own children, and the father was obligated to maintain his children even when they resided with their mother, conditions that were more favorable to women than social expectations had been before Islam. Understanding the history of women and Islam in West Africa depends on knowledge of each local community.

Nana Asma'u

Some women played a notable role in expanding the reach of Islam, and during the eighteenth and nineteenth centuries they benefited from the spread of Qur'anic education for women. Nana Asma'u was the daughter of Usman dan Fodio and was a prominent educator and writer.[5] Born in 1793, she was raised in a household where writing and studying Islamic texts was expected and encouraged. She followed her father's practice by seeking the Sunna path of pure devotion, with the Prophet Mohammed as the model of a proper Islamic life. Their home in Sokoto was modeled on the Prophet's home at Medina. A devout life included participation in daily tasks; Usman dan Fodio was known to make rope, and his daughter Nana Asma'u was certainly involved in the domestic chores required to run a large household. The jihadist wars began when she was ten, and for many years her life was itinerant and disrupted by conflict. She married Gidado dan Laima at age fourteen; he later became the chief advisor of the Sokoto Caliphate. They had six sons, the first born when Nana Asma'u was twenty.

She began writing poetry and short essays, and in 1820 she wrote her first book, a study of morality called *The Way of the Pious*. She continued throughout her life to write materials that dealt with the teachings of the Sunna, the ongoing war, and the role of women. In addition to her own writings, she actively worked to educate women, developing a traveling school that could be brought to women in seclusion and in isolated and distant rural locations. Her work with the teachers also involved her with social welfare efforts, as non-Muslim women as well as Muslims were suffering from the war. She was recognized as a leader from a young age, and by the time she was forty she was known as Mother of All.

Nana Asma'u prepared lessons for a group of close disciples who then taught teachers who went to rural areas to spread the principles of Qur'anic verses and prayers. The instruction also included stories of important Sufi women in history, the biography of Mohammed, reports of victories in battle, and other materials such as vignettes of pious individuals that could aid women in leading an exemplary Muslim life. Nana Asma'u also contributed verses that allowed illiterate and semiliterate women to memorize important concepts and historical events. The corps of teachers was able to travel more freely because they were past childbearing age, or were younger and unmarried. Asma'u recognized the instructors' contributions by distributing special hats with red cloth strips. The hats were copied from official insignia that had previously been associated with male leaders, and her appropriation of the hats reduced their unique male associations and simultaneously raised women's status.

Nana Asma'u was a follower of Sufism, a form of Islam that encouraged devotees to live a life of simplicity and commitment to Islam, and to avoid materialism. Greed and vanity were particularly condemned. Sometimes described as Islamic mysticism, not all adherents retreated from the world, though some did. Sufi writings included rules to guide a pure life, but they also taught that the core of the belief was not only in how strictly a person followed the regulations concerning food preparation and cleanliness, but was found in the heart of the believer.

Although Asma'u was an exceptional scholar and leader, she was not the only educated Muslim woman who worked to improve her community and contribute to the growth of Islam in West Africa. She was not even the first woman to lead a scholarly life, since her grandmother and aunts were also literate believers who taught her father. She learned from her foremothers and developed into an influential leader and educator because of her upbringing. Long after her death in 1864, her life provided a model for African female scholars. Women who were teachers and writers more than one hundred years later commonly cited her example as one they respected and tried to emulate.

Mam Diarra Bousso

Another notable woman in West African Muslim history was Mam Diarra Bousso, who was born in Senegal in 1833. She was raised by very devout parents who taught her to be familiar with the Qur'an. She married and had three children, but she died of illness at the age of thirty-three. Her son, Sheik Amadou Bamba (1850–1927), founded the Islamic Mouride movement in Senegal. His followers included many women, and they came to revere his mother as well. Initially honored as the mother of a saint, she came to be honored as a saintly person herself, and her burial place in the village of Porokhane became a site of pilgrimage for pious women who venerated her generosity and kindness. The shrine was especially important for dealing with women's concerns over infertility, marital problems, and economic difficulties. The effort and expense of traveling to Porokhane was understood as bringing blessings to the women who made the pilgrimage.[6]

Islam in East Africa

Islam had spread along the East Coast of Africa by the eighth century, though it arrived incrementally as Muslim traders conducted business in the port cities and was more prevalent in northern regions such as Somalia before taking hold along the coast to the south. By the fourteenth century, Kilwa, a small island off the coast of what is now Tanzania, was the center of Muslim and Arab authority. After the arrival of the Portuguese and other Europeans, there was a power struggle that ended in the seventeenth century with political control in the hands of Arabian sheiks who were from Oman on the Arabian peninsula and were headquartered at Zanzibar, also an island off the coast of present-day Tanzania (after independence in 1964, Zanzibar became part of the nation of Tanzania). Swahili culture, found in the East African coastal communities mainly present in Kenya and Tanzania, developed out of the centuries of interaction between Africans and Arabs. The Swahili language (Kiswahili) has elements of both African languages and Arabic, and it can be written in Arabic or Western scripts. Nonetheless, the term *Swahili* was a flexible ethnic identifier. While most Swahili followed Islam, many Kiswahili-speaking people did not; likewise, Kiswahili speakers were often described as coastal, yet many lived throughout the region and were found in central Africa including in the Congo.

Princess Salme of Zanzibar (Emily Ruete)

One unusual source for information on coastal Muslim women's lives was a memoir written in the 1880s by Salme, the daughter and youngest child of Seyyid Said BuSaid, Sultan of Oman and Zanzibar. It was published under her married name of Emily Ruete.[7] Though her life was not an ordinary one, Salme recorded many details of life in the palace of Zanzibar. She was born in 1844 to one of her father's many concubines. After her father died, her brother, Madjid, became sultan; however, he faced opposition from within his family, and Salme sided with those who wished to replace Madjid. Her brother then apparently refused to arrange for an appropriate marriage for her. She began a courtship with a neighboring German merchant and eventually left for Germany with him amidst rumors that she was pregnant. She converted to Christianity, and they married. Her husband died in a streetcar accident just three years later in 1870, leaving her with three small children. She traveled back to Zanzibar, though

Fig. 3.2 Young women of Zanzibar, studio portrait, 1908. Photograph courtesy of the Melville J. Herskovits Library of African Studies Winterton Collection, Northwestern University.

she was not welcomed by her family. She subsequently spent many years in Beirut, Lebanon, before returning to Germany, where she passed away in 1924. Her memoir was initially published in German, and she was also fluent in Arabic and Kiswahili.

Her story of life in a stone palace in Zanzibar includes accounts of the interactions between the women who were confined to the women's quarters, often referred to by outsiders as a harem. Her father had one legitimate wife, and he gradually purchased as many as seventy-five other girls and women who between them had thirty-six children. She says very little about her personal religious beliefs, noting that she had been "once a Mahometan, and raised up as such," and later describing a celebration of her birthday in the 1880s that took place on a ship off the coast of Zanzibar. As she commented, "In honour of my birthday (a born Mahometan's!) a pig was killed on board the *Adler*, and almost in sight of Islam's most faithful worshippers."[8] Religious Muslims do not eat pork, so providing a pig suggests that she was not known as a devout follower of Islam.

Nonetheless her story provides details of the privileged lives of women whose family wealth derived from commerce in ivory, cloves, and slaves. The presence of slaves in the household was simply accepted as a reality and was not further discussed in the memoir. She had personal slaves who cared for her when she was young and one slave who traveled with her when she fled to Germany. She was fully conscious of writing about a life that was considered exotic and even barbaric by her primarily Western audience, yet she refrained from embellishing the story or otherwise pandering to that audience. In a chapter outlining the position of women, she argued that women of privileged rank were equal to men, and they were able to travel about town freely, though veiled. In her view the women who suffered more were women who were poor or enslaved, and their difficulties were a result of economics not of religion. She provided examples of educated women, wives who stood up to misbehaving husbands, and other women whose lives she considered to be on a par with the European women she observed. Ruete was particularly pleased to recall the story of her great aunt who ruled in Oman when her son (Ruete's nephew) was next in line but was too young to act as sultan, concluding, "I trust the above will suffice to demonstrate that woman in the East is not at all the degraded or oppressed and outlawed being she is generally believed; she is by no means a cipher."[9]

Mwana Kupona and Muslim Ideals

There is another published account from the mid-nineteenth century that illuminates some aspects of East African Muslim women's lives. Written in the 1850s by Mwana Kupona, a well-known female poet, *Utendi wa Mwana Kupona* (*The Epic Poem of Mwana Kupona*) was a notable literary achievement that has been translated and published in many different formats. It was still remembered and recited by Kenyan women in the late twentieth century.[10] Born around 1810, Mwana Kupona lived on the Kenyan island of Lamu and was the wife of a sheik. She wrote poems within the canon of Kiswahili poetry, which included educational and religious topics. Shortly before her death in 1860, she composed *Utendi wa Mwana Kupona* in order to provide guidance for her daughter, who was about to be married. Due to that instructional content, the epic is sometimes referred to as *Lessons* or *Advice of Mwana Kupona*. Dealing in part with the theme of wifely virtue, the poem outlined key behaviors that would bring happiness, including being trustworthy, faithful to Islam, respectful, and avoiding the company of slaves and ignorant people. Some lessons reminded the daughter to bathe often, speak jokingly, and to dress beautifully with ankle bracelets and wrist bangles. Other verses focused on the proper treatment of her husband. Lines included counsel that has been interpreted as teaching women to be subservient, such as the following:

> Be in harmony with him.
> Deny him not what he desires.
> Do not quarrel with him;
> If you do, you will be the loser.[11]

While the domestic and personal sections are important, the poem's longevity as the only epic by a woman in the accepted canon of Kiswahili texts rests equally on its attention to religion and Muslim philosophy.[12] Although the beginning verses focused on the daughter and proper behavior, the latter part of the epic was primarily about Mwana Kupona's hope for divine blessings and for relief from the illness that was taking her life. She ended with the following plea:

Keep me in the world
Among the blessed people
When I die may I go to heaven
The dwelling of the saved.[13]

The poem illustrated the detailed knowledge of Islam that was held by Swahili women. Because Muslim women in East Africa seldom attended services at a mosque, some observers suggested that they were not devout. The sentiments in Mwana Kupona's text demonstrated that women were familiar with the Qur'an and used pious writings to further their study of Islam.[14]

Although very different from the religious texts written by the West African scholar Nana Asma'u, the integration of family life, personal virtue, and Islamic beliefs and practices are seen in both women's writings. All of the publications and actions by Muslim women in Africa demonstrated the ways that they practiced their faith, the ideas that motivated their lives, and the importance of women's participation in developing specifically African forms of Islam.

Islam and Spirit Possession

In Hausa communities in northern Nigeria and neighboring Niger, female leaders of spirit possession cults, known as *bori*, played a role in integrating bori into Islamic beliefs. Though the origins of bori are not entirely clear, it was most likely based on pre-Islamic practices, though it gained greater prominence during the nineteenth century following a period of social disruption and community dispersal. Although often associated with Islam, it was not a recognized Muslim custom, and it was occasionally was a source of conflict between spirit mediums and Muslim clerics. Women were particularly associated with bori, and at times their spirit possession has been an avenue to redress economic and social inequalities. Bori was also a healing ritual, with the onset of the possession experience indicating that the person who believed they were possessed had problems that they understood could be resolved through following the instructions of the spirits.

Zaar (sometimes spelled as *zar* in older publications), a similar form of spirit possession known in Sudan, Somalia, Ethiopia, and parts of the Arab world, was dominated by female adherents as well. It was common in Muslim areas but was not an Islamic rite; rather, it provided an alternative religious experience. Zaar referred to a spirit that people believed could cause illness in human beings, and it could only be managed through rituals organized by spiritual leaders. Commonly, a woman came to zaar after being afflicted and the process of learning to live with the zaar spirits was also part of the learning arc that trained new adepts. Zaar was a complex set of cultural practices that could free women to act in uncharacteristic ways, and it also provided a profound set of social connections infused with deep spirituality that enabled believers to make sense of the world around them.

The experience and practice of bori and zaar were so similar that they were sometimes referred to as "zaar-bori," or similar terminology.[15] In studies in both East and West Africa, the cult was presumed to have been present in many societies for some time, but it began to spread and grow in the mid-nineteenth century. European travelers observed people who were affected by an illness that could not be explained, who fell into a trance, and who danced wildly. Women were noted as being susceptible to experiencing possession, and when a woman came under the influence of a zaar spirit, her home became a site where women gathered to eat, drink, and dance. Sometimes women would dress in male clothing and behave in ways considered to be uncivilized for women, such as burping, smoking, and talking loudly in a rude way. A spirit leader would always be present to supervise the assembly and guide the affected women through the encounter with spirit possession.[16]

Women sometimes found the bori or zaar experience to be a route to making requests of their husbands or other male kin and community members. Those men were then required to respond because of the power of the spirits. The spirits themselves were known personalities, sometimes named and recognized as representing a deceased person, someone of note, or someone causing difficulties. Women who were seen as possessed were most often married women; unmarried, virgin women were not expected to experience possession. A woman would sometimes believe she experienced the onset of possession at a time of marital crisis or problems with fertility. A woman might become ill, and during her trance condition ask for certain favors, new clothing, or other items or actions. Male concern about easing the affliction while honoring the spirits resulted in men fulfilling such appeals, hoping to appease both the unseen spirits who were making the request and their wives who were captured by the spirit. Spirit possession had complex and nuanced meanings for people who encountered it, with many varieties of practice. Women who otherwise faced restrictions and obstacles in their lives could find fulfillment and support through a community of women who shared their beliefs.

Christianity

Most of the African continent only encountered Christianity with the arrival of Catholic and Protestant missionaries from the sixteenth century onward, and particularly in the nineteenth century. Ethiopia was exceptional as there was an indigenous Christian presence from biblical times. In the early nineteenth century, missionaries were more likely to be men and to be interested in recruiting male Africans, although Western women missionaries were present as wives and as single women from the beginning. As various denominations of Catholic and Protestant churches became more interested in converting Africans to Christianity, they staked out areas of influence and built mission stations. Those small settlements provided a home base for the European missionaries, and were centers for education and evangelization. Women missionaries, both nuns and laywomen, often contributed to outreach efforts through their work as teachers and nurses.

By the mid-nineteenth century, some African women were seeking refuge in mission stations, and women had become an important part of the Christianizing project. Many peoples' experiences with Christianity in Africa were historically connected to oppressive aspects of colonialism, and some Africans rejected Christianity as part of the colonial project and as a distinctly non-African expression of spirituality. Others adopted aspects of Christian beliefs and developed new forms of worship that integrated local practices into the Christian liturgy. Missionaries often focused on elements in African societies that they deemed particularly pagan and uncivilized, and these were frequently centered on marriage and family concerns that directly involved women, such as mission disapproval of polygyny, bridewealth, and initiation rites.

Mission Education

Western-style classroom education for girls in Africa was introduced by missionaries in the nineteenth century. They generally wished to train girls to be suitable wives for male converts to Christianity, and so they emphasized enough literacy so students could read religious materials, and they taught domestic skills including sewing. In many areas the missions included boarding schools for girls, in order to facilitate their access to regular classroom attendance. Some of the better known schools included the Inanda Seminary in South Africa, the Gayaza Girls' Boarding School in Uganda, and the Mbereshi Girls' Boarding School in Zambia (then Northern Rhodesia). One issue was the much smaller presence of girls than boys in the mission schools. In many African societies, girls had daily responsibilities for agriculture and they tended to marry while still young. Many African families believed that mission education was useless with regard to the main tasks African women faced, and they allowed and even encouraged early marriage and responsibilities for work on family agriculture to curtail the time available for attending school. The lack of access to schooling at lower levels also resulted in fewer girls pursuing higher education.

The European missionaries encouraged African women to wear Western dress. It was assumed that women who converted to Christianity would dress in appropriately modest clothing. Much of the effort to teach sewing skills to girls in mission schools was related to those concerns, and African girls learned to sew their own new garments. Women in Congo-Brazzaville had training in sewing that was similar to the routine in missions across the continent, as women's desire to learn to sew became a central aspect of African women's attachment to the mission and to the women teachers. Access to the new skill and to Western-style clothing enhanced a woman's status, as women had been responsible for clothing themselves and their families in precolonial society as well. The shift from using local materials to imported cotton cloth indicated a person's connection to the wider world. Not all women began wearing dresses, but the introduction of cotton cloth greatly expanded women's wardrobe choices.

The earliest classes were devoted to hand-sewing modest dresses and infant clothing. By the 1920s in most areas, the missionaries were importing sewing machines and women were learning to use them. Other materials related to sewing, such as needles, scissors, thread, and cloth itself, were coveted gift items. Although few women found work in garment factories until after independence in the 1960s, many African women were able to gain an income with the dressmaking skills that they learned at the missions. While sewing was a strongly gendered course of study for girls and young women, for many of those women it also offered access to a livelihood that had not been an option in the traditional rural milieu. The new style of dress became a mark of respectability for some women, because covering one's body differentiated the converts from African women who continued to wear older styles that often left the upper body bare, and sometimes had only minimal coverings below the waist.

MISSION EDUCATION IN SOUTHERN AFRICA

The most common place where southern African women and girls encountered Christianity was through formal schooling. Inanda Seminary was a landmark educational institution for girls in southern Africa, founded in 1869 by Protestant missionaries affiliated with the American Board of Commissioners for Foreign Missions. Although girls were admitted to the Lovedale Institute in South Africa, Inanda was the first all-female boarding school for African girls. It was established at a long-standing mission station that served a rural population in Natal, South Africa, and it initially was geared toward training girls in middle-class domesticity that would enable them to be "respectable" wives to educated mission men. Basic literacy was taught along with sewing skills, and the students' lives were closely regulated to ensure their proper upbringing. The American Board Women's Auxiliary funded female missionaries to teach at Inanda, including Mary Kelley Edwards, who led the seminary from 1869 until 1892. She continued to live at the school until her death in 1927 at age ninety-eight. There was a limit to the number of women teachers that could be sent from the United States, and given the need to expand primary school classrooms, one of the goals at Inanda was to train African women to teach the younger children.

As was common at most mission schools, the students were expected to contribute to the daily functioning of the institution by working in the garden plots, cleaning their rooms and grounds, collecting water and firewood, and preparing food including the daily task of grinding the maize into flour. An ideal of self-sufficiency and the hope of controlling expenses were at the root of these labor demands.

Inanda was noted for its adherence to a Western standard of education and daily living. English was to be used at all times, in the classroom and between the students in their personal interactions. The missionaries confiscated beads and other items perceived as "charms," and no local rituals were allowed. Letters were subject to approval by Mary Edwards as headmistress. This approach diverged from some other schools in the region, such as the Mbereshi School, which permitted students to incorporate some elements of their initiation rites and did not strictly prohibit bridewealth and polygyny, with the view that such adaptations made it easier for Africans to accept Christianity. The American missionaries in Natal sought "a profound reorientation in the girls' world-view, an exacting task for the teachers and a daunting one for their charges."[17]

At first the school served the local area, with just over two hundred girls enrolled by 1885. As time passed, the school attracted adolescents from a wider region, many of them seeking to escape an unwanted early marriage. New laws in Natal in the 1870s and 1880s allowed women to refuse forced marriage and to divorce husbands who treated them badly, though it continued to be difficult for women to take advantage of even these limited options. The school was a visible site of refuge and escape that represented the possibility for a future different from the constrained choices of rural African life. The school registers noted many new enrollees as "runaways," girls who had fled their villages and sought protection. While this development did bring hostility from local people, who sometimes came to the school to reclaim their recalcitrant daughters, the local chief supported the school. In his view, with women's ability to avoid unwanted marriage, the school was a safer place for them than wandering about "as prostitutes."[18]

In the early twentieth century, the school began to introduce a more rigorous domestic science curriculum, with courses in sewing, cooking, laundry, and general housekeeping. They continued with an academic program as well, but many of the students were drawn to the practical skills taught in what was termed the "industrial course." According to anecdotal evidence, the most common careers followed by graduates during the 1920s and 1930s were teaching and nursing, followed by women who most likely were married and who said they were "at home," a reference to being housewives. By the 1930s, the school's reputation was such that elite African girls from all regions of South Africa dominated the student body, marking a shift from the earlier years when Inanda served the local community.

<small>MISSION EDUCATION FOR GIRLS IN SIERRA LEONE</small>

Sierra Leone was the site of some of the earliest mission schools for girls in Africa. The goals of the missionaries encompassed several interconnected ideals. The Europeans wished to expand the rate of conversion to Christianity, and they believed that the education and conversion of girls was an essential component. The boys and young men who had converted to Christianity preferred to marry Christian wives in order to establish families and homes that were monogamous and that mimicked European practices of marriage and child-raising. Thus education for girls included some training in literacy and arithmetic. In addition, a key component of girls' education was the sewing course, so that they could make their own more modest European style of dress. And there was a theme of moral education that introduced new ideas about sexuality and subservience. Mission education established new boundaries in girls' lives as the European teachers tried to set a standard of sexual purity that was very different from local practices.[19]

The first schools in Sierra Leone were established by the Anglican Church Mission Society (CMS), a Protestant denomination based in England. Though most missionaries in Africa in general were men, the CMS urged British women to travel with their husbands in order to serve as role models for monogamy, service, and domestic work. Despite a high rate of death among the European immigrants that made it difficult to sustain some mission stations, many of the women who arrived in Sierra Leone in the early nineteenth century began a process of training African girls in the ways of white middle-class lives.

Sierra Leone was home to diverse immigrants from an early date. As discussed in chapter 2, in the late eighteenth century freed slaves from Britain and North America were settled along the coast, and when the international trade in slaves was abolished by Great Britain in 1807, it became a site of resettling Africans from an assortment of West African societies who were removed from slave ships. Those Africans, who were displaced from their home communities, were more receptive to missionary overtures than indigenous peoples in the region.

The missionaries were especially concerned with controlling girls' behavior by instilling an ethic of sexual virtue. They urged monogamous marriage as a way of suppressing promiscuity, and they formulated Christian marriage to embody not only monogamy, but a focus on domesticity. The primary methods of introducing these values included sex-segregated classrooms, the regulation of female dress, and advocating sex-differentiated lessons. Those three approaches were interconnected, as the girls attended single-sex classrooms, where their training often included hours of sewing, reinforcing the emphasis on domestic duty while resulting in new, more modest Victorian-style clothing for girls. Boys' schooling included some manual training, but since the goal was to prepare them to earn a living, their courses did not have the domestic focus of the girls' schools.

Reports and letters written by the missionary teachers, both male and female, often remarked on the pleasing sight of clean children in their school uniforms. For the missionaries, the neat presentation reflected a more orderly individual in the most intimate way. The focus on domestic activities for girls, their reduced classroom time on academic subjects when compared to boys, and the concern about dress and cleanliness, especially for girls wearing appropriately concealing clothing, demonstrated the centrality of gender from the earliest days of Western-style education in Africa. The pattern seen in the schools in Sierra Leone was repeated in mission schools across the continent for more than a century.

Slavery

Women continued to operate as slave owners, especially in West Africa, while suffering from the slave trade across the continent. In many areas, women were more vulnerable than men to being captured and enslaved. Women in nineteenth-century southern and central Africa were dependent on men, whether their fathers or husbands or other male kin, in order to have access to land for cultivation. If they lost such connections through death or other misfortune, they were susceptible to being sold to slave traders or to a man who wished to expand his household. The British ended the external slave trade in 1807, though that trade continued clandestinely for several decades, and internal slavery was not immediately affected.

Slavery in West Africa

Aurélia Correira was a member of a prominent family with links to Portuguese authorities in Cape Verde, as well as to leading African households in the region.[20] Her position was bolstered by her aunt, Júlia da Silva Cardoso, who had been an active trader and political mediator. The two women lived in neighboring stone houses with tiled roofs close to the beach at Bissau, where they were easily able to monitor arrivals and departures and to oversee import and export activities. Aurélia Correira married Caetano José Nozolini, a governor and a wealthy slave trader. When he died in 1850, she was able to use her connections to local powers in the Bijagó community to maneuver into a position of commercial strength and political power. Some evidence suggests that her mother was a leader among women in the matrilineal Bijagó society, and was possibly an *okinko*, or regent, a position which held political and religious significance. It cannot be proven from existing sources, but it was possible that Aurélia was able to follow her mother as okinko. Though erroneously referred to as a "queen" by at least one Portuguese chronicler, like her mother, she most likely held an influential rank among African women.

Aurélia was responsible for groundnut, rice, and cotton plantations, which relied on the labor of her reported four hundred slaves in the mid-nineteenth century. She and her husband continued trading in slaves after it was outlawed by the British, using the geography of the islands along the coast to conceal that commerce. When ships with her slaves were captured, as happened on more than one occasion, Aurélia, not her husband or other male kin, pursued legal and financial reparations, claiming the slaves were her personal domestic slaves and therefore not part of the international slave trade and not subject to capture. She continued to use slave labor to cultivate her export crops for several decades, and to actively mediate to maintain a peaceful society conducive to successful trade. She appears in archival documents as a key person, whom the Portuguese relied on to assist in their own commercial dealings.

But even Aurélia Correira eventually had to reduce her slave trading and turn to increasing the cultivation of groundnuts (peanuts), which were exported to Great Britain to be used for cooking oil. She was recognized for her management of a series of large farms, and she passed control of that agriculture and the international trade in commodities to her three daughters and their families. By the early twentieth century, the dominance of Aurélia Correira and others involved in the international commercial networks had diminished, subject to changing patterns of trade, demand for different commodities, and the weakness of the European authorities who could not act decisively to protect the import and export commerce. The impact on the status and influence of the female traders was severe; although they had persisted for several centuries, they could not maintain their wealth and power when confronted with global economic changes.

Slavery in Central Africa

In many areas, women did similar work whether they were slaves or free. The arduous work of growing and preparing food was the primary activity of all adult women. For example, women's work cultivating and preparing cassava (also called manioc), a root vegetable commonly grown throughout Africa, was a task for all of the women in villages along the Congo River basin.[21] Turning the potentially toxic root into edible flour was labor intensive, as cassava contained cyanide that had to be leached out by repeated soakings. Once cassava flour had been properly treated, many long-distance river traders preferred it because it was easy to store and to cook with while traveling.

Women, whether slave or free, began by clearing brush and preparing fields where they planted cassava. When it was ready to be harvested, they pulled the tubers from the ground and brought them to the riverbank, where they had easier access to water. The cassava was cut into pieces and left to soak for three days. The women then peeled the root and immersed it in fresh water for an additional day. To make flour, the cassava was grated and stored in large baskets lined with leaves. The river traders used large canoes, and each canoe would take as many as four oversized baskets, which were stored in the river at night and brought back into the canoe to travel by day. When a traveler wished to eat, he (the canoe traders were primarily men) would take a couple of handfuls of flour, knead and shape it into a loaf, steam it, knead it again, and steam it once more before eating it.

When an enslaved woman was married, she continued to perform the same labor, participating as a member of a household and contributing her share of cassava and other crops. As a wife, she sold surplus produce in the market and accumulated her own income, which some husbands would eventually use to purchase girls to assist their wives. As a slave wife began to have control over other captive or purchased workers, her own status would mutate so that she was like a free person, if not entirely free herself. The advantage for men in marrying a slave woman was that her kinless situation gave the husband complete control over any offspring. Usually, the cost of buying a slave was less than the cost of paying bridewealth for a woman of free or high status, so a man benefited by paying less and avoiding conflict with the woman's relatives.

A slave woman lacked support or recourse if the marriage was unhappy or violent; a free woman could leave and return to her family home. But while a slave woman had no control over her marriage, she could refuse to bear children with her master and husband. Missionaries in the nineteenth century observed a marked paucity of children along the Congo River. While the trading towns had more enslaved women than smaller villages along the river, they were otherwise similar in terms of diet and environment. The low numbers of children suggested that women took control over their own fertility, likely relying on known contraceptives and abortifacients. Most common were herbs, roots, and tree bark that would be prepared and used as a douche.[22]

The Mangbetu, who also lived in the Congo, preferred women as slave labor because their labor was valued and they were not a threat to the male patrilineal system.[23] Male slaves had on occasion gathered a following and disrupted the established lineage hierarchies, while female slaves, for various cultural and social reasons, were not a threat. As mentioned previously, women were more easily incorporated into patrilineal societies. Matrilineal societies presented a somewhat different experience, as seen among the matrilineal Bakongo from the same region of the continent. Female slaves provided labor but did not have the same social and legal rights as sisters, who had authority in the matrilineal clans.[24] Women's daily lives followed similar patterns of cultivation, food preparation, and child care, regardless if they were slave or free, poor or elite.

Vulnerability of Women in Southern Africa

In southern Africa's patrilineal societies, most women were subordinate to their husbands and other male kin. In the early nineteenth century, the area was witness to a series of raids and wars, in response in part to extensive food shortages and famine. The violence included the movements of the African leaders Moshoeshoe and Shaka, which led to the Mfecane, a widening ripple of disruption throughout the region. While most of the historical attention has been focused on prominent male authorities, women were subjected to greater suffering and were also victims of violence.

In the best of times, women were not allowed to participate in their communities' central political courts. An example from the southern African region that was later Botswana suggested the presence of what might be called hypermasculinity. When an age grade of newly-initiated young men was preparing to return to their village after the extended initiation rites, men from the previously initiated group would run through the settlement, cursing the women who had remained behind, breaking their cooking pots, extinguishing the fires, and forcing women to go inside their thatched sleeping huts, as they repeatedly called out, "Those who are being killed!" This activity demonstrated how a ritual designed to make boys into men culminated with an overt attack on women and homesteads.[25]

Given that kind of attitude, it should not be surprising that even during relatively peaceful times women were routinely captured and forced to marry, often after being raped or otherwise sexually abused. While young men claimed they were seeking cattle and land in their raids, they also referred to women as "hornless cattle." Reports of eloping couples might suggest that a consenting man and woman were running away to marry in defiance of family wishes, but it was also a euphemism for men kidnapping women and carrying them off.

Young men also were noted for taking food, especially the stored sorghum that was a staple crop. In these patrilineal herding cultures, where cattle were considered a center of wealth, women were the primary farmers. In addition to doing the agricultural labor in the fields, they were responsible for storing the harvest and saving seed for the next year's planting. When the men raided rural communities, they not only stole cattle and women, but they broke into the storage huts and took the sorghum and other food.[26]

SARA BAARTMAN

Sara Baartman was a Khoesan woman from southern Africa who was brought to Europe as a household slave around 1810 by her owner, English army surgeon Alexander Dunlop. She was born around 1787 and lived what was apparently an ordinary life in Cape Town, where she worked in domestic service before marrying and having children. After moving to England with her owner, she continued working as a household servant for a time. She had extremely large buttocks, a condition known as steatopygia, and she was soon exhibited in London as an exemplar of African exoticism. She was sometimes referred to as the "Hottentot Venus," that name placing her as part of a group long seen by Europeans as the most bestial of Africans. The term Hottentot was most likely a reference to the click languages spoken by the Khoesan and other southern Africans, which Europeans once believed was not a true language but somewhere between animal grunts and human speech. The display of Sara Baartman's thinly veiled body in London and Paris was marketed as part of the existing practice of displaying humans with unusual physical features, often called freaks, but it also was one of the first exhibits that claimed a scientific, and therefore educational, motive. In Britain, a group of abolitionists took her case to court in a failed attempt to free her. After her death in 1815 in Paris, her genitals were put on display at the Musée de l'Homme until possibly as late as 1982. Her story became emblematic of the misrepresentation of black sexuality and of the exploitation of African women. After an international outcry, her remains were returned to South Africa in 2002, where she was welcomed by Griqua people (whose ancestors were Khoesan) in a ceremony in Cape Town.[27]

Vulnerability of Women in East Africa

Many of the stories of individual women in nineteenth century East Africa report on their susceptibility to being captured and enslaved. In part this perspective reflects the kinds of sources that have survived, as women who joined new Christian communities had sometimes escaped from being captive or from unhappy marriages. One document relates the personal history of Swema, a girl from the Yao people in northern Mozambique. After she was rescued from near death, her story was recorded and published as an uplifting example of finding new life through conversion to Christianity.[28]

Swema was born in the mid-nineteenth century in an agricultural village. Her father was a successful hunter, providing meat for the family to eat and ivory elephant tusks to passing caravans, earning an income that enabled them to live a comfortable life. She recalled her mother and older sisters wearing a lot of beads and imported cloth, a clear indication of their prosperity. But that idyllic time came to an abrupt end after her father was killed by a lion while participating in a village hunt. Her mother continued to cultivate food crops and care for their goats and chickens, but then locusts descended on the village and consumed all the crops. Within three days there was nothing left; once their small livestock were eaten or died, they faced famine. Her sisters and an infant brother died. It was not clear from her narrative why there was no assistance from fellow villagers, some of whom must have been related by blood or marriage to either Swema's mother or father.

But for whatever reasons, Swema and her mother left that village and settled in another that was three days distant. Her mother borrowed some sorghum from a neighbor, hoping to make a new beginning. They were thwarted again by a bad harvest. Though her mother made pots for sale, they were unable to repay the debt. At that juncture, an Arab caravan arrived, en route to the Indian Ocean coast, transporting slaves for sale in the market. The neighbor claimed the repayment of the debt by taking Swema to sell to the slave traders, with the approval of the village elders. Her mother pleaded to be taken also, entering into a kind of voluntary pawnship or slavery, a common recourse for people who were unable to survive otherwise.

Once they began the trek with the caravan, Swema and her mother worked as porters, carrying elephant tusks and other belongings. But her mother, probably already weakened from the extended period of famine and poverty, could not survive when the caravan crossed an area that had been laid waste by fire, where not even famine foods could be found. The caravan leaders forcibly took Swema from her mother's arms and left her mother to perish by side of the caravan route. Since they had not paid for her, they had no qualms about abandoning her. When Swema likewise weakened, however, the slave trader was not willing to leave her behind, because he had paid for her and hoped to make a profit by selling her at the coast. After reaching Kilwa, in present day Tanzania, the slaves were packed into a boat and taken to Zanzibar Island. By the time they were taken to the slave merchant, Swema was too weak to stand, and the merchant chastised the trader for investing time and rations on a dying person. He ordered her wrapped in a mat and readied for burial.

Swema's cries from the shallow grave where she was left drew the attention of a man who rescued her and took her to a Catholic mission on Zanzibar. There she recovered and received a mission education, and she worked in an infirmary at the mission. To her horror, an injured man who arrived one day was the Arab leader of the caravan. She was able to care for him, and she found salvation in that act. She was then baptized and joined the Sisters of Mercy on the Indian Ocean island of Réunion.

Swema's story included many cherished Christian metaphors, including the obvious one of rising from the (near) dead. The published document was shaped by the priest who recorded her story, and while some incidents may have been embellished or even fabricated, the section about her childhood and capture reflect the situation of women and girls in East Africa. They depended on male protection to survive, and they were vulnerable to capture and sale during the decades of the slave trade in the late nineteenth century. While many men and boys were also captured and enslaved, women and girls faced a particular set of circumstances that affected their experience of the slave trade.

The life history of Bwanikwa provides another example of female vulnerability in eastern Africa. The narrative serves as an entry point for discussing nineteenth century changes that had an impact on women and on slavery, and it also illustrates the fluid boundary between marriage and slavery for women.[29] The rise of international commerce allowed men to gain new sources of wealth and power, and it gave them increased control over women. The centrality of lineage systems of local governance was also strengthened by men's increased access to wealth through trade. As seen with Swema, if women found themselves with no kin to care for them, they were easily made victims of the slave trade. Bwanikwa's story followed a similar trajectory.

Bwanikwa's narrative was first told to the world by missionary Dugald Campbell, in a narrative published in Scotland in 1916 and titled, *Ten Times a Slave but Freed at Last.* She was born in the early 1880s, and as a child she lived with her family in Central Africa in what are now Zambia and the Democratic Republic of the Congo. Her family was wealthy, as seen in the dozen wives her father had. But when the head wife passed away, her father had to pay compensatory death fees to her family in the amount of three slaves. He had two slaves, but without a third, he was forced to pawn a child; Bwanikwa as the second daughter, was selected. He intended to redeem her, but when he was unable to do so, she remained in slavery. She was then subject to a series of transactions, first being sold to some passing slave traders for "a packet of gun-powder." That new master transferred her as part of a fine he owed for some unspecified crimes, and that next owner gave her to one of his warriors as a wife. Since she was still very young, that warrior traded her again to a man named Mukoka who married her and with whom she had a child who lived for three days.

In 1891, Msiri, who was a recognized ruler in the region, was killed by Belgian forces. His death brought about a period of instability, and for the remainder of that decade, there was conflict and uncertainty in the area, as European military and missionaries settled in some villages while others remained independent. The village where Bwanikwa was living was abandoned by all of its inhabitants, and she and some other slaves took the opportunity to flee. Kabongo, a man who had been a slave and was a recognized elephant hunter, took her with him. They first tried to settle with Kazembe, a well-known chief who ruled over a large area of Central Africa. But when Kazembe showed interest in Bwanikwa, she and her husband moved on, eventually settling again with their former owner and Bwanikwa's former husband, Mukoka, who claimed her again. As a result of disputes between the two men, Mukoka decided to sell her to a passing slave caravan, and once she was gone he killed Kabongo.

Bwanikwa was headed west, and she was able to find refuge with one of Msiri's sisters, who protected her until she (the sister) was killed by a lion. After a short time without a guardian, she was convinced to marry again, this time to a man who lived near a mission station. When the missionaries sent him to build a station in British territory, he took her with him but sold her to Arab slave traders. She managed again to escape, this time from a room with female guards and barred windows. Her husband took her back, but she refused to live with him any longer and sought refuge at the mission station. An African man traveling with Dugald Campbell wanted to marry her, so her husband agreed to let her marry the new man in exchange for a gun. She considered that new relationship to be slavery as well.

Bwanikwa's story, and the flexibility of her considering the men who controlled her life either master or husband, provides a stark example of the vulnerable situation that women could experience. She was at risk both on her own and when she was with a man; she might call a man her husband, but he was as likely to sell her to the next man as someone referred to as a master. Bwanikwa continued to live with the last man in a somewhat happy relationship, though "at times he would taunt her with the gun he had paid for her." She began to work in Campbell's household and also earned an income from making pottery, from breeding goats, and from selling surplus produce. With her earnings, she bought an elephant gun and a shawl, which she then presented to her husband in order to redeem herself, and at last she became a free woman. They remained married, but in the eyes of those around them, their relationship was more equal since people noted their mutual respect. She became a role model and a Christian leader.

It was not uncommon for domestic slaves to be incorporated into families, and at times to be called by kinship terms. But it was also the case that a person's servile origins were remembered and were often applied to their descendents as well. In trying to understand the social standing of someone like Bwanikwa, it seems evident that in communities where women had little control over their lives, including who they would marry, the line dividing the condition of wives and slaves was flexible. The work done by women, as noted above, was similar whether done by an enslaved woman or by a wife, particularly in poorer families. Women who were wealthy and could themselves command labor were able to avoid performing daily agricultural work and other onerous tasks. There was little evidence of people accumulating slaves simply to perform particular tasks. David Livingstone, the well-known missionary and explorer of the mid-nineteenth century, observed that female slaves were desired only as wives. Women were subject to capture and were purchased, but they were considered wives not slaves.

The other aspect of Bwanikwa's story that was not easy to discern was how she viewed her own marriages and enslavement. In the words that were written down, as mediated by Campbell, the distinction between marriage and slavery appears to be minor; she was sold to a man and then he claimed her as his wife. In societies where goods in the form of bridewealth were exchanged to formalize a marriage, there was only a slight shift from such interactions between clans that cemented a marriage and the exchange of goods between individual men to pass along a woman who might also become a wife. When Bwanikwa joined the mission community, she learned about other possibilities, and she was then able to earn the money needed to buy her own freedom. She was no longer owned as a slave, but she continued as a wife to the same man who had bought her.

At the end of her life, Bwanikwa returned to her childhood village. Many women who were considered to be free by European missionaries did not really feel free until they returned to their home. The ability to travel and the freedom to go where they wished was proof of the end of their enslavement. As European authorities were often concerned about maintaining control over women, they did not see restrictions on female mobility as a part of enslavement, but they encouraged marriage as a way to keep women under male control. The complications of this approach can be seen in the similarity of women's experiences as slaves and as wives.

Missionaries as mediators of our knowledge of the lives of slave women in Africa were also found in a study of Uganda in the last half of the nineteenth century.[30] Dozens of personal histories, discovered in the files of a Catholic mission station, illustrated how the missionaries were concerned with sorting out peoples' marital history and status in order to proceed with their baptism as Catholics. In broad outline, the life histories suggested that the widespread practices of kidnapping and capture were the primary avenues for being enslaved, with purchase being a secondary method. The decades of the late 1800s were a time of general disruption, and many of the women were kidnapped directly from their families by individuals, though others were captured by war parties.

In the mission files, women reported being purchased in exchange for cowry shells or guns, which indicated the encroachment of the international slave trade. The lack of their consent and the payment of goods outside the normal bride-wealth or dowry exchange pointed toward these events as enslavement rather than marriage. The Ganda histories provided further evidence of the fluidity of the slave and wife division. Women described performing the same or similar agricultural and household labor, regardless of their status. None of the women reported a more formal marriage exchange or ceremony taking place, though a few men did claim that the women were legitimate wives. The women were primarily domestic workers, and much of their labor was focused on growing and preparing *matoke*, the standard local food of steamed starchy bananas.

Many of the women were captured when young and then subjected to a series of exchanges and purchases, with the result that they lost contact with kin who might have come to their aid and were unable to find their way home. Men had much greater control over enslaved workers than they had over legitimate wives, who could return home and enlist kin to help end the marriage if they were unhappy with their treatment by their husbands. Even with those obstacles, women did flee when the opportunity arose, and there was some evidence that the many stories that were recorded by missionaries of runaway wives referred to enslaved women seeking their freedom. The mission stations in many areas became a refuge for women who wished to leave an abusive situation, whether in a recognized marriage or as captive workers.

South African Women Leaders

Women were also visible in leadership positions in southern Africa in the early nineteenth century. The three stories presented here suggest the ways that women were recognized as powerful, and act as a counterweight to the many stories of vulnerability.

Zulu

Zulu society in southern Africa was strongly patrilineal. Cattle herding was a primary focus of the economy, and as with many pastoral societies, women were brought in as wives to men and their clans. Cattle were the basic form of bride-wealth, and the interconnections of wealth in cattle, acquiring wives, and male political leadership were complex. Nonetheless, women could use the alliances between their birth families and their new marital clan as a source of authority, though their position was ambiguous since they were simultaneously insiders and outsiders.

The rise of Shaka in the early nineteenth century marked a turning point in Zulu history. His story begins with his mother, Nandi, who was born around 1760 and was a key figure in South African Zulu history. She was the daughter of a Langeni chief, and she had a relationship with Senzangakona, who was a Zulu chief. Problems arose when she became pregnant before they married; some sources suggested that Nandi and Senzangakona were considered to be too closely related to marry. When she gave birth to Shaka outside of a legitimate marriage, she was poorly treated by the Zulu community.

She took Shaka back to the Langeni when he was six, but they were forced to leave the Langeni community during a famine. Nandi and Shaka then settled among the Mtewa, where Shaka rose through the ranks of the army of Dingiswayo. When Senzangakona died in 1815, Shaka claimed his seat and Nandi, as queen mother, came to be known as Ndlorukazi, "The Great She-Elephant." When she died of dysentery in 1827, Shaka instituted an extreme expression of public mourning. Although it was not unusual for some attendants to be put to death when a ruler died, various reports suggested that Shaka began a massacre that resulted in seven thousand deaths and that he placed twelve thousand warriors to guard her grave for a year. He also commanded that people pour out their milk and stop cultivating crops. In reaction to such orders his aunt Mnkabayi (his father's sister and a friend of his mother) sponsored a coup that brought another nephew, Dingane, into power.

Nandi was particularly noted in Zulu society and history as a result of her son's fame, though other women such as Mnkabayi were able to profoundly influence Zulu political power. The role of royal women in Zulu society, both those born into the nobility and others who were captured and served the royal clan, was transformed under Shaka. The numbers of captive women increased as Shaka began to develop alliances through acquiring women from neighboring communities. Male lineage elites who supported Shaka's military expansionism sent female family members to join the royal household, and they also gained wives when those new household members were redistributed. Shaka cultivated personal relations and alliances through that practice, and he also collected bridewealth in the form of cattle for each woman whose marriage he arranged. Questions remain about women's roles at that time in Zulu history, including why many women were kept rather than being married off, as well as how much agricultural and other physical labor they performed. Nonetheless, those women did gain some measure of political power that was not possible prior to the rise of Shaka and the development of a centralized state. Their power was seen in the increased role of female diviners and healers, who were responsible for maintaining links with Zulu ancestors through rites held at prominent gravesites. As protectors of certain royal relics, women potentially could control royal succession and therefore wield serious political power, as seen with Mnkabayi.[31]

Mmanthatisi

Mmanthatisi led the Tlokwa group of Sotho in South Africa and Lesotho during the mass migration, known as Mfecane, in the early nineteenth century. She was born around the year 1784 in what became the Free State Province, South Africa, and was the daughter of a chief named Mothaha; her name at birth was Monyalue. She married the Tlokwa chief Mokotjo, who was her cousin. After the birth of her first child around the year 1800, she was given the name Mmanthatisi, indicating that she was the mother of a daughter named Nthatisi. The couple had a son in 1804 named Sekonyela and a second son named Mota. When her husband died in 1813 (some sources say 1819), she held the position of regent for Sekonyela, who later became chief. She also had a daughter with her brother-in-law after Mokotjo's death, as a consequence of the common practice of levirate marriage in which a widow becomes the wife of her deceased husband's brother, demonstrating a continued connection to her husband's clan.

As the Zulu wars began to encroach on Mmanthatisi's territory in the 1810s, the Tlokwa began to move to the west. At the time it was estimated that there were between thirty-five thousand and forty thousand Tlokwa. In one of her first raids, she led them in a successful attack on Zwide, chief of the Ndwandwe, and captured many cattle. Over the next few years she organized their military campaigns as they joined in the generalized migration and raiding of that era. She clashed with the well-known leader, Moshoeshoe, and with the Hlubi chief Motsholi. Some accounts suggest that she tricked the Hlubi when they attacked her community while her warriors were away, by arraying women and older children along a hilltop so that the attackers believed there was an army ready for them. These events were followed by further encounters with groups along the Caledon River, and at one point the Tlokwa were joined by the Sia, a related Sotho group.

Though Mmanthatisi was credited with leading her troops, it was also claimed that while she planned strategy, she did not personally lead her people in raids and attacks. Nonetheless, it was unusual for a woman to have this position in a patrilineal society, and her activities attracted attention throughout the region. Roaming groups in the Vaal and Orange Rivers region were called *mantatees,* in a mispronunciation of her name, and she was held responsible for many actions taken by other groups. Sekonyela joined her when she settled in northern Lesotho, though she continued to be active in Tlokwa politics after he assumed the chieftainship around 1824. Mmanthatisi lived until 1847.[32]

Mujaji, the Rain Queen of the Lovedu

The Lovedu of southern Africa recognized both an actual woman, who was referred to as a Rain Queen or Mujaji (sometimes Modjadji), and a spiritual leader who was embodied by those queens. The first woman who represented the Rain Queen was Dzugudini, who came from the north (what is today Zimbabwe) around 1600. She was the daughter of a chief, and when she had a child out of wedlock and refused to disclose the identity of the baby's father (who was possibly her brother), she was forced to leave. She was recognized as founding the dynastic leadership among the Lovedu.

In the early nineteenth century, after two centuries of troubled rule by kings, the elderly male ruler Mugodo decided that his daughter Mujaji was better suited to rule. He requested that she consent to be queen if she agreed secretly to bear a daughter as her heir, with Mugodo as the father. She agreed, and after bearing a daughter, she reigned for fifty years and gained a reputation for bringing peace and prosperity to the Lovedu. The incestual relationships may be factual or may indicate the legendary aspects of her claim to authority. Her fame as a rainmaker spread throughout southern Africa and leaders from across the region paid tribute, brought gifts, and at times sought her hand in marriage. She protected the Lovedu from Zulu incursions, reportedly striking down enemies as they approached the Lovedu realm. The Lovedu were strongly matrilineal and took special pride in the role of women in their spiritual world and in their physical community.

Local people sent their daughters to her to become wives of the queen and cement alliances. Woman-woman marriage was practiced in many African societies, and it often facilitated political connections. Among the Lovedu, the wives came from different sources. If sent from the families of district heads, the queen would send payment to those local chiefs as bridewealth. Other wives came from noble families or foreign chiefs who were seeking favors, who wanted support in bringing rain, or who were entering into complex exchange relationships. Politically, the wives from the district heads were the most important since their redistribution brought support from her subordinates. Some of those wives served the queen directly, while others were sent as wives to other district heads, becoming part of an elaborate cycle of obligation. The women who lived in the royal compound performed the work of all women, cultivating crops, preparing food, and making beer. Women were often able to exert some authority in the districts as well, a result of their essential place in the circular exchanges. While "the ramifications of exchanges and re-exchanges are so complex as to defy analysis," the women themselves and the reciprocity of the process demonstrated the extent of Mujaji's authority throughout a wide geographic area and with a series of families, clans, and communities.[33]

The Rain Queen's renown inspired Rider Haggard's novel, *She: A History of Adventure*, a classic tale that presented the queen as the immortal white ruler of a lost primitive community that had fallen from its ancient status as a center of civilization. The book was published in 1886, and though it was a completely fictional story of imperial conquest, it played a role in spreading the word about the Lovedu and their queen, referred to in the novel as "She-who-must-be-obeyed."[34]

Mujaji II and Mujaji III succeeded their mother and grandmother, though they were not able to sustain the same level of protection, particularly as Europeans began to settle on the land. Research in the early twentieth century found the Lovedu society to be based on agriculture with patrilineal descent, though with a continuing strong role for sisters within family groups.

Mujaji III was responsible for ensuring the timely arrival of seasonal rain and overseeing the general welfare of the Lovedu. Being a spiritual and a political leader, the queen's accession was surrounded by rites that emphasized the special nature of the queen as a person and as a symbol of divine power. Her authority relied on "compromise, the aversion from military institutions, and the subtlety of feminine persuasion."[35] She controlled the rain through her store of secret medicines and objects that allowed her to bring rain during the proper season, though she also collaborated with other healers and spiritual leaders. The ingredients in special animal horns and designated storage pots included natural items such as sea water, feathers, and roots and bark from forest plants. The animal horns would be burned in a special ceremony, producing smoke that rose into the sky and resulted in rainfall. The rite of burning the horns also involved special drumming ceremonies that were commonly practiced in the nineteenth century but fell into disuse. The combination of the materials, the timing of the rites, and the involvement of district heads with rain pots of their own were all elements regulated by the queen, and the Lovedu believed completely in her ability to bring the rain that was required for agricultural success.[36]

Though the Rain Queen gained some fame beyond the borders of her realm as an unusual example of female leadership, her role as a political ruler with divine attributes was not uncommon. Many societies recognized female spiritual leaders, and though few women emerged as queens, many African women played highly influential roles in determining who would rule their communities, which marriages would be approved, what rites were needed to ensure prosperity, and how to manage the seasonal cycle of agriculture on which everyone depended.

Conclusion

This chapter has discussed some very different experiences faced by women in the nineteenth century. By presenting arenas where women held religious authority, as well as sites of extreme vulnerability and oppression, the idea of African women as a single cohort has been decisively dismantled. During the nineteenth century, most women continued to live in small rural villages where they cultivated crops for their families, sometimes traded a surplus in local markets, and performed seasonal and life-course rites that were designed to ensure continued well-being for themselves and their communities.

The spread of Islam and Christianity introduced innovative forms of religious practice and access to new educational possibilities both of which altered women's daily lives and brought opportunities for themselves and their families. The spread of the slave trade was built on existing vulnerability, as well as women's work as traders. Individual women experienced greater oppression and increased personal independence, since the major changes of the nineteenth century brought new disruptions to innumerable societies and resulted in change that was positive and negative. The forces set in motion continued to reverberate in the decades that followed, as women responded with efforts to protect themselves and to thrive in the new conditions.

Notes

1. Jell-Bahlsen, *The Water Goddess in Igbo Cosmology*.
2. Roberts, "The King is a Woman."
3. Ibid., 68.

4. Callaway, and Creevey, *The Heritage of Islam*, 31–33.

5. Mack and Boyd, *One Woman's Jihad*.

6. Rosander, "Mam Diarra Bousso."

7. Ruete, *Memoirs of an Arabian Princess from Zanzibar*.

8. Ibid., 16, 286.

9. Ruete, *Memoirs of an Arabian Princess from Zanzibar*, 154.

10. Mwana Kupona binti Msham, "From *A Mother's Advice and Prayer*."

11. Ibid., verse 29, translated by Ann Bierstecker and Naomi Shitemi.

12. Biersteker, "Language, Poetry, and Power."

13. Ibid., verse 89, p. 65.

14. Werner, "Introduction," *The Advice of Mwana Kupona Upon the Wifely Duty*, 23–24.

15. Constantinides, "The History of *Zar* in the Sudan."

16. Boddy, *Wombs and Alien Spirits*.

17. Hughes, "'A Lighthouse for African Womanhood,'" 204.

18. Ibid., 211.

19. Leach, "African Girls, Nineteenth-Century Mission Education and the Patriarchal Imperative."

20. Havik, *Silences and Soundbytes*.

21. Harms, "Sustaining the System."

22. Ibid.

23. Keim, "Women in Slavery among the Mangbetu."

24. Broadhead, "Slave Wives, Free Sisters."

25. Landau, *Popular Politics in the History of South Africa*, 40.

26. Ibid., 38–39.

27. Crais and Scully. *Sara Baartman and the Hottentot Venus*.

28. Alpers, "The Story of Swema."

29. Wright, *Strategies of Slaves and Women*.

30. Tuck, "Women's Experiences of Enslavement and Slavery."

31. Hanretta, "Women, Marginality and the Zulu State" and Weir, "'I Shall Need to Use Her to Rule.'"

32. Lye, "The Difaqane," 115–121.

33. Krige and Krige, *The Realm of the Rain-Queen*, 177.

34. Ibid.

35. Ibid., 164.

36. Ibid., 271–281.

4 Colonial Era, 1850s to 1945: Work and Family

THE ERA OF colonialism when European powers had political authority over African societies does not coincide neatly with a set of years. Europeans began arriving in Africa in the fifteenth century, most frequently settling in coastal enclaves where they entered into the slave trade and became merchants of goods such as ivory and gold. Although some areas were under European authority from those early years, it was not until the late nineteenth century that the European nations of England, France, Germany, Belgium, and Portugal met in a famous conference in Berlin in 1884–1885 and divided areas of influence among themselves. The most intense colonialism then followed, with increased warfare when Europeans attempted, and in most areas succeeded, in enforcing their own political control over African communities.

While all Africans endured difficulties from different aspects of colonial rule, women were subjected to particular kinds of repression related to their work in agriculture and as traders, because of their role as mothers, and because of their impact in local political events prior to European incursions. The colonial experience varied widely and not only between men and women. There were important regional differences, variations among the British, French, Portuguese, and other colonizers, and differences along lines of ethnicity, religion, and class. Some specific aspects of colonialism that had an impact on women included new economic and political structures, the introduction of new legal systems, the expansion of missionary activities, and the increased access to Western education for girls and women. While there were arenas where women suffered and were oppressed, there were also some women who benefited from the expanded opportunities that came with increased urbanization and work possibilities. Some women were able to use access to new religions and education to find relief from certain oppressive elements in traditional rural society. It was a time of great changes, with both positive and negative outcomes.

Overview of Major Changes

The European powers expected their colonies to generate the income that would pay for their own subordination. They made some of that profit from the commerce in crops and minerals that they controlled. They introduced new taxation schemes that were often based on households, following the European model where the husband and father was considered the head of the household and was responsible for paying taxes and for other interactions with the state. These systems intersected, as the colonial agents recruited Africans, especially African men, to labor in the new export-oriented endeavors. And when people refused to work under conditions that were frequently dangerous and humiliating, they were fined. In many parts of Africa, the refusal to work for a wage or to pay taxes meant that workers were forced to labor on colonial farms or mines or for government projects such as building roads. These changes in local economies had a direct impact on women's work and family life.

Because the site of taxation and forced labor was centered on the household, women's prior experience of work and income that was under their own control was both overlooked and diminished. Men, seen as household heads, gained authority in relation to dealing with the political system. Women were marginalized. Women also faced new burdens in areas where men were removed from local work and responsibilities and forced to labor in colonial enterprises, usually for little or no remuneration. In many cases, women remained in the rural home with increased work in family agriculture and for the household, including maintaining ties with kin, upholding ritual activities, and enduring months and sometimes years of the absence of a husband and other male kin.

Studies of women's work during the colonial period often showed that women lost power and economic autonomy with the arrival of cash crops and their exclusion from the global marketplace, in contrast to men who were more likely to benefit from those economic changes. Even further, men, and international commerce, benefited because they were able to rely to some extent on women's unremunerated labor. The dynamic varied from place to place.

One area of African women's lives that consistently drew the attention of colonial agents was all aspects of sexuality and reproduction. Across the continent, Europeans were concerned about marriage, pregnancy, birth rates, motherhood practices, and female circumcision or genital cutting. Attempts to control and change African practices included introducing new laws and offering classes that taught African women European-style customs. A common theme was the assumed ignorance of proper modern habits among African women. Specific experiences will be described later in the chapter.

The presence of European settlers and trading companies was gradually augmented by a number of missionaries, traders, and officials throughout the sixteenth to nineteenth centuries. Trade in such items as rubber, gold, salt, and cloth had an impact on African societies and on international markets. By the late nineteenth century, the conflicts between European powers (England, France, Portugal, Germany, and Belgium) resulted in negotiations that concluded with a plan for dividing up spheres of interest on the African continent, with absolutely no African input. The 1884–1885 decision led to the greatly increased presence of Europeans, as they laid claim on the ground to territories they had obtained only on paper. Africans did not passively accept European rule, and their resistance meant an increased role for European military forces who engaged in a series of incursions designed to subdue African populations. By the early twentieth century, parts of southern and eastern Africa were home to numerous settlers as Europeans arrived to seek their fortunes in plantations and mining. West Africa did not experience the same level of settler colonialism, though European authorities were present.

Research on the colonial era exhibits a tension between women's experiences as victims or as powerful agents within their communities. Women's formal political activity was generally ignored and denigrated by the colonial authorities, mainly men themselves, who turned exclusively to men when they established local political offices. Although much of the writing about African women under colonialism emphasized the economic and political losses they suffered, when scholars turned to women's specific experiences they discovered evidence of women who found ways to progress and succeed in the face of blatant discrimination. Sometimes the new forms of oppression spurred women to new kinds of activities. Female agricultural innovations were described as essential to community survival because they shared knowledge about crops and cultivation methods, for example. Women became politically active, as seen in Nigeria with the development of three different market women's associations in Lagos that mirrored ethnic and class divisions present in the city. Women also found new ways of working and initiated new family forms as urbanization accelerated. For instance, the development of mining compounds, though designed primarily as male workplaces, opened opportunities for women to move from their rural homes, establish new marital and kin relationships, develop fresh ways of earning an income, and enter into innovative community endeavors.

Labor Under Colonialism

Agriculture

Women across the continent bore the major responsibility for the day-to-day work of growing food for their families' sustenance. Men usually helped with preparing land for planting, especially if that required removing trees or other heavy labor. But the daily round of planting seeds, tending the crops, weeding, chasing away birds and small animals that might eat or damage the plants, and then harvesting the food and preparing it for consumption was all the work of women.

A European observer in late nineteenth-century Mozambique described one aspect of that work when he detailed the process of winnowing grain to remove

Fig. 4.1 Women in Mozambique preparing food with a mortar and pestle and a winnowing basket. Source: *O Occidente* 4, No. 99 (September 21, 1881), 228.

the inedible parts, recognizing the physical strength required and also noting how women shared the labor:

> In their domestic life women perform all household chores, as well as the farm labor. . . . The principal basis of the diet of the black is vegetable, as they are sustained almost exclusively on cereals, such as maize, sorghum, and rice, either as a grain or ground to flour. To separate the grain from the surrounding husk, which is too tough to digest, they pound it in a very large mortar of wood, made from a large tree trunk hollowed out inside, working with two

people alternating, and sometimes three, each with a pestle in her hand. This work requires a lot of force, given by the expansion of the chest cavity, and develops the arm muscles of those who do this.

After removing the grain from the husk that covered it, they go on to separate the two things, putting them in a *supo* [shallow basket] which is properly a concave tray of woven grass with a hoop of flexible wood, giving it a circular shape. Shaking this *supo* in a place where the air flows freely, the little bits of cereal are blown away by the wind, leaving in the bottom the perfectly clean grain.[1]

Though he was describing women's work in a particular place and time, the daily task of preparing grains for consumption was seen across the continent, where women performed the work of pounding grain and sifting out the chaff on a daily basis.

WOMEN AND RURAL LAND IN KENYA

Women in western Kenya experienced a loss of control over land and their agricultural production as a result of colonial practices.[2] The Luyia, Gikuyu, and other communities in western Kenya were patrilineal, and women's access to the land they needed to produce food for their families was only available through their husbands. As in most areas of rural Africa, land was not owned by individuals, but it was considered to be a community resource. The allocation of land was controlled by the clan head or local chief, usually a man, who distributed access to male household heads. That man then allocated strips of land for cultivation to his wife or wives. Polygyny was preferred by men and women alike, as the additional labor contributed to the household in a material way. Women had little control over the food they produced, and inheritance of access to land went from father to son. Women were recognized as managers of land as well as of cattle belonging to the household. Though their legal rights were minimal, in practice their work and knowledge were acknowledged as central to the success of the family.

The lack of legal standing meant that women were vulnerable to economic change, as was experienced with the arrival of British colonialism. The troubles began in the 1890s when British settlers started claiming land that they believed was unused. In many instances the land was not being cultivated, but it was in a fallow period, an essential part of successful cultivation techniques. Africans considered all land to be under the jurisdiction of a Kenyan clan. By 1913, British administrators had expanded their territorial claims, effectively taking land from African communities and families that still lived and farmed their fields on that property. As the colonial government began leasing and selling land to white settlers, rural Africans lost access and control. By the 1930s, European settlers controlled one-fifth of all the land, and half of the land deemed worth cultivating.[3] They invested in crops such as tobacco, which could be sold, but, as with many cash crops, could not be used as sustenance for families. Cash crops also required a great deal of hired labor to do the hard work in the fields, which most settlers were not willing to carry out themselves.

Many Africans found themselves restricted to living on special reserves, where they were expected to follow their customary practices of land access and inheritance. However, the disruptions and restrictions meant that it was no longer possible to allow women the same support and access they had held historically. There was much less available land in the crowded reserves. Land entered the market, was owned by individuals rather than the clan, and came to be associated with specific ethnic groups. As arable land became scarce, its value rose and the higher prices kept Africans, and especially African women, out of the market and out of land ownership. The settlers wanted Africans to become landless, so that they would be forced to enter the labor market and work for European farmers, sometimes on the same land that Africans and their ancestors had once cultivated. As disputes over land entered into the courts, women were further removed from the processes of land ownership and control.

By the 1950s, problems in agricultural production led the British to adopt plans to improve the conditions for farming. As one governor analyzed the situation, the fact that women were the primary producers was at the root of the difficulties, and his solution was to focus on men when introducing new methods and other support. When land titles were allocated, they were given to men. When cattle ownership was registered, it was in men's names. Conflicts within households increased, especially during planting season, when women found they did not have access to the plots of land they needed. As cooperatives were formed to deal with cash crops such as maize and tobacco, women were excluded from membership. At each step along the way, as colonialism became more entrenched in western Kenya, women lost ground both literally and figuratively. While women had been dependent on men in the precolonial patrilineal societies, they had enjoyed some recognition and support from their community. With the escalation of colonialism, women were often unable to practice the most basic agricultural work, and they faced greater poverty and hardship. Their resistance to that experience, including the formation of the protest movement called Mau Mau, will be discussed in chapter 6.

Cocoa Production in Ghana

In Ghana when cocoa trees were introduced in the late nineteenth century, it quickly became clear that cultivating cocoa for export was a lucrative business.[4] That new source of income was dependent on women continuing their cultivation of crops for household consumption, in effect underwriting the expansion of cash crop agriculture. The unpaid inputs of women's labor both to support their families and as additional labor on the cocoa farms were key elements in the success of growing cocoa cheaply and for greater profit. As men cooperated with the interests of international capital, women worked harder and suffered more.

The Akan of southern Ghana were a matrilineal society in the precolonial era. As seen in other African communities, control over labor was at the center of village relations, with intersecting and competing interests between men and women, elders and youth, and slaves and free individuals. Chiefs were generally older men, and along with councilors they made judicial decisions and performed religious rites that contributed to the success of agriculture and lineage continuity. In most families, following matrilineal ideals, the senior man in a household had primary control over the kin on his mother's side of the family, such as his younger siblings and his sisters' daughters, and less influence over his own wives and children, who were more closely affiliated with their own female lineage. Enslaved household members were also under his control.

A man's authority over his nieces meant that he could decide who they would marry, and he could pawn them in return for a loan when he needed income. A pawned individual could be redeemed when a debt was repaid, but frequently the debtor could not afford to do that, and the pawned person could become fully enslaved instead. An uncle could demand a loan from the husband of a niece, and when the husband agreed, his wife would become the pawn, or collateral for the debt, which placed her in a reduced legal position within that community. The Akan system of relationships could be quite complicated, and girls and women were subject to ill-treatment as a result of their vulnerability to being pawned. Even free-born women were legal minors and subject to the control of their uncles and other male kin.

Men in precolonial Akan communities also had the right to sell land to non-lineage members. During the nineteenth century, as the British increasingly outlawed slavery and worked to switch their African commerce from trade in people to trade in commodities such as palm oil, Akan men sold land to Africans from outside of Akan lineages. The interest in owning land increased at first as the trade in palm oil expanded. By the 1890s, it was found that cocoa grew very successfully in the Akan areas, and the buying, selling, and mortgaging of land became even more common.

Women were involved in three ways in the expansion of cocoa farming and the trade that went with it. They were often the monetary security that allowed men to buy land that they could devote to cocoa trees, because in most cases men bought such land on credit and used female kin collateral. Because men generally had greater mobility, an impoverished young man might migrate to an urban area or a new region seeking work, and thus avoid being pawned. Women were less able to leave their villages, and were therefore more likely to be pawned when a male relative needed to borrow capital to get started in the cocoa farming business. If the man could not repay the loan, women were transferred to the creditor.

Women and children made up the major share of the labor force on the cocoa plantations. Men relied on female kin to contribute to the initial intense work of clearing land and planting new trees, as well as the daily tasks of weeding, drying, and fermenting the cocoa before it was taken to the market. When cocoa was sold, the male land (and tree) owner kept the proceeds, and he was not obligated to pay any wages to the women who had labored on the cocoa cultivation. Some women did own land themselves, but they were the minority. Women also continued to perform nearly all of the agricultural work that fed their families and the necessary daily responsibilities such as collecting water and firewood, caring for small children, and preparing meals for the household.

One of the labor requirements was to transport the sacks of cocoa beans to the coast for export, and this work was another area where women were seen, carrying sacks on their heads that weighed up to two hundred pounds. British observers noted the reliance on female porters for this work, and they also described the poor health of the women who struggled under excessively heavy burdens. Once trains and roads were constructed beginning in the 1920s, head-loading sacks of cocoa became less common.

Though Akan women had long been involved in market trading, men generally controlled more lucrative goods, including marketing cocoa. Some women did sell cocoa, and at times pawned individuals, male and female, were allowed by their masters to sell some cocoa, though never in quantities that would undercut the senior man's profits. And in some cases women were able to enter into cocoa marketing as a route to greater freedom. But generally, despite the centrality of female labor to the entire cocoa enterprise, from obtaining land through the daily labor of maintaining cocoa trees, to marketing the product, women did not gain an income from that work.

By the early twentieth century, the British outlawed pawning, though families continued to count on receiving some money or gift for the marriage of their niece, and women were expected to remain in a marriage in order to fulfill the demands of the loan. The payment began to be referred to as "thanks money" rather than a loan, but the obligation of a wife to tolerate an unhappy marriage for the sake of her extended family remained the same. Despite changes in pawning, women's options were restricted and their labor continued to support men's cash crop endeavors. Many men found the cocoa business to be a route to personal prosperity, wealth they gained from collaborating with the colonial authorities in the exploitation of women's labor and subordinate social status.

Fig. 4.2 Women carrying bags of cocoa beans in Ghana, mid-twentieth century. Source: the American Geographical Society Library, University of Wisconsin-Milwaukee Libraries.

Textiles and Clothing

The production of textiles has often been at least partly women's responsibility, and the process has been marked by a gender division of labor. For example, indigo cloth produced in nineteenth-century Mali was a joint production of men and women. Typically, men grew the cotton and women cultivated the indigo plant. Women spun and dyed the cotton to produce the indigo cloth for the luxury market, while slave labor did the weaving. Plain white cloth, which men produced, was for household use rather than for sale. The process changed after slave emancipation in 1905 and with the spread of Islam. Women were more often secluded, which restricted their access to their agricultural fields and to the markets. Men were able to move into those areas, and eventually women lost control over the marketing of the indigo cloth.[5]

Women's tasks varied in different locations. Mali was also the site of women who produced a distinctive mud cloth called *bogolan* ("bogo" means river mud), printing repetitive geometrical designs in shades of brown and tan. Historically, the cloth was made by mothers and grandmothers for a bride-to-be, and the symbols were reminders of proper behavior and advice from their female kin. In the nineteenth-century Sokoto Caliphate (present-day northern Nigeria), women were spinners, weavers, and dyers.

In the southern Nigerian town of Abeokuta, Yoruba women were renowned for dyeing imported cloth with indigo designs. Known as *adire*, women gained economic influence through their control over the process of dyeing.[6] As the colonial economy grew at the end of the nineteenth century, exports of cocoa and other products increased and brought wealth to many residents. People used their new disposable income to purchase imported cloth, which local women then dyed to meet African markets. The development of the colonial infrastructure, including roads, railways, and European firms that extended credit to both cocoa and cloth merchants, facilitated the export of cocoa and the importation of cloth.

Local hand-woven cloth was available but was more costly, and because it was somewhat stiffer than the imported cloth, it was not as easy to dye. The dyers used a variety of resist methods to transfer the design onto the cloth, including tie-dyeing, folding, and using a paste or other material to block out a pattern on the white cloth. The knowledge was commonly passed from mother to daughter, and the dyers were recognized as skilled artisans. The dyers owned their own pots and hired people to help with the work, and therefore they controlled the production of the cloth. The complex process of transforming the leaves of the indigo plant into a usable dye could be unreliable, and the women often turned to religious and spiritual leaders for support in their efforts. Wealthy women could hire workers or bring in slave labor, but many women relied on kin to participate in a family-based industry, with the dye pots being located in family residential compounds. The importance of adire production in the local economy, in regional trading networks, and as a part of global commerce, indicates how women's work was essential to southern Nigeria's economy in the early twentieth century.

Urban Work

The increasing economic activity associated with colonialism contributed to the development of urban areas. Often there had been a population center located on the coast or along a river where it was easier for traders and others to meet. In the nineteenth century, such centers began to grow more rapidly and became home to Africans who were educated in mission schools and who worked in colonial enterprises. Many urban centers were the site of the development of new elites. Though they comprised a relatively small sector of society, they were very influential since they practiced Christianity or Islam, were literate, and earned a wage.

They developed new patterns and expectations of personal areas of life such as marriage and family. The choices they made in housing, dress, and food were often noticeably different from people in nearby rural villages.

WEST AFRICAN MARKET TRADERS

Women throughout Africa have been active in market trading, but especially in West Africa, they have been noted for the extent and strength of the markets. From the earliest days of European contact, women were involved in the exchange of goods with traders along the coast. For many years, women were able to exploit their position between the newcomer Europeans and established coastal communities to regulate trade and limit the expansion of European economic power. In some cases, they married or formed other intimate relationships with European men who could provide access to imported goods. Some women became wealthy and renowned as a result of their trade. The nineteenth century marked a waning of the international slave trade, which was slowly replaced with crops such as palm oil and palm kernels, peanuts (often called groundnuts), and rice. Although in many areas of West Africa agricultural producers relied on local slaves to cultivate export crops, slaves were withdrawn from the international market.

European travelers in nineteenth-century Hausa areas reported seeing many markets throughout the region. Women in the 1820s were described as selling prepared food such as bean cakes from roadside markets where customers could also find fresh fruits and vegetables, groundnuts, and yams. Spreading their goods out on mats under shade trees, a vendor sometimes would build a fire and roast skewers of small pieces of meat, serving clients from a mat spread across her lap while seated on the ground. Women also sold milk, sweet potatoes, and other supplies to travelers. As they were everywhere, markets were centers of commerce and offered vendors and shoppers an opportunity to share news and discuss family and community events.[7]

In Sierra Leone, the active trading described in chapter 2 continued to develop in the nineteenth century. While some women did travel and engage in trade between different communities, most women were vendors in local markets.[8] By the mid-nineteenth century, women were able to collectively pressure the government of Freetown to build a new stone market to accommodate the requirements of those who regularly sold vegetables and other items. The new market developed into a crucial economic center in the city, and many women rented a space by the month to guarantee a regular site where customers could find them. In the 1860s, they could usually be seen with large baskets displaying their yams, bananas, limes, eggplant, avocado, and okra for sale. They also marketed local and imported goods such as thread, mirrors, beads, cowries, cotton cloth, rice, groundnuts, smoked and dried fish, and other items that were in demand. Visitors at various times described the noise of the bartering and the liveliness of the exchanges as the vendors and their customers discussed their purchases. The market also served as a social meeting ground where women of different ethnic origins gathered and worked together to control and advance their common interest in maintaining a successful market.

Women were able to travel widely, and they were found as traders at all levels of society—from local vendors selling produce from their own families' garden plots to regional dealers playing a significant role in the kola nut trade throughout the region. Kola nut was a stimulant that was used throughout West Africa and was an essential part of greeting and welcoming rituals in many cultures. From the mid-nineteenth century, women in Sierra Leone, especially those with kin connections to Nigerian communities, took an increasingly large role in growing and trading kola nut. Their marketing activities also included sesame seed, rubber, rice, and palm tree products, but kola was the driving commodity. From their base in Freetown, Sierra Leone's capital, they ventured into Guinea-Bissau, Senegal, and the Gambia, where there were eager customers waiting to purchase the desired nut. As the trade developed, the women deliberately fostered personal and commercial relationships throughout the region that enabled them to act as intercultural brokers.

The nineteenth century in Sierra Leone was a time of achievement for many women because they brought skills from a diverse set of geographic, religious, and ethnic backgrounds and established themselves as market women. While some engaged in local trade in primarily perishable goods in Freetown, others were able to travel great distances and connect with economic and social networks that brought them material success as well as a notable role at the center of the development of a multicultural community.

In other areas of coastal West Africa, the experience of women traders demonstrated the shift from trading in people to exporting crops. Ña Rosa de Carvalho Alvarenga organized her agricultural business close to the areas where Bibiana Vaz had her trading concerns in the previous century (see chapter 2). Ña Rosa's family connections, which included her Cape Verdean father who was commander of the garrison, may have allowed her to control a key parcel of land along the river close to Cacheu in Guinea Bissau. She also maintained relations with local communities where her African kin resided. She owned slaves who worked in her rice fields, and she marketed the rice in exchange for imported cloth. In addition to her commercial activities, she was noted in various European reports for acting as a mediator when local sailors and canoemen threatened to rise up against the Portuguese authorities, and she was acknowledged as the final authority in working out differences. The apparent arrangement where the Portuguese relied on a local person to assist in keeping the peace also indicated the weakness of the colonial power in the region.[9]

NIGERIAN TRADERS

Several women traders rose to prominence in nineteenth-century Nigeria. The stories of their individual lives provide some insight into women's situation more generally in the urban and coastal communities where they resided.

Madam Efinroye Tinubu was an influential businesswoman in Abeokuta, Nigeria. After learning market women's work from her mother and grandmother, she set up her own trade in tobacco and salt. After she was widowed and left with two children, she remarried a man who had been a king in Lagos, but was living in exile in Abeokuta. When he was recalled to Lagos, she followed him and began trading near Lagos, where she started dealing with European slave traders. Madam Tinubu got involved in local politics in the 1830s, due to her support of her husband, and then backed his son in a succession dispute. She expanded her commercial networks, and by the 1840s was dealing in salt, tobacco, palm oil, firearms, and slaves. Her political connections intersected with her business interests, and she found success in both arenas.

In 1855, she was involved in an attempt to end the power of wealthy immigrants from Brazil who were active in Lagos and Sierra Leone, but her efforts brought in British military forces as her influence was opposed by the British consul. As a result she was exiled from Lagos. She then reestablished her business in Abeokuta, adding cotton production to her network of products. She stepped forward to protect Abeokuta when the town was threatened with an invasion in the 1860s. Her actions in recruiting local women to support soldiers led to her being given the title of *Iyalode* of Abeokuta in 1864 (the role of iyalode is discussed in chapter 2). She died in 1887. Tinubu Square in Lagos was named to commemorate her contributions to Nigerian history.[10]

Born in 1872, Omu Okwei was a major trader and Igbo market woman in Onitsha, Nigeria. As a member of a royal family in Ossomari, she was descended from formidable merchants and apprenticed at the age of nine to a maternal aunt to learn the market business. She built her own trading empire from nothing, as she forfeited her dowry by marrying men who were not approved by her parents. She began by trading food and expanded to include tobacco and cotton cloth. As British control grew in the region, she became an agent of the Niger Company in 1904 and began to market vegetable oil in exchange for gin, lamps, matches, and dishes and pots. She benefited from the inter-city trade, and used her profits to acquire girls and young women who she then placed in arranged marriages with prominent businessmen. That system of slavery meant that all children and goods accrued to Okwei as the owner of the women, and it gave her favorable terms of credit as well as privileged access to men who traded in ivory and gunpowder. She was named to the Native Court in 1912 and played an important role in the social life of her city. In 1935, she was crowned as Omu (queen) in recognition of her central role in the economy and society of Onitsha. She lived several more years, passing away in 1943. A life-sized marble statue of her in Onitsha was unveiled in 1963, and one of the city's main roads bore her name.[11]

MINING COMPOUNDS

Some of the newly established urban areas under colonialism were centered on mining enterprises following the discovery of deposits of gold, diamonds, and copper which European investors began to exploit. While the miners were almost entirely African men, many women moved to the communities that developed near the mines, some with their husbands and others seeking new opportunities for work. In South Africa, where diamonds and gold were discovered in the 1870s, the authorities provided housing for single male workers and discouraged women from living in the mining communities. Women were expected to remain in their rural home areas while men were away on lengthy work contracts at the mines.

A somewhat different pattern emerged in Northern Rhodesia, later known as Zambia, where copper was extracted in the mining region known as the Copperbelt. Copper mining was initiated in the 1920s, and at first men were recruited without their families.[12] At some locations, the mining company management found that there were advantages if they allowed the male workers to bring their wives or to establish new relationships with single women living in the mining towns. At the same time, the colonial government was actively opposed to women leaving the rural areas. In part they were responding to concerns by rural men, who feared that if women were allowed to freely leave the villages the rural male leaders would lose their authority over women, and local food cultivation would be disrupted. In the 1930s, the government required unmarried women to remain in the rural areas, and enforced this restriction by introducing marriage certificates and setting up checkpoints along the roads leading to the Copperbelt. Women without proper documents were returned to their villages. They also created African courts in the urban areas, where the vast majority of cases were related to marriage disputes. While urban marriages were being regularized, a woman was allowed to marry only when the urban court obtained the approval of male elders in her village of origin.

While some mines discouraged family residences due to the perception that it would involve greater costs to provide appropriate housing, others realized that if the men were accompanied by their wives they were more content and had access to better shelter, cleanliness, and food. As one mining compound manager in the 1940s observed, "the married employee is undoubtedly more contented than the single, he is better fed, looked after and clothed, and has the rudiments of a sense of responsibility which tends to make him a more suitable and efficient worker."[13] While his comments were paternalistic, the result was that women were allowed to live with their husbands in the compounds.

Single women were also able to move to the mining towns and find situations where they could earn an income. The services they provided might include sex, but in most cases they also cooked meals and did laundry for the male workers. The availability of such domestic services meant that the relationship, though often short-lived, was more complicated than sex work or simple prostitution.

Both married and single women were occupied with the extensive daily round of work, caring for children, collecting firewood, waiting in line to purchase food, and preparing food for consumption. Many of them maintained gardens where they grew produce primarily for their families' tables, and also sold any small surplus in the urban markets. In addition to selling the surplus from their gardens, some women sold handicrafts such as baskets. A few women were able to find employment in the hospital and welfare offices.

When possible, women engaged in income-generating activities, and the colonial government introduced measures to control or prohibit many of the projects that women attempted. Beer-brewing was a major source of income. In the rural areas, women commonly made beer for work parties and for other social and religious events. In the urban settlements they produced beer for sale, using their knowledge of the process of making beer from sorghum and other local grains. The colonial authorities banned private beer brewing, and they launched beer halls where the men could drink and the profits would go to the colonial officials to use for other programs aimed at maintaining order in the urban neighborhoods. But women continued to brew beer illegally, which was a popular activity because it could be done in the home and the brewers could potentially earn a substantial income.

The low wages and the restrictions on women's activities led to urban unrest, as people protested the constraints they faced in their efforts to earn an income. The response of the mining companies was to offer classes in domestic skills, including hygiene and baby care, sewing and knitting, and cooking. As seen elsewhere, missionaries were involved and often Christian values such as monogamy and marital fidelity were part of the training course.

Despite the attempts by the colonial authorities to control women's work and to stabilize urban marriages, the new towns offered women greater independence than found in the rural areas. They had enough personal freedom to live without a husband, earning an income from their own work. Though their lives were not easy, some of the worst hardships of rural life were mitigated. Urban living brought new opportunities for women that they sought even with the many obstacles placed in their path by both rural men and urban colonial governments.

PROSTITUTION

Prostitution, at least in forms which are recognized as the practice of exchanging money for sexual favors, was rarely practiced in precolonial African societies. The few exceptions involved slave women who were sometimes destitute and usually far from their home communities, as was the case for some of the slave women who lived in the royal household of Dahomey or those who were "public women" in the Gold Coast (see chapter 2).

With the onset of colonialism and the development of urban centers and market economies, some African women found that prostitution was a way to earn an income. Prostitution in African societies seldom involved the presence of a pimp or other male control, and it did not necessarily rely on brothels. More common was the individual woman who accepted money for sexual intimacy with men for whom she frequently also provided domestic comforts such as a cooked meal and laundry services. As seen in the example of the mining communities, sex work was often part of a set of domestic services that women could perform and that male laborers desired or required. There were instances where women entered into relationships with men, and while these were sometimes of short duration, they could last many years and include the birth of children. There were local terms for women who went from man to man, or who sought sexual relationships outside of marriage, including *adana* and *mgboto* (Igbo), and *malaya* and *watembezi* (Swahili). Those words seldom translated easily to "prostitute," but more often referred to aspects of the prostitute's behavior, such as her ease in undressing, or her habit of walking on the streets.[14]

Research in Nairobi discovered how the types of prostitution shifted over the decades of colonialism. In the early part of the twentieth century, when British colonialism expanded and rural societies lost cattle to the devastating rinderpest epidemic, women began to leave their villages in search of a more secure livelihood. At first the women added sex work to other urban work they performed, including gathering food and firewood or engaging in petty trade. Along the way they would meet men and accept money for having sex with them. The money they earned was substantial in local terms, and it enabled the women to support their families in the rural areas and to purchase land and houses in the developing urban settlements. Many women viewed the opportunity to live in an urban neighborhood and earn an income from cooking meals, doing laundry, and providing sex for male workers as a way to support themselves and their families and yet continue to have control of their own lives. By the 1920s, women had their own rooms and small houses where they lived and accepted male visitors. As one woman commented, "[Men] knew that the house belonged to a woman who never had a husband, so they knew it was a safe place to come because the owner had no husband to beat them. . . .The best way to find men was for them to come to your room and you talk, you make tea for him, and you keep your house clean, you keep your bed clean, you have sex with him, and then he gives you money."[15] By taking the money at the end of the session, the woman was able to charge for all of the services that she provided. The availability of domestic services often brought the same men back to the same women, and the relationships sometimes became long term. By the 1930s during the Depression, men were more often out of work and short of funds, and the women found they needed to ask for money upfront, or the men were likely to take advantage of them, using their sexual and domestic services, and then leaving without paying. By investigating women's sex work as part of the colonial urban economy, the complex connections between rural communities, women's typical domestic work, and changing livelihoods in the cities is evident.

Urban women were sometimes perceived as prostitutes if they dressed in Western styles, especially in revealing or form-fitting clothing, and if they appeared to be financially independent. During the colonial era, authorities subjected African women to hygiene controls including forced physical examinations in an attempt to stem the spread of venereal diseases. Though not practiced everywhere, in Southern Rhodesia (now Zimbabwe) from the mid-1920s to the late 1950s, urban women were regularly examined in a practice they called *chibheura* (open your legs).[16] As seen in many colonial initiatives, the European authorities were concerned with controlling women, especially in the cities, and they focused on female health and hygiene through of the implementation of new laws and regulations.

Religion under Colonialism

Missions

For many African women, their first encounter with European colonialism was at a Christian mission station. Missionaries played a central role in introducing new ideas about health and hygiene, and they often focused on motherhood as a point of entrance into African women's lives. Mission ideas about health and family life were not always easily accepted and sometimes came into conflict with African preferences. African women sometimes opposed missionary efforts to end practices such as bridewealth and polygyny, as seen in Kenya in the 1930s. Missionaries tried to end Gikuyu initiation rites, which included the practice of female genital cutting, but their efforts led to some Gikuyu embracing their own culture, with a renewed observance of the rites. As African societies suffered the disruptions of colonialism, some people turned to Christianity as a source of salvation and relief from the difficulties they faced, gladly embracing monogamous marriage and denouncing bridewealth and initiation rites. Women also approached Western missionaries for assistance with infertility or illness.

Some women joined convents such as Bannabikiira in Uganda or the Congregation of the Daughters of the Sacred Heart of Mary, which was established in Senegal in 1858. The converts lived celibate lives, renouncing motherhood and family life. As African societies generally expected all adult women to marry and have many children, the African nuns were occasionally taunted for making what was perceived as a non-African choice. Women who wished to avoid a forced marriage sometimes found refuge in mission stations, and their negative stories about polygyny contributed to missionary ideas about the oppression experienced by African women. Other women who married monogamously according to Christian expectations found that life was too limiting, as they faced restrictions when wishing to leave an unhappy marriage.

European women came with the White Sisters, the Immaculate Conception order of nuns, other Catholic orders, and Protestant missionary groups. Many Western women came as missionaries with the hope of converting Africans through the introduction of "modern" schooling and health care, though too often their starting point was the rejection of most aspects of African society. Mary Slessor was a well-known missionary who arrived in Nigeria in 1876 and devoted herself to serving local people. Other European female missionaries came as the wives of male missionaries or married a male missionary. Many suffered and died in Africa. One of the best known was Mary Livingstone, wife of the famed Scottish missionary-explorer David Livingstone, who was buried on the banks of the Zambezi River after a fatal illness. Missionary work was also the task that brought African American women such as Susie Wiseman Yergan to Africa.

Bannabikiira was one of the oldest Catholic sisterhoods in Africa. The White Sisters had begun work at Buddu in Uganda in 1902 under the leadership of Mother Mechtilde. Within a year the first group of girls trained as catechists, and their numbers grew rapidly. In 1907, when there were 140 girls living at the mission, wearing distinguishing dress, and working with children, some of them asked to become nuns. Mother Mechtilde established a novitiate in 1908, and in 1910 the first three girls were professed. The order applied rules specific to their community that differed from the European system, as the African sisters kept their own names, did not take a vow of poverty, and made an annual rather than a lifetime commitment. The name Bannabikiira, meaning "Daughters of the Virgin" in Baganda, a language spoken in Uganda, was also adopted in 1910. By 1926, the order had a new permanent headquarters in Buddu and a Ugandan nun, Mama Cecilia Nalube, was named as the first African mother superior, taking the name Mother Ursula. At that time the congregation adopted the practices of accepting new names, vowing poverty, and making a lifetime commitment to the order. Their numbers and influence continued to grow, and there were 256 nuns in 1956 accompanied by a growing number of sister congregations in other regions of Uganda, which counted over 1,000 Ugandan sisters. Other prominent Ugandan orders included the Franciscan Missionary Sisters of Africa, founded by the dynamic leader from Ireland, Mother Kevin (1875–1957). African nuns chose a life course that veered sharply from what most African women chose, and they used that choice to serve their communities as teachers and nurses.

Haya Women and Catholic Missionaries in Tanzania

The experience at the White Fathers Catholic Mission among the Haya in northern Tanzania suggested some of the motivations that brought women to stay at the mission.[17] Men and women came to the mission stations for a variety of reasons, though certain categories of women were more likely to seek a haven among missionaries. Missionaries allowed girls and women to participate in mission activities rather than coercing them to return to household or community situations that were deemed dangerous or were considered in opposition to Christian ideals. In the early twentieth century, many of the converts were ex-slaves. Some of these women were Haya and had been subject to local domestic slavery, while others were rescued from slaving caravans that passed through Haya territory. The missionaries were interested in ending slavery entirely, and as long as various forms of slavery continued they offered sanctuary for enslaved people on their grounds.

Among the Haya, it was common for some girls to go live in the king's compound, where he could choose one of them when he was selecting future wives. Widows of lower chiefs and subchiefs were also expected to join the royal household, where the king might marry them. Several of the stories recorded by the missionaries involved girls who refused to submit themselves to the process of joining the chief's entourage of wives. Diary entries by the mission Sisters recorded such events as the following: "1913, Febr. 7. Three more girls from the Kiziba king came to take refuge with us. . . . Febr. 22. A man from the king came to look at the Sisters' place for three of his *baisiki* [girls]. They refused absolutely and the good prince left them in peace."[18] In a similar case in 1914, an unnamed subchief died with no sons or male heirs; his widows and daughters, following his wish that they become Christian, eluded the king's soldiers and found refuge at the mission. At times the kings brought legal cases in order to reclaim the girls, and in one reported instance a girl was returned, only to commit suicide some months later. Sometimes the girls had a desired fiancé or other friend or relative who would pay the bridewealth to the king in order to end the royal claim and allow the girl to continue her training as a Christian.

In some Haya localities, a few girls were chosen to guard the tomb of a deceased king, remaining virgin and in attendance for their entire lives, and several reports of girls or women arriving at the mission station concerned those tomb guardians escaping that unwanted duty. Girls increasingly were able to leave such situations, in which previously they had felt a strong imperative to ful-fill their cultural obligations. That development indicated that local institutions were weakening, allowing an opportunity for missionaries to intervene.

A further group of women were those who were escaping from marriages, especially young girls who were avoiding forced and arranged marriage. In many of the recorded cases, the girls' parents had already collected and spent the bridewealth and were committed to the marriage of their daughter. Older men were more likely to have access to cows and other resources that comprised bridewealth, making marriages between older men and young girls a common occurrence. Older prospective husbands likely had the additional encumbrance of a prior wife or two. Girls who rejected marriage to an older man often sought protection from the missionaries. Not only were the girls dodging an undesirable husband, but the missionaries were happy to gather up such examples of what they considered barbaric practices. As with the ex-slaves who found shelter, there was a neat fit between the interests of the missionaries in exposing what they described as pagan customs, and the pursuit of safety on the part of Haya girls and women.

Several of the stories entered in the mission diaries told of women who had begun taking instruction in Christian practices and encountered resistance from their husbands, who did not want them to pray. It was not uncommon previ-ously for Haya women to leave their husbands following a disagreement, though they used to return to their natal home and their parents would then help work out a settlement. Once the mission stations were established, those became an alternate place of retreat, and the missionaries began to act as mediators. Not all women who arrived at the mission stations intended to remain there perma-nently; occasionally they simply required some time away from their husbands to indicate their sincerity in adopting Christian beliefs.

Others who came to the missionaries had practical interests, such as seeking medical care for injuries and illnesses that local medicines had not cured. For many, the dispensaries were an initial point of contact between Africans and Europeans. Among the Haya in the early twentieth century, the White Sisters mission averaged 1,500 visits to the dispensary every month. Certainly that was an opportunity for the Sisters to introduce Catholic teachings, and for local peo-ple to observe an alternative to Haya customs that they found troublesome.

CONGOLESE WOMEN AND CATHOLIC MISSIONARIES

Women on the opposite coast, in Congo-Brazzaville, had similar interactions with the Catholic missionaries from France who settled along the Congo River and established a mission there.[19] African women were not a homogenous group, and likewise the various European missionaries were from a variety of countries and spiritual traditions. Each location was the site of a nuanced interaction of specific missionaries with a particular African community. In Congo-Brazzaville, local people still followed a matrilineal ideal of recognizing kin relationships. Women were valued for their agricultural work and their child-bearing abilities, especially as that region was not densely populated in the early twentieth century. Local concerns about family intersected with French worries about population growth and labor supply. Congolese women who identified primarily as mothers and sisters found much to admire in the Sisters of Saint Joseph of Cluny who came to live among them at the end of the nineteenth century.

As with other areas, local rural societies experienced violent disruption from colonial incursions. As the French military sought control over the region and moved to gain access to the interior, the African communities they passed through viewed the European caravans as a source of taxes. Both Africans and Europeans suffered from thefts, kidnapping, and other attacks. Villages were further damaged by the spread of disease and climatic problems that brought drought and famine. In societies that relied on control over human labor and where women's agricultural work was valued, these factors made life in general very unstable.

The French missionaries arrived in the coastal area called Loango, now in Congo-Brazzaville, in the 1880s. They immediately began recruiting men and women as catechists. At first, in contrast to many other parts of Africa, they found that many more men than women were coming to the mission station. This demographic was a cause for concern, because they wanted to establish Christian families, which required women to convert and be available as wives to the newly-Christian African men. But women not only performed essential agricultural and household labor, they had rights to their own land and controlled the distribution and income from their produce. Observers commented that a husband would not take even "an egg from her chicken coop" without permission from his wife.[20]

Women also led local religious gatherings, especially groups concerned with fertility and therapeutic activities that worked to bring prosperity and health to individuals and the community as a whole. It was no wonder, then, that chiefs and elder men were reluctant to allow women to join the mission project. And the women themselves were often uninterested, as they already had a satisfying and fulfilling set of beliefs and rituals that were specifically centered on women's roles in society. Initiation rites, as in other parts of Africa, were important events at which older women taught girls about their roles and responsibilities. Women were not willing to forego a treasured custom in order to participate in something new and unproven. The continued widespread practice of the rites was a major obstacle for the missionaries, who designated the rituals as witchcraft, a pagan activity that had to be stopped. At just the age when the mission sisters wanted the girls to identify as Christian, they were opting to join their village mates and undergo a lengthy rite that would confirm them as proper adult women with a recognized status in their own familiar society.

With circumstances that encouraged women to remain committed to their own culture, the first girls to join the missionaries were often outsiders, in the Congo and elsewhere. As with the Haya in Tanzania, some of the most successful recruits were girls who were redeemed from slave caravans, who had already been removed from their home villages. The missionaries believed that older Africans were too set in their "pagan" ways to be successful converts. Older men in patri- lineal societies could buy slave girls and eventually marry them or arrange a mar- riage with a kinsman, as a method of controlling people and increasing the power and reach of their clan. The missionaries entered into the slave trade when they purchased children themselves, in what they considered a kind of ransom, hoping to save them from an enslaved life. The mission stations became a home for girls from different societies in the Congo, and many of the ransomed girls grew up to become mothers of large Christian families, part of an entirely new society that was separate from already existing African villages. In the early years of the mis- sion at the end of the nineteenth century, the rate of illness and death among the European Sisters was quite high; without European women to train local women, the male missionaries turned to recruits to play a leadership role, giving the ran- somed girls an even stronger loyalty to the missionaries and to Christian life.

Those early converts became the center of an expanding Congolese mission, as the men and women established families and worked to recruit other Afri- cans in part by their example of living a comfortable life. The women worked closely with nonconverts in the traditional arenas of women's interest, such as agricultural work, issues of fertility and motherhood, and women-centered religious beliefs and practices. By the 1920s and 1930s, the mission station wit- nessed an increase in the number of girls and women who sought education and potential marriage to the educated male converts who frequented the station. In those years, the missionaries no longer rescued girls from slave markets, but they focused on finding suitable marriage partners and in some cases providing bridewealth for the male catechists, allowing them to marry and establish Chris- tian families. As with the Haya and elsewhere, disruptions such as maltreatment, early widowhood, and a desire to avoid an arranged marriage brought women to the mission stations seeking refuge, and many stayed to contribute to the estab- lishment of African Christian communities.

CHRISTIANITY IN SOUTHERN AFRICA

In southern Africa, women found other ways of being involved with the Chris- tian missions. Some women attended prayer groups called *manyano*; in Lesotho, similar groups are called *kopanos*.[21] The name was derived from the Xhosa term meaning "to join" or "unite." The groups were started by African women within Christian missions and churches, especially among Methodists. In South Africa the Swiss Mission reported that in the 1870s women were meeting to share prayer and religious discussion. The groups also offered support for women with problems in their marriages, in raising their children as Christians, and with other common issues; for these reasons they were sometimes considered mothers' groups. A particular concern was maintaining the sexual purity of their daughters, who were growing up in rapidly changing communities as men left to work in the urban centers and mines. Urban life also brought new experiences as girls attended social affairs and events that had been unknown in the rural lives of their mothers. Most of the prayer groups followed strict rules for membership and attendance, including abstinence from alcohol, and members often wore matching attire. They were sometimes known as Women's Prayer and Service Unions, or similar designations. In Zimbabwe, where they were first established at the Methodist mission in 1929, they were called *ruwadzano*.

Women who were active with the Christian missions also became evangelizers known as biblewomen. These were African women who converted to Christianity and who devoted themselves to proselytizing by traveling to distant rural areas and conducting study sessions with local women.[22] Most evident in South Africa, they performed this work in the first half of the twentieth century under the auspices of the Methodist Women's Auxiliaries. These individual women visited villages where men remained opposed to the women in their household getting involved with the missions. The biblewomen noted that a major obstacle to gaining adherents to Christianity was the continuing power of local spirits who resented the influx of a rival set of beliefs. Another obstacle was male alcohol consumption; in addition to problems associated with drunkenness, when men frequented urban beer halls, women's traditional brewing was less lucrative. The missionary women urged abstinence from alcohol as one way of dealing with bad behavior by drunken men, though alcohol avoidance also hurt women brewers and contributed to women's lack of opportunities in small rural settlements. Nonetheless, biblewomen made significant contributions in spreading the word about Christian religious beliefs and winning converts.

East African Independent Churches

The early colonial period was a time when numerous independent churches emerged. Most of these churches drew in part on Christian teachings, while also including some local beliefs and practices. Though apparently Christian in some key aspects, they were not part of any official hierarchy or administration. Women were prominent in these churches, and even in churches which were founded by men, women often played a crucial role as faithful followers.

The history of the Roho church, which arose among the Luo of western Kenya in the 1930s, exemplifies some of the contradictory experiences of such churches. Colonial officials viewed the founder, Alfayo Odongo Mango, as a man who was using religious teachings to expand his own ethnic concerns about access to land. Missionaries from the main formal branches of Christianity were fearful that they would not be able to control the activities of new Christians or of local people whose first interaction with any form of Christianity was when they were recruited to unorthodox Roho beliefs. But many Luo viewed Mango as a revered local leader who founded a truly African church that addressed many of their own concerns and spiritual desires.[23]

The role of women in the central structures of the early Roho church was a key factor in the success of the church among the Luo. The church first became known in the early twentieth century when people experienced the Holy Spirit in their communities. In the 1930s, after two decades of expansion, the church came to the attention of missionaries, who began to speak against the unorthodox expression of Christianity found in the Roho community. As the missionaries and colonial officials tried to halt the spread of Roho beliefs, Luo women risked beatings and imprisonment in order to attend prayer meetings in peoples' homes. When persecution increased in 1934, women protected themselves and their families by acting as soldiers and guardians. The local colonial administration eventually banned the church, but while many men then left Roho, female members remained faithful and kept the church alive.

Women felt drawn to the Roho church for a variety of reasons. It was a space where they were free to express their spirituality through speaking in tongues, going into trances, and exhibiting physical activity such as jumping and dancing. Luo women appreciated the opportunity to preach and lead worshippers in the Roho church, practices which were forbidden to them in the mission-sponsored churches. An early hymn, "We Are Women of War," acknowledged female leadership in the face of violent attacks, including a fire that claimed several Roho leaders and members who were commemorated as martyrs in later years. Women were important in local Luo beliefs and customs, as seen in their historic experience of spirit possession and as healers in possession cults. They were not able to adequately include such experiences in the mission churches, and they were attracted to the more familiar practice that arose among Roho believers.

West African Independent Churches

Christianah Abiodun Emmanuel, born in 1907, was a founder and leader of a Christian sect known as the Cherubim and Seraphim Society, which was based in Nigeria. It was considered a part of the Aladura movement, from the Yoruba word for "owners of prayer," which referred to several West African sects that grew into churches in their own right. In 1925, Emmanuel reported seeing visions and claimed that angels had taken her up to heaven. She fell into a coma that lasted for seven days until Moses Orimolade Tunolase arrived; he already had a reputation as a healer and was known as the "praying man." When he prayed for Emmanuel, she awoke from her coma and described her vision of a heavenly city. Soon people were traveling great distances to visit her and hear about her visions. She and Orimolade began holding regular prayer sessions, and by September 1925, they formed an interdenominational prayer society called the Seraphim Society (Egbe Serafu). During the late 1920s, the organization spread throughout southern Nigeria and Ghana, encouraging prayer and fasting, condemning witchcraft, and calling on people to end their worship of traditional gods. After a disagreement between Emmanuel and Orimolade in 1929, they formed separate organizations; Emmanuel was leader of the Cherubim and Seraphim Society while Orimolade called his group the Eternal Sacred Order of the Cherubim and Seraphim. Further splits continued into the 1930s. Following Orimolade's death in 1933, Emmanuel tried to assert her leadership over his society but was not successful. Another woman, Christianah Olatunrinle (known as Mama Ondo) emerged as the leader in 1935 and served until her death in 1941.

One of the most renowned religious activists was Alinesitoué Diatta, a Dioula prophet in Senegal.[24] Born around 1920, she came to prominence in the early 1940s when she claimed that the supreme being, Emitai, spoke to her. That announcement, as the first woman to make such a declaration, brought her into a realm that had been reserved for male leadership. Her experience appeared to be related to the oppression of French colonialism because her first visions came when the French were pushing for increased rice production and were allowing both Islamic and Christian incursions into local Dioula communities. Diatta used methods traditionally associated with male prophets and brought women and young men into the process, allowing them increased access to religious authority. She also challenged French development schemes that introduced peanuts as a male crop, leaving all rice cultivation to women. She argued that peanuts were alien to Dioula ecological beliefs because they resulted in a decreased role for women in agriculture while increasing Dioula dependence on the French. As her followers increased in number, the French feared she would instigate a rebellion. They arrested her in 1942, and she died of starvation the following year in exile in Timbuktu. She was followed by over two dozen female prophets who carried on her work.

Marriage and Politics

The late nineteenth century brought some changes in the ways that Africans practiced marriage. Increased urbanization, the impact of the slave trade, conflict within Africa and as a result of European incursions, the increasing influence of Islam and Christianity, and major shifts in local economies all had a bearing on how African women and men arranged their families. While some aspects of the history of marriage and family life are difficult to discover, other information has been recovered and analyzed by historians.

Lagos, Nigeria, under Colonialism

The experience of nineteenth century people in the urban center of Lagos, Nigeria, demonstrates some of the factors that altered marital practice. One key development was the establishment of an elite urban community, which was in part a product of Western education and conversion to Christianity. As residents began to accept the importance of monogamous marriage where women were primarily responsible for domestic tasks, they came into conflict with the prevailing African norms of polygamy, where women more often worked in agriculture and in markets outside the home. The shift acknowledged changes in relationships between men and women and in legal expectations and responsibilities.[25]

Lagos was a primarily Yoruba settlement on the coast of southwestern Nigeria, made up of a series of islands within a watery site. Though communities based on fishing and agriculture had settled there in past centuries, as an urban center it remained relatively small, with a population of about five thousand in 1800. But the general circumstances of economic equality and lack of hierarchy began to change with the growth of the slave trade. As Lagos was positioned in a strategic location for international trade, the slave trade brought a growing population and changes in the distribution of wealth. Chiefs had access to new and greater income from the trade, and they used that wealth to solidify their political control of areas around Lagos. With Great Britain's decision to end the international slave trade in 1807, the British turned to Lagos and the surrounding area as a place to control and stop the trade.

In the mid-nineteenth century, Britain annexed the island of Lagos and a piece of mainland territory and settled their own governmental and social structures there in order to support their antislave trade efforts. In the 1860s, British laws began to have supremacy over the city, which was by then a formal colony of the British Crown. Despite legal language in those laws that could have protected the existing Yoruba government and legal system, British structures took over. Simultaneously, as the slave trade decreased, trade in what were considered "legitimate" products increased, in a pattern that was seen elsewhere in Africa. In Lagos this change meant a dramatic increase in the trade in palm oil. Another factor was rapid population growth, with the number of Lagos residents reaching twenty-five thousand in the 1860s, as the influx of new people overwhelmed the smaller group that had been resident there. Among the new inhabitants were people who had been enslaved and were returned from Brazil (called Amaro) and from initial resettlement in Sierra Leone (known as Saro). The new settlers possessed different ethnic and religious identities, but they included an appreciable number of literate Christians, whose work in the colonial offices and in the construction trades made a notable imprint on Lagos society. All of these events had striking impacts on Africans' daily life.

The intersection of the Christian elite with local Yoruba communities was evident in all aspects of peoples' lives. Marriage was one central relationship that illustrated the effect of the changes taking place. Yoruba marriages exhibited some common characteristics, though not all were always strictly followed. Generally, descent was patrilineal, and residence was patrilocal. Bridewealth was commonly exchanged, representing the idea that marriage was a relationship between lineages and families, not simply between individuals. Kin could prohibit a marriage if they believed the union was not a good one. Women maintained ties to their biological kin, but they usually moved to their husbands' compound after marriage. Though many married couples loved each other, love was not necessarily a precursor to marriage.

Bridewealth was part of a series of exchanges between the lineages during the process of formalizing a marital bond. Typically, elder members of a man's lineage initiated negotiations with the woman's family. Though the relationship was considered legitimate following the first gifts of kola nut, the intended bride remained living with her family for as long as several years, while her husband had exclusive rights over her and any children who were born. He brought part of his agricultural harvest to his wife's family each year and was expected to help out with clearing fields and with large expenses, such as for funerals. A final bridewealth payment, required for the marriage to be considered complete, was made just before the woman moved to her husband's household.

Historically, the items in bridewealth exchanges consisted of kola nuts, honey, cloth, and other objects with symbolic significance. During the nineteenth century monetary sums entered into the mix, as men began to earn wages in the newly developing colonial economy. By the end of the century, many men felt the amount of money that was expected had become onerous, and letters to the editor, a useful source for gauging public opinion, often included complaints about the expense of marrying.

Economic production in Yoruba communities was organized by household. Men in farming areas cleared land and tilled the soil, while women worked in the fields, harvested crops, prepared food, and traded any surplus. Men also gathered palm nuts and hunted, while women performed other domestic tasks. Many households included slaves who also did much of the farm labor. As elsewhere, the economic strength of a household depended on the available workforce; more wives and slaves meant a much greater opportunity to cultivate agricultural crops, process them for consumption, and trade raw or prepared goods. While polygyny was an ideal, most men had no more than two wives. Some elite men had up to ten, but that situation was uncommon. While the division of labor followed gender lines and men and women within a household worked coopera-tively, they each also had their own area of work and their own sources of income. Typically, a woman could earn her own money from trading, and her husband did not have access to that income.

Though actual practice varied within these expected norms, most marriages aspired to follow the Yoruba pattern. But as colonialism, Christianity, chang-ing economic activities, and other transformations entered into Lagos, there was more and more deviance from those norms. While some of the changes were partial or subtle in reaction to economic and social transformations, Christian-ity brought the most changes because it brought its own set of norms regarding marriage.

Christian marriages also fell within a range of practices. In the mid-nine-teenth century, many of the norms reflected the Victorian expectations of Europe and especially England during that era. The clearest difference was seen in the emphasis on monogamy and rejection of polygyny. Among the local practices that the British viewed as repugnant, polygyny was at or near the top. Yoruba people who wished to convert and join a Christian congregation had to be monogamous. Other aspects that set European-style marriage apart included the idea that marriage brought together two individuals rather than two families or lineages, and that personal compatibility and happiness held primacy over eco-nomic and family interests. Love came to be seen as the basis for a successful marriage, and the importance of feelings of love between a husband and wife was the topic of pamphlets and letters.

Further, European marriage included a notable shift in the division of labor within the household, with the expectation that men would be breadwinners and women would be wives, mothers, and homemakers responsible for all domes-tic tasks. In a pamphlet written by Abigail C. Oluwole, wife of an Anglican bishop, she extolled the contribution women could make by their industrious labor, cooking and cleaning, making and mending clothing, and otherwise keep-ing occupied within the house. Although Yoruba women had long worked in the fields and markets, a Christian wife was not supposed to work outside the home. New laws concerned the registration of Christian marriages, defined as "the voluntary union for life of one man and one woman only," clearly setting aside any consideration of polygamous marriage (and, though less significant in nineteenth-century Lagos, excluding homosexual unions). People in Lagos rec-ognized that this approach could be a problem, as it ignored an important basic tenet of Yoruba society. As discussed in an editorial in the *Lagos Weekly Record* (March 13, 1909), the implementation of the law would mean "the disruption and overthrow of the social fabric" and could "produce social chaos."

Despite these concerns, elite women in Lagos preferred Christian mar-riage to conventional Yoruba unions. Conversion to Christian religious beliefs was intertwined with aspirations for an elite lifestyle, so that Christian families educated their children, boys and girls, in schools that emphasized the ideal of Western civilization. Young women commented that a Yoruba marriage rite was not a legitimate marriage, and they could never consider anything other than a Christian marriage. For both men and women, marrying another Christian was a marker of their own status and expectations for their lifestyle and their future. In a colonial situation where women's economic activity and political authority was being undermined by the expansion of a global economy that favored men, claiming certain rights via Christian marriage was a realistic response to such adverse changes.

Nonetheless, the new laws did little to protect women. There were many men who entered into outside relationships despite being married in a Christian ceremony. They expected to be able to have more than one wife, and the Christian wives found little support among other Yoruba or in the law for filing for divorce. People commented that polygyny was the norm, and elite wives should accept their husbands' other liaisons. If they did divorce a philandering husband (from a Christian perspective), there was no law requiring maintenance of an ex-wife, and the women were so unused to working that they were unable to support themselves. Kin who did not wish to become financially responsible for divorced or separated women were known to encourage the women to remain in their Christian marriages, no matter how miserable.

The actual experience of couples in both traditional and Christian marriages was diverse, with loving and caring partnerships, as well as troubled ones, found in both. But the story of these changes in one urban center indicates how women's intimate lives were affected by broader changes in society, politics, and the economy. Though the number of Christian marriages remained small during the nineteenth century, the elites who tended to be Christian and practice some form of an idealized Christian marriage set an example because of their education, work, and prestigious place in Lagos society. The position of elite women, however, was not always to be envied. Similar shifts in marital practice and expectations were occurring throughout Africa because colonialism brought sweeping changes to local economies, social customs, and political authority.

Ethiopian Nobility: Marriage and Politics

In the last half of the nineteenth century, the rulers of Amharic Ethiopia acted to consolidate their power by encouraging marriages among particular families. Never a European colony, the state was becoming more centralized, and the suicide of Emperor Tewodros in 1868 brought on several decades of scheming and plotting to determine who would rule. Each of the next three men who ascended to the throne benefited from calculated marriages: Takla Giorgis, who ruled from 1868 to1871, Yohannes from 1872 to 1889, and Menilek, from 1889 to 1913.[26]

Arranging for royal princesses to marry into ruling families had the advantage for the woman's kin of improved access to the royal family, and the emperor had the advantage of expanded access and control over dispersed territories. Uncovering the multiple interconnections of the often unacknowledged elite women, whose identities could be difficult to confirm, involved research into family histories and genealogical studies of gravesites, newspaper obituaries, wedding reports, and oral histories collected from descendants.

Though the repeated conflicts of the era are better known, negotiations over marriage illustrate a more peaceful method of consolidating power. Takla Giorgis benefited from the marriage of a male clan member to Lady Tisseme Darge, Menilek's cousin. Giorgis also arranged for his sister to wed the youngest son of a rebel leader from regions that had threatened his rule. When that son rebelled as well, Giorgis initiated an alliance with a rival leader in the region, naming him as governor and arranging a marriage between the new gubernatorial ally and another sister. Without belaboring the many confusing familial relationships, these instances are examples of repeated alliances between members of the ruling elite, where political requirements were supported by marriages that connected families.

It is difficult to know how much influence the women themselves had in the negotiations and alliances. Takla Giorgis married Dinqinesh, a sister of his rival Kassa. But that relationship did not deter Kassa from rising up against his brother-in-law, Takla Giorgis. Kassa won, and he was crowned Emperor Yohannes IV in 1872. In a poignant suggestion of her untenable position, Dinqinesh was credited with this brief verse:

> The winner my brother
> The victim my husband
> My grief is incomprehensible
> All contained in my house/family

A later important marriage involved Menilek, who was attacking the rule of Yohannes in the 1880s. Yohannes, attempting to maintain control when confronted by a strong rival, advocated that his young son, Ras Araya Sellassie, marry Menilek's daughter, Zauditu. As Yohannes had just redistributed land and authority in order to decrease Menilek's power in the region, the idea of such a marriage was apparently designed to ameliorate any hurt feelings on the part of Menilek. Another result for Yohannes was to keep an enemy close by way of this important connection. As the two children were quite young (Zauditu was only six, while Araya was thirteen), and Araya died at age nineteen, the marriage was important primarily as an emblem of a political alliance. The wedding ceremony took place in February 1883, and was a spectacle of wealth with feasting, elaborate clothing, and the exchange of luxurious gifts. It was difficult for Menilek to contest the loss of his land and authority, as it was transferred to his son-in-law Araya and thus remained in Menilek's family through the connection to his young daughter. Zauditu's later rise to rule as an empress herself is discussed in chapter 5.

These Ethiopian women were part of a privileged class and were not the recognized leaders, yet their position as elite women made them a crucial aspect of ongoing political consolidation and rivalry that were more often portrayed as masculine activities with little acknowledgement of the gendered aspects of all politics. The elite women in Lagos illustrate a similar point for a colonial society: marriage and family relations were central features of social, political, and economic transformation, and women's involvement and contributions were essential to fully understanding the complex processes of historical change.

Women's Bodies, Women's Health

Colonial officials focused on projects concerning health and hygiene as a major part of their desire to develop African societies to meet a Western standard. The colonial ambition of ending female genital cutting and shifting women's practices of motherhood meant that women were particularly subject to interference in relation to their sexuality. The inclusion of such goals under colonialism suggests how central African women's lives were in the overall scheme of conquest.

Female Genital Cutting in Sudan

Sudan was governed by the British, though few British settled there in contrast to Kenya or South Africa. One of their primary concerns related to women's reproductive behavior was the practice of female genital cutting, often erroneously referred to as female circumcision. Though the practice is commonly called "female genital mutilation" (FGM), that term is avoided in this book because of the negative and judgmental meanings attached to the idea of mutilation, while "cutting" is considered a more neutral description.[27] Women in Sudan more often performed infibulation, an extreme form of cutting involving the removal of all outer genitalia including the labia and the clitoris and stitching the resulting wound shut with only the most minimal openings left for urine and menstrual blood to exit. Campaigns to end the practice began in the late nineteenth century, as the British not only felt horror at the practice, but they believed it had a negative impact on population growth, necessary to supply labor and consumers for the expansion of colonial capitalist society.

The colonial presence in Sudan was marked by the notorious action by General Gordon against a Muslim ruler in Khartoum. Sudan was under Egyptian rule at the time, but people were not pleased with that overrule and in the early 1880s had come together under Muhammad Ahmad. He was a rising religious leader who people came to believe was a Mahdi, a divinely guided member of the

Prophet's family who would lead them out of oppression. The increasing level of Mahdist revolts against Egyptian rule in Khartoum lead to British involvement. In a military attack in 1885 that explicitly countered Muslim "barbarism" with Christian "civilization," Britain and Egypt combined their forces under General Gordon and attempted to remove the Mahdi, but they were defeated following a months-long siege by the Mahdi's army. The entire British garrison was killed and General Gordon became a martyr to British colonialism. In 1898, the British returned when Lord Kitchener led a renewed British force and defeated the Mahdi's regime, ushering in the British colonial administration.

The British occupied Sudan in what was initially a select men's club. The colonial agents were not allowed to marry during their first years of being posted in Sudan, and most believed that the climate both politically and in terms of heat and disease was not suitable for British women. Though more women came to Sudan after World War I, it remained the case that British men, who were often the products of all-male schools and who remained single and involved in all-male social and work milieus, were responsible for legal decisions concerning Sudanese women. Even when British women were recruited to serve in Sudan after World War I, those women were primarily unmarried as well. These generally well-meaning foreigners, with their wide-ranging powers to intervene in the intimate lives of Sudanese families, had an immense impact on women and men.[28]

Many Sudanese people held interconnected beliefs that accepted the influence of spirits and the practice of spirit possession through their zaar practice (discussed in chapter 3) and involved continuing the custom of female genital cutting. The intersection of spiritual and physical cleanliness also informed their ideas about proper adult behavior, and for women in particular the social assumption was that infibulation was a requirement for true maturity. The British arrived with nearly opposite beliefs since they assumed that spirit possession indicated paganism and infibulation was a barbaric practice. With little appreciation for the role of these rituals in Sudanese society, they set a goal of eradicating both customs through the introduction of Western education and modern medicine.

British women who were employed as teachers or health workers in the colonial administration had the primary task of reeducating Sudanese women. The teachers, nurses, and midwives were caught in a colonial dilemma, however, because they needed to tread a careful line between preserving a modicum of indigenous behavior that could be used in the system of indirect rule and introducing new ideas about female bodies and minds, molding them to accept Western ideals. Female genital cutting was the key issue in this regard, though the British approach suffered from contradictory colonial goals. Some agents wished to end the practice and hoped their teachings would lead local women to avoid putting their daughters through the ritual. Others were reluctant to interfere too strongly in local customs and avoided outright campaigns to end infibulation. Somewhere in the middle, British women taught girls and assisted with pregnancy and childbirth, trying to influence Sudanese women to become more Western, but not too Western.

Colonial ambitions were broad, yet their reach was quite restricted. They relied on mission schools for girls, and in the 1920s and 1930s only a tiny fraction of the local population ever attended for even a limited time. The progress of bringing Western education to Sudan was marked by the divergent interests of missionaries, British colonial administrators, and local Islamic community leaders, with classrooms under the control of Catholic, Protestant, or Islamic boards. Even as schooling for girls expanded, in 1932 an official report stated that only two-thirds of one percent of the eligible population of girls was in an elementary school.

In addition to elementary education, British women established a Maternity Training School, where the main emphasis was on improving women's experience of pregnancy and childbirth, couched in terms of overcoming "harmful rites and customs." The British in Sudan pursued that goal through teaching traditional birth attendants some Western methods of health and hygiene. To a limited degree, the British had to accept the local custom concerning female genital cutting because they had to deal with the effects of infibulation with every birth. In order to allow for childbirth, women had to be cut open and later restitched to conform to Sudanese requirements. But while the British women accepted handling women's bodies that had been cut and sewn back together, they simultaneously undermined social beliefs when they tried to bend local custom to accept less severe practices.

An example was the procedure of what the British called "rope" childbirth, in which a woman remained upright throughout the birth, gripping a rope and being supported by attendants and kin. While the British were not able to end the expectation that women should be upright, they insisted that women lie down as they neared the end of the birthing process. Conflict between local and colonial practices was evident in the most intimate aspects of women's lives, as female bodies became the terrain of debate between indigenous (seen as primitive by colonialists) and Western (seen as modern) beliefs and practices.

The debate shifted in the late 1930s with a new administration in Sudan, including a new head of the Maternity Training School. That new administrator was so appalled after witnessing the cutting ritual that she forbade the midwives, who were on the government payroll part-time, from continuing their traditional role in performing the procedure. This rule was one that the local women could not obey because they had to be involved in Sudanese customs in order to be trusted by their own communities. Nonetheless, with the support of other British officials, the colonial position became more inflexible as time passed, with a 1946 law forbidding infibulation. The law, coming near the end of the colonial era, was met with protests and was never enforced in Sudan.

The British and other European colonizers had similar approaches in all of the African colonies. Though zaar spirit possession and infibulations were particular to Sudan, the larger ideal of ending local religious and ritual customs that were deemed abhorrent to European sensibilities was at the base of the ideal of bringing Western "civilization" to "backward" nations. In most locations, this principle was directed at women, and local women were the measure of European perceptions of barbarism and of the pace of improvements. In Sudan, the fact that women wished to perpetuate the genital cutting that they believed defined them as women was itself an indicator for the British of the generally uncivilized nature of Sudan. And Sudan's advance into the modern world, as seen by the British, was also measured by women's willingness to forgo infibulation. While the Europeans worked to stop the practice of extreme cutting that was common in Sudan and they understood those efforts in terms of women's health, their motives were intricately tied up with their larger interests in the economic development of their colony. British colonial documents suggest and sometimes state outright that infibulation was a product of backward beliefs, and it also led to continued backwardness as a result of the trauma inflicted on girls who underwent the cutting. Ideas about nationalism, modernity, and capitalist development were all factors in the focus on ending infibulation.

Female Genital Cutting in Kenya

In neighboring Kenya, the British colonial administration also wished to control the practice of female genital cutting, but in a somewhat different social context and with different results. The history of the interaction between missionaries, colonial agents, and girls and women, particularly in Meru District, was informative regarding the complex situation. As with other colonized areas, the colonial authorities were worried about the African labor force, and they wished to increase both the number of people, especially men, who were available and to develop circumstances that would induce workers to join the waged labor force and continue working for a wage.[29]

In Meru, one of the issues related to population growth was deemed to be a high rate of abortion among young girls. The interpretation of British observers was that the late initiation of girls allowed them time to engage in sexual activity before they were initiated and married. Pregnancies that resulted from the extramarital youthful encounters were often aborted, with a resulting negative impact on the size of the labor force. The approach adopted by colonial representatives was to get local leaders to lower the age of initiation, so that girls would marry at a younger age and would therefore carry any teenage pregnancies to birth.

Although missionaries and some other colonial officials, especially those affiliated with Gikuyu communities, focused their efforts on ending what they considered the abhorrent practice of female genital cutting, in Meru the goal shifted to controlling the initiation and cutting procedure in an effort to stop abortions. The opposition to abortion was not on religious grounds, but it was expressed in terms of population growth and the need for a larger labor force.

Colonial attempts to impose an outright ban on female genital cutting were met with opposition from local people. When colonial agents and missionaries tried to prohibit the practice in the 1920s in Gikuyu areas of Kenya, they were met with widespread protests. Young Gikuyu men and women staged a dance that incorporated a song that accused those who aimed to end genital cutting of wanting to seduce young girls, steal land, and disrupt local customs. Such resistance became an essential element in the incipient nationalism seen in the stance of the Kikuyu Central Association (KCA). Nationalist leader Jomo Kenyatta initially supported efforts to make the procedure more hygienic, but he changed his position when criticized by the KCA. Kenyatta earned a Ph.D. in anthropology and wrote a fundamental ethnology of the Gikuyu, in which he commented that female genital cutting "has enormous educational, social, moral, and religious implications" that were a basic component of Gikuyu cultural identity.[30] The British retreated somewhat from trying to ban the practice when it appeared such an approach was feeding into growing anticolonial attitudes.

Among the Meru, girls' initiation rites were actually a series of events that could take place over several years, beginning with ear piercing, then abdominal tattooing or scarification, and only when girls had reached puberty and were in their mid-to late teens, the genital cutting ceremony. All three stages involved the community in feasting and dancing. For the final stage of the rite, the girls were secluded for three months during which time they were cared for by older women who not only supervised the genital cutting, but taught the girls about adult sexuality and other responsibilities of adult women. As in many societies, the ritual was considered to be a kind of second birth, with the girls emerging as women, physically and socially ready to marry and bear children.

Because the initiation rite marked girls as adults, it was deemed a serious breach of social norms if an uninitiated girl became pregnant. A child born to a girl who had not been properly prepared to bear a child was regarded as a danger to the community as a whole and was an emblem of disruption to social harmony. In order to control that eventuality, it was not uncommon for an uncircumcised pregnant girl to abort her fetus. The British who learned of this procedure were concerned about the impact of abortions on population growth and the availability of labor, though they did not recognize the role of colonial policies in what appeared to be an increase in pre-initiation pregnancies. Families who paid taxes to the colonial authorities then faced shortages of cattle and other stock needed to perform a proper initiation, which led to holding the rites at a later age, and this led to more girls becoming pregnant at earlier ages. The British simultaneously insisted on the reduction of punishment for couples who became pregnant prior to the girl's initiation, thus reducing community control over such breeches.

As one British district officer noted, "public opinion [did] not seem to be in sympathy with the cause" of restricting genital cutting, and as the colonial officials were unable to stop abortions, they turned to a program of lowering the age of girls' initiation, so as to reduce the numbers of fecund but uninitiated girls. They also continued to introduce measures to lessen the extent of genital cutting, policies that then required male police to intervene and determine if the women were following the law. Such intrusions of men into what were considered solely female affairs were shocking to many in Meru. The experience of the British colonial representatives in Meru in the 1920s and 1930s was complex, with some policies leading to unintended consequences that then posed new problems for the colonial government. Often larger concerns about politics and economics were played out on women's bodies and in women's lives.

The colonial attempts to limit or ban female genital cutting in the 1930s brought together female Protestant missionaries and women legislators in England, who voiced their policies in maternalist terms of protecting women from potential harm during childbirth. Western women would express a desire to end female genital cutting repeatedly throughout the twentieth century, often from a position of limited information but with a sense that they knew better than African women how to control African bodies and how to deal with such intimate issues as childbirth and sexuality. Not until the 1980s and later did African women begin to take a lead in introducing less harmful genital cutting procedures that were acceptable to Africans.

Motherhood

Most African societies assumed that motherhood was a major purpose of female adult life, and becoming a mother was a common measure of adulthood, as fatherhood was for men. Mothers were frequently treated with respect and even reverence, as they had contributed to the continuation of a lineage and to the ongoing development of the community. Motherhood was an essential step in the ritual life of the society as well, and various stages of pregnancy, childbirth, and child-raising were all marked by special events. Mothers were recognized when their children reached puberty, and attention to the mothers of the new initiates was an important part of initiation rites.

None of those attributes were found in the attitudes of colonial authorities. During the colonial period many missionaries were concerned with introducing health and hygiene standards that would lower infant mortality rates, and they initiated courses and training programs designed to teach "mothercraft" to

African women. The prior knowledge and experience of African mothers was not generally recognized by colonial authorities.

In Uganda in the early twentieth century, the British were concerned with a low birth rate, similar to their concerns in the Sudan.[31] They saw the spread of venereal disease as a major factor in the high rate of infant mortality, and they introduced medical and social projects to both treat the disease and to shame Africans for nonmonogamous relationships that were perceived as licentious and promiscuous. The second part of their campaign to increase the birth rate was a direct approach to women as mothers. They recruited midwives and missionary women to teach African women how to care for their infants. As one British woman wrote in 1900, "Many of our dear Christian women who are quite intelligent about reading are quite ignorant about caring for their little ones."[32] The effort to change mothering practices was centered on a joint government and missionary project to train midwives in both medical skills and to model conduct that met morally upstanding Christian ideals. A school for midwives and a series of maternity centers were established, which were kept under the watchful and censorious control of the mission women. Concerns that had been private and familial increasingly were considered to be within the purview of public policy since the colonial establishment focused on individual women in their campaign to transform sexual behaviors and mothering practices. Women were a crucial element in the colonial structure that required healthy bodies to enter the labor force, and their responsibility began with their treatment of their infants.

Health Education in West Africa

The British were not the only colonial power to establish a school for midwives in Africa when they opened the maternity school in Khartoum in 1921. The French had previously introduced L'École des sages-femmes (The School of Midwives) in 1918 in Dakar, later part of Senegal. The French colonial officials had similar goals of bringing modern health care and civilization to West African women, and they found that training local women facilitated their access to African communities. That approach also improved the colonial administration's ability to introduce new methods of treatment concerned with such private issues as sexuality and childbirth. Simultaneously with courses in anatomy, obstetrics, and infant care, the behavior of the student midwives was subjected to scrutiny. They lived in a dormitory supervised by two European women who gave them "moral guidance" and strove to "inculcate habits of order and regularity and proper behavior."[33]

Health education was often directed at mothers, and again the attitude was paternalistic. European missionaries assumed that African women were ignorant about caring for their children, beginning with pregnancy and continuing into infancy and early childhood. In Ghana, the European authorities engaged in "making mothers," which involved teaching new methods of childcare to African women, countering what were viewed as unhygienic, careless, and superstitious practices.[34] Colonialism had introduced major changes into African societies, including migrant labor primarily for men that disrupted family life, cultivating cash crops that interfered with women's agricultural work, and a demand for taxes that had a negative impact of household economies. Yet they judged that any problem with infant mortality or child health in general was primarily a result of mothers' ignorance of proper childcare rather than increased poverty and instability in local communities.

Embedding the new educational effort in Asante as part of a public health campaign, the British administration opened a school for girls in the 1920s. They also introduced other projects, including an annual baby show, an affair that became very popular, with hundreds of mothers registering their babies in order to be included in the event. Not only did mothers have to officially register the births, preference was given to those who went to the welfare center and received vaccinations. The women who were more likely to be affiliated with the welfare center were those who were already connected to Western colonial society in some way—for instance, if their husbands worked for a wage in the colonial economy, if they were involved with the mission churches, or if they lived in Kumasi rather than a more rural locale. Their interest in new ideas about proper motherhood was part of their experience of broader changes in the economy and political structures. They did not necessarily feel that British policies about child welfare were paternalistic because they came to agree that Western methods were preferred to the old-fashioned ways of their grandmothers. While some women avoided going to the clinics and maintained prior baby-care practices, many women struggled to find their own way in the intersection between the old and the new. As one Asante woman commented about the births of her three children, "Sometimes I would take some herbs and sometimes I would go to the hospital."[35]

Another example of colonial intrusion into African women's intimate lives as mothers was seen in the Belgian Congo, where the familiar concerns over depopulation and low rates of birth led the authorities to attempt to bring about changes in marital structures and relations.[36] The missionaries, not surprisingly, advocated monogamy rather than polygamy, and they then pushed for couples to resume sexual relations soon after the birth of a child. In polygamous families, it was possible for a woman to breastfeed an infant for two or three years, abstaining from sexual intercourse and also benefiting from the dampening of fertility related to breastfeeding. Her husband would have access to her cowives, and she would be able to space the births to the best advantage of her health and the child's well-being. But the officials believed that prolonged breastfeeding that led to widely spaced births was a key element in their concern with increasing the labor force, and they began to urge women to wean their children at a younger age. This practice required a supply of infant food at an earlier age also, thus altering the amount of work involved in feeding children. Women in more urban areas or whose husbands worked in the mines or plantations were especially susceptible to colonial offers of gifts and salary bonuses for giving birth in maternity wards, as well as to handouts of soap and other supplies for attending classes and educational programs. Distributing soap underlined the public health side of the colonial project, which consistently emphasized hygiene rather than the labor needs of the colonial economy. All aspects of marriage and family were interconnected in a fluid workable unit, and when one part was altered, the reverberations carried through to all facets of African sexual behavior, marital relationships, family development, and child welfare.

Conclusion

African women faced many difficulties as a result of the expansion of European colonialism in the late nineteenth and early twentieth centuries. The impact on women's labor was often negative, and the new forms of marital choice were unpredictable. Missionaries had a profound influence on communities were they settled, and they brought new educational and religious opportunities as well as disapproving attitudes toward women's customary religious and social authority. Colonial intrusion into the most intimate spheres of women's lives was seen in the campaigns to end female genital cutting and to alter women's practice of motherhood and family life. Though this chapter has focused on the impact, often damaging, of colonial development, women and men resisted the unwanted European authorities, and that resistance is the subject of chapter 5.

Notes

1. de Castilho, "O Pilão Africano."
2. Nasimiyu, "Changing Women's Rights over Property in Western Kenya."
3. Ibid., 291.
4. Grier, "Pawns, Porters, and Petty Traders."
5. Roberts, "Women's Work and Women's Property."
6. Byfield, *The Bluest Hands.*
7. Bivins, *Telling Stories, Making Histories.*
8. White, *Sierra Leone's Settler Women Traders.*
9. Havik, *Silences and Soundbytes.*
10. Biobaku, "Madame Tinubu"; Chuku, "Tinubu, Efinroye."
11. Ekejiuba, "Omu Okwei of Osomari."
12. Parpart, "Class and Gender on the Copperbelt."
13. Ibid., 142.
14. White, *The Comforts of Home.*
15. Ibid., 55.

16. Jackson, "Sex and the Politics of Space in Colonial Zimbabwe."

17. Larsson, *Conversion to Greater Freedom?*

18. Ibid., 38.

19. Martin, *Catholic Women of Congo-Brazzaville.*

20. Ibid., 21.

21. Gaitskell, "Wailing for Purity."

22. Gaitskell, "Hot Meetings and Hard Kraals."

23. Hoehler-Fatton, *Women of Fire and Spirit.*

24. Toliver-Diallo, "'The Woman Who Was More Than a Man.'"

25. Mann, *Marrying Well.*

26. Sereke-Brhan, "'Like Adding Water to Milk.'"

27. For discussion of terminology and Western responses, see the contributions to James and Robertson, *Genital Cutting and Transnational Sisterhood.*

28. Boddy, *Civilizing Women.*

29. Thomas, *Politics of the Womb.*

30. Kenyatta, *Facing Mount Kenya*, 128.

31. Summers, "Intimate Colonialism."

32. Ibid., 799.

33. Turrittin, "Colonial Midwives and Modernizing Childbirth in French West Africa," quoting Mumford and Orde-Browne, *Africans Learn to be French*, 1935.

34. Allman, "Making Mothers."

35. Allman and Tashjian, *"I Will Not Eat Stone,"* 191.

36. Hunt, *A Colonial Lexicon*, 244.

5 Politics, Leadership, and Resistance to Colonialism until 1945

THROUGHOUT THE LATE nineteenth and early twentieth centuries, women claimed positions of power and leadership in communities across the continent. Some women emerged as rulers because they represented established royal families. Others became known as leaders as a result of their customary roles as religious authorities. Many became active as a direct consequence of colonial policies that had a negative impact on their work in their families and communities.

Women's precolonial political activity was generally disregarded by the colonial authorities, who turned exclusively to men when they established local political offices. In many parts of West Africa, women had participated in local organizations that were managed by and for women. Women had the final say in disputes over markets or agriculture, sectors where they were the primary actors. Some of those associations included elaborate systems of ranking, and women's groups were viewed as complementary to men's within the community. The colonial agents, nearly always men, ignored that reality.

Women played a central though sometimes unacknowledged role in early resistance to colonial rule. The best known action occurred in 1929 at Aba in southeastern Nigeria, but there were many other events where women publically protested colonial oppression and contributed to the development of nationalism and political parties. Some women took action through their position as spiritual leaders, while others were more overtly political in opposing taxes or encroachments on their agricultural work. Women's associations, including women's auxiliaries that were formed within male political organizations, were active in the decades prior to World War II. Political events that occurred after World War II will be discussed in chapter 6.

From the earliest years, Africans resisted the increasing control that Europeans exerted over African societies. The modern nationalist movements gained strength in the early twentieth century as organizations across the continent pushed for local African political control. Women played significant roles in nationalist movements and were involved in activities in every region of Africa. They protested the extension of taxes and agitated to be included in political decision-making. The role of women in anticolonial and nationalist organizations offers further evidence of a vibrant community of women who were central to the eventual success of those movements.

East Africa

Female Leaders in East Africa

Women held positions of authority through their leadership regarding traditional practices and as part of royal or noble families in several east African communities. Royal women ruled in independent Ethiopia and during the early years of colonialism in the Comoros Islands, as well as during troubled times in Kenya.

ETHIOPIAN WOMEN LEADERS

Ethiopia was never a colony, so women who emerged as leaders there were not part of an anticolonial campaign. However, those women played a significant role advocating for their own communities and making their mark as powerful women. Ileni Hagos, who was born in 1805, was an important leader among the Tigrayan communities in what is today Eritrea. The region was marked by feuds and succession disputes. When her husband died around 1837, she defended her son's right to rule. With the support of an important military leader, she ruled as regent for her son, though her ascent was opposed by those who did not want to see a woman in power. She also lost popularity by imposing high taxes and by engaging in quarrels with other regional rulers. Though deposed in 1841, she continued to play an influential role until her torture and murder at the hands of an opponent in 1851. Her sons avenged her death, and the blood feud was ended only when her daughter married the nephew of her main opponent.

Zauditu, the daughter of Ethiopia's monarch Menelik II, ruled as empress from 1916 to 1930. Also known as Judith, she was born in 1876. Her arranged marriage when she was a young girl was discussed in chapter 4. Her father had resisted naming her as his heir, but since he had no sons, his grandson, Iyasu V, became ruler upon his death, and Zauditu acted as regent for her son. When Iyasu was overthrown in 1916, Zauditu was named empress. She was forced to renounce her husband, Gugsa Wolie (Wele), whom she had married as her fourth husband in 1902. In a complex situation, she was titular head while simultaneously, her second cousin, Haile Selassie, was named regent and heir apparent. After more than a decade as empress, she observed that Haile Selassie was encroaching on her authority and taking more power for himself. In 1928, Zauditu attempted to forestall his plan by usurping the throne for herself with no shared command, but her actions prompted Selassie to stage a coup and oust her as empress. In the aftermath, as power changed hands, she had to crown Haile Selassie as king.

Her estranged husband also tried to take power in 1930, but he was defeated and killed. She died of pneumonia two days after his death.

WOMEN LEADERS IN COLONIAL EAST AFRICA

In some cases, women ruled in situations where it was more common to see men. Though they did not necessarily push for women's issues when they were in positions of authority, their presence helped ensure that women were not completely marginalized and shut out of powerful roles in government.

Djoumbe Fatima was queen of Mwali in the Comoros Islands between 1842 and 1878. Born in 1837, both her father and mother were members of the Merina royal family that was based in Madagascar. She ascended to the throne at age five when her father, Ramanataka, died, though her mother and stepfather (who had been a close advisor to her father) ruled as regents for some years. Djoumbe Fatima ruled at a time of contesting powers, and her position on the throne reflected that turbulence, as the French tried to gain influence while the Comoron rulers continued to favor the Arabs based on Zanzibar. The French provided a governess for her when her mother divorced, and they arranged for her coronation in 1849 when she was only twelve. In 1851, Djoumbe Fatima expelled the governess and married Saïd Mohammed Nasser M'Kadar, a cousin of the sultan of Zanzibar, who ruled with her as prince consort until the French ousted him in 1860. Djoumbe Fatima remained in power, marrying two sultans in succession and making commercial agreements with a French trader in 1865, which she rescinded two years later. She renewed her ties with Zanzibar, abdicated in favor of her son, and later was restored to the throne when the French returned in 1871. Subsequently, she ruled without further interruption until her death in 1878.

Wangu wa Makeri was named "headman" of a Gikuyu community at Weithaga in Kenya at a time when it was an unusual and notable achievement.[1] She was born around 1856 and raised in a traditional Gikuyu household, marrying and bearing six children as most Gikuyu women did. By the time she reached a mature age and her children were grown, British colonial authorities were in place in Kenya. They established a system of indirect rule, in which Africans, nearly always men, acted as local authorities regarding tax collection, road maintenance, and other tasks related to keeping order. Wangu was a popular and charismatic woman who was named to the position of headman or local authority in 1902. She played an important role in mediating the early contacts between the Gikuyu and British settlers. Wangu set an example when she sent her own son to the mission school in 1903. But she was a controversial figure, in part because of her responsibility for carrying out colonial demands, and sentiment began to turn against her. In 1909, she participated in a *kibaata* dance, where her abbreviated traditional dress led to accusations that she had danced naked. Those who wanted to remove her from power used that incident to force her resignation. She lived until 1915.

Spirit Mediums and Cultural Resistance in East Africa

Women became spirit mediums in many societies and circumstances, and such religious authority was related to political influence as well. Spirit mediums were responsible for guiding people's access to ancestors and for assisting in important decisions concerning social well-being. Because of those undertakings, some women used their position to get involved with anticolonial movements. Accounts from nineteenth-century Uganda and Tanzania tell of spirit possession cults that were primarily female, and which counted nearly all of the women in a community as members. Often women who became healers had special authority over women's activities such as childbirth or agriculture. For some women, taking on that role offered an outlet for exercising authority to which they otherwise would not have had access. In a few cases, women holding positions of ritual power were treated as men. While in a trance, women would be allowed and even expected to criticize the social order; their comments could be directed at the general situation such as the dominance of men, or they could focus on a particular man such as a husband. They would also expect or demand gifts from members of their community. In a few notable cases, women who were spiritual leaders rose to prominence as anticolonial activists.

The colonial attitude toward those who exhibited spiritual leadership in African societies was to label the activities as "witchcraft," a negative term for diverse spiritual customs. There existed immense variations in witchcraft, and Africans held both positive and negative views about the role witches played in society. Witches included diviners, who were believed to have the ability to view the future, and sorcerers capable of performing transformative and redemptive acts. The incidence of reported witchcraft sometimes increased when a community was undergoing unusual stress. Witchcraft was often noticed among family, kin, and close neighbors; in patrilineal societies, wives who married in from other communities were vulnerable to complaints that they were witches. Conflicts over ordinary issues could have an outcome in witchcraft. For instance, any inexplicable illness might be blamed on an individual who was labeled a witch, or a woman who was unusually successful might bring on jealous complaints that she relied on witchcraft. Those accused of being witches were subjected to rituals to identify and condemn them. Some rites, such as those that relied on poison ordeals or other physical tests, could result in further illness and death. European colonial officials regularly tried to end what they considered witchcraft, and anticolonial leaders who held religious powers and leadership were subject to arrest and trial in colonial courts as witches.

Nyabingi, East Central African Leader

A long-lasting example of female spiritual leadership in eastern Africa was Nyabingi. She became notorious among colonial officials for her role in opposing European rule in Uganda and in neighboring regions of Rwanda and Burundi.[2] Nyabingi was the name for a type of healer, and it was therefore considered a title; it was also the name used to refer to individual healers in the Central Lakes area of Africa. The variety of stories told about Nyabingi makes it difficult to write a straightforward history, though she and her followers were part of an established tradition of spirit possession called *kubandwa*. The origins of what is sometimes called the Nyabingi "cult" are obscure; reported as originating in Rwanda, adherents were also noted in Uganda, Tanzania, and the Belgian Congo (now the Democratic Republic of the Congo), where women had a longstanding tradition of spirit mediumship that focused on issues of fertility.

Nyabingi first appeared in written sources in the late nineteenth century, where she was described as a queen in Mpororo. Mediums known as Nyabingi—who could be either male or female, though women predominated—were also leaders of anticolonial movements, with a series of notable uprisings from 1914 to the 1920s. The British responded by outlawing all activity by spirit mediums, condemning their endeavors as witchcraft. It is likely that there was an individual known as Nyabingi who was famous for her skill and whose spirit was believed to be later manifested in other individuals, appearing in various contexts over a lengthy period of time. Thus Nyabingi emerged as the granddaughter of a king, but also as the servant of a king, and as an ordinary woman.

Muhumusa, a woman described as an "extraordinary character," came to prominence in the area that is today southern Uganda and Rwanda, in a region where many communities honored religious leaders who were believed to be possessed by spirits.[3] It was also an era of severe economic disruption, especially as the devastation of the rinderpest livestock disease resulted in increased cattle raids further in the interior. European interests were also moving inland, as British and German forces divided up the area. Muhumusa was a member of the ruling family in Rwanda. When her husband died, her son was initially named as his successor. However, when that son lost his position to a half-brother, Muhumusa fled north into the area that is now Uganda. She called on the power of the locally familiar spirit of Nyabingi to build up a center of support and raise opposition to the new ruler. European observers cynically implied that she adopted a connection to Nyabingi as a way to gain a following, though she was recognized by local people as the legitimate representative of that potent presence. She led raids and protests against the colonial authorities.

Muhumusa's attempts to establish control over settlements in the region drew the attention of the colonial authorities, who were threatened by her activities and her claim to have a connection with ancestral powers. The German colonialists imprisoned her from 1908 to 1910; when released she continued to try and organize a power base for her son. In 1911, the Germans began to measure land and erect stone boundary markers that carved a route through the middle of the small kingdom that had been established as a seat of power by Muhumusa and her son. When the Africans disputed the new boundaries, the British staged a surprise attack in 1911. Her followers had believed that her power gave them the ability to resist bullets; that proved to be false when forty of them died in the raid and she was injured and captured by the British, who imprisoned her for the second time.

Muhumusa's followers continued to resist colonial incursions for many years. She was joined by Kaigirirwa, another woman who rose to prominence in the region. The protesters invoked their connection to the Nyabingi spirit and attacked colonial military posts and communications lines into the 1920s. Kaigirirwa was killed when she resisted capture during one of their attacks. In 1928, the Nyabingi resistance was revived when people in the region began singing, "The queen has come to her country," though that group was poorly organized and easily defeated by British colonial forces. In the 1930s, when she was probably in her sixties, she continued to have the support of an entourage, and she was described as a "lively talker."[4] She remained a prisoner of the British in Kampala until her death in 1945.

MEKATALILI, ON THE KENYAN COAST

Mekatalili was active among the Giriama, a Kenyan coastal people who were part of the Mijikenda ethnic group.[5] She exemplified another permutation of women leaders who drew from their roles as spiritual authorities and who focused on maintaining local cultural practices in the face of deep changes introduced by the colonial powers. Mekatalili led a revolt beginning in July 1913 against colonial labor recruitment and in favor of strengthening Giriama traditional government and reclaiming Giriama for the Giriama people. Her campaign succeeded in part because she called women together and drew on the tradition of Mepoho, a female prophet who had predicted that the land would deteriorate, youth would not respect their elders, and the Giriama would no longer bear healthy children. Mekatalili argued that the Europeans were causing these forecasts to come true. She was not from a leading family, but she was a widow (a stage of life that can allow women some freedom of movement and action) and was noted as a charismatic speaker who commanded respect. She helped call the Giriama together to make sacrifices and take oaths regarding the reinvigoration of Giriama political culture. As a result, local people refused to work with the British, the colonial officials could no longer recruit porters or collect taxes, and their attempt to extend their control was halted. Mekatalili was arrested in October 1913 and exiled to Kisii, one thousand miles away, where she was sentenced to remain for five years. She escaped from prison and apparently returned to the coast, though she was recaptured and again sent to Kisii before the 1914 war between the British and the Giriama. By 1919, the British were still unable to govern directly, and they decided to reintroduce traditional local government as an avenue to controlling indigenous communities. Mekatalili was pardoned and returned to become head of the women's council, a new formation that had not been part of traditional Giriama government. She died in the mid-1920s.

Maji Maji Revolt in Tanzania

The profound shifts in gender relations, particularly regarding women's control over their agricultural labor, were discussed in chapter 4. There were similar patterns across the continent of Africa, and the disruption to gender norms was a factor in resistance to colonialism. In the region of East Africa that is now Tanzania, people in southern and coastal areas rebelled against German colonization from 1905 to 1907. In most accounts of the uprising, women are nearly invisible, but it has become clear from renewed research that women's roles in ongoing social and economic relations had a central place in the events that the Germans recorded as "Maji Maji," *maji* meaning water in Kiswahili. The Maji Maji story is not an account of women leading a rebellion as some other events in this chapter suggest. Understanding the central role of gender to this event involves a complex description of longstanding relations of conflict and appeasement between several ethnic groups.[6]

The standard version of Maji Maji explains that in the face of increasing German incursions into land holdings and demands for labor for agriculture and construction, men from several groups, including the Hehe and the Bena, worked together in a pan-ethnic resistance movement. They relied in part on precolonial ideas about the power of local spirits to give supernatural strength to adherents. In a situation where people lived in small nonhierarchical societies, there was no local ruler to lead people in protest. People did revere local spiritual leaders—in this instance, a man called Kinjikitile, who controlled a sect or cult of believers. He gained followers, and he distributed a medicine called *maji maji*, which was believed to protect people from injury or death from bullets.

Although maji maji has been understood as a war medicine, its beginnings are in agriculture. Women were the primary laborers in the family plots, and they had control of a protective medicine that they called maji maji. The consecrated water was sprinkled on fields to ensure a good harvest and to protect the crops from predators such as wild pigs. It was used in conjunction with special fertility dances that were also designed to avert hunger by bringing food to the family hearth. When famine threatened, people were known to travel to neighboring localities to join in fertility dances and to collect potent protective medicines. In 1905, German observers noted that people were participating in large-scale dances, and they interpreted the gatherings as anti-German, in one case arresting dozens of men and women who had gathered for a ceremony to protect their crops. The German interpretation, and later analyses by historians who viewed the Maji Maji events through a nationalist lens, obscured the roots of the uprising, which could be found in women's grievances related to increasing problems with their responsibility for agricultural well-being. Maji Maji suggests the centrality of women's work and gender issues to nationalism, even in situations where women were not at the forefront of protest.

SITI BINTI SAAD, TANZANIAN PERFORMER

Another example of women's involvement in anticolonial resistance in Tanzania is seen in the songs made famous in the 1920s by Siti binti Saad.[7] Born in the 1880s in the countryside near Zanzibar town to slave parents (her given name, Mtumwa, referred to her slave background), she eventually was known as "Siti," a term of honor for Arab women on the island. Siti was a prominent *taarab* singer from Zanzibar who recorded over two hundred and fifty songs in Kiswahili between 1928 and 1930.

Taarab had been introduced into Zanzibar in the late nineteenth century as an elite form of music that relied on primarily Middle Eastern instruments, was exclusively sung in Arabic, and whose performance was restricted to events within upper class households. Taarab-style music had begun to be performed in more public spaces in the early twentieth century. Siti was recognized as an innovator, as she and her band began singing music that was considered taarab though it was performed in Zanzibar's urban neighborhoods rather than remaining limited to the sultan's palace. And though she often sang Arabic songs, she broke new ground by writing and performing songs in Kiswahili that reflected the social and political concerns of ordinary Zanzibaris. She was the first East African to have her voice recorded onto 78-rpm records, an event that is remembered with pride by Zanzibar residents.

Siti's songs were based on Kiswahili poems and often referred to local history and politics, as with the song "Kwa Heri Rupia" ("Good-bye Rupee"), which marked the introduction of the British shilling to replace the rupee in local currency, and which is associated with demonstrations opposed to the change. Another popular song, "Wala Hapana Hasara" ("There Is No Loss"), told the story of a powerful Arab clerk who embezzled state money to pay for his daughter's wedding. He did hard labor in the local rock quarry, commemorated in the song's refrain, "The rock is on your head."

Her songs also questioned gender inequalities. "Kijiti" told the story of a woman who was raped and murdered, while Kijiti, the man who committed the crime, was allowed to escape to mainland Tanganyika. The man avoided prosecution, but the victim's female companions, who had witnessed the events, were found responsible because they had been out on the town and were seen as loose women by the British authorities. In addition to such legal cases, her songs investigated relations between men and women. "Wewe Paka" ("You Cat") came directly from Siti's personal experience of sexual harassment and lamented the power imbalance between elite men and poor women. The widespread familiarity of such songs provided evidence of the power of ordinary people's perceptions, which ran counter to images officials held of themselves as benevolent bureaucrats.

Throughout her career, Siti's songs were an important local method for distributing news and information and for suggesting alternate views to official pronouncements and legal decisions. The lyrics often acknowledged the difficulties of life for working people and poor neighborhoods. Siti and her band performed regularly and provided a space for creating community while enjoying urban life on Zanzibar. In the 1970s, her name was the inspiration for the name of the Tanzanian women's journal, *Sauti ya Siti*, the *Voice of Siti*.

Protests against Taxation and Forced Labor in Kenya

Mary Nyanjiru and Harry Thuku

Kenyan women who participated in anticolonial protests were generally less visible than the men who founded and were active in organizations such as the East African Association (EAA; it had originally been called the Young Kikuyu Association, but the name was changed to enhance a wider appeal). Women's political work was most often related to their agricultural responsibilities in dispersed rural communities as they faced the disruptions of colonial rule.

One of the best known incidents involved Mary Muthoni Nyanjiru, a political activist in Kenya in the 1920s.[8] She worked with Harry Thuku, a leader of the anticolonial EAA. Thuku was typical of the leaders of the EAA, who were primarily mission-educated Gikuyu men. The main grievances against the colonial regime were the familiar ones related to taxation, police repression, and coerced labor. In Kenya, women and children had also been subject to forced labor requirements, and in some cases they had been sexually harassed and raped while working on plantations at the demand of British officials. Thuku and the EAA paid particular attention to the issue of women's forced labor and abuse, and their awareness of the problem attracted support from women. Thuku spoke to large crowds throughout Kenya, especially in Gikuyu areas in the early 1920s, enumerating injustices that Africans experienced from missionaries, the colonial government, and local chiefs who were on the government payroll. Thuku worked in the treasury department, and his political activism made him vulnerable to retribution from colonial authorities.

In early March 1922, Thuku visited an area where women and girls were cutting reeds under the direction of local police. He described the scene in his autobiography, saying, "I saw a large number of young girls and women cutting reeds under the supervision of the tribal police. I called over one of these, the one who seemed to be in charge, and asked him what the women were doing. He said they had been ordered to cut reeds to thatch the police-lines in Nyeri." Thuku told him that Winston Churchill (then in the British Colonial Office) had ordered an end to forced labor, so the women's work was illegal, and they should be sent home. As Thuku explains, "The policeman made no trouble because he himself was angry at this forced labour, seeing his sisters going out to work for no reward."[9]

The local police may have been sympathetic, but the colonial administration was increasingly aggravated with Harry Thuku's activities, and in 1922 they declared him a threat to the British colonial government and imprisoned him. He had been outspoken in support of women, so much so that some called him "the chief of the women." Women sang songs acknowledging his leadership and protesting his arrest, including one that invoked the traditional shaming gesture where women exposed their buttocks or genitals; as the song claimed, "When Harry Thuku left, that is the time I started scratching my buttocks."[10]

Members of the EAA went on strike to protest Harry Thuku's detention, and a crowd of seven or eight thousand people assembled at the Nairobi police station, including many women and Mary Nyanjiru, who had been present when he was arrested. The first day the demonstrators simply prayed and then dispersed. The second day, a delegation of African men met with European officials to demand Thuku's release, and they then returned to the demonstration to ask the people to go home. The crowd was unhappy with what they considered an ineffective outcome, and women, who initially expected men to take the lead, became angry. Government reports on the incident told how women taunted the men, adding to the tension in the crowd. Though there were very few women in the crowd, perhaps as few as 150 or 200, their jeers "prevented a peaceful termination of the episode," according to an account by the British governor.[11]

British observers believed that the men were about to leave the area when the women began calling them cowards. Mary Nyanjiru went to the front of the crowd, and in a typical shaming practice, raised her skirt up and challenged the men to take her dress and give her their trousers, as they were too cowardly to take action. Her behavior and comments brought a rousing response from the women who ululated in agreement and then rushed to the prison door, pushing against the armed guards until the soldiers opened fire. Twenty-one people, including Nyanjiru and three other women, were killed, and a further twenty-eight were injured. Harry Thuku was not released, but her example was important to ensuing generations of anticolonial activists, who learned the political song "Kanyegenuri," which commemorates the actions of women in Nairobi in 1922.

Little is known of Mary Nyanjiru's life before she came to the front of the crowd that day, though it is probable that she was a Gikuyu woman who was a member of the Church Mission Society at Weithaga. She and the other women at the protest had likely moved to the city from their rural homes in search of work or to escape family difficulties, and they had thus already taken steps to get out from under traditional patriarchal authority. With few jobs available to women in towns, many turned to prostitution, and one British observer commented that the women that day were "mostly town prostitutes."

As seen in Mary Muthoni Nyanjiru's act, traditional shaming practices were invoked in modern political protests. In many African communities (as well as other world regions), a traditional shaming practice involved women removing their clothes or lifting their coverings to display their nude bodies, sometimes making such comments as "Do you want to see where you came from?" Actions that showed or suggested female nudity, women dressing as men, and other signs meant to shame men, were also found in Nigeria with the Aba Women's War and during a tax revolt in Togo, both events discussed later in this chapter. It was considered a potent way for women to control bad behavior by men, though it was also a method for women to insult other women. By violating norms of dress and behavior by exhibiting their buttocks or genitalia, women called attention to female sexuality and reminded men that they were born of women. It was a dramatic method by which women used their authority as women and as mothers to shame men into acting to support women's work and family responsibilities.

Southern Africa

Women in southern Africa resisted their increased subordination to European rule by turning to religious action, by overt political reaction to colonial laws that restricted their movement, and by turning to women who were leaders. Women used traditional roles to agitate for privileges they expected to have, and they turned to new avenues of organizing in their persistent attempts to protect their families and themselves as colonial authorities continued to restrict their freedom.

Women Leaders in Southern Africa

Even when women in general were in a weak position, there was a simultaneous tradition of charismatic women who became chiefs. As with the female rulers in East Africa discussed earlier in this chapter, they sometimes reflected precolonial positions of authority for women and sometimes were examples of new activities for women when they confronted colonial subjugation. Their attempts to protect their communities were not always successful and sometimes made them unpopular, but their efforts demonstrated their strength and ingenuity in the face of international shifts in power that extended far beyond their own territories.

Lozikeyi Dlodlo

At the end of the nineteenth century, a queen came into prominence in the area that became Zimbabwe. Lozikeyi Dlodlo, who was born around 1855, was the senior wife of the renowned Ndebele king Lobengula. During a period of increasing British presence, she ruled with her husband and had input into many important policy decisions. More detail about Lobengula and the British is included later in this chapter, as this brief section is about Lozikeyi. Lobengula married her in 1880 in order to improve his relations with her powerful family. As a ruler herself, she worked to maintain and later restore the Ndebele monarchy, having responsibility for preparing medicines, supporting the king, and implementing policies especially related to women. Lobengula and Lozikeyi encouraged young Ndebele women of lower status to engage in relations with European men, seeing that as an extension of Ndebele practice that strengthened alliances among different groups. The practice resulted in the birth of mixed-race children, a source of concern to many Ndebele who worried about encroaching British colonial governance. Lobengula was forced into exile in 1893 by the British South African Company under Cecil Rhodes and died under mysterious circumstances, but Lozikeyi remained and acted as queen regent to maintain the Ndebele monarchy. With her brother she began a war in 1896 designed to drive out the British, but they were defeated by imperial forces and lost control over most of their land. Lozikeyi continued to rule and came to terms with the British presence. In 1909, she encouraged the establishment of Western mission schools in her territory, and she welcomed representatives from the London Missionary Society. She died in 1919 during the international influenza pandemic.[12]

Labotsibeni Gwamile LaMdluli

Labotsibeni Gwamile LaMdluli was a key figure in ruling circles in Swaziland during a crucial historic period.[13] She was born in 1858 into a family with close connections to the ruling Dlamini clan, and she was raised within the royal household. She was the senior wife of Mbandzeni when he ruled from 1874 to 1889, served as queen mother when their son Bhunu was on the throne from 1894–1899, and was then queen regent from December 1899 to 1921 for her infant grandson Mona, who eventually ruled as Sobhuza II. In the Swazi system of dual leadership, Labotsibeni was viewed as a co-ruler and was not subservient to the male kin with whom she ruled. She was an intelligent and forceful personality who played a central role in maintaining the cohesiveness of Swazi political structures in the face of aggressive colonialism. Her desire to negotiate was in opposition to Bhunu's wish to engage in all-out warfare with the encroaching British interests. She was particularly noted for her role in regaining Swazi land that had been signed away to British concession holders, as well as for introducing an extensive system of education. Labotsibeni remarked that European power "lies in money and in books; we too will learn. We too will be rich." She died in 1925.

Religious Revolts

Southern African communities responded to the intensification of colonial control with protests that often found inspiration in religious beliefs and practices. Women who represented traditional African religions as well as personal manifestations of Christian beliefs were responsible for some of the most memorable events. Three of the best known involve Nongqawuse, Nontetha, and Nehanda. Once again, their efforts were not always successful and sometimes had unexpected and contradictory outcomes, but they represent women who were willing to come forward and take chances when confronted with assaults on their societies.

Nongqawuse

Nongqawuse was a Xhosa girl in South Africa who was born in 1841. When still a young woman in the 1850s, she was recognized as a prophet. She reported that she had a vision of strangers who were revealed as Xhosa ancestors; those ancestors called for the Xhosa to halt cultivating and to kill their cattle, economic activities that formed the basis of Xhosa society and economy. Nongqawuse quoted the ancestors as prophesying that taking such a drastic action would allow "the dead to arise" and the Xhosa to live free of European rule.[14] The result of this millenarian action was a terrible famine through the loss of corn and cattle, and that weakened the Xhosa people, allowing the British to impose colonial rule. When a feminist scholar investigated the original sources, she added to the analysis by suggesting that Nongqawuse, an orphan who was dependent on her uncle, might have been responding to abuse from male kin living in her community by calling for a communal cleansing.[15] It is not possible to prove her motives, but much of her testimony concerned bad behavior by unnamed Xhosa men, though for decades her words about those actions were systematically ignored by researchers. The events Nongqawuse precipitated are often referred to as the Xhosa cattle killing, but the more damaging aspect of those events was her related call for the Xhosa to refuse to plant their maize. That action was the real root of the ensuing famine, and it resulted in the death of many thousands of Xhosa. Nongqawuse later lived in the household of Major Gawler, a magistrate in the British colonial administration. In 1858, it was recorded that she sailed to Cape Town and was placed in the Paupers' Lodge, a women's prison. Her name then disappears from the public record, as she was not listed as an inmate in 1859 when the Lodge was disbanded. Oral testimony indicated that she settled near Alexandria in the Eastern Cape where she married and had two daughters and perhaps survived until 1898 or as late as 1910. Her story illustrates how private matters involving women could have a far-reaching impact on society. The recovery of her testimony about possible abuse by her male kin was the key to a new analysis that placed women's experiences and women's labor at the center of a controversial historic event.

NONTETHA

Nontetha Nkwenkwe was a South African prophet.[16] Born around 1875, little is known of her earlier years. She married and had ten children, and when her husband died she struggled to raise her large family. After surviving the international influenza epidemic that devastated Xhosa areas of South Africa, she reported that she had a series of dreams that showed her that the epidemic had been a punishment and she had been chosen to lead reforms in her society. She then established the Church of the Prophetess Nontetha in 1918. Nontetha never had any formal education and spoke no English, but she developed religious beliefs that incorporated local practices and an idiosyncratic interpretation of Christianity. Her church addressed women's concerns, and it attracted many female diviners as followers. Women found a place in the church where they could articulate their problems and develop a network of support.

She was not the only prophet in South Africa during that time. There was a similar cult in nearby Bulhoek that drew thousands of followers who squatted on property and refused to pay taxes. Government officials raided their encampment in 1922, killing two hundred people in what became known as the Bullhoek Massacre. As officials feared Nontetha's sect might provoke further violence, they declared her insane and kept her in jail or hospitalized until her death in 1935 at the Pretoria Mental Hospital. Her followers staged numerous protests, marching on the hospitals where she was held and encountering officials who stopped them on each occasion. Though her career was short and her church never grew beyond a small congregation of several hundred, she was typical of other African prophets who preached from the Bible, advocated abstinence from alcohol, and spoke out against witchcraft. Female adherents to her church continued to revere her memory.

NEHANDA

Charwe was a woman and spirit medium who was a member of the Shona community in Rhodesia (now Zimbabwe). She reported that she experienced possession by the female spirit of Nehanda, and she became a pivotal actor during the late nineteenth century protest against British colonialism.[17] Nehanda was initially a relatively innocuous rainmaking spirit among the Shona, and Charwe was an individual woman who was a medium for that spirit. Some earlier examples of possession by Nehanda were reported in the 1880s prior to the most serious British incursions, but those were possibly other mediums and not Charwe. Nehanda exemplified the way that a known spirit could emerge in a new guise during the anticolonial struggle, and Charwe's story illustrates the potential for older practices reappearing with a new purpose in the face of oppression. As a person believed to be possessed by the Nehanda spirit, she came to be seen as a leader of the Ndebele and Shona resistance to British colonial activity in Zimbabwe in 1896–1897. After setting the scene in colonial Rhodesia, we will return to the story of Nehanda and her medium, Charwe.

The British had moved into central Africa from their settlements in South Africa under the leadership of Cecil Rhodes, whose name was given to the colonies of Northern and Southern Rhodesia. He had earned a fortune in the diamond and gold mines of South Africa when they were exploited beginning in the 1870s and 1880s, and he was searching for more wealth in other African areas. In 1890, he organized a small force of two hundred men (and only men) to travel north into Mashonaland, as they called the region inhabited by the Shona people. The Shona were ruled by the Ndebele leader Lobengula, who was based at Bulawayo in the western part of what became Rhodesia. The story of his wife, Lozikeyi Dlodlo, was covered earlier in this chapter. With wealth and land as their goal, Rhodes and his associates resorted to lies to convince Lobengula to sign a concession, which resulted in giving long-term land and mining rights to the British South Africa Company (BSAC). Lobengula did not intend to give away land rights to the extent that were eventually claimed by colonial authorities, but the British made many false promises, including claims that no more than ten European miners would operate in his territory. That stipulation was not included in the document that Lobengula eventually signed; when he learned of the deception, he tried to get it annulled but with no success. With that shaky groundwork, the small armed group of Europeans, mainly British, moved north into the contested area.

An 1893 incident related to cattle raiding between the Shona and Ndebele became a pretext for Rhodes and his cronies to end several years of uneasy peace, as they advanced on Bulawayo and, with superior military strength, forced Lobengula to flee. When Lobengula learned that his soldiers had been routed, some sources claim he took poison, leaving a message to his people stating that, "now here are your masters." The British proceeded to reward their soldiers with grants of six thousand acres of looted land, and within a year nearly all of the most fertile terrain surrounding Bulawayo had been given away to Europeans who dreamed of becoming farmers. In addition to taking over the land, the British treated all cattle as war plunder to be redistributed to the BSAC and the settlers, destroying not only the local economy but also the whole system of bridewealth and family formation. Ndebele homes were burned down, and in the face of such complete devastation, local people were forced to work for the new European settlers in order to survive. The Ndebele men had been warriors, and their new situation of doing manual labor for the British destroyed their sense of self worth. The Shona found themselves in a similar situation, and though they had not liked being under the rule of Lobengula and the Ndebele, they liked the British even less. The British proceeded to consolidate their rule by imposing a hut tax of ten shillings per hut on the Shona. As discussed in chapter 4, colonial taxes, which were based on marriage and family size, forced Africans into the waged labor force and marginalized women's work and social position. A man who was well-off and able to marry more than one wife was required to pay more in taxes based on the number of huts in his household.

The hardships were clearly the result of white settler activity and had already initiated resentment. But in the early 1890s, there were further incidents that finally made the burden too much to bear. Locusts came first, and returned for several years of devastation; they were joined by a disastrous drought in 1894. And in 1896, the deadly cattle disease called rinderpest, which had already wreaked havoc in East and South Africa, reached the Bulawayo area. The impact was immense, as sick cattle died from the disease and healthy cattle were killed by British officials in a futile attempt to stop the spread of the contagion.

In March 1896, the Ndebele learned that most of the British police had left the area with the infamous Jameson Raid, a convoluted and unsuccessful attempt by some British to gain control over areas in South Africa. The Ndebele were prepared to drive the settlers out, and they saw their opportunity in the absence of the official protectors. Some said they were given support from a spiritual source, an oracle in a cave in the Matopo Hills. They launched attacks on settler farms around Bulawayo, and they had some initial success, though there were difficulties in sustaining their efforts. Then in June the Shona also rose up against the settler communities on advice from the same cave oracle. The rebellion became widespread, and a number of British settlers and colonial officials were killed.

The Shona were encouraged by their spiritual leaders who promised protection from the bullets. One of the prominent leaders was Charwe, who was introduced at the beginning of this section. Born around 1862 to a noble Shona family in the Mazowe valley, she married and gave birth to two daughters and one son. Charwe first experienced possession by Nehanda years earlier, possibly in 1884. In 1896, Charwe was held responsible for the death of an oppressive British colonial official, H. H. Pollard. She was captured in 1897, and after continuing to resist and refusing to convert to Christianity, she was hanged in 1898. Renewed research into her actions found that she never claimed to be possessed by Nehanda when she was leading the rebellion, that she was no more important than other local

Fig. 5.1 Charwe, the medium of Nehanda (left), with the medium of Kagubi, under arrest in colonial Rhodesia, 1897. Photograph held at the National Archives of Zimbabwe.

leaders at that time, and that it was likely she had little or nothing to do with Pollard's death. Nonetheless, her reputation grew after she was hanged and she came to be considered a legendary resistance leader in Zimbabwe. The image and name of Nehanda have taken root in Zimbabwean society as emblematic of a national spirit of independence, with her name given to streets, hospitals, and other public venues. One of Zimbabwe's best known novelists, Yvonne Vera, wrote a novel about the events of the 1890s called *Nehanda*, in which she evocatively imagined the rural life and motivations of an African woman, unnamed in the novel, who embodies the ancient spirit.[18]

Charwe was exceptional in some ways, in part because she became prominent as an anticolonial icon. However, she was otherwise an ordinary rural African woman, with no particular event marking her as special. Even experiencing possession by Nehanda was not a singular experience because others had been mediums for Nehanda, and African women in many societies were mediums for well-known and venerated spirits. Spirit possession and leadership were expected from women who helped direct their communities' seasonal round of cultivation, were consulted about marriage and other family issues, and were sometimes councilors to local male chiefs. The imposition of colonial rule resulted in Charwe being singled out by the British authorities, and both Charwe as an individual and Nehanda as a particular spirit were remembered and honored.

Resistance to Pass Laws in South Africa

Governments in many areas introduced laws that required women to carry passes giving them permission to leave their rural homes and move to urban areas. Such laws were common as well in South Africa, which was ruled by a white minority government. While men had long been subject to pass laws in South Africa, women had been exempt until African men and government authorities became concerned about the numbers of women moving to urban areas. There were variations in the specific provisions in the laws, but many were similar to those in Southern Rhodesia that required women seeking employment in the towns to obtain official approval from the authorities. Such laws were designed to keep women under the control of men as they moved away from the influence of male family members. The motivation was similar in South Africa, though that country was an independent nation after 1910. While the European authorities imposed a new legal structure that controlled African lives, those settlers were not under the direct control of a European country, as was the case in Kenya, Rhodesia, and other settler colonies. The most stringent laws were imposed under the apartheid government of South Africa, which was also the site of some of the largest protests against such laws.

In eastern and southern Africa, women were at the forefront of overtly anti-colonial protest activities, writing articles in local newspapers, working in organizations, and often struggling on two fronts as they fought for African political control and simultaneously for the inclusion of women at all levels of government. In South Africa, women protested against the extension of pass laws, which already controlled men's employment and freedom of movement into towns.

Focusing on the respect women were due because of their status as mothers, one of the earliest anti-pass demonstrations occurred in 1913 in the Orange Free State (OFS).[19] The Orange Free State had initially introduced passes for women in 1893, and women first protested the requirement that they carry passes in 1898. South African politics at that time was dominated by conflict between Dutch (Boer or Afrikaner) and British settlers, marked by the wrenching impact of the South African War, sometimes referred to as the Boer War or the Anglo-Boer War. The war ended in 1902. In the aftermath, passbook protests were spearheaded by the Orange Free State Native Vigilance Association, a male-dominated African organization that sent petitions and letters to the mayor of Bloemfontein (the OFS capital) and to King Edward VII of England.

The Orange Free State added to the burden when it introduced a series of regulations that required that Africans obtain special permits and pay fees for various urban services. Included was a new law that demanded that women have a permit to simply live in urban areas. At that time, the OFS was the only province that had a requirement that women carry passes; but when the Union of South Africa was formed in 1910, protesters had to shift their focus from local actions in Bloemfontein to national complaints sent to the parliament in Cape Town. In 1912 the OFS Native Vigilance Association joined the South African Native National Congress (SANNC), which later became the African National Congress. The initial SANNC meeting was held in Bloemfontein, with local women present, though they primarily served food and acted as hostesses. But because the meeting took place in Bloemfontein, African leaders from across the Union learned of the injustice of women's passes.

CHARLOTTE MAXEKE AND ANTI-PASS PROTESTS

Charlotte Maxeke was on the executive board of SANNC and was one of the out-of-town participants who learned about the problems with women's pass laws at the 1912 meeting in Bloemfontein. Born in 1874, she had the opportunity as a young woman in the early 1890s to travel to England and the United States as part of a singing group, the African Native Choir (the group included Charlotte's younger sister, Katie Makanya).[20] While in the United States, Maxeke was offered entrance to Wilberforce University in Ohio, which was under the auspices of the African Methodist Episcopal (AME) Church. She met and married a fellow South African, Rev. Marshall Maxeke, while in the United States. She earned her B.Sc. degree in 1905 and was recognized as the first African woman from South Africa to earn a college degree. Back in South Africa, Maxeke and her husband worked to establish the AME Church and organized the Wilberforce Institute as an institution of higher learning for Africans. She was later president of the Women's Missionary Society of the AME Church.

In the months immediately after the SANNC convention, women circulated petitions throughout the Orange Free State that called for an end to women being forced to carry passes. Once they collected five thousand signatures, they sent a delegation of six women to Cape Town where they met with the Minister of Native Affairs. He verbally agreed to remove the pass requirements for women, though he did not in fact introduce any changes that would end or mitigate the pass laws.

When no action was taken for a year, the women and their supporters resolved to continue their protests, but they turned to passive resistance. Maxeke was a leader in the 1913 women's demonstrations against the government's plan to extend identity passes to women. There were two main sources of inspiration for the decision to protest, both rooted in non-African practices and both indicative of the increasing integration of African women into global politics. The Indian lawyer and activist, Mahatma Gandhi, was based in nearby Transvaal. He first developed some of his important tenets of non-violent resistance in South Africa while organizing Indians and Africans. There were thousands of Indian laborers who had been brought to South Africa as indentured servants to work in the sugar industry and had begun to protest their poor conditions. Gandhi also found support in the Coloured community, Africans who were of mixed-race descent and were placed in their own legal category that was neither black nor white. Some of the women protesting the pass laws in the Orange Free State were also Coloured and knew about Gandhi's activities by reading about his exploits in the Coloured press. The second impulse was also found in the press, where people read about the ongoing struggle for votes by women in the suffragist movement in England, which was particularly active at that time.

The role of civic leaders and the influence of press reports suggest a further factor in the activities of the women of Bloemfontein. The city by that time was a center of African community and social endeavors, and many Africans performed skilled labor, owned property, and enjoyed a comfortable standard of living. Educated women were involved in cultural pursuits; their husbands were political leaders, and the women expected some respect as a result of their social standing. Even women who were active in market trading, beer brewing, sewing, and most importantly, as laundry women, were able to make a secure living. The laundry women enjoyed a great deal of personal freedom since they worked out of their own homes. But they were visible in the urban landscape because they traveled to and from the homes of their white clients, and the police began to target the city laundry house as a site of potentially illegal activity. Police attention to the laundry women often included inappropriate bodily searches and rough treatment, leading to resentment at the disrespect the women experienced.

The women decided to risk arrest by refusing to carry their passes. As increasing numbers of individual women were jailed for not having a pass, women called a community meeting. One of the leaders was Georgina Taaibosch, who was known as a member of women's prayer groups (manyanos) and regularly read the newspapers. Her connections and knowledge contributed to her boldness in confronting the authorities, and she was arrested twice during the anti-pass protests. At a meeting in May 1913, the women agreed to collectively reject the passes and to serve the prescribed punishment term in jail. They marched to downtown Bloemfontein and ripped up their passes in front of the police. The mayor intervened and suspended arrests for pass law violations. But just two weeks later, the police reneged on the agreement and arrested one woman who did not have her pass. Other women then came to her aid and violence erupted between a crowd of women and the police, resulting in two months imprisonment and hard labor for thirty-four women.

Women formed the Orange Free State Native and Coloured Women's Association, a new organization that raised funds and supported the jailed women. The founders included Katie Louw, who was president of a manyano, and Catharina Simmons, a member of a prominent local family. White women from a neighboring town came out in support, and women wore blue ribbons after their models, the British suffragists. Another organization, the Bantu Women's League (BWL) was founded in 1918 by Charlotte Maxeke. It was the forerunner of the Women's League of the African National Congress (ANC), though it was not formally acknowledged as part of the ANC until 1931, when women were allowed in as members of the auxiliary but not as full ANC members. Women were finally welcomed as members of the ANC in 1943, and the ANC Women's League was then established with Madie Hall Xuma as the first president.

Regarding the anti-pass activities, they enjoyed one of the few positive outcomes in the history of South African women's early twentieth century resistance movements, when the national Union leaders in Cape Town relaxed the pass requirements. In 1923, women were exempted from carrying passes throughout the Union, a step that was a direct outgrowth of the activist women in the Orange Free State and their refusal to carry passes. Passes continued to be required of African men in South Africa, but women were spared that burden for several decades longer. One factor in their success in those early decades was related to economic conditions throughout the Union. Passes were always primarily economic since white settlers wished to control the availability and freedom of black labor. But at that time, with greater ease of travel and employment for Africans throughout the region, many simply moved away from the Orange Free State to avoid the more stringent restrictions. Thus the extension of pass laws became a drag on the local economy, and that added to the pressure to end the requirement that women also carry passes.

Although the women were free from the pass burden for a time, the government continued to introduce restrictions on women's migration into the urban areas throughout the 1920s and 1930s. Charlotte Maxeke continued her activism, including delivering a well-known speech, "Social Conditions among Bantu Women and Girls" at a conference at Fort Hare in 1930. In that speech, she detailed how the migratory labor system and the pass requirements acted to disrupt African family life and forced women into beer brewing and other illegal activities.

Lilian Tshabalala and the Daughters of Africa

Other women in South Africa combined their concern for their homes and families with their nationalist political activities by joining the Daughters of Africa (DOA). The DOA appeared in the 1930s and gained some public presence through articles in *Bantu World*, an independent newspaper that regularly covered African cultural activities and politics. The Daughters of Africa, founded by

Lilian Tshabalala, was at times viewed as being focused solely on domesticity and family concerns. Public speeches and writings by Tshabalala and others demonstrated their understanding that new family formations reflected modern urban experiences, and they were the basis for a stronger political role for both men and women.[21] Tshabalala was born around 1892 in South Africa, and she spent nearly twenty years in the United States, where she was educated and worked with the American Board of Commissioners for Foreign Missions. The opportunity to attend college and to interact with American black activists was formative for both Tshabalala and Charlotte Maxeke, as well as others who pursued higher education in the United States. After she returned to South Africa, she began to organize women into the Daughters of Africa. The group was founded around 1932, but it did not register a constitution until 1940, and its main years of activity were in the early 1940s. The DOA's members included some women who were clearly part of the African elite, such as Madie Hall Xuma, as well as women from working class backgrounds and women active in manyanos.

Tshabalala believed that women were essential to the overall improvement of township life, where people were building new urban communities in the racially restricted areas. She wrote essays in *Bantu World* that outlined her understanding that women's concerns with domestic issues such as health and family were inextricably connected to a broader political world. Poverty, male migration for work, and malnutrition all required women to become "club women." She wanted the clubs to nurture leadership among African women in order to ensure that women's concerns with their families were a fundamental part of political organizing.[22]

Tshabalala was a leader of the Women's Brigade that worked with the Workers' Transport Action Committee, a coalition that organized the 1940s bus boycotts in Alexandra township outside Johannesburg. The white-run municipal bus company raised its rates in 1943. Although this issue affected both men and women, it had a more severe impact on urban working women whose wages were significantly less than men's. Tshabalala and other leaders led blockades to stop the busses from running, organized alternate transportation for workers until the authorities forbade trucks from carrying people, and defied a ban on meetings of more than twenty people. Tshabalala encouraged protestors to accept a coupon system that mitigated the fare increase, a decision that was considered a victory for the boycott.[23]

Women in South Africa were not forced to carry passes until 1948, when a new government introduced the laws that codified apartheid. The history of protest and women's activism in the first half of the twentieth century demonstrated the types of endeavors and the depth of political analysis that women contributed. The convergence of racial, national, and gender protests offered a powerful example of effective dissent to oppressive laws. Women in South Africa confirmed their seriousness and determination, as well as their essential role in the development of African nationalism.

West Africa

Queen Mothers

Queen mothers were women of real power and authority in their societies. They were usually but not always the biological mother of the king, and they often had a much wider role as royal counselor and sometimes co-equal sovereign. Although political offices were generally held by men, in many instances the men had gained that position because of the active support of their female kin. The Akan proverb, "It is a woman who gave birth to a man, it is a woman who gave birth to a chief," encapsulates the philosophy of queen mothers' authority. Queen mothers were long-established in many African societies. Such a position provided a major platform for women to have political authority, and it gave them the opportunity to voice and sometimes act on anticolonial issues.

"Queen mother" is the most common English rendering of a wide variety of local expressions for royal or noble women in leadership positions, though it is not always the best translation of such terms. The queen mother in the area that is now Rwanda was called *umugabekasi*, and she lived at the court, controlled her own land holdings, owned cattle, and earned the loyalty of people who served her as clients. Further examples of specific terminology for female titles include *magira*, for the Kanuri queen mother in Bornu in northern Nigeria; *ndlovukazi*, for the Swazi queen mother; *ndlorukazi* in Zulu; *kpojito* among the Fon in Dahomey (discussed in chapter 2); and *mafo*, the term for the Bamileke queen mother in Cameroon.

Historically among the Yoruba in Nigeria, the female Omu ruled in parallel to the male Obi ruler, representing the dual-sex system of political organization. For instance, in 1884 Omu Nwagboka of Onitsha was a signatory to a treaty with the British, and two years later she led the women in a boycott that compelled the Obi to seek peace negotiations. Her actions made it clear to the Obi that he needed the support of the women in order to rule effectively. Omu Okwei was one such woman; she was a prominent trader in Nigeria who was discussed in chapter 4.

QUEEN MOTHERS IN GHANA

Ahemaa (singular *ohemaa*) is the Akan word for female chiefs, more often translated as queen mothers. Ahemaa were considered co-rulers with chiefs because they had joint responsibility for the affairs of state and when there was no male heir they could rule. An ohemaa, as the senior woman in a lineage, could be the actual mother of the chief, though sisters, aunts, and other female kin who had the requisite diplomatic and leadership skills could be ahemaa as well. Ahemaa symbolized motherhood, though they most often took on the queen mother role after their own children were grown. Because women were restricted from many ritual activities and from military action during menstruation, ahemaa often came to power after reaching menopause. As the chief genealogist for the lineage, she nominated the candidate for chief, confirmed his legitimacy, and had veto power over the council in determining the next male chief. She was obliged to be present at the meetings of the governing council, and she also had her own court with female retinue and councilors. In the court of the king, she sat at his side, offered advice, and was the only person allowed to reprimand him. The highest queen mother among the Asante was the *asantehemaa*. The ahemaa could amass great wealth through trade in kola nuts, gold, or rubber, and reports from the early nineteenth century included descriptions of vast estates farmed by slave laborers who were held by the ahemaa. Three of the most prominent women in Asante history—Afua Kobi, Yaa Akyaa, and Yaa Asantewaa—were asantehemaa.

Afua Kobi, who was prominent from 1834 to 1884, advised the Asante council to avoid war with the British. In 1873, she made a powerful speech before the military chiefs—which included her son, Asantehene Kofi Karikari—arguing that such a war would destroy Asante. The chiefs decided to fight; they lost to the British and Kofi Karikari was replaced by Afua Kobi's younger son, Mensa Bonsu. Afua Kobi continued as senior counselor, though neither of her sons was notably successful during their reigns. She faced competition from her daughter (and Mensa Bonsu's sister) Yaa Akyaa, who worked to get her own children named to the Golden Stool, as the ruling seat of the Asantehene was known.

Yaa Akyaa was born in 1840 and became asantehemaa when her son Kwaku Dua II took the Golden Stool after she ousted her brother Mensa Bonsu and exiled him and their mother Afua Kobi in 1884. When Kwaku Dua II died after only forty-four days in office, Yaa Akyaa succeeded in having another son, Prempe I, named at age fifteen, and was able to exert a strong influence over him while she remained asantehemaa. She was resolutely anti-British, and though astute about royal politics, she was ruthless in getting rid of her enemies. When the British subjugated Asante, they focused on removing her, and in 1896 she was exiled with her son Prempe I and other Asante chiefs to the Seychelles Islands, where she remained until her death in 1917. Though many people revere her memory, Yaa Akyaa's reputation for violence against those who opposed her has meant her legacy as a positive figure in Ghanaian history is disputed.

Yaa Asantewaa, born around 1830, was ahemaa of the Asante sub-group known as Edweso (Ejisu).[24] Her grandson was among the chiefs exiled in 1896 with Prempe I and Yaa Akyaa. Yaa Asantewaa, a respected older woman of seventy years of age at the end of the nineteenth century, worked to end British rule after the British victory in 1896. In 1900, she exhorted a group of leaderless Asante chiefs to fight back when the British governor Francis Hodgson demanded the Golden Stool. She told them, "How can a proud and brave people like the Asante sit back and look while white men take away their king and chiefs . . . If you, the chiefs of Asante, are going to behave like cowards and not fight, you should exchange your loincloths for my undergarments."[25] She followed her comments by taking a gun and firing it into the air, and the chiefs vowed to force the British out of Asante as a result of her example. The struggle, which lasted from 1900 to 1901 and included keeping the British under siege for six months, is sometimes called the Yaa Asantewaa War. She was commander-in-chief of the combined Asante forces and also had her own army. When the British were ultimately victorious in 1901, Yaa Asantewaa and others were exiled to the Seychelles Islands, where she died in 1921. The centenary of the war was marked by celebrations in Ghana in 2000.

All three of these women held their office as a result of Asante institutionalized political expectations. The actions they took, including counseling the chiefs and speaking out in council meetings, had been part of the asantehemaa repertoire of authority for many generations. While in the past such forceful leadership might have been seen during conflict between different Asante groups or between Asante and other regional communities, they continued to voice their opinions and push the male leaders to take action when they faced British colonialism. They modeled the behavior that they expected the men to perform, and as the official mother figure for the community, men were obligated to honor their mothers by accepting the reprimands and orders that came from the asantehemaa. Despite the eventual British victory over Asante, the queen mothers continued to be held in high regard.

Female Leaders in West Africa

Other female leaders, though not queen mothers, played a similar role. They drew on the history of female authority and continued to expect that women's work would be recognized and supported. The women discussed in this section all looked back to their foremothers for examples of how to lead, and they courageously faced new situations that arose with the spread of colonialism. They emphasized the centrality of women's contributions to family formation, agriculture, trade, and spirituality as they moved through the nineteenth and early twentieth centuries.

Madam Yoko was born around 1849 and rose to power among the Kpa Mende of Sierra Leone in the late nineteenth century, establishing a confederacy of splinter Mende groups and confronting British imperial forces.[26] She left her first husband when he grew too jealous for her to be happy in that marriage. Her second husband was so impressed with her abilities that she was promoted to be his senior wife, though she was not the first woman he married. He passed away from illness, and she married Gbanye, a relation of her second husband, in a leviratic marriage, as was expected in the patrilineal Mende society. Gbanye was a successful warrior who rose to be chief in the Bumpe River region. He was acknowledged as chief by the British colonial officials as well, who included him and his warriors when the British were fighting with the Asante in Ghana in the 1870s. He also elevated Yoko to be his head wife, and she was widely known for her success in agricultural production, food storage, and trading. As seen in other geographic areas, her skill in supporting a large group of kin and followers brought political advantages to herself and her husband; a woman who could offer such hospitality was viewed as a leader among women and men. When Gbanye fell mortally ill in 1878, he told his followers that he wished Yoko to succeed him, and she therefore ascended to his seat and was recognized as a paramount chief by the British. Madam Yoko extended the area under her jurisdiction to regions that had not been controlled by her husband. She began with an advantageous social position and combined traditional strategies, such as her leadership of the Sande society, with her intellect and diplomatic skills to expand her area of influence. She passed away in 1906.

Ahebi Ugbabe, an Igbo woman in Nigeria, drew attention as the only female warrant chief appointed by the British colonial authorities in 1918.[27] The vagaries of oral history and memory mean that while much has been learned about this unusual woman, there is still much that is unclear. As a child she fled her home village for reasons related to personal freedom; she may have been raped and forced to marry the man who assaulted her, and she was likely expected to serve a local goddess in payment for crimes committed by her father. She was a sex worker for a time, enabling her to earn enough to set herself up as a market trader.

As British colonialism spread, she began to act as an intermediary between local people and the new political authorities, perhaps even as an informant. Given her unhappy experiences as a child, she might have viewed the British as a route to ending oppressive practices such as deity marriage. As a result, she was well-regarded by officials, who appointed her as a "headman" and then to a seat on the Native Council as a warrant chief. Women had held high office in Igbo society, but the British had not honored that history and Ahebi Ugbabe was the only African woman given a "warrant," the paper that conferred authority in the colonial system. Over the years she had acted as a man, subverting local ideas about gendered political power. That conduct eased her access to high positions both in the colonial system and in Igbo society, where she was later invested as "king" of Enugu-Ezike. She established a palace where she lived much as male rulers had, surrounded by courtiers including many young women. She married some of them in the tradition of woman-to-woman marriage, which gave her control over any offspring. Women sometimes found refuge in the palace when fleeing difficult marriages. But her attempt in the 1930s to stage her own masquerade, a ritual performance that men in power routinely organized, was seen as overstepping gender boundaries. As British support for her ambitions also declined at that time, she lost standing that she was not able to recover before her death in 1948.

In the Yoruba town of Kétu in Benin, on the border with Nigeria, there was a similar history of strong women who held leadership positions under French colonial rule.[28] As with Yoruba society more generally, women historically held positions as councilors to male rulers and were part of a parallel system of governance where women earned titles and had particular responsibilities for the markets and other areas of female activity. These women, called *iyalode*, were discussed in chapter 2, as they were observed and written about as early as the eighteenth century. By the late nineteenth century, African societies were resisting the increasing control of European imperialist forces; in the region where Kétu is located, the French recognized that they might benefit by placing women in leadership positions. There were two noted women, both called "queen" by the French, though neither was given the official colonial title of *chef de canton*. Both ran afoul of French desires and lost their seats.

Alaba Ida was often referred to as Queen Ida in the colonial documents, though Alaba was her given name, and Ida simply meant "senior wife." She was born in Kétu around 1854, and she was a royal wife there until her husband was killed in a conflict with nearby Dahomey. She was then taken by the Dahomey ruler, until he was defeated in a battle with the French; Alaba Ida then asked to return to her home. She initially worked closely with the French, who were seeking local people who could act as district chiefs and would support the French colonial authority.

A second woman, known as Yá Sègén and sometimes referred to as Mother Sègén, was from a village just outside Kétu. She rose to prominence as a religious leader and adherent of the orisha deity Ondo. In the early twentieth century, both Yá Sègén and Alaba Ida acted as local representatives of French colonialism. Though neither of them was officially part of the colonial government, they held judicial and executive responsibilities. Throughout the region during the last decades of the nineteenth century and into the early twentieth, Africans resisted the French expansion of power in myriad small ways, refusing to pay taxes, hiding when military recruiters came to their towns and villages, and otherwise evading control. In 1911, issues escalated when an African interpreter came to Kétu. He was viewed as representative of the French bureaucracy, and thus was shot by another African man who was embroiled in a complicated dispute and wanted to show the French how unhappy Africans were with their rule.

Following the attack on the interpreter, the French feared the spread of what they considered anarchy and they came to believe that female rule was not traditional and was unacceptable in Kétu. Though both Yá Sègén and Alaba Ida remained in their positions for six years, holding on after the French first called for them to leave, they were removed by 1915. Their rule was limited and vulnerable to colonial whims, but at the same time it reflected historic female authority in West Africa.

Another way that women in West Africa voiced their political opinions was through journalism. Some of the first literate women initially turned to publishing in community newspapers. During the colonial era, elite educated women in Ghana used local newspapers to publish articles extolling the need for girls' education and women's rights. Mabel Dove Danquah was one of the best known journalists. She began by writing letters about current events to the local newspapers, and in the early 1930s she was asked to write a regular column for women for the *Times of West Africa*, which she did under the byline "Marjorie Mensah." She wrote short stories as well, publishing her first, "The Happenings of a Night," in serial form in her column in 1931. A supporter of Kwame Nkrumah's Convention People's Party, she wrote articles in the party publication, the *Accra Evening News*. In 1951 she was appointed as editor of the newspaper, the first African woman to hold such a position, though she was dismissed after five months when she disagreed with Nkrumah over editorial methods.[29]

Through both historic and new approaches, women were active in their efforts to end colonialism and stop the expansion of European control in their communities. Though they had some successful experiences, the colonial powers steadily encroached on African territories and defeated African communities.

Tax Revolts in West Africa

African women have a history of resistance to paying taxes, though often defying tax assessments symbolized wider disagreements with authorities. Some of the best known activities by women in the colonial era were related to increased taxation; for instance, the Aba Women's War in 1929 in Nigeria, illustrates how a combination of motivations could bring women to the point of resistance, while their move into political action was crystallized by the threat of taxation.

Aba Women's War

In 1929, Igbo women in southeastern Nigeria demonstrated against the extension of taxation to women; their protest became known as the Aba Women's War, an event that is recognized as one of the touchstone political activities by African women protesting colonial abuse. Sometimes referred to in colonial documents as the Aba riots, calling the activity a women's war brings the focus to the women who led the event and to the organized nature of their demonstrations, and it more accurately reflects the Igbo term for the events, Ogu Umunwaanyi.[30]

Igbo people had been increasingly tormented by British actions, in particular by a key event in 1902 when the British had enforced their rule by destroying an ancient shrine at Aro. The British then instituted a system of indirect rule and appointed "warrant chiefs" to represent British interests in local districts. Warrant chiefs were local men who had a document, or warrant, that gave them authority to act as agents of the British colonial government. This region had not historically had an extensive hierarchy of chiefs, and women also had a role in local governance. Often the British appointed men who were not local, but simply had some minimal level of education, and those men frequently used their new position to exploit the local community.

The expansion of British rule coincided with a series of difficulties. In 1918, the international influenza pandemic sickened and killed many Igbo people. In 1925, a woman gave birth to a baby that was outside the norms; though the exact issue or deformity is not clear from the available evidence, it was considered a monstrous or miraculous birth. Some people interpreted that event as a sign that the Igbo were suffering these afflictions because they were turning away from their ancestral gods and spirits and accepting Christianity. Others came to believe that European political and religious beliefs were to be valued, since the older Igbo beliefs were not strong enough to withstand a conflict with the British. Thus disagreements rose not only between Igbo and British, but within Igbo communities between Christians and those who maintained their traditional values.

Apparently influenced by the unusual birth, women in the region came together in November 1925 to take action to "sweep" out the polluting elements.[31] Sometimes called the Dancing Women Movement, groups of women arrived at the compound of a warrant chief and danced in the courtyard as they swept the area, symbolically and ritually asking that the chief clean house. After a crowd had gathered to observe the unusual activity, the women presented their demands for a return to the old customs and a rejection of British practices. They specifically called for an end to the use of English currency, a halt to the new reliance on the Native Courts, a return to the expectation that girls should not wear clothing until after their first baby was born, and they asked that Christian men not be given wives in arranged marriages. Significantly, they also asked that the prices for food and for bridewealth be reduced to their former levels. The women also required that any chief who was the object of a dancing demonstration pay a fee of ten shillings to the dancers. The colonial reports indicated that "the dance and the chant created a strong impression in the division through which it spread in three days."[32] African chiefs acquiesced in great fear and, in opposition to the orders of the British Divisional Officer, they assisted in spreading the word as the dancing women requested. The dancers were not well coordinated enough to sustain their movement in the face of British opposition, however, and by early 1926 the movement had collapsed.

To pay for the new colonial administration, the British began imposing taxes. The system of taxation that was first introduced in the southeastern region of Nigeria in 1927 began with a census as preparation for collecting taxes, a process that raised many concerns. Because the local understanding was that a person could only count what was his or hers, and no one could count people, locals feared that counting individuals might bring unwanted attention from evil spirits. Elders and chiefs worried that counting meant that people had become slaves or property belonging to those doing the counting, that is, the agents of the British colonial system.

Thus the issue of taking a census and collecting taxes was a problem as soon as it was introduced. The new procedures only became more contentious in 1929 when local chiefs began counting women as part of a census, an activity that convinced many people that women were about to be taxed as well as men. There were several reasons why the tax was particularly onerous for women. The broader explanation was that people experienced political oppression as the British extended their rule and put unwanted chiefs in authority in villages and towns, and made local people pay for maintaining the colonial system. Women had an extensive network of local authority that was specifically concerned with women's work in farming and trading, and was also related to protecting women with marital or other family problems. The British political system completely disregarded the important role of women leaders and did not include women in any way in the new colonial system of government.

Economically, women in that part of Nigeria were central to the functioning of the local and long distance markets and trading networks. Palm seed oil and palm kernels were a particular focus of their work, and the 1920s were years of falling production and increased mechanization in oil processing. Women saw their livelihoods being threatened, and just at that moment a new danger appeared in the form of potential fees for colonial taxation. Women's economic fears were intertwined with increasing concerns about their role as mothers and the central position of fertility in Igbo female psychology. Women had held recognized political, reproductive, and economic realms of control in precolonial Igbo society, and they were losing authority in all areas.

In 1929, women around the market town of Aba protested British colonial activities by using a traditional method of critiquing male authority. The action of "sitting on a man" involved singing insulting songs and otherwise ostracizing men who were not following the proper norms of respecting women and their work. The initial contact was with Nwanyeruwa Ojim, who was preparing the red-colored palm oil in her own compound. When an official dressed in his white colonial uniform asked her how many people and livestock were in her compound, she responded, "Was your mother counted?" In the scuffle that ensued, she was able to call on neighboring women who began "sitting on" the official to demonstrate their displeasure with his intrusion into women's affairs.

The news of the women's situation spread quickly through existing trading and kin networks in Owerri and Calabar provinces. The local market organizations and trading networks under women's authority became a conduit for rapidly spreading the word of the escalation of events throughout the region. Women carrying palm branches traveled their familiar market paths to villages to report on the situation, recruiting more women to join them and further distribute the news. They called themselves Ohandum, Women of All Towns, in a reflection of the cooperative aspect of the gatherings that brought women together from many villages.

The women articulated demands to end any tax on women, to remove corrupt chiefs, and to institute female judges, and they also voiced more general complaints about declining fertility and fears about British practices cutting into women's trading. Although their grievances were related to contemporary political conditions, they drew on older traditions to express their objections. Women had a history of maintaining their market and agricultural labor in part by censuring men who encroached on those areas or who damaged women's crops. In rural Nigeria in the 1930s, an observer learned of women killing two pigs when those animals had entered into the women's gardens and destroyed some crops. When a local man was asked whether there was any recourse for the man who had lost those pigs, he commented, "It is the women who own us," referring to the reality that it was women who grew and prepared all the food. If the case went to court, the women would state, "Do we not feed the men morning, afternoon, and evening?" In that situation, it was a problem if a man's pigs ate the women's cassava plants, and women had a right to take drastic measures to protect their labor and production.[33]

When faced with the incursion of British colonial policies into their work, the Igbo women took similar steps. They wore wreathes of leaves on their heads, dressed in sack cloth, and carried palm fronds. Their appearance was deliberately designed to alert officials that they were women who were drawing attention to injustice. When they arrived at British court buildings and other official sites, they danced and sang songs that insulted the men who claimed authority over them. In many cases they were nude or they raised their clothing as part of the demonstration. The nudity was deliberate, as it called attention to their womanly mandate to control women's arenas. It also reflected the older practice of "sitting on a man," in which women sang scurrilous songs and performed their anger by slapping their bellies in a gesture that was understood locally as an insult to men's manhood and courage.[34]

Despite the fact that the women carried only branches and were clearly unarmed, the police felt threatened on several occasions. As one male witness claimed during the subsequent inquiry, the women "appeared to have been seized by some evil spirit."[35] They did dismantle Native Court buildings and blockade roads. In one early episode near Aba, two women were killed by a car trying to maneuver past a group of women as they walked along the road. In another incident, the official response to a boisterous crowd of dancing women was to open fire, killing over thirty of them. Attacks on women in other locales resulted in an official total of fifty-two deaths and fifty injuries, though the actual total may never be known. No British residents and only one Nigerian man were killed.

Following an inquiry into the events, the British introduced some changes in colonial policy, especially related to taxation, as taxes were not introduced in the eastern region until the 1950s. Women also gained some rights in removing corrupt officials, and the warrant chief system was ended. The new policies reverted to a reliance on traditional leaders, but did not result in the restoration of political or economic power to women. The British even added a few women to seats on the Native Courts.[36] But at the same time, women's market grievances were not addressed, and complaints about women's loss of land rights, decreasing fertility, and diminished control over arranged marriages were ignored.[37]

YORUBA MARKET WOMEN ORGANIZE

Women in other parts of Nigeria also organized to protect their economic interests in the face of colonial interference. Yoruba market women in southwestern Nigeria began to form ongoing organizations to press their interests in the 1920s and 1930s. Designed to bring attention and renewed authority to women's activities, they often arose from market women's precolonial associations. One of the earliest groups recognized as participating in the development of Nigerian nationalism was the Lagos Market Women's Association (LMWA). Organized in the 1920s following the suggestion of Nigerian nationalist Herbert Macauley, the LMWA brought together over eight thousand female vendors who played a major role in supporting Nigerian nationalist movements. Under the leadership of Alimotu Pelewura, they backed the efforts of the Nigerian National Democratic Party.[38]

Pelewura was born around 1865 and became a prominent leader in Nigeria in the first half of the twentieth century. She was a Yoruba woman like most of her fellow vendors, and she followed her mother into the fish trade where she was well-established by 1900. She married and was widowed while young, and she never had children and never remarried. Pelewura was appointed to the council of Yoruba authorities in Lagos in 1932, where she represented eighty-four women's market associations. She led the market women in a series of protests, first to stop the threatened government effort to relocate their market in the mid-1930s. Her actions brought complaints from colonial officials, who reported on their difficulties with the powerful women's guilds in the markets. She continued to lead the LMWA against successive attempts to tax women in the 1930s and 1940s, and to resist the imposition of price controls during World War II. The women paid three pence weekly into a common fund used to pay clerks and hire lawyers when needed. Pelewura passed away in 1951, having organized women for decades and just before Nigeria finally became independent.

La Révolte des Femmes (The Women's Revolt), Lomé, Togo, 1933

In the early 1930s, Togo was suffering from the worldwide Depression and the French governor, Robert de Guise, introduced new taxes as a measure to alleviate the economic setbacks. Market women had faced problems with the French colonial officials for several years. The French wanted to impose order on the markets, and they tried to control the locations of market stalls and restrict the market days. They wanted the markets to meet less often and to be centered in the urban areas, where they could be more closely watched by the authorities. Other innovations, such as the introduction of French currency, had created confusion and hardships for women involved in local and cross-border trading.[39]

Political debate in Togo in the 1920s and 1930s was ineffectually divided between the French colonial officials, the local council made up of elite African men, and a nationalist group called Duawo, meaning "the people" in the local Ewe language, with women sidelined from the political discussions. African residents of Lomé, the capital of Togo, resisted de Guise's attempt to impose taxes by staging a notable revolt, and de Guise responded by arresting two of the Duawo leaders. Women from the urban markets, who had been subject to new market fees themselves, immediately began gathering in front of the prison. According to some reports, women made up about 80 percent of the crowd of several thousand that demanded their leaders' release.

Although the protesters met with initial success and secured the release of the two men, word spread to outlying rural districts overnight. The next day there was further unrest, with colonial institutions such as the wharf and railway offices suffering damage from crowds of young men. The governor brought in more soldiers, and the violence escalated when one troubled rifleman killed seven people in an African neighborhood.

Women's traditional activities were marked by their use of voudun (voodoo) rituals, a key part of the Ewe cultural experience. They believed the community had been polluted by the violence, and their role was to cleanse that pollution through a weeklong series of ceremonies invoking customary song and dance performances in public places. But they altered lyrics to place the focus on ideas of liberation, in one example chanting, "Today we are the Alaga! Today we seek vengeance against the affront of the French!" In actions that recall the Aba Women's War and were likely drawn from similar precolonial endeavors, the women in Lomé carried palm fronds, removed their footwear, and spread ashes on their clothing while singing songs that accused the French of empty bluster. They particularly insulted one French official by lifting their clothing and turning their bare buttocks in his direction, thus using one of their most potent weapons of shaming; even decades later some who witnessed the events would not name the women involved for fear of their power.

The colonial administration arrested and tried leaders of the revolt, levying fines on those who were convicted. The women made it clear that they would close the markets in order to perform a proper cleansing. In the voudun belief system, the deaths by gunfire required a special ceremony to remove the pollution of the market that had resulted from the violence. Thus the women priestesses led ritual prayers, bathed with herbal solutions, and organized the collection of trash that was swept up with palm fronds. They abstained from sex and from eating salt and spices for the week of the ritual. The women took the action they felt was required to cleanse the community after the violence that had been so harmful materially and spiritually. The French commandant, apparently unwittingly, decided to mark the city-center location of the shooting by establishing a garden, and that action was accepted as reconciliation by the women and their supporters.

West African Women Working in Anticolonial Organizations

While many women were involved in organizations and actions the focused on women's changing circumstances, other women gained prominence through their contributions to broader anticolonial movements. In Ghana, Mary Lokko was involved in the West African Youth League in the 1930s.[40] She initially had an interest in national and international politics in general, and she was concerned with the issue of the Italian-Abyssinian conflict. As she participated in meetings, she drew attention because of the intensity of her beliefs. An editorial in the local paper, *Vox Populi,* commented that she was a "noble example of sincere racial sympathy," and in January 1936, the political leader I. T. A. Wallace-Johnson suggested to the organization that she be named as his assistant. In that function, she was perhaps the first West African woman to hold an official position in a modern political organization. She often spoke up to encourage and support women's involvement in the Youth League, and she lamented that women in Accra seemed to be more interested in fashion than politics. She commented that it was not necessary to have a university education in order to be politically active because she was not college educated, but was self-motivated to follow the news. In particular, she took a female member of the British parliament as a model after she was encouraged to read about Eleanor Rathbone speaking out on colonial issues related to Ghana. There is little information about Lokko's background or her life after the 1930s.

Another woman who worked closely with I. T. A. Wallace-Johnson was Constance Cummings-John.[41] Born in 1918 to the Horton family, an elite Krio (Creole) family in Sierra Leone, she was educated at private schools in Freetown, and at age seventeen she went to England where she trained as a teacher at Whitelands College, an affiliate of the University of London. She was first involved in political organizations while in London, participating in the West African Students' Union and the League of Coloured Peoples, both groups whose members actively worked to end colonialism. She then moved to the United States, where she attended a six-month course at Cornell University in 1936 and also went to the southern American Jeanes schools, which promoted education for black students. Her experience of racism, especially in the South, focused her politics, and she became militantly anticolonial. She also encountered men who told her she could not be politically active, especially after she married the lawyer Ethan Cummings-John when she returned to London. Each experience of being told how to behave simply enraged her and pushed her to be even more involved in politics.

She returned to Sierra Leone in 1937 and took a position as principal at the A.M.E. Industrial and Literary School for Girls. She also worked with Wallace-Johnson in 1938 to found the West African Youth League, which claimed over forty-two thousand members within a year. Cummings-John was the first woman elected to office in a colonial governing body when she was elected to the Freetown Municipal Council that same year at the age of twenty, and where she served until 1945. She lived in the United States from 1945 to 1951, where she was active in the American Council on African Affairs and had the opportunity to meet Eleanor Roosevelt. Back in Sierra Leone, Cummings-John established a new school for girls. She also worked closely with women leaders from the markets, and with them she founded the Sierra Leone Women's Movement (SLWM) in 1951. Cummings-John was elected to the legislature in 1957, but she did not take her seat as a result of internal factionalist conflicts. She continued to be politically active after Sierra Leone gained its independence, becoming mayor of Freetown in 1966, the first woman to be a mayor of an African city. She was forced to live in exile after a military coup in 1967. She was active in Labour Party politics in London until she returned to Sierra Leone in 1976 and worked for the SLWM until she was forced to return again to London to as political conditions worsened.

Several of the women who were active in West Africa, as with South Africa and other regions, were influenced by reading about European women activists or by travels to England and the United States, where they gained experience and political contacts. The encounters with women who were political leaders made a strong impression on African women who wanted to improve conditions in their own countries.

Conclusion

Women were essential to anticolonial movements across the continent in the late nineteenth and early twentieth centuries. Even when they were not overtly evident as activists, their experience of loss of access to land and marginalization from political decisions was pivotal to the development of anticolonial sentiment in their communities. They emerged as local leaders, activists who roused their compatriots, and strategic organizers. They relied on existing roles as spiritual adepts, marketplace managers, knowledgeable farmers, and neighborhood coordinators, always concerned with providing for their families. The increased colonial intrusions into their lives in the form of new taxes, pass laws, and other bureaucratic measures motivated them to take action. They focused on problems particular to women, and they contributed to broader actions that had an impact on their communities. The movements against colonialism succeeded as a result of the important involvement of women from varied class, ethnic, religious, and other backgrounds.

Notes

1. Wanyoike, *Wangu wa Makeri.*
2. Hopkins, "The Nyabingi Cult of Southwestern Uganda," and Freedman, *Nyabingi.*
3. Hopkins, "The Nyabingi Cult of Southwestern Uganda," 61.
4. Bessell, "Nyabingi," 81.
5. Brantley, "Mekatalili and the Role of Women in Giriama Resistance."
6. Monson, "Relocating Maji Maji," and Sunseri, "Famine and Wild Pigs."
7. Fair, "The Music of Siti binti Saad."
8. Wipper, "Kikuyu Women and the Harry Thuku Disturbances," and Presley, *Kikuyu Women, the Mau Mau Rebellion, and Social Change in Kenya.*
9. Thuku, *Harry Thuku,* 32.
10. Wipper, "Kikuyu Women and the Harry Thuku Disturbances," 304–305.
11. Ibid., 313–314.
12. Clarke and Nyathi, *Lozikeyi Dlodlo.*
13. Kanduza, "'You Are Tearing My Skirt: Labotsibeni Gwamile LaMdluli.'"
14. Peires, *The Dead Will Arise.*
15. Bradford, "Women, Gender and Colonialism."
16. Edgar and Sapire, *African Apocalypse.*
17. Beach, "An Innocent Woman, Unjustly Accused?"
18. Vera, *Nehanda.*
19. Wells, "Why Women Rebel," and Wells, "Passes and Bypasses."
20. McCord, *The Calling of Katie Makanya.*
21. Healy-Clancy, "Women and the Problem of Family."
22. Ibid., 465–469.
23. Nauright, "'I Am With You as Never Before.'"
24. Boahen, *Yaa Asantewaa.*
25. Aidoo, "Asante Queen Mothers in Government and Politics," 75.
26. Hoffer, "Madam Yoko."
27. Achebe, *The Female King of Colonial Nigeria.*
28. Semley, *Mother is Gold, Father is Glass.*
29. Opoku-Agyemang, "Recovering Lost Voices: The Short Stories of Mabel Dove-Danquah."
30. Van Allen, "'Aba Riots' or Igbo 'Women's War?'" and Bastian, "'Vultures of the Marketplace.'"

31. Bastian, "Dancing Women and Colonial Men," and Afigbo, "Revolution and Reaction in Eastern Nigeria."

32. Afigbo, "Revolution and Reaction in Eastern Nigeria," 549–550.

33. Green, *Ibo Village Affairs*, 173–174.

34. Van Allen, "'Sitting on a Man,'" and Ifeka-Moller, "Female Militancy and Colonial Revolt."

35. Ifeka-Moller, "Female Militancy and Colonial Revolt," 129.

36. Mba, "Heroines of the Women's War."

37. There is an immense literature on this event. Two valuable recent publications are Matera, Bastian, and Kent, *The Women's War of 1929* and Falola and Paddock, *The Women's War of 1929*.

38. Mba, *Nigerian Women Mobilized*, 228–231.

39. Lawrance, "La Révolte des Femmes."

40. Denzer, "Towards a Study of the History of West African Women's Participation in Nationalist Politics," 67–69.

41. Denzer, "Women in Freetown Politics," and Cummings-John, *Memoirs of a Krio Leader*.

6 Liberation Struggles and Politics from the 1950s to the 1970s

In the years after World War II, women's political involvement gained prominence. The nationalist movements for most African colonies culminated in a wave of newly independent nations beginning with Ghana in 1957. By 1965, around thirty countries were no longer colonies, though other nations continued their liberation struggles. Women participated in nationalist movements in the 1950s and 1960s and developed new international connections as well. This chapter examines the role of women in significant events and organizations, including the Mau Mau struggle in Kenya, the development of nationalism in Tanzania, and women's involvement in new political parties in West Africa and elsewhere. Some activities can be seen as extensions of earlier protests, such as the Anlu movement in Cameroon, which bore some similarities to the Aba Women's War of 1929 in Nigeria, and the women's march on Grand Bassam in Côte d'Ivoire, which mirrored earlier actions in Togo and Kenya where women protested the imprisonment of male leaders.

Other activities connected women to newly developing nationalist movements. In one example, the recovery of the history of women's role in organizing the Tanganyika (later Tanzania) African National Union (TANU) altered what was accepted knowledge about men and women and nationalism. TANU was conventionally seen as an organization of Western-educated Christian men, but it became clear that their success in ending British rule was equally due to the activism of Muslim women, led by Bibi Titi Mohammed, who had specific grievances against British colonial rule. In Nigeria, important protests were also registered by women's organizations such as the Abeokuta Women's Union, which organized a tax revolt by Egba women led by Funmilayo Ransome-Kuti and which resulted in the temporary deposition of the Alake, the male ruler. Kwame Nkrumah in Ghana depended on Hannah Kudjoe and the crucial support of market women who provided food and other material that ensured his ability to lead the Convention People's Party (CPP). Similar patterns of women's participation were seen with the Nationalist Party, Rassemblement Démocratique Africain (RDA) in Guinea.

Women were also crucial in the liberation movements in the Portuguese colonies, in the struggles in Namibia (then called South West Africa) and Rhodesia (renamed Zimbabwe after independence in 1980), and in the anti-apartheid movement in South Africa. In the 1960s and 1970s, as Portugal refused to relinquish its African territories of Angola, Mozambique, Guinea-Bissau, and Cape Verde, the local people initiated armed struggles. Women were included only after they came forward to raise the issue with the male leaders.

Zimbabwe, Namibia, and South Africa endured grueling armed revolts that eventually brought about majority rule despite the intransigence of white settler populations. Women were vital to the success of all of these resistance efforts through their work in supplying food, acting as couriers, and building an alternative social order in the liberated zones. They were also found in combat roles, though they faced many more obstacles to full acceptance than did men. Nonetheless, women are today recognized as national heroines for the sacrifices they made for the freedom of their countries. Across the continent, and stretching over several decades, the success of nationalist and liberation movements was the result of both men's and women's involvement. Women's perspectives, contributions, and participation at all levels of anticolonial activism were essential to the eventual independence of African nations.

Anticolonialism in West Africa

Women were involved in many actions aimed at ending colonial rule. Areas of West Africa that were under French colonial authority were gathered into large regions that only after independence separated into the individual countries more familiar in the late twentieth century. French West Africa, or Afrique occidentale française (AOF) was a federation of eight French colonial territories in Africa: Côte d'Ivoire (Ivory Coast), Dahomey (now Benin), French Guinea, French Sudan (now Mali), Mauritania, Niger, Senegal, and Upper Volta (now Burkina Faso). The French also established a federation in Central Africa in 1910, which include five territories: French Congo (the Republic of Congo), Gabon, Oubangui-Chari (later the Central African Republic), Chad, and, added later, the French sector of Cameroon. The liberation movements also worked on two levels, both in local political parties in Senegal, Côte d'Ivoire, Mali, and other countries, while also often being involved in the broader regional organization, the Rassemblement Démocratique Africain, or the Democratic African Assembly (RDA).

The British colonial territories in West Africa were much smaller, though Nigeria's large size insured that it had a major influence. Nigeria was initially administered as three subregions, with northern, eastern, and western areas under separate British governors and governments; even after they were formally unified, each region maintained a high level of autonomy. The Gold Coast was the first African nation to gain independence as Ghana in 1957. Other British colonies in West Africa included The Gambia, a tiny strip of land along the Gambia River and surrounded by Senegal, and Sierra Leone.

There is information on elite women who rose to leadership positions and who are profiled below, but the participation of countless less well-known women

Fig. 6.1 Statue commemorating the Women's March of 1949, Grand Bassam, Côte d'Ivoire. Photograph courtesy of Ezzoura Errami.

was the key element to the success of various protests as well as the base of support for those few women who gained more prominent public roles. The stories of individual women should not obscure the many who contributed their time and energy. At the same time, their lives, though exceptional, offer insights into all women's lives and opportunities.

The March on Grand Bassam in Côte d'Ivoire

Grand Bassam, a city outside of Abidjan, Côte d'Ivoire, was the site of a prison that was the focus of a major anticolonial demonstration by women in 1949.[1] The local party leading the political protests was the Parti Démocratique de Côte d'Ivoire (PDCI, the Democratic Party of Ivory Coast), which was affiliated with the RDA; the party names are commonly linked as PDCI-RDA. Male leaders of the party had been jailed by the French colonial authorities, and in December 1949 they began a hunger strike. Five hundred women sang and danced for thirty miles during a dramatic march from Abidjan to the prison. The demonstrators were attacked by French colonial troops, who injured forty women and arrested four of them. It was a pivotal event that influenced the French decision to agree to African independence.

Among the leaders was Célestine-Marie-Marthe Ouezzin Coulibaly, who was born in the Ivory Coast around 1910 with the name Makoukou Traoré. Her father was Balla Traoré, the chief of the canton of Sindou with twenty-one wives and thirty-nine children among them. Makoukou married Daniel Ouezzin Coulibaly in 1930 and adopted the name Célestine in 1931 when they both were baptized in the Catholic Church. Célestine Ouezzin Coulibaly became an important anticolonial leader in French West Africa in the 1940s, when she helped institute the women's section of the PCDI-RDA in Ivory Coast and Upper Volta, and was elected as general secretary of the women's section in 1948. When the PCDI-RDA leadership was imprisoned, she helped lead the successful women's march to Grand Bassam calling for their release. After independence in 1958, she was appointed minister of social affairs, housing, and work in the new government of Upper Volta, serving until 1959 when she was elected to represent Upper Volta in the French Community senate (1959–1961). Ouezzin Coulibaly was probably the first female cabinet member in any Francophone West African government.

Aoua Kéita and Nationalism in Mali

Another woman leader in French West Africa was Aoua Kéita.[2] She was born in Bamako, Mali, in 1912, and was educated there and in Dakar, Senegal, where she trained as a midwife. She became acutely aware of women's difficulties through her midwifery contacts, and she brought that knowledge to her political work. She and her first husband, Daouda Diawara, joined the socialist party, Union Soudanaise-Rassemblement Démocratique Africain (US-RDA, the Sudanese Union-Democratic African Assembly), where they were involved in anticolonial politics. They were known for their egalitarian relationship; nonetheless, the marriage ended in 1949 when it became clear she could not have children and her mother-in-law pressured them to divorce.

Kéita was exiled to Senegal and later to a remote region of Mali near the Mauritanian border, as a result of her political militancy. In 1956, she returned to Bamako and later won a seat on the US-RDA Central Committee; at the time of the country's independence, Kéita was the only woman in the party's leadership. Kéita and Aissata Sow formed an early women's organization, the Union des Femmes Travailleuses (Union of Women Workers), which she served as president. She was the only woman elected to Mali's National Assembly in 1960, where she continued her activism for women's rights, and she was named as secretary-general of the Commission Sociale des Femmes when it was formed in 1962. After a military coup in 1968, she left Mali and lived in Brazzaville, Republic of the Congo, for most of the 1970s, where she wrote her autobiography.[3] She returned to Mali where she passed away in 1979.

Hannah Kudjoe in Ghana

Hannah Kudjoe (her name was also spelled *Cudjoe*) was a Ghanaian political activist who was influenced by the political leader Kwame Nkrumah.[4] Born Asi Badu in 1918, she was part of a politically prominent family, including her brother E. K. Dadson, who introduced her to Nkrumah. While she worked as a dress-maker, she began participating with Ghana's nationalist party, the United Gold Coast Convention (UGCC), in developing anticolonial propaganda. In 1948, Kudjoe organized a mass demonstration to protest the arrest of UGCC leaders by the British colonial authorities, using her dressmaking work as a cover for visiting households to spread information about the protest. The women spread clay over their bodies and wore white cloth, possibly the first time women dressed in a nationalist uniform in Ghana. In the 1950s, she was a founding member of the Convention People's Party (CPP), and she was elected as the CPP national propaganda secretary. She was also involved in an antinudity campaign designed to encourage women in northern Ghana to wear more modest clothing.

The Ghanaian Women's League (GWL) was headed by Kudjoe. In the late 1950s, Nkrumah decided that the GWL and a second women's group led by Evelyn Amarteifio were to be brought together as a single organization in order to facilitate control over the women by the male-dominated party leadership. Comments by John Tettegah, who was given the task of bringing the groups together, were strikingly misogynistic and revealed male fears that women would take over Ghanaian politics. In his words, "When you had its leadership bristling with dynamic women intellectuals and revolutionaries and the organization had become conscious of its strength, it could break off in rebellion, form a party by itself and sweep everything before it at the polls. The ratio of women voters to men then was about three or more to one and the position could well arise, where Ghana would be ruled by a woman president and an all-woman cabinet and the principal secretaries and Regional Commissioners were all women and men would be relegated to the back room!"[5]

Kudjoe was instrumental in founding the transnational Conference of Women of Africa and African Descent, which met in Accra in 1960 and evolved into the All African Women's Conference. She fell out of favor when Nkrumah was ousted by a coup in 1966, and her contributions were largely lost to the public record of nationalism in Ghana. She returned to public life in the mid-1980s, and she died soon after making a speech for International Women's Day in 1986.

Funmilayo Ransome-Kuti and the Abeokuta Women's Union in Nigeria

In Nigeria, women were also active in opposing British colonial rule. In one prominent example, women in the Abeokuta Ladies' Club, originally founded in 1932, began to get involved in broader political issues related to promoting women's rights and African political independence. The club was transformed into a vibrant political organization that fought for market women's rights, and in 1946 it changed its name to Abeokuta Women's Union (AWU). Funmilayo Ransome-Kuti served as president from its founding until her death.

Funmilayo Ransome-Kuti was born in Abeokuta in 1900 and named Frances Abigail Thomas. She was a pioneering leader in women's political action and in promoting girls' education.[6] Though much of her inspiration came from her Egba community (a Yoruba subgroup) she was involved in national and international projects. Her family was well-known as Christian converts and community leaders from the nineteenth century, and the prominence of her lineage continued with her children, who included two medical doctors and the musician Fela Kuti. She was the first girl to enter the Abeokuta Grammar School (AGS), and after finishing there she went to England for further education. While in England, she began using the Yoruba first name Funmilayo. Her marriage to Rev. Israel Oludotun Ransome-Kuti was a major factor in her political development, as he was headmaster of the AGS and with him she became deeply involved in educational politics. Both of them were charter members in the Nigerian Union of Teachers, founded in 1931, and were active in numerous other organizations.

During the colonial period she began to demonstrate her outspoken nationalism by wearing Yoruba dress exclusively and making all of her public speeches in Yoruba. She was a leader not only for women throughout Nigeria and an advocate of Nigerian culture, but she also had a high profile on the international scene during and after the colonial period, when she attended meetings of the Women's International Democratic Federation and the Women's International League for Peace and Freedom. She also traveled to England in 1947 as the only woman in the delegation of the National Council of Nigeria and the Cameroons political party when they protested a proposed constitution.

Before the expansion of British colonial power, women had controlled their own market work through women's councils and leaders (see chapter 2). But by the 1940s, women were being increasingly taxed, and they had almost no representation in the government. The market vendors complained that they were forced to accept "conditional sales," which was a requirement that in order to buy desired items such as sugar for resale, they had to also buy slower-moving goods such as cutlasses or scythes that they did not want. The women's groups worked with the market vendors to end such onerous practices, in particular calling for an end to government control over the markets, and for no further increases in women's tax burden. Ransome-Kuti and others stepped into the vacuum created by women being excluded from government office and advocated for women— especially for the market women. They recommended that foreign companies pay more taxes in order to diminish the burden on market women. The popularity of the AWU among women was seen in their support; there were twenty thousand dues-paying members and as many as another one hundred thousand supporters who could be counted on to turn out and demonstrate when needed.

In one of its first campaigns in Abeokuta, the members of the AWU focused on the problem of the taxation of market women and criticized the local authorities for the misuse of funds. The market women had some very specific grievances about the burdens placed on them by the colonial government. In the mid-1940s, the administration began confiscating rice being sold by market women, as part of a campaign to control perceived shortages related to World War II. Ransome-Kuti and the Abeokuta Ladies' Club began contacting District Officers, but with no response. They then took the story to the media, and local newspapers published reports of the situation in the markets. Within a week the government stopped seizing rice from the market women. The revolt was notable for lasting for nine months, for involving rural and urban women as well as women from different class backgrounds, and for using their local circumstances to make connections with the Nigerian nationalist movement and with women throughout the country.[7]

Following on that positive result, the women's group expanded to include more market women as members and was renamed Abeokuta Women's Union, indicating a shift to a more political stance and more open membership. They recruited women from diverse backgrounds; many of the market women were Muslim, and though the initial impetus for the group came from Christian women, they were subsequently welcoming to women of all faiths and backgrounds.

After 1949, the AWU was a chapter of the national organization, the Nigerian Women's Union, and in 1953 the Nigerian Women's Union called a conference that led to the founding of the Federation of Nigerian Women's Societies (FNWS). The members passed resolutions that called for the inclusion of more women on local councils, for universal adult suffrage, and for the FNWS to be consulted about any legislation, so that the group could assess the impact on women. The organization also advocated for women's education, encouraged women to be involved in all sectors of the community, and worked to improve women's economic activities, until it was overshadowed by a rival organization, the National Council of Women's Societies. The FNWS continued to exist, but it was most active in Abeokuta.

Ransome-Kuti was honored with the Order of the Niger in 1963, the Lenin Peace Prize in 1968, and was awarded an honorary doctor of laws from the University of Ibadan in 1968. In the 1970s, following the example of her son, the well-known musician Fela Kuti, she began using the name Anikulapo-Kuti, as a way of further supporting Yoruba culture. She often stayed at her property in Lagos, which had been transformed by Fela into the Kalakuta Republic, a center of antigovernment activity. In 1977, she was severely injured when police threw her from a second-story window during a raid that resulted in the complete destruction of the property. That incident was generally believed to have led to her death the following year. She is remembered for her fierce advocacy for women.

The Anlu Movement in Cameroon

In Cameroon, a country adjacent to Nigeria that had been colonized by France, Britain, and Germany (which lost its colonial holdings following World War I), women were also active in politics during the nationalist struggle. Cameroon was divided administratively between French and British regions, and in 1952 women in the French sector formed the Union Démocratique des Femmes Camerounaises (UDEFEC, Democratic Union of Cameroonian Women), the women's wing of the Union des Populations du Cameroun (UPC, Union of the Cameroon People). There had been a Women's Committee of the UPC established in 1949, but that association had been relatively ineffectual until the international Communist organization, Women's International Democratic Federation, took an interest in funding and supporting women's groups throughout the world. Cameroonian activist Emma Ngom Mbem attended a meeting in Vienna, Austria, and when she returned to Cameroon she and Marie-Irène Ngapeth-Biyong called together women in the capital, Douala, and formed UDEFEC with Ngapeth-Biyong as the first president.

The UDEFEC was nominally part of the UPC, though they did have some autonomy that allowed them to put women's issues at the forefront. At the same time, their activities were strongly connected to the attempt to end French colonialism, and as they grew more militant the French administrators introduced more stringent controls, culminating in July 1955 when the UPC, UDEFEC, and other related organizations were banned and many leaders were persecuted, arrested, imprisoned, and executed. Other leaders fled to British Cameroon in order to avoid French harassment. Since most of the leaders who were recognized by the French were men, more women were able to move into decision-making positions in their absence.

One of the key UPC activities was to collect petitions demanding independence, detailing maltreatment, and calling for the release of imprisoned leaders.[8] These documents were forwarded to the United Nations. Women, working through UDEFEC, were instrumental in collecting the information and arranging for the papers to be sent to the United Nations. Gathering information was itself a political act, as women contacted their neighbors, traders they patronized in the markets, relatives who shared their agricultural labor in the fields, and people they knew from working in European households and from school contacts.

Women had experienced colonial oppression in their own lives as new laws restricted their control over markets and agricultural work, and as arrests and imprisonment disrupted family life. They faced increased bureaucratic regulations and fees related to their market trading, and they documented instances of arrest for leaving a marketing license at home or for selling goods from their houses rather than traveling to the market. They were unhappy with their experience with Western medicine related to pregnancy and childbirth, and they detailed cases where pregnant women and small children were injured or killed as a result of official raids against nationalist activities. They perceived a vaccination campaign in 1957 as an attack on children and fertility, and they feared birthing clinics as potential sites of disease and death. Women viewed schools, which focused on teaching French history and culture, as places where the colonialists gained control over their children. The women concentrated their political activity on supporting their work as mothers, traders, and farmers.

At many of the meetings the women kept meticulous records, including their observations of colonial oppression. They formulated petitions that were not simply a list of names, but they also presented an account of grievances. The details in the petitions demonstrated how urban women joined with rural women to frame their demands for the release of prisoners while also calling for improved economic development in neglected rural communities. Although the petitions were ultimately written documents, they began with the oral testimony collected in local committee meetings, where a literate member of the group wrote down the stories told by those in attendance.

Hundreds of petitions from the 1950s were rediscovered in the archives, and those documents indicated the increasing role of women in formulating political demands. In 1957, there were 36 petitions from women; the remarkable increase to 293 petitions the following year was partly a result of increased colonial repression of male nationalists but also testified to the key participation of women. Petitions often came from groups identified as UDEFEC committees, though individual women also sent in documents that included information about their marital status and occupation. Women's experience in discussing the possibility of ending French colonial rule spread the idea of Cameroonian nationalism at the grassroots level through women-led meetings, and they helped connect individual complaints to the national and international anticolonial movement.

Anlu

A protest developed in Cameroon in the late 1950s that was reminiscent of earlier anticolonial demonstrations such as the Aba Women's War in Nigeria. In 1958, British colonial authorities tried to introduce agrarian reform in the sector of Cameroon under their control, including innovative methods of farming that undercut women's authority. In July 1958, a group of Kom women in the Fon kingdom rejected new British colonial regulations calling for contoured farming. The rules had been introduced by a school teacher named Chia Bartholomew, and the women went to his school and to his home, singing scurrilous songs, chant-ing, carrying tree leaves, and dressed in trousers and rags. In November 1958, an all-woman delegation marched to the government offices in Bamenda, where Nawain Mwana, one of the delegation leaders, expressed fears about women's loss of control over fertility and food production. The women carried tree branches and sang abusive songs that reportedly brought fear to those who were present.

The protest lasted for three years and was called *anlu*, which was a tradi-tional method of protest used by Kom women in the Cameroon Grassfields to protect women's near-absolute authority in agriculture and to ostracize commu-nity members, male or female, who transgressed behavioral norms. Women in other regions of Cameroon were also known to hold leadership positions and to have recourse to public protest when their rights were encroached upon. Some villages had male and female co-chiefs, and queen mothers were seen in many areas. An early reference to public political protest came in 1925 in the Belo area, when a priest and his entourage reportedly tried to take food from a woman; women and men turned against them, booing and jeering, hitting them with sticks, and forcing them to leave the town.[9]

Although the 1958 anlu began as an autonomous protest focused on women and agriculture, within a few months there were seven thousand members meet-ing in branches throughout the region, and the demands grew to include broader political issues such as resentment about Nigerian migration into Kom areas. The women's movement was eventually affiliated with the anticolonial political party, Kameruns National Democratic Party (KNDP), which was in the midst of a dis-pute about Cameroon's future as part of the British or French colonial sphere. The KNDP favored unity between the French and British sectors of Cameroon; the Kameruns National Congress (KNC), the ruling party in 1958, preferred inte-gration of the British sector into a federal system in Nigeria.[10]

The 1958, anlu was noted for the disruption of both colonial and traditional authority in the region, as women blocked roads and obstructed the rule of the Fon, the traditional male ruler. When the Fon palace was burned, anlu actions kept people from rebuilding it. During the years of protest, school attendance fell and anlu participants closed markets and blocked other activities. In the end, elections held in 1961 demonstrated the influence of the women of anlu, as KNDP won over the KNC party, and Cameroon remained independent of Nigeria while uniting the British and French regions.

Observers and scholars have concluded that "in Kom eyes women had the right to take over Kom governance, that the women did rule Kom for three years, and that the movement's main thrust was anti-colonial in nature."[11] The move-ment was controlled by women who acted to extend their traditional rights to defend their agricultural and market activities to the protection of the kingdom as a whole. Women's rights were a factor, but that was not the main thrust of anlu.

It was a significant event because of the length of time the women were active, and because the outcome was a positive one for the women, at least in the short term.

Political Activism in Southern Africa

The history of southern African usually focuses on South Africa and the increasing repression introduced under the apartheid regime, which enforced racial divisions and white minority rule. Other parts of the region also had women leaders and female involvement in anticolonial and anti-apartheid protests.

Mantse Bo in Lesotho

In some cases an individual woman was able to use a position of power to bring about improvements for women. One example was Mantse Bo, also known as Amelia 'Matsaba Seeiso Griffith, in Lesotho. Born in 1902, she was the first wife of Paramount Chief Seeiso Griffith, who ruled for only eighteen months before his death in 1940. A council of leading men, the sons of Lesotho's founding king Moshoeshoe, named her to act as regent for her stepson Bereng, who was only two years old when his father died. Lesotho was under British control, and the British high commissioner accepted her appointment, but it was contested by her husband's brother who took her to court. The high court confirmed her as regent in a special session in 1943, and Mantse Bo ruled until 1960 when Bereng was installed as Paramount Chief Moshoeshoe II. During her twenty years as regent, she brought issues concerning women to the forefront, as when she overturned a colonial law that allowed authorities to harass female beer brewers, or when she argued in 1962 that women should have equal access to credit and inheritance. She was also an early supporter of women chiefs as equal to male chiefs in status and salary, advocating this position in 1950 with the Basutoland National Council (Basutoland was the colonial name for Lesotho). She passed away in 1964.

South African Apartheid

South Africa was a site of racial segregation beginning with the arrival of the first European settlers. Restrictive laws had been introduced over the years, but a new era began after World War II when the white-dominated government passed a set of extreme laws that imposed virulent segregation governed by brutal rules about racial categories. The new system was known as *apartheid*, literally "apartness" in Afrikaans, the language of the white Afrikaner population. Individuals were assigned to a racial category, sometimes quite arbitrarily, dependent on their appearance. Marriage, residence, and employment were strictly regulated, with any potential mixing of people of different races severely restricted and subject to punishment. People of all racial backgrounds resisted the new laws through legal and extra-legal methods.

Fig. 6.2 Women protesting pass laws, Cape Town, South Africa, August 1956, on the same day as the massive national women's protest in Pretoria. Source: the *Cape Times* negative collection, courtesy of the National Library of South Africa (Cape Town).

Women were involved in all phases of the anti-apartheid resistance movement. In the 1950s they protested the extension of restrictive pass laws to women (see chapter 5 for earlier pass law protests). African men had carried detailed identity cards called passes for decades, and the passes were central to the apartheid system of racial oppression and control. After the election of 1948 brought in a white-dominated government intent on expanding racial segregation, women faced new attempts to force them to carry passes as well, though the government initially called them "reference books" and claimed they were not actual passes. Those affected were primarily urban women who had moved into the cities looking for work as they lost access to rural land for cultivation. Women responded by organizing the Federation of South African Women (FEDSAW) and sponsoring demonstrations throughout the country.

The Federation was founded as a non-racial organization in 1954 by Lilian Ngoyi, Ray Alexander, Florence Mkhize, Helen Joseph, Fatima Meer and others. Within months there were over ten thousand members, primarily urban African women, and including such activists as Frances Baard, a trade union leader who later wrote an autobiography.[12] FEDSAW was involved in many activities, but focused on bringing women into the anti-apartheid struggle.

After a number of smaller protests, FEDSAW organized the Defiance Campaign, a demonstration in 1956, where they handed in petitions opposing the new pass laws. That march was their most successful action, as twenty thousand women descended on government buildings in Pretoria, chanting "You have touched the women, you have struck a rock." Their struggle highlighted three primary objections to passes for women: that passes would restrict women from easily seeking work, that women would be subject to sexual abuse by officials, and that the inevitable arrest and detention of women for pass offenses (breaking pass laws was the most common cause of male arrests) would have a negative effect on their homes and families. Despite a massive response by women, in the end they were obliged to carry passes.

While many women's lives followed similar paths, looking at some of the individual activist leaders of that era clarifies why women had particular difficulties with the new laws as they faced increased limitations on their work and family lives. Lilian Ngoyi, who lived from 1911 to 1980, was an important leader of the anti-apartheid movement. The daughter of a clergyman in Pretoria, her family could not afford to keep her in school through high school. After she was widowed when her daughter was three, she began to work in a garment factory. By 1952 she was deeply involved in the Garment Workers Union, and she was later elected to the union executive committee. A pivotal experience in her political education was a trip to attend the World Congress of Women in Switzerland in 1954, when she was able to visit several European countries. The 1956 Defiance Campaign, protesting the expansion of restrictive pass laws, brought her into the African National Congress (ANC), where she served as president of the African National Congress Women's League in 1953 and then as president of the Federation of South African Women in 1956. Known to all as MaNgoyi, she was a powerful orator. She was charged with treason as part of a famous trial of the 1950s, and she spent most of the subsequent years under banning orders that restricted her public activities.[13]

Winnie Mandela was another prominent leader of the anti-apartheid movement. Though known primarily as the wife of Nelson Mandela, she was an activist in her own right. She was born in 1936 in Pondoland, South Africa, and trained as a medical social worker. She married Nelson Mandela in 1958, and he was imprisoned from 1962 to 1990. Winnie Mandela was active in the ANC and was also subjected to repeated banning orders (meaning she could not speak publicly or publish any of her writings) and imprisonment for her activities. During the 1950s and 1960s she was often at the forefront of ANC and women's protests. She remained popular, though in the 1990s she faced charges of fraud and some people held her responsible for a murder committed by young men who were associated with a community group she sponsored.

As government repression escalated in the 1960s and 1970s, it became increasingly difficult for the Federation to organize. The ANC leadership also placed less emphasis on massive demonstrations in general because growing repression forced the organization to shift to sabotage and eventually to clandestine armed struggle. Some observers suggested that the male ANC leaders wanted to keep women from playing a central political role, though it was also true that the ANC did not have the resources to defend thousands of arrested activists, whether male or female. FEDSAW ceased to be active after 1963.

The ANC Women's League focused on recruiting women to the ANC and on raising issues of importance to women within the ANC. As was the case with many political party organizations, the Women's League followed the ANC's leadership and its organizing efforts were defined by ANC priorities. It was periodically banned by the white-minority government and then reestablished. It was part of the coalition of the Federation of South African Women and participated in the Defiance Campaign.

White women also worked in coalition with all South African women in opposition to the apartheid laws. When the government passed the Senate Act in 1955 that legalized removing Coloured citizens (the official term for mixed-race residents) from the voter rolls, a group of white women formed the Women's Defence of the Constitution League, later known as Black Sash, to protest. In the 1950s and 1960s, Black Sash members held silent vigils in public locations, where they stood with political posters and wore black sashes diagonally across white dresses as a symbol of mourning for the death of constitutional rights under the apartheid government. In the 1970s and 1980s, they shifted their work to support services for women in urban areas, offering advice about employment, pass laws, housing, and pensions.[14]

Helen Joseph was a white woman who played a prominent role in South African anti-apartheid politics, particularly as a leader of the Federation of South African Women.[15] She was born in 1905 in Sussex, England, and earned a degree in English at King's College, University of London. She taught in India before moving to South Africa in 1931. There she married, got involved in women's issues, took courses in social studies at the University of the Witwatersrand, and went to work for the Garment Workers' Union. In the 1950s she helped found the Congress of Democrats, a primarily white organization that worked to end apartheid, and she was one of the founders of the FEDSAW and a primary architect of the Defiance Campaign.

Joseph was arrested in 1956 and was one of those who stood trial at the Treason Trial.[16] She was acquitted in 1961. In 1962, she was the first person to be placed under house arrest, a method used by the apartheid government to restrict political protest activity. She was generally banned or under house arrest throughout the 1960s. Joseph was an honorary president of the National Union of South

African Students and in 1983 was elected a patron of the United Democratic Front. During her years of house arrest, she completed a degree in theology from the University of London. Joseph was awarded the African National Congress's highest award, the Isitwalandwe, for "the one who wears the plumes of the rare bird," traditionally given to brave warriors. She passed away in 1992.

The years following the 1948 implementation of the oppressive system of apartheid laws were marked by protests and demonstrations by individual women and by organizations that worked tirelessly to bring about a democratic system of government based on majority rule. They finally succeeded after decades of struggle, when the first democratic elections in South African history were held in 1994, resulting in Nelson Mandela becoming president of a newly free South Africa.

Nationalism in East Africa

Women in East Africa faced some of the same problems under colonialism seen in other regions of Africa, as the colonial governments increasingly sought to control women's agricultural labor, family opportunities, and public activities. In the histories below from Tanzania and Kenya, two prominent protests are discussed with women's participation at the center. In both countries, women's contributions were essential to the success of the movements for independence, though their involvement is too often omitted or marginalized in the histories and scholarly reports.

Urban Women Mobilize in Tanzania

In the 1950s Tanzanians began to organize to end the rule of Great Britain in their territory. Tanzania was not technically a colony, but was a British mandate. Originally a German colony known as Tanganyika or German East Africa, Britain had gained control after Germany lost World War I and was forced to relinquish jurisdiction over their African colonies. Most of the initial analyses of Tanzanian nationalism focused on Julius Nyerere, who was a founder of the Tanganyika African National Union (TANU) and Tanzania's first president after independence. He was Zanaki, a minority ethnic group in Tanzania, and he was an educated Christian, a status shared by many of the men who were TANU members.

That analysis of Tanzanian political history was altered when feminist historians investigated the role of Bibi Titi Mohamed, who lived from 1926 to 2000.[17] She was a Muslim woman who emerged as a nationalist leader in Tanzania, and she was responsible for bringing women into TANU. Women had not been involved in TANU, but the party leadership was motivated to seek them out when John Hatch, of the British socialist organization the Fabian Society, visited in 1955 and asked where the women were in the new political organization. Bibi Titi, who held one of the earliest TANU membership cards, was asked by the male leaders to develop a women's section in TANU. Though men might have been influential in prompting the women, the rapid growth of the women's section can only be explained by appreciating the ways in which women were already organized, and their reasons for being interested in ending British colonialism.

Urban women's dance groups in East Africa were a widespread and popular form of organization and leisure activity. Celebrating their time together, women wearing coordinated outfits performed and held competitions on a regular basis. Bibi Titi was a leader in one group in Tanzania's capital city, Dar es Salaam. She already had recognition among urban women and experience in using her extensive contacts to organize dance competitions. She knew women from all sectors of the city through the dance groups, and she turned to the dancers to find women to recruit to the nationalist cause, another example of how women used existing practices and networks to advantage in a climate of political change. Within four months of establishing the women's section of TANU, there were five thousand members, largely drawn from already existing networks of women who were actively involved in city life. The women were all or nearly all Muslim, though of different ethnic backgrounds, and they shared not only the dance competitions, but also the Kiswahili language. Although many educated men, including Julius Nyerere, were fluent in English, most women had not attended formal schools and were not familiar with or comfortable speaking English. Kiswahili offered a shared language and cultural connection, whatever other differences might be apparent. Bibi Titi described how she helped Nyerere improve his fluency in colloquial Kiswahili so that he could more easily connect with ordinary Tanzanians.

Bibi Titi traveled to rural areas to recruit women as well, where she found local women who shared her interest in ending colonialism. In areas such as Moshi in northern Tanzania, the most public form of women's organization was found in clubs that focused on teaching domestic science, offering classes in child nutrition, baking scones, and home nursing. In their orientation they were very similar to groups found throughout colonial Africa. In the context of Tanzanian nationalism, the groups offered an entry point to local women's interests, and many of them joined TANU once they had the opportunity.

The lack of education was one of the key issues that women in Dar es Salaam, Moshi, and elsewhere brought to their political organizing. They blamed the colonial government for blocking women from having the same educational opportunities as men, and many women knew that TANU had promised to provide schooling for girls. Bibi Titi had completed Standard 4 (similar to fourth grade in the United States) in government schools, a level of education that was not common for Muslim women at that time. Women understood that education was an important step in bringing them greater options in work, family life, and political involvement. But beyond the specificity of that concern, the women expressed a desire for dignity, the ability to rule themselves, and an end to the discrimination that they observed and experienced under colonialism. They frequently described the problems they faced in their marriages, in their attempts to find economic success, and in the obstacles they faced when becoming politically active. They had a basic sense of what was fair, and they held the colonial system responsible in part for the inequality they encountered as women in urban Tanzania. When Bibi Titi and her colleagues visited various dance groups and talked about TANU and its goals of independence, equality, and development, the members immediately joined because they wanted independence for Tanzania and equality for themselves and their daughters.

Bibi Titi became general secretary of the TANU Women's Section beginning in 1959. Tanganyika won its independence in 1961, and in 1964 it merged with the island of Zanzibar to form the independent nation of Tanzania. In 1962, all women's groups were merged into the Umoja wa Wanawake wa Tanganyika (UWT, the Tanzanian Women's Union), and Bibi Titi served as president of the UWT until 1967. She was also involved in regional organizations such as the East African Women's Seminars and the All African Women's Conference. Bibi Titi was arrested in 1969 and charged with treason, a result of her friendship with a leading dissident and her own involvement with a constitutional reform campaign. She was convicted and sentenced to life in prison, though she was released through a presidential pardon in 1972. In 1985 she was finally recognized by Tanzanian President Julius Nyerere for her early nationalist work, and his public actions served as an apology for the time of the treason trial.

Discovering the history of Muslim women in Dar es Salaam as well as of women throughout Tanzania fundamentally changed the conventional view that the Tanzanian anticolonial movement was led solely by men who were products of Christian mission education. Researchers had previously argued that the colonial powers brought about their own end by educating the men who formed the anticolonial organizations and then came to power after independence. Bibi Titi Mohammed and women she recruited, who were not Christian and were mostly outside the colonial educational system, were essential to the successful struggle to end colonialism. Without the widespread involvement of Tanzanian women, it was doubtful that TANU would have been as successful as it was, both in ending colonialism and in bringing new inclusive policies of development to the country.

Agricultural Protest and Mau Mau in Kenya

Mau Mau was the name given by the British to a nationalist revolt in Kenya in the 1950s, which was led by the Land and Freedom Army. The goal was to end British colonialism and reclaim land that the colonial government had taken from African farmers. While women played an important role, they have been neglected in the conventional histories of the movement. Kenyans, especially Gikuyu who lived in fertile agricultural areas in central Kenya, had been subjected to British colonial control for decades, and from the beginning of that experience they had been struggling to retain or regain land and rights (see chapter 5). Similarly to what happened in other colonial settler societies, the British seized over seven million acres of the best agricultural land, put themselves in control of key political and economic institutions, and introduced a series of laws that restricted African freedom of movement. African farmers were forced to work on British plantations that grew coffee for export where they were paid low wages and had to pay taxes from those earnings. They were prohibited from growing coffee or other export crops themselves, making it difficult to earn an income except by working for British settlers. Taxation and an onerous pass system combined to control the lives of Africans in Kenya.

GIKUYU RESISTANCE IN THE 1940S

The Gikuyu areas were the hardest hit, as people were removed from their traditional lands and restricted to living on reserves where the land was insufficient for the numbers of people and less fertile than the land claimed by British and other European settlers. Significantly, land access and ownership were not simply economic issues, but were at the foundation of Gikuyu family formation and social life. Young men were only considered to be adults who could marry when they had land under their control, and women's responsibility for providing food crops for their family meant that they were also regarded as adults only when they could fulfill that obligation. Land expropriation by the British damaged Gikuyu society in the most basic ways, giving rise to intense anger and resentment.

Africans began organizing in opposition to the British incursions into their lives in the 1920s. As the years passed, the land in the reserves became more crowded and the land was subject to erosion and overuse, which made it increasingly less fertile. In the late 1940s, the British introduced land management programs designed to control the erosion, promoting such practices as terracing and intercropping. They wanted trees to be planted on hillsides so the roots would help hold the soil in place. They also wanted to regulate cattle breeding by requiring culling and vaccinations.

These agricultural requirements became women's burden because women were responsible for growing the family food crops, though men had usually prepared land that women then planted. But in the late 1940s, as many as 50 percent of Gikuyu men were away from their home villages doing short term migrant labor, so women experienced increasing demands on their time and energy. In July 1947, the Kenyan African Union (KAU) held a meeting to discuss the difficulties women were facing, and determined that women should refuse to perform the terracing that the colonial authorities were asking them to do. They could not complete the work normally required in their family homes and their fields while also meeting official demands.

In April 1948, twenty-five hundred women in Muranga district, where over two thousand acres had already been terraced, converged on the district headquarters to protest the new agricultural obligations. The government report described the women as singing and dancing at the local chief's household, as they "informed everyone that they would not take part in soil conservation measures mainly because they felt they had enough work to do at home."[18] In protesting, women defied African male leaders and representatives of the British colonial system, they widely publicized their views, and they directly confronted their exclusion from political discussion.

The district commissioner (DC) retorted that "the soil could not wait for a few men to terrace it," but the women continued to avoid terracing their land for several weeks until the DC ordered their arrest for refusing to comply with the law. The women persisted in their protest, forcing the release of those who had been jailed when "a large crowd" of women came to the government offices "brandishing sticks and shouting Amazonian war-cries," in the words of the DC's account. When the DC tried to fine all the women who were involved, they maintained their dissent and eventually won some minor lessening of the demands and a reduction in the terracing requirement.[19]

Wanjiru Nyamaratu was a political activist in the 1940s, when she joined the KAU and became treasurer of one of the local branches. Beginning in 1947, people in her region protested the agricultural demands, and she emerged in the leadership that recruited thousands of local residents who had lost access to their land and were forced to work on European projects. She was a dedicated advocate for Gikuyu rights, and was among those who rejected Western clothing and instead wore hand-sewn cloth wrapped in a more traditional Gikuyu style.[20]

Women in Muranga rose up again in 1951, when the colonial government began the mandatory vaccination of all cattle to control the spread of the devastating disease rinderpest. The cattle began to die in great numbers at the same time, so the women attacked the inoculation centers and chased away the officials who were implementing the program. Five hundred women were arrested, and several women were injured in the fracas that occurred. The women's perspective on the events was captured in a song:

> We women of Muranga were arrested for refusing
> To have our cattle poisoned. And because we
> Rejected such colonial laws we were thrown into
> Prison cells and our children were wailing because
> They had no milk to drink.
> (Chorus) We beseech you, our God
> Take us away from this slavery.[21]

Fig. 6.3 Woman picking coffee beans on a plantation in Kenya, 1957. Source: the American Geographical Society Library, University of Wisconsin-Milwaukee Libraries.

In nearby Kiambu, where many women worked as paid laborers on coffee plantations, women had also protested in 1947.[22] When their demands for an increase in their compensation were refused, they went on strike. They refused to pick coffee, they blocked roads, and their leaders were taken into custody for questioning. Notably, as a precursor to women's involvement in Mau Mau, they threatened to place a curse on any woman who broke ranks and went to pick coffee. This form of sanctioning was an older Gikuyu tradition that was directly related to oath-taking ceremonies that appeared in the spread of Mau Mau adherents.

Mau Mau

Women in Kenya thus had a history of protesting colonial intrusion into their agricultural and familial responsibilities, and when the Land and Freedom Army began to meet secretly in forests in central Kenya, women were prepared to join and offer support. While the most noted leaders in the Land and Freedom Army were men, they could not have survived in the forests without women supplying food and other necessities, acting as spies and messengers, and performing other tasks.

Women were present at the oath-taking ceremonies that marked membership in the Land and Freedom Army, though few women administered the oaths despite earlier similar practices by women. Men and women took a series of oaths with escalating levels of secrecy and commitment. The later oaths involved bloodletting and sexual activities, including animal sacrifice and the use of women's menstrual blood in ceremonies. Some observances demanded greater loyalty by having participants perform public sexual acts that were normally considered taboo, such as having male candidates engage in ritual intercourse with menstruating women. While the reasoning behind such unconventional practices was not clear, it was likely assumed that once people observed and participated in activities normally considered perverse they would feel a greater commitment to the organization and be less likely to report such activities to the authorities.

Women were recognized as district organizers, they were judges in the forest communities, and a small number rose to high positions within the organization with at least one woman ascending to the rank of field marshal. But gaining those promotions was not straightforward, as precolonial Gikuyu society had not included women's councils or other mechanisms for women to exercise authority in an official capacity. Mau Mau opened some new opportunities as women were able to prove their ability to contribute to the anticolonial movement. As a result, councils that were established included both men and women, and women's opinions were allowed to be heard.

While few women were warriors on a par with men, some did fight alongside men while others performed support activities such as cleaning and manufacturing weapons and ammunition. But much of their work in the forest Mau Mau communities repeated the domestic work they had previously carried out, including preparing food and collecting firewood and water. As commonly occurs in war, some women became "wives" of warriors, especially for officers who could require women to provide sexual as well as other domestic services. But women's involvement was widespread, and according to the estimates made by women in later decades, one-fourth of all adult women in Kiambu district participated in Mau Mau activities and support.

Women who remained in their villages and towns were able to make important contributions because, at least at first, the British and the Kenyan police who worked for the colonial government did not view women as a threat and allowed them greater freedom of movement. Thus thousands of women were able to travel in the region, and to deliver food, medicine, clothing, weapons, and other supplies to the forest communities. They also operated as spies by carrying messages and reporting on colonial government activities.

Wanjiru Nyamaratu, the KAU treasurer and organizer introduced above, was active from the earliest days of Mau Mau endeavors. She began with the assignment of coordinating food for the forest warriors in the area around Njoro and Nakuru. Her success brought her the title of General in Charge of Food, or Genero wa Rigu in Gikuyu. She recruited both men and women whose task was to raise funds and gather food, medicine, and other supplies. Her successful efforts to enlist new combatants earned her another promotion and she was known as the Mother of Senior Warriors. She eventually served as a judge in the Mau Mau courts, dispensing punishment to Mau Mau members who were found to be working in opposition to the group's aims.

As the fighting and violence increased, the British tried to control the activities of African communities in general. They fenced and guarded women's fields and livestock and many villages were turned into stockades with controlled access. At the same time, Mau Mau anticolonial measures penalized European settlers who supported the British colonial government, and also Africans who worked for the authorities or who were judged to be working counter to Mau Mau goals. Many Kenyans who lived through the political activities of the 1950s felt that they were subject to punishment no matter what they decided to do, as they were likely to be imprisoned by the British if they were caught helping the forest fighters, and they could be disciplined by Mau Mau representatives even if they tried to remain neutral.

Wanjiru Nyamaratu was among the fiercest adherents of Mau Mau, whose goal was to return land to the landless farmers. Her history of activism, beginning in the early 1940s and spanning the agricultural protests and participation with the Mau Mau forest fighters, continued in later years when she became a leader in a Nakuru women's group that focused on buying land and property for women.[23] Though just one woman, her story suggests some of the ways that women's roles changed, bringing them new options to enter expanded arenas for political activity and take on public positions such as judges.

Women suffered a great deal during the conflict of the 1950s. Though most British assumed that women in Mau Mau had been recruited by their husbands or other male kin, testimony from women indicated that their involvement was a result of their own experience of colonial oppression. One British colonial authority noted in a 1954 report that "wives have in many cases persuaded their husbands to take the oath and are often very militant."[24] Many thousands of women were imprisoned, including some who later became prominent in Kenyan politics such as Margaret Kenyatta. Born in 1928, she was the daughter of Jomo Kenyatta, a Gikuyu leader and the first president after independence; she served as mayor of Kenya's capital Nairobi from 1970 to 1976. Wambui Otieno, who was born in 1936, was deeply involved in the Mau Mau anticolonial struggle in the 1950s, where she was a central figure organizing women as scouts and providers of food. She was detained by the British authorities more than once.[25] In the post-independence years she also was prominent in Kenyan political and cultural events (chapter 9).

WOMEN IN PRISON DURING THE EMERGENCY

The British colonial authorities called the events surrounding the Mau Mau resistance "the Emergency." They eventually recognized the importance of women to the struggle, incarcerating thirteen thousand female sympathizers in camps and holding areas, and they fortified villages to keep residents from leaving to aid or join the resistance. When the Emergency ended, women still made up over 10 percent of Gikuyu prisoners (3,103 women in a total population of 27,841). But many thousands more women had passed through the jail system, imprisoned for their work with Mau Mau. The numbers remain disputed due to incomplete tallies by the authorities.

The prison conditions were poor, with women prisoners subjected to beatings, torture, and forced labor, and suffering from inadequate food, with even those meager amounts sometimes withheld as further punishment. If women prisoners renounced their Mau Mau oath, they were given lighter work in the prison orchards and vegetable plots. In a particularly ironic case, women prisoners at Kamiti prison were required to terrace the prison agricultural fields in 1954.

Women performed forced labor such as building roads, quarrying stone, and transporting the cut stone blocks on their heads. For the road building project women had to dig out the stony laterite and carry the heavy load in metal basins to a gathering site some distance away. Women sometimes bent the basin bottoms inward and threw handfuls out along the way to lessen the amount of laterite they were forced to haul. Some who had been detained reported sexual abuse and torture, with foreign objects being shoved into their vaginas. Women who had been incarcerated recalled the horrific work of handling bodies of Kenyans killed in the struggle, a task considered the worst in the prison. Male prisoners dug huge pits, and the women had to unload bodies from the truckloads that were brought to Kamiti prison on a daily basis.[26]

An additional experience that primarily affected women was their attempts to protect their children. Many women brought small children with them when they were imprisoned, and others gave birth while jailed. The British estimated that as many as 15 percent of the four thousand women in Kamiti in 1956 had one or more children with them, for a possible total of six hundred children sharing appalling conditions with their mothers. Most of them did not survive; the burial of children was a chore allocated to the women considered to be the most militant adherents of Mau Mau.

It would be difficult to exaggerate the dreadful conditions of the prisons that held both convicted women activists and other female detainees. But the British hid the extent of incarcerations of both men and women, destroying most of the records and hiding other information. The official British story of the Emergency described savage Africans attacking well-meaning white settlers who only wanted to bring "civilization" to Kenya, and that description became the narrative familiar to people around the world in the 1950s. The reality was far more complex and was filled with contradictions and difficulties, with events rarely conforming to the version promoted by the British.

The colonial authorities used the gated locations and prisons to expand training in Western-style domesticity, which was introduced by colonial women through the women's organization, Maendeleo ya Wanawake, meaning Women's Progress or Women's Advancement. Maendeleo later became the official women's organization in independent Kenya. In the 1950s, the British women who ran the local meetings gave priority to those who renounced Mau Mau and were known to be loyal to the colonial system. Thus women whose families were in the colonial Home Guard police force and served the British in various capacities were more likely to have access to the cooking and sewing classes, as well as famine relief. With such incentives, in 1954 there were thirty-seven thousand members of Maendeleo. Women were taught about their responsibility for creating a Western-style home, in classes that deliberately countered the new gender roles that were found within the Mau Mau resistance. The British hoped to use certain cohorts of women to undermine the effectiveness of the anticolonial struggle.[27] Though it appeared that the colonial forces were victorious in 1956 when the Land and Freedom Army was defeated by the British military, African grievances were far from resolved. Within a few years, growing international pressure to end colonialism in Africa compelled Britain to abandon Kenya, which gained its independence in 1963 with Jomo Kenyatta as the first president.

Maendeleo ya Wanawake continued to organize women into the independence era. A prominent leader of Maendeleo was Jane Kiano, who was chair from 1971 to 1984 and was responsible for a huge growth in the numbers of branches and members, to three hundred twenty-seven thousand members in 1983. Beginning in 1967, the organization published *Sauti ya Mabibi* (*Voice of Women*), though it apparently ceased publication in the 1970s. In 1986 the government dissolved the executive and integrated Maendeleo's activities into the ruling party, though it was restored to autonomy in 1991. By 2000 it claimed a membership of 1.5 million women. In 2004, the organization sponsored projects in maternal and child health and family planning, HIV/AIDS, environment and energy conservation, leadership training, and income generation.[28]

Kenyan history during these decades demonstrates women's changing experiences, from their extreme oppression under colonialism, to their ability to take on new tasks in the anticolonial struggle, and the ways they moved into positions of authority in the postcolonial years. Women's persistence in their efforts to maintain their families while figuring out how to be part of local and national politics illustrates how crucial female contributions were to the eventual emergence of an independent nation.

Religious Activism in Zambia

Zambia was the location of a religious revolt that threatened the government in the 1960s. As seen in the rise of other independent churches in Africa, such religious structures allowed a space for women to reclaim some of their spiritual leadership and to press for change in their societies. The Lumpa Church in Zambia was founded by a woman, and it had a particular connection to women's prior role as spiritual guides, before it developed into a political threat to the newly independent nation of Zambia.

Alice Mulenga Lenshina was a postwar religious leader whose church became a center of anti-government activity in the 1950s and later.[29] Born around 1924, she married a Bemba man who was a convert to the Free Church of Scotland's Lubwa Mission. In 1953 she fell into a coma while ill with malaria, and she regained consciousness as she was about to be buried. She claimed that Jesus Christ called her to be a prophet after she had died four times, "rising again" after each death. She said she had been given a true Bible, from which she preached an anti-witchcraft doctrine. As a result of her experiences, she founded the Lumpa Church in 1953. She adopted the name Lenshina, a corruption of "regina," for queen; the church name, "Lumpa," was Bemba for "better than the rest." She quickly gathered a large following, estimated at fifty thousand to one hundred thousand during the peak years in the 1950s. People were initially drawn by the strict moral code of the church, which did not allow drinking, smoking, dancing, or adultery in addition to a complete renunciation of magic and witchcraft.

By the early 1960s, many of her followers left the church and became involved in party politics, especially in the United National Independence Party (UNIP), which was the leading nationalist political party in Zambia. UNIP and the Lumpa church developed a strong mutual animosity, and many churches were burned in arson attacks blamed on UNIP supporters. After Zambia became independent in 1964, serious battles broke out between government authorities and church members, who refused to pay taxes. Over five hundred people died in a three-week time span. On August 3, 1964, the new president, Kenneth Kaunda, outlawed the church, and Alice Lenshina surrendered on August 12. Some church members continued to fight, though most moved to the Democratic Republic of the Congo where they settled. Lenshina was detained until December 1975 and was restricted to Zambia's capital, Lusaka, upon her release. She died in 1978. The church continued with a new name, as the Jerusalem Church of Christ.

A close reading of hymns that Lenshina wrote demonstrated how she combined Christian imagery with traditional Bemba ideas. The lyrics drew on concepts of honesty and cleanliness as the basis for a strong monogamous marriage. The introduction of modified ceremonies re-introduced women, with Lenshina in the lead, as mediators between individuals and a supreme deity. She positioned herself as a shrine builder, and women became primarily responsible for building village churches. In one example of how she combined traditions, she accepted the Western wedding ring as a symbol of a committed marriage, and she combined it with the older African idea of the bored stone, which represented women's spiritual leadership in rural communities. The stone can be traced back to prehistoric practices, and it was commonly used to weight women's digging sticks (see chapter 1). It came to be used in girls' initiation rites and in a smaller size as an amulet.[30]

Alice Lenshina and the Lumpa Church had been well-received as a witchcraft eradication movement, and many people supported the church's opposition to what were viewed as modern vices that were damaging African families and communities. Such responses to modernization and urbanization were seen in other local churches, some of which rose independently and others that broke away from more mainstream Protestant and Catholic congregations. Many Zambians became active in the movement as a way to return to a society that was remembered as being more orderly. Women in particular were restored as church leaders and intermediaries, assisting people in accessing God and Jesus Christ. Lenshina was one of the few women to gain national and international attention for her leadership, and many of her followers continued to be committed to her despite her decade of detention.

Portuguese Colonies

Most of the British and French colonies became independent in the 1960s, while Portugal remained determined to hold onto their African territories of Angola, Cape Verde, Guinea-Bissau, Mozambique, and São Tomé e Príncipe. As Africans in those countries realized that Portugal would deny their peaceful political attempts to gain their freedom, they turned to armed struggle. Though each country had its own liberation movement or movements, there were some parallels among the countries that shared a history of Portuguese colonialism.

Beginning in the 1950s, Africans formed new organizations to promote their liberation from the Portuguese colonial system. Groups such as FRELIMO (Front for Liberation of Mozambique) in Mozambique, and MPLA (People's Movement for the Liberation of Angola) and UNITA (National Union for the Total Independence of Angola) in Angola were formed. But even that limited pursuit of independence brought a strong response from the Portuguese government, which since a coup in 1926 had been a fascist dictatorship. After António Salazar came to power in 1932 he introduced the New State, a reactionary regime opposed to any form of liberalism or socialism. After decades of repressive colonial governance, there was little opportunity for nationalism to grow in the Portuguese colonies as it had in other African nations.

In 1951, the Portuguese renamed their overseas colonies as Overseas Provinces, thus emphasizing that they were part of Portugal and not eligible for independence. Beginning in the 1950s African intellectuals wrote about the abuses of colonial rule and sometimes organized groups that worked for reforms. Some were based in urban centers in the African colonies, while others met in Lisbon where they had traveled for more education and where they found themselves part of a growing anticolonial movement. By the early 1960s nationalists in all of the Portuguese colonies had determined that they would need to engage in an armed struggle to end colonialism, as the Portuguese had made it clear that they would never voluntarily transfer power.

Cultural Nationalism: Noémia de Sousa in Mozambique

Noémia de Sousa was a writer and poet in Mozambique.[31] She was born in 1926 in the Mozambican capital Lourenço Marques (now Maputo), the child of two mixed-race parents. She was proud that her background included German, Portuguese, and Goan (Indian) ancestors, as well as Ronga and Makua from Mozambique. Her early education was in Maputo, though after her father died she was not able to attend an academic high school. She trained at a commercial school, learning to type and do stenography, as well as more traditional academic subjects and English and French. De Sousa initially worked at a local business as a secretary in order to support her mother.

She published her first poem, "O Irmão Negro" ("The Black Brother") at age nineteen in the local literary magazine *Mocidade* (*Youth*). She soon began working for a political organization called the African Association, where she was responsible for reviving their newspaper, *O Brado Africano* (*The African Cry*) and worked with the renowned Mozambican poet José Craveirinha. She wrote several well-received and much anthologized poems during those years, though after 1951 she no longer wrote poetry. Her early poems are often cited as representative of the Negritude school of writing, extolling black African culture and history, though she was writing in isolation from the better-known French school of Negritude.

Her poems celebrated Mozambican culture and history. One of the most often cited was a poem about migrant workers in South Africa's gold and diamond mines, "Magaiça," which concluded,

Youth and health,
the lost illusions

which will shine like stars
on some Lady's neck in some City's night.

Her celebration of "my mother Africa" (in the poem "Black Blood") was continued in "If You Want to Know Me," which cataloged the diversity of Mozambican lives:

If you want to understand me
come, bend over this soul of Africa
in the black dockworker's groans
the Chope's frenzied dances
the Changanas' rebellion.[32]

In 1951 she moved to Portugal to escape the vigilance of the Portuguese secret police, who were interested in her work with *O Brado Africano*. In Portugal she met and married her husband, Gualtar Soares, and they later moved to France. She worked as a journalist there, writing under the name Vera Micaia. She returned to Portugal and was living there when she died in 2002.

Political Nationalism in Mozambique

During the 1960s, Mozambicans in the armed struggle espoused differing nationalist politics, though with the primary goal of ending Portuguese colonialism and developing Mozambican identity. FRELIMO was founded in 1962, when three earlier nationalist groups united in their struggle to end Portuguese colonialism. Eduardo Mondlane was elected president. From the beginning there were fundamental differences of opinion about the character of Mozambique's oppression, and consequently about what the appropriate response should be. Some activists viewed the war as a racial and nationalist war of African Mozambicans against European colonialists, and their goal was simply to rid Mozambique of the Portuguese. Others believed it was a class war pitting Mozambican peasants and workers against Portuguese capitalism and imperialism, and their objective was to organize a new society along socialist lines.

Divergent analyses also emerged over women's emancipation, as those who favored the first tendency were less open to women becoming involved, while those who were developing a socialist consciousness began to see that women suffered a particular oppression that they needed to address. Efforts to improve women's access to education and military training met with opposition from some members of FRELIMO, while even those who favored including women when it was discussed in the abstract sometimes had difficulty in implementing new directions for women's involvement. Despite these debates, formal recognition of women's important role in the struggle emerged at an early date.[33]

In September 1962 the newly formed organization adopted a series of resolutions to be acted on immediately by the Central Committee. Two important items were "to promote the unity of Mozambicans" (as number 2 on the list) and "to promote by all methods the social and cultural development of the Mozambican woman" (number 6). A further resolution called for the formation of organizations of workers, youth, and women. The League of Mozambican Women (LIFEMO for *Liga Feminina Moçambicana*) was established in 1962, soon after FRELIMO itself, as a way of bringing women into the struggle. LIFEMO's main objectives were to unite Mozambican women in the anticolonial struggle, to promote the well-being of Mozambican women and children, and to combat illiteracy. By 1963 Celina Simango, a LIFEMO member, represented Mozambique at the International Women's Congress in Moscow. Thus attention was directed at women's participation from the earliest days of the struggle to end colonialism.

The armed phase of the struggle against Portuguese colonialism began in northern Mozambique in 1964. Initially women were only marginally involved and were excluded from guerrilla training. The first women who became active were seen as role models for others, and when they spoke about FRELIMO in the villages of the northern province of Cabo Delgado, other women took note. Mozambican women became known as exemplars of revolutionary spirit, promoting equality, pictured carrying arms and embodying ideas about the possibilities for women under socialism. Women faced many obstacles to full participation in the struggle, but nonetheless the work they did in the bush was essential to the success of the military branch of FRELIMO.

Women's motives for joining FRELIMO were varied. Some women or their family members had experienced Portuguese brutality personally. Joanina Mbawa described seeing Portuguese soldiers maim and kill her sister, arrest her father and brother, and burn her village. She managed to escape into the bush with her five-year-old brother, and she subsequently joined FRELIMO. Another woman, Conescence, told how she and her cousin, Gloria David, joined after Conescence's father was arrested and killed by the Portuguese secret police. Her brother was already a FRELIMO member. Teresinha Mblale saw her uncle killed during an infamous massacre at Mueda in Cabo Delgado in 1960, and she described her father's difficulties making a living in the Portuguese colonial system, both factors in her joining FRELIMO in 1965. Another woman from near Mueda had seen her father and cousin maltreated under colonialism, and was ready to listen when her father came to her and her sister to tell them about FRELIMO.

Other testimony recalled how, because their husbands had not paid their taxes, women were imprisoned, made to do forced labor where they faced rape from the policemen in charge of their work details, and suffered torture and death at the hands of Portuguese settlers and administrators. All of these occurrences influenced women to join. These stories were published as part of FRELIMO's campaign to gain support from outside of Mozambique, and it reflected FRELIMO's political approach in emphasizing the difficulties of the system of colonialism rather than individual experiences.

Many women, especially those who were younger, joined along with their families. Women who became leaders often were influenced by their fathers and uncles, who taught them about colonialism and resistance. Josina Machel, who became a heroine of the Mozambican revolution, was the niece of FRELIMO Central Committee member Mateus Sansao Muthemba, who was killed in 1968. Her father was also active and was imprisoned by the Portuguese. Josina was a leader in agitating for a stronger role for women at the top levels of FRELIMO, and she was director of FRELIMO's Section of Social Affairs. She married Samora Machel, who was president of FRELIMO after Eduardo Mondlane was assassinated in 1969, and who was the first president of an independent Mozambique in 1975. She died of illness on April 7, 1971, at the age of twenty-five, and the date of her death is commemorated as Mozambican Women's Day.

As Paulina Mateus told her story, her family was active in the struggle against Portuguese colonialism. She helped her father distribute FRELIMO membership cards when she was just twelve years old herself. She and her family lived near the Nangololo mission where her father taught and she attended school. Her life changed when Daniel Boorman, a Dutch missionary supportive of FRELIMO, was killed in August 1964 by a man active in nationalist groups opposed to FRELIMO. Because Paulina's father was involved in those intrigues, he was suspected of the murder. Paulina claimed her father was an active member of FRELIMO and not involved in Boorman's murder. Her family was in the process of fleeing when her father was killed, leaving her as head of the family. Her cousin led her to FRELIMO activists, who she recalls were speaking about Portuguese imperialism, and she joined as an adolescent. She later was president of the Mozambican women's organization, OMM (Organização da Mulher Moçambicana).

Mozambique was noted for the public ways in which the liberation movement incorporated policies designed to support women, despite some continued marginalization of women activists. Exhausted by the seemingly endless warfare, in 1974 progressive military officers in Portugal staged a coup that ended the decades of fascist government and led to independence for Portugal's African colonies in 1975. FRELIMO became the ruling party, known as Partido Frelimo, and began implementing many of the policies designed to support women. The liberation struggle could not have succeeded without the material contributions of women and their work, and women's political interventions dramatically shifted those fighting the anticolonial war to take a broader and more inclusive approach.

Zimbabwe

Politics in Southern Rhodesia followed a familiar pattern for women in the 1950s. From the 1890s when the area first came under British control, the white population increasingly claimed African land for their own agriculture. Rural women faced problems as they lost access to farming land and were restricted from settling in urban areas if they were unmarried. After World War II, increasing numbers of urban residents were female, and many more were arriving independently as they sought employment and wished to support themselves. Although there were small examples of resistance, there were no large-scale demonstrations such as were seen in South Africa and other areas. African urban communities were divided by ethnic and class differences, and gender-related tensions reflected those disparities as well.

By the late 1950s, Africans in Southern Rhodesia expected to become independent, a course of action that was proceeding in other British colonies. But a series of proposed constitutions were rejected, and in 1962 the white-dominated Rhodesian Front Party won elections. In 1964, the Rhodesian Front leader and one of its founders, Ian Smith, became prime minister. Once Smith was elected he wasted no time in declaring a Unilateral Declaration of Independence (UDI). Rather than negotiating independence with Great Britain, a process which would likely have allowed governance by the African majority, he simply declared that Rhodesia was no longer a British colony, and it could establish a white-minority independent government. Although the nation was no longer a colony of Britain, it suffered under white minority rule until independence with majority rule was finally negotiated in 1980.

Africans formed the Zimbabwe African People's Union (ZAPU) under Joshua Nkomo in 1961; ZAPU was banned in1962. The Zimbabwe African National Union (ZANU), initially led by Rev. Ndabamingi Sithole, was founded in 1963 and was then banned in 1964. The long struggle to end white-minority rule brought out vicious differences between the African parties, ZANU and ZAPU, as well as between the white minority and black majority populations. While the political differences were complicated by ethnic and personal antagonisms, ZANU espoused a more confrontational approach and developed a socialist perspective. ZANU was also identified as the Shona party; the Shona were the majority ethnic group, making up 80 percent of Zimbabwe's population.

As Africans were repeatedly banned from organizing their own political parties, they were forced to turn to underground and guerrilla tactics. By 1967 ZANU had its own army, the Zimbabwe African National Liberation Army (ZANLA), which began a guerrilla war, attacking colonial and minority-rule offices. The liberation war in Zimbabwe was brutal, with the struggle being carried out not only against white minority rule but between liberation movements with differing views of what an independent Zimbabwe should look like politically. The war only ended in 1979 when the British brokered the Lancaster House agreement, which allowed for majority rule while including regulations that safeguarded some limited positions for white Zimbabweans in government. Zimbabwe was finally an independent nation in 1980.

Urban Struggles in the 1950s

In Salisbury, Southern Rhodesia's main city (later known as Harare, Zimbabwe), the British authorities had imposed strict residential segregation that assumed that most urban dwellers were men working in urban industries. When women arrived, they confronted an extremely limited set of job possibilities. Urban women were more likely to be impoverished and to find an income through illicit beer brewing and prostitution. Defining prostitution in this context continues to be a fraught issue; while many women did perform sexual acts in exchange for money or goods, they frequently had long-term relationships with a man for whom they also cooked and kept house, as seen with women in Kenya (see chapter 4). They were not controlled by pimps or restricted to working out of brothels, but were most often independent women who were left few options when seeking an income. Women in long-standing relationships with men, but who were not legally married, also had little recourse when harassed by colonial officials for being in the city illegally.

Two political events in 1950s Salisbury were directly related to the racial and gender segregation of that place and time.[34] The first was associated with a trade union organization, the Reformed Industrial and Commercial Workers' Union, known as RICU. Started in the 1930s by Charles Mzingeli, it mainly catered to male workers until the early 1950s. British colonial rulers, following the example of South Africa, introduced new laws requiring Africans to carry identity passes and restricting where they could live in the city. They also began to crack down on unwanted urban residents, especially women who were illegally brewing beer or working as prostitutes. Unmarried women were subject to being sent back to rural areas.

Women fought back by aligning themselves with existing organizations, and RICU found its membership growing from a few hundred to nearly seven thousand by 1954. But it was not an easy alliance, as many of the married women and men in RICU were disdainful of the poor women seeking support for their choice to live in the city. The poor women had their own experiences that led to their own anticolonial attitudes. They were targeted for removal from their homes, and they were unable to make a formal complaint without being subjected to sexual assault and repeated raids on their residences. The class conflict, evident at RICU meetings and seen in the minutes that reported remarks made by attendees, was a major obstacle to the development of a mass movement as was seen in South Africa and in the interclass alliances of Nigeria.

One result of the housing crisis was that colonial authorities agreed to build a hostel for single women workers, similar to several such hostels for men that existed in Salisbury. Most of the women living in the hostel worked as domestic workers and nannies, and their income was noticeably higher than that of men employed in factories. In a situation of deteriorating services, African men formed a new organization, the City Youth League (CYL) in order to demand improvements. One of their first actions was to call for a bus boycott, similar to that seen in Johannesburg, South Africa, with the intention of stopping a proposed rate increase. While the increased rates were difficult for working men to pay, the women had a much higher income and some women defied the boycott and rode the bus to their jobs. The men, angry at the lack of compliance, attacked women at the hostel, raping some and causing injury to residents and damage to the hostel. Twenty-one men were charged and six finally sentenced for their part in the attacks.

Zimbabwe urban experiences were parallel to what was seen in many other African colonies, but the response to new encounters and events was not the same. Class and gender conflict seemed to hold the upper hand, making it difficult to build alliances that could more successfully struggle against colonial rule. Poor women and their concerns were not supported by married women and men, and urban Africans did not find common cause in an anticolonial organization in the 1950s. In the bus boycott incident, gender hostilities combined with incipient class differences to thwart any possibility for an alliance between men and women, and instead led to a violent attack on urban working women.

Rural Struggles in Zimbabwe

Although much of the documented political activity was in urban areas, rural communities and rural women who had been deeply affected by the colonial presence were involved, often in clandestine ways, in the anticolonial struggle.[35] Shona society had been based on a gender division of labor, with women primarily responsible for agriculture and men performing seasonal tasks such as clearing fields and maintaining control over cattle and family labor allocation. As described for other regions of Africa, marriage patterns, bridewealth exchange, and household configuration were all part of a coherent social structure. When European settlers arrived and began to claim land for themselves, hiring Africans to work in their fields and imposing taxes that forced African men in particular to seek waged work, the balance was shifted in ways that brought greater disadvantages to rural women.

By the 1950s, the colonial government sought to regularize its control of land transactions with the Native Land Husbandry Act (1951). African farmers resisted because that law instituted individual land tenure and ignored the existence of communal lands and local knowledge about access to land, clan ownership, and other practices that were unfamiliar or unfavorable to the settler authorities. Women were expected to expand their agricultural production in order to help raise taxes; at the same time they often faced such increased burdens alone, if their husbands had migrated to the mines or urban areas to find waged labor.

As the guerrilla war spread into the rural areas, the liberation fighters often found willing partners in rural women, who resented their increased work and reduced authority under white-minority rule. Women were specific in their complaints about local men and the colonial authorities. They said their husbands refused to let them work, yet they lacked transport to carry their goods to sell in the market, and government price controls restricted what they could earn.

The women sometimes knew—and, on occasion, welcomed—individual combatants, who might be family members or offspring of neighbors. At times, they also feared the arrival of the guerrillas; if there was a Rhodesian camp nearby, rural communities could face repercussions for assisting ZANLA members. The women, when they could, provided shelter and food, and carried messages. Many villages formed committees to organize their support, and those committees were also responsible for reporting those who failed to support the liberation struggle. Both women and men were involved in the village committees. Women who had been active in the colonial clubs that taught domesticity and home economics ascribed their ability to participate in the committees and lead activities to the earlier club experience. There were also reports of guerrillas intervening in village disputes, at times making men support their wives rather than abandon them, or telling men not to beat their wives. Women could observe that the ZANLA combatants brought visible and specific remedies to gender conflicts, while making vital connections to the larger project of national liberation.[36]

Although ZANU developed an official policy that advocated for advancing women, the actual practice was so limited that some viewed it as a "myth" of female liberation.[37] Ideas about sexual equality and stated policies calling for respect for women and abstinence from sexual intimacy during the armed struggle were not followed, with many reports of forced and consensual sexual relationships in the guerrilla camps. There were enough pregnant women and nursing mothers to warrant establishing a special camp for them across the border in Mozambique, with the result that those women were isolated from most activities and shamed as promiscuous women.[38]

As with other liberation struggles, women in general were marginalized, though a few individuals did gain leadership positions. While many rural women carried messages, prepared food, and provided shelter to combatants, a few women taught in the liberated areas in camps and schools, and sometimes were trained in weapons and warfare. Perhaps the best known female guerrilla fighter in Zimbabwe's struggle was Joice Nhongo, who was given the honorary name "Teurai Ropa," or Spill Blood. Born in 1955, she joined the military wing of the liberation struggle in 1973, headed the Women's Detachment of ZANLA, and rose to the rank of general. In 1977, she joined the central command of the army. She married another ZANLA combatant, Solomon Mujuru, during the struggle in 1977.

Margaret Dongo walked with school friends to join the struggle at a ZANLA camp in Mozambique in 1975. When she spoke about her experience in later years she remained critical of the terrible conditions she found and of the continuing gender differences that made life difficult for women. Women did not find equality in the struggle, she stated, commenting that while "women and men received the same military or political training. . . . It is only [when it came to] power sharing, or making decisions, that women could not participate—no, not at all."[39] Dongo continued to fight for women's rights after independence as a member of the government, but she always was aware that despite some new opportunities for women that resulted from the liberation struggle, the vast majority of women did not experience equality.

Joice Nhongo Mujuru eventually became vice president under Robert Mugabe in 2004. She and her husband amassed land and wealth, and Mujuru succeeded for a while because of her loyalty to Mugabe. But Mujuru remained vulnerable, as Mugabe began to prepare his second wife, Grace, to succeed him, and allowed or encouraged her to engage in a power struggle within the ruling party, ZANU-PF. In 2014, as tensions escalated between the two women, he abruptly removed Mujuru from the vice presidency, accusing her of corruption and of plotting to kill him. She then initiated a legal challenge to Robert Mugabe's leadership.

Despite the example of Dongo and Mujuru in their role on the national political scene, most female veterans did not gain power commensurate with their efforts in the liberation struggle. Zimbabwe suffered further in the post-independence years as Robert Mugabe refused to leave the presidency, holding on to the office by suppressing free speech and political opposition.

Suffrage

In most African countries under colonialism both men and women had very limited or no voting rights. As nations gained independence they most often granted universal suffrage. Women thus gained the right to vote as their countries became independent, and there was no history of widespread women's suffrage movements agitating for the vote for women.

In a few countries the issue of women's suffrage intersected with racial restrictions on who could vote. During the early twentieth century in South Africa, white women fought for the right to vote, which was won when the Women's Enfranchisement Bill of 1930 was passed. They were much influenced by the British women's suffrage struggles and maintained contact with the international movement for the right to vote for women through the Women's Enfranchisement Association of the Union, which was established in 1911 when it brought several regional suffrage organizations into a single national association. Racial politics were integral to the South African suffrage movement, as women emphasized their potential as white voters while anti-suffrage men argued that if white women gained the vote, black women would perforce have to be included, thus claiming that no women should be able to vote. Black men in some provinces had been able to vote, but their rights were eroded throughout the twentieth century; black women did not gain the vote at the national level until apartheid was ended in 1992. In Southern Rhodesia white women formed the Women's Franchise Society, and they gained the vote in 1919.

Men in Senegal who lived in certain urban districts had the right to vote from 1848, as they held voting rights equal to men in France. When French women finally gained the vote in 1944, French fears of being outvoted by Senegalese citizens meant that they did not extend the vote to Senegalese women. Senegalese men, however, argued that women should have the vote, basing their claims on racial equality. Thus, when women in Senegal gained the vote in 1945, it was not a result of a campaign for gender equivalence, but on the basis of racial fairness.[40]

In some countries men and women did not gain the vote simultaneously; for example, in Cameroon the male franchise was introduced in 1955, while women did not have the vote until January 1959. In northern Nigeria, where Islamic law dominated, women did not gain voting rights until 1977, seventeen years after the rest of the country adopted universal suffrage at independence.

Ethiopia and Liberia, which were not colonized, granted women's suffrage in 1955 and 1956. Women's suffrage spread more rapidly as countries approached independence and ended colonial rule. Ghana's women gained the suffrage in 1955, and 1956 saw women gain the right to vote in Benin, Cameroon, Central African Republic, Chad, Republic of Congo, Gabon, Guinea, Ivory Coast, Madagascar, Mali, Mauritania, Niger, Sudan, and Upper Volta (now Burkina Faso), in anticipation of the end of colonial rule. Somalia (1958) and Mauritius (1959) were the next two nations, followed by Nigeria, and the Congo (Kinshasa) in 1960; and Burundi, the Gambia, Rwanda, Sierra Leone, and Tanzania in 1961. The rest of the decade brought new additions each year: Uganda (1962), Equatorial Guinea and Kenya (1963), Malawi and Zambia (1964), Botswana (1965), Lesotho (1966), and Swaziland (1968). The final nations to grant women the right to vote were the former Portuguese colonies which gained their independence in the 1970s: Angola, Cape Verde, and Mozambique in 1975, and Guinea-Bissau in 1977. African women only gained the right to vote in white-minority ruled nations when majority rule was won: Zimbabwe (formerly Rhodesia) in 1980, Namibia in 1990, and South Africa in 1992.

Gaining the right to vote was an important first step to women's further involvement in electoral politics, where they continued to face obstacles while making incremental gains throughout the late twentieth century.

Conclusion

Women were crucial members in anticolonial political movements across the continent. Whether they formed women's organizations, such as the market women in Nigeria, joined guerrilla movements such as Mau Mau, or worked in women's auxiliaries during armed struggles in southern Africa, they were motivated by losing access to land for their farming, facing restrictions to their ability to move freely into urban areas, and being marginalized by colonial governments. In several locales it was clear that women's particular experience of suffering under colonialism was a key factor in the rise of nationalism and in the eventual success of the independence movements across the continent.

Notes

1. Diabate, *La marche des femmes sur Grand-Bassam.*
2. Turrittin, "Aoua Kéita and the Nascent Women's Movement in the French Soudan."
3. Kéita, *Femme d'Afrique.*
4. Allman, "The Disappearing of Hannah Kudjoe."
5. Tettegah, quoted in Allman, "The Disappearing of Hannah Kudjoe," 26.
6. Johnson-Odim and Mba, *For Women and the Nation.*
7. Byfield, "Taxation, Women, and the Colonial State."
8. Terretta, "A Miscarriage of Revolution."
9. Shanklin, "*Anlu* Remembered," 172.
10. Ibid.
11. Ibid., 164.
12. Baard and Schreiner, *My Spirit is Not Banned.*
13. Stewart, *Lilian Ngoyi.*
14. Spink, *Black Sash.*
15. Joseph, *Side by Side.*
16. Joseph, *If This Be Treason.*
17. Geiger, *TANU Women.*
18. Quoted in Kanogo, "Kikuyu Women and the Politics of Protest," 83.
19. Ibid., 83–84.
20. Kanogo, "Kikuyu Women and the Politics of Protest," 93–95.
21. Ibid., 85.
22. Presley, *Kikuyu Women*, 74–80 and throughout.
23. Kanogo, "Kikuyu Women and the Politics of Protest," 93–96.
24. Quoted in Elkins, *Imperial Reckoning*, 222.
25. Otieno and Presley, *Mau Mau's Daughter.*
26. Elkins, *Imperial Reckoning*, 226.
27. Santoru, "The Colonial Idea of Women and Direct Intervention."

28. Aubrey, *The Politics of Development Cooperation*.

29. Hinfelaar, *Bemba-Speaking Women of Zambia*, especially chapter 5, pp. 73–100.

30. Ibid., 10.

31. Owen, *Mother Africa, Father Marx*, 43-105.

32. de Sousa, "Magaiça," 45–46; "Black Blood," 58; "If You Want to Know Me," 59–60, in Dickinson, *When Bullets Begin to Flower*.

33. Sheldon, *Pounders of Grain*.

34. Scarnecchia, "Poor Women and Nationalist Politics."

35. Ranchod-Nilsson, "'This, Too, is a Way of Fighting.'"

36. Ibid.

37. Nhongo-Simbanegavi, *For Better or Worse?*, 133.

38. Ibid.70–73.

39. Interview with Margaret Dongo, 121–129 in Zimbabwe Women Writers, *Women of Resilience*, quote on page 129.

40. Beck, "Democratization and the Hidden Public," 153.

7 Work, Family, and Urbanization from the 1970s to the 1990s

IN THE MID- to late-twentieth century, most African women found themselves in a new situation of political independence and a postcolonial array of Western influences. This chapter will examine the history of women and gender and development, assessing the theoretical ideas and practical experiences that informed the programs that affected women. Case studies of rural and urban work describe how women in different circumstances continued their efforts to support their families. They faced unexpected obstacles in the 1980s when the World Bank and the International Monetary Fund introduced structural adjustment programs to many nations as a condition for continued aid funding. It became clear that the initial programs did not consider the social impact of economic restructuring, which had a disproportionately negative effect on women. Discussion of development in the late twentieth century will address legal issues, health, and education. The chapter will also consider women's contributions to art, literature, music, and sport.

Development

Broadly speaking "development" refers to political, social, and economic efforts to improve people's daily lives. Over the years there have been a number of debates about the best approaches to achieve that goal. Programs in the 1950s and 1960s tended to take a welfare approach, which provided women with programs on childcare and housework, tied to the perception that women's primary social role was as mothers. Other practitioners introduced methods that took a different slant, whether through human rights, or by training women in crafts with the goal of enabling them to generate an income. In the 1980s and 1990s, "gender" began to replace "women" in development discussions, recognizing that development involved both men and women, though differently.

Typically, a development project involved money from outside, whether from an international source or from a national government. In some places the immediate alleviation of women's chores was the focus, with money going to such projects as digging wells in order to bring water supplies closer to women's rural homes so they would not have to spend hours walking to a more distant water source. Introducing fuel efficient stoves and mechanical mills for grinding grains had a similar motive. Other development projects might have involved building a meeting hall so that a women's organization would have a center for gathering together and for storing materials. Related efforts included education for women about their legal rights pertaining to land ownership, marriage, and divorce. Inputs to help women with agricultural support, improving chicken or livestock husbandry, or developing fruit orchards or fisheries, were all designed to expand women's usual rural work and to add to their potential for earning an income.[1] All of the varied approaches made some contributions since women were able to see real improvements in certain areas of their lives despite various drawbacks.

Rural Work

Most African women worked in agriculture, with an average rate of 75 percent of working women in that sector (compared to 61 percent of men), primarily cultivating food for their own families' use. Although Africa experienced rapid urbanization in the late twentieth century, most people still lived in rural villages. Women's agricultural work in rural locations followed a similar pattern across the continent. Other rural activities included wage labor on plantations, and fishing.

Women's Work in a Mande Village in Mali

The daily round of labor in a Mande village in Mali in the 1990s began early when a woman, usually one of several wives in a compound, rose and went to the well to collect water in a bucket, which she carried back to the cooking hut in the compound.[2] She repeated this activity several times in order to accumulate enough water in the pots to allow her to cook throughout the day. She then began preparing breakfast, adding sorghum flour to boiling water to produce a thin porridge that was eaten by family members from a common bowl. As that cooked, she prepared more sorghum for the next day. The grain was primarily cultivated by men in distant fields, and it was kept in a storage hut in the compound. She pounded it in her mortar to remove the husks and chaff, and she then pounded the cleaned grain into flour. Mortars were usually made from a tree trunk and pounding grain required intense work with a heavy pestle or staff.

After the men left for the fields, the woman began preparing a midday meal, which was again sorghum, cooked to a thicker stiff consistency for that meal and served with a sauce, usually made from local plants and produce. The afternoon found both men and women pursuing other tasks, such as making baskets and mats, working in vegetable plots that were closer to the homestead, or, for many women, engaging in the arduous task of making charcoal. The evening meal was more sorghum porridge with a vegetable sauce. The dishes were washed by the woman responsible for cooking for that day; the tasks were rotated among the wives who lived in a compound together. Allowing for cultural differences in the food that was prepared and served and in the specific organization of household compounds, this routine was paralleled in rural communities across Africa.

Women were responsible for the domestic chores and men tended distant sorghum fields. Women also cultivated plots of vegetables, and both men and women participated in the harvest, where men gathered the sorghum and women used large baskets balanced on their heads to carry the collected grain to the storage sheds. The Mande community viewed the grain cultivation and harvest as essential for life, not only nutritionally but socially. The process was perceived as being a gender-shared activity, with men growing the grain and women making the sauce, both tasks needed to create a meal that was shared within a household. While the shared ethos of the harvest might imply that it was a practice carried on for generations, in fact it was a more recent innovation that was adopted to allow people, especially young men, more time with their individual garden plots, where they grew vegetables for sale.

Women were assigned specific "women's fields" where they cultivated the crops they would need to make the sauce for everyday meals. The women were typically married women from outside the community, so they did not own land, but they were allocated rights to specific plots by men in authority. During the rainy season the women were very busy, working in the fields for many hours each day. A typical plot would include peanuts, cowpeas, okra, and other produce, most of it destined for the sauces cooked for lunch and dinner each day.

Rural women did not engage in much market trading, though the men in the village did take surplus horticultural crops to urban areas where they sold it to market vendors, who were usually urban women. Older rural women, who had less of the physical strength required to engage in farming, collected firewood or made brooms that were sold to the urban vendors as well. The increasing role of men in vegetable gardening for sale in the market was a recent change, and that was also paralleled in other areas of Africa, where men controlled the most lucrative sources of monetary income, even when it meant that they took over areas where women had previously had more control. In this Mande example, women formerly had more access to certain low-lying plots for their "sauce" gardens, but they had lost out to men who were growing crops for sale.[3]

Fisheries Development in Rural Tanzania

Women and men living in a village on the banks of Lake Victoria in western Tanzania devoted much of their time to fishing and preparing the fish for sale.[4] Typically, families engaged in agriculture, including animal husbandry, as well as fishing. The division of labor was similar to many other African societies, with women responsible for the daily agricultural work of hoeing, weeding, and harvesting while men cleared the land, at times helped with the harvest, and cared for livestock. Some men also owned a boat and fished on a regular basis, while women smoked the fish to preserve it and then sold it in small local markets.

While some men earned cash in caring for animals belonging to others, women found that their money from selling fish was the most reliable source of income. Women earned a meager income from selling fish, and they used that cash to purchase such household items as oil, flour, and soap. Selling was not easy work; women met the fishers who brought their catch to the shore in the early morning, and they bargained in competition with other female vendors. After smoking the fish over holes filled with burning dried cow dung, women had to carry the preserved fish in baskets on their heads, walking five miles to the market. There were no fishers or sellers groups, and all fishing and selling were privately organized within each household.

After independence the Tanzanian government decided to introduce an industrialized fishing project to encourage development and improve livelihoods for people in the village of Sota. Sota was a multi-ethnic community, with people mainly living in ethnically-based neighborhoods. During the 1970s, the development project constructed offices and classrooms and provided houses and motorboats, but the declining economy of the 1980s put an end to the scheme. Nonetheless, some Tanzanian fisheries project officers remained in the village, and by the end of that decade they were involved in a fresh attempt to develop the local industry.

The new idea was to target women and their activities in preserving and selling fish. The development officers wanted to set up a kiln for smoking the fish, which they expected would improve quality control and ease the work load of individual women. The process of using a kiln, however, indicated some of the perhaps unexpected issues that became obstacles. The idea was introduced informally to the community, and the women quickly elected two from their group to attend management committee meetings. The first problem that arose was conflict over where to place the new community kiln. Women were used to smoking fish in their own yards, and they did not want to lose that local control over the process. The reality of ethnic antagonism and clan tension also entered into the discussions about where the new kiln should be located. Women made some bricks for the kiln, expressing hopefulness about the ultimate results. Almost immediately further discord arose, as some men were concerned that they had not been included in the plans. A formal meeting did not resolve the problem since people preferred to remain silent in a public setting about their misgivings and almost no women were present. Within a few weeks the bricks dissolved in the rain and no kiln was built.

The development officers did not give up, however, and the following year they made a fresh start on building a kiln, using borrowed bricks. They recruited the Tanzanian women's organization to assist in bringing local women into the project. With funding from national and international donors, the women's organization established new local associations which held training classes for the village women. Nonetheless, women continued with their individual fish smoking and the kiln was only used as a demonstration when visitors came to the village. The newly formed associations were expected to distribute their income to help fund yet more new groups. The result was that the first groups that had direct donor funding did not get the benefit of their initial income because that money was used to start more groups. Other aspects of the development project, including bringing bicycles to the village, training women to fish at night, and the arrival of male trainers, all added to the unhappiness that many felt with the project.

Some of the tensions were related to neighborhood and kin concerns about favoritism, and issues of personality that intruded into the projects. Other worries were gender based, as men did not want their wives out fishing at night or going to a kiln that was located in an undesirable zone. As one observer noted, "the more assistance and goods offered from outside, the more visible did the aspects of clan, ethnicity and neighbourhood become. . . . [The] organized women's activities [challenged] the traditional pattern" of men holding political power.[5] While some improvements were introduced, the process of bettering women's lives was filled with obstacles. Local perceptions of women's work did shift in reaction to the increased role of the women's organization and the material inputs related to the kilns. But the process of development was not as simple as it might appear to agents from outside a village.

Thus, even development projects that appeared to be specifically designed for a particular locale often foundered. Conflict within a village, differences between local people and urban project managers, gendered expectations that emphasized the different perspectives of men and women, and the impact of international funding all contributed both to certain kinds of progress and simultaneously introduced serious hindrances.

Debate about how to best distribute development funding has led to an increased call to simply give money directly to the poor, and let them decide how to spend or invest the cash infusion.[6] Such a program would eliminate the huge overhead of international staff, the costs of their travel, and the expense of conducting extensive follow-up surveys to ensure that the money was being properly used. When international donors provide money, they require that the recipients be accountable. If donors could let go of that expectation, the costs would decrease while people in poverty would gain control over their own lives.

Urbanization

Women continued to play a central role in the development of African cities, building on the conditions discussed in chapter 4. In West Africa there was a higher level of urban residence historically, and as seen in prior chapters of this book, women were noted as active participants in the markets and other activities. In eastern and southern Africa, cities more often emerged in connection with colonial settlements, and Africans moved into urban areas in response to new work opportunities as well as to escape deteriorating rural conditions. Although conventional studies have emphasized the male-dominant character of urbanization, as men found employment and women remained in rural areas engaged in agriculture, it was also true that many women moved to the cities. And although women did migrate with male family members, there were also women who traveled alone or with female kin when they sought a new and different life.

In the urban areas, some women were able to find factory employment while others entered new occupations as professionals such as teachers or nurses, or they worked in the informal sector, including market vending. Other women continued rural activities such as urban farming and beer brewing as a way to support themselves and their families; such work indicated the permeable boundaries between urban and rural life. Family life was under less scrutiny in the more impersonal conditions of urban living, and although most women still married and raised their children, some women remained single or lived in female-headed households, and many women were more likely to use contraceptives and live in a monogamous relationship than rural women. Urban residence also brought women into contact with organizations that were not available in rural locations, including neighborhood groups, religious communities, work-related associations, and political alliances.

In southern and eastern Africa, many women began working as market vendors in the 1980s and 1990s as they faced increasing economic constraints that resulted from structural adjustment. By the late 1990s in Maputo, Mozambique, it was estimated that between 55 and 75 percent of women were involved in market trading, though many of them could not afford to rent space in the formal cement markets and simply set up a mat or spread out a cloth on a curb where they displayed the items for sale.[7] Market women have been the focus of government criticism in many areas, resulting from perceptions of their wealth and political influence as well as from fears that their operations were a source of disease. At times officials razed markets in an attempt to control the female vendors.

Urban Work

The skewed nature of women's limited access to salaried jobs continued into the post-independence era. Across the continent, only 5 percent of working women were found in industry compared to 15 percent of men, and 20 percent in services (23 percent of men). Many women earned an income through informal sector activities, especially selling goods in markets, work that typically was not counted in formal statistics. It was also common for people with a waged job to perform informal sector work in addition to their formal position, as a supplement to chronically low wages.

The *Women's Indicators and Statistics Database* of the United Nations presented a breakdown of African women's share within the following professional job categories in 1990: Liberal and technical professions, 36 percent female; management and administrative personnel, 15 percent; office clerks and related functions, 37 percent; sales people, 52 percent; and production, transportation, domestic service, unskilled workers and operators, 20 percent.[8]

Domestic service included women working as cleaners, cooks, and doing home-based childcare. Although domestic service was considered primarily women's work in much of the world, in Africa far more men than women found employment in that sector. South Africa was the exception, though even there paid household work was more often done by men until the early twentieth century. In general across the continent, and especially in eastern and southern Africa, women were not expected to leave their agricultural responsibilities to work for wages, so waged work more often went to men. It was difficult to bring improvements to working conditions for domestic servants as they were employed as individuals within isolated households, making them particularly subject to maltreatment and poverty-level wages. In some countries domestic workers began to organize into trade unions to improve their situation, notably in the South African Domestic Workers Association and the Namibia Domestic and Allied Workers' Union.

As the modern clothing and textile industry developed in Africa, women rarely found employment in the new factories. In Mozambique the garment factories had an almost entirely male labor force until new government policies promoted hiring women in the 1980s.[9] In Lesotho, in contrast, the rapid growth of a new textile industry in the 1980s relied on women workers as many men were migrant mine workers in neighboring South Africa. In 1990, the labor force in Lesotho's clothing and textile factories was 92 percent female.[10] South Africa's own textile industry began to develop in the 1920s and 1930s with a primarily white labor force. Only in later decades, as the industry grew to be the largest on the continent, did black women find employment there as well. Nigeria, which was second in Africa in the size of its textile industry, had a minority of women in the textile labor force. In many regions the textile industry did have an impact on cloth production because cheaper mass-produced cloth replaced the labor-intensive cloth that had previously been woven by hand in African communities. Women have rarely owned businesses that produced textiles, though there were women in Nairobi, Kenya, and elsewhere who owned small garment factories.

Structural Adjustment Programs

In the 1980s the World Bank and the International Monetary Fund introduced a series of economic reforms that poor nations had to adopt in order to have access to loans. The economic restructuring programs came to be collectively called "structural adjustment." With an underlying perspective that free markets were better for people than more government involvement, structural adjustment was a mandatory policy that emphasized privatizing government services such as health clinics and education programs. The main goal was to encourage economic growth and efficiency. For the World Bank leaders, that meant dismantling government services while liberalizing the markets through reducing price controls, subsidies, and other mechanisms that helped governments control their economies. But the very nature of these goals meant that the social impact was disregarded or discounted, as economic and social sectors were viewed as disconnected rather than intertwined.

While many economists looked at macroeconomic guidelines and felt the reforms were successful in reinvigorating agriculture and industry, other researchers found that the economic changes ignored the social impact, particularly on women. That impact was often negative, as salaries stagnated and prices for agricultural goods fell. People lost access to important services, and farmers' and workers' livelihoods were disrupted by the sudden shift in economic policy. Women suffered from increased levels of poverty as they found themselves working longer hours but earning less money; they often sought additional work when their first occupation no longer supported their families. With lower incomes and fewer state services to turn to, girls and women faced malnutrition and other health problems including anemia and declining fertility. Evidence also pointed to such family problems as increased domestic violence and more men abandoning their families, leaving women as the heads of their impoverished households.[11] Two specific stories about the impact of structural adjustment on urban and rural women will suggest the wide ramifications of the new economic policies. Cashew factories in Mozambique and agriculture in Nigeria both suffered under the new mandates from the World Bank.

Cashew Factories in Mozambique

The cashew industry in Mozambique had hired women beginning in the 1950s.[12] During the 1970s and 1980s as the business expanded, many thousands of women found employment mainly in the shelling and sorting sheds, where the cashew nuts were prepared for packaging. While the Maputo factory was still largely female (80 percent of twenty-five hundred workers at Caju de Chamanculo), factories in other parts of the country were mainly or entirely male, including factories at Angoche and Mozambique Island.

By December 1993, workers at the cashew factories in Inhambane, Angoche, and Manjacaze were owed several months of back wages. Workers at the plant in Xai-Xai in Gaza province went on strike over non-payment of wages. The difficulty was that cashews had not been arriving at the factories to be processed.

With no cashews being produced for the market, the factories were unable to pay the workers. The dismissal of those workers was representative of the new economic policies. Previously, the Frelimo government had attempted to keep workers on the payroll even when there was no work, but structural adjustment programs called for reducing the work force in that situation. Cashew workers had been guaranteed a lifetime retirement pension of thirteen thousand meticais a month (approximately $13.00), and they faced a rapidly changing financial reality that meant their pension would buy less than ten loaves of bread a month; bread was a staple food item for urban residents.

An instructive case study of the impact of World Bank policies on women can be seen decisions in the late 1990s about cashew exports. Cashews had long been a major export and foreign exchange earner for Mozambique, with a high of two hundred sixty-five thousand US tons exported in the early 1970s. The combined impact of an internal war, disrupted production, and aging trees meant that the level had plummeted to only fifty-five thousand tons by the early 1990s, when the World Bank set a goal of exporting one hundred ten thousand tons. Following IMF structural adjustment guidelines, the cashew industry was privatized in 1994–1995, along with many of the other industries that had been in the public sector or that had been nationalized after independence in 1975. Then in 1995, the World Bank country director in Mozambique, Phyllis Pomerantz, decided that it was more efficient to remove trade protection by reducing the surtax on exports of raw cashews. The result was that it became more profitable for cashew traders to export raw nuts to India, rather than having them processed domestically. In the early 1990s, the cashew processing factories employed over ten thousand women, representing an important source of income for many families in Maputo and other areas in Mozambique. When these tax and export changes resulted in unprocessed nuts being exported, the factories could not remain open and those women, many the sole income-earners in their families, were out of work.

The argument was based in part on a flawed study that claimed that Mozambican peasants, who grew the cashews, would benefit if raw rather than processed nuts were exported. In fact the beneficiaries were the traders, and the peasants did not gain appreciably, if at all. In 1995, representatives of the Mozambican cashew industry were already arguing that changes in tariff policy would amount to "suicide" because the Mozambican factories simply did not have the productive infrastructure that would allow them to compete with the Indian industry. An outside review of the policy in 1997 found that it was a disastrous approach. But the government could not halt the export of raw nuts without IMF approval for fear of being considered "off-track" by the IMF, which would have resulted in development funds being frozen. By the time a review of the policy determined that imposing trade liberalization before domestic industry was ready to compete

Fig. 7.1 Women shelling cashews in Maputo, Mozambique, 1993. Photograph courtesy of Jeanne Marie Penvenne.

was not an economically sound approach to cashew production and exports, ten factories had closed their doors, with more than five thousand women losing their jobs. Five factories remained active for a time, but by February 2000, the leader of the cashew workers' union reported that only two of sixteen sizable processing factories continued to produce. That meant that a further twenty-five hundred workers were unemployed, while five thousand still had contracts but in reality were not working in the cashew factories. While a project to plant over one million new trees a year in order to replenish the available cashew harvest was welcomed, it did not address the problem of factory processing.

In February 1999, Frelimo representatives in parliament submitted a bill that would have banned the export of raw cashew nuts for ten years, to give the local industry a chance to recover. The minister of industry commented that the policy of tariff liberalization that was imposed by the World Bank was opposed by the Mozambican government, which was forced to acquiesce because other loans that the country needed were conditional on Mozambican agreement with World Bank policy. Mozambicans protested vigorously, and they convinced James Wolfensohn, president of the World Bank, to reconsider the policy, but it had already brought greater hardship to the lives of women who worked in the cashew factories. The cashew export case exemplifies the dissension within the World Bank itself, where Wolfensohn pushed for a policy of decentralization in policy-making and more input from the countries themselves, while others in the Bank continued to advocate a top-down approach to fiscal decision-making. In Mozambique those policies confirmed the shift from a socialist economy that promoted citizens' participation in such decisions to an economy dominated by a handful of international "experts." At that time there was little debate of the devastating impact on women in the Third World as a result of the authoritarian economic policy-making process of the World Bank and the IMF.

Agriculture in Nigeria

Women across rural Nigeria held the primary responsibility for agricultural production, performing about 70 percent of all farm work. Food production, including such tasks as planting, weeding, and harvesting, as well as food processing and transportation, was done by 80 percent of women, while around 20 percent were involved in marketing food. Because many women farmed and also marketed their produce, those numbers did not refer to discrete groups of women or work. Yet women routinely faced obstacles to their efforts to improve their lives. Such barriers included their responsibility for child care, their burden of housework including the time-consuming tasks of collecting water and firewood for cooking, and the overarching social attitudes that formed the unequal division of labor and discriminatory ideas about women's place in society.[13]

As an example of women's specific labor, women in Ogun State typically cleared farmland, and planted yams, cassava, plantains, and maize. About half of their maize and cassava harvest was eaten in their household along with other vegetables and fruit, with the surplus sold in local markets. Generally women did not own their farms, but relied on access to land through their husbands. They used hoes and large machete-like blades for the labor-intensive work in their fields, and they had limited access to hired labor. When food was ready to be harvested, they performed that labor and then carried the harvested produce home in loaded baskets on their heads. Once home they began the sometimes lengthy process of making their crops edible.

Beginning during the colonial era, projects designed to advance Nigerian life focused on men and often women's contributions to agricultural work were not recognized, leading to the protests discussed in earlier chapters. Those attitudes persisted into the post-independence years, with male-dominated export crops receiving subsidies and other supports, while women's work was usually ignored despite its essential nature. In the 1960s and 1970s domestic food production began to fall, and Nigeria relied more and more on imported food to feed its population. There was no central program, but only piecemeal projects that favored food imports over local production. Small farmers, who were mainly women, were left out of national economic planning and did not have adequate access to credit and other inputs. They were rarely even the subject of studies and research that might have informed the economic planners.

When Nigeria's oil industry entered a crisis period, the rest of the economy was poorly placed to succeed. Political corruption and poor management played a role as well. By the early 1980s, the country was vulnerable to the demands of the World Bank to stabilize the economy by imposing structural adjustment policies. Nigeria was required to comply with World Bank reform policies in order to have access to loans and to control of their debt. The result of the efforts to reduce oil subsidies, extend new credit lines, privatize public corporations, and deregulate interest rates was a series of negative impacts on social programs that women had counted on.

Cutbacks affected the supply of such necessities as water, electricity, health care, and education. People who were already poor lost access to services that might have helped them improve their own and their families' lives. Following structural adjustment requirements, the government cut back on subsidies for agricultural supplies including fertilizer, pesticides, and seeds. Subsidies to other sectors such as transportation and credit were also reduced, adding to the negative results in rural areas. Other policies included devaluing Nigeria's currency and eliminating certain food imports, bringing greater hardships to small farmers.

The structural adjustment program in Nigeria involved a series of Agricultural Development Projects, which were designed to increase cash crop yields by making improved seeds, fertilizer, and other supports available. In Nigeria, however, such supports went to wealthier farmers and did not reach the poorest small farmers, who were mainly women. The aim of such programs, though not articulated as such, was to encourage agrarian capitalism by promoting farmers who were already better off. Those farmers were positioned as a buffer between the truly large-scale cash crop farmers and the small-scale female farmers who primarily were growing food for their own families. Even training programs that women could have benefited from were run by male extension workers who saw male farmers as their target clientele.

A 1990s study of the impact of Agricultural Development Projects on female farmers in Bendel and Ogun states found that they were not benefitting and at times were suffering. When asked about access to credit from banks, 4.4 percent of the women replied that they had gotten bank credit, while 30 percent of men in the study had received credit from a bank. Women had approached banks in search of a loan, but they were rejected because they lacked collateral. Bank agents stated that helping women apply for a loan was not part of their mandate. Gender-based differences were also seen in access to farming inputs such as fertilizer and seeds, which 24 percent of women said were readily available compared to 80 percent of men; and extension training, with 14.4 percent of women and 70 percent of men being visited by an agent on a weekly basis.

The adverse impact of the new economic policies was evident. As food became more expensive and scarce, 85 percent of those surveyed said they had reduced their daily consumption from three meals a day to two and had cut back on eating protein sources such as fish, beef, and chicken. As a consequence, malnutrition and disease increased, but cases of kwashiorkor and anemia were not treated because health centers and hospitals were underfunded and understaffed. As this study concluded, "With the SAP's [structural adjustment program's] emphasis on the production of cash and non-food crops for export . . . women are relegated to producing food crops mainly for subsistence. . . . The overall result is a fall in women's quality of life."[14]

Similar results were seen across the entire continent, in rural and urban areas. Women's needs were not accounted for in the large-scale economic policy shifts, and they suffered more because the planners were blind to the potential impacts on real people. Ideas about financial markets and national debt led to policies that looked only at economic spreadsheets and ignored peoples' daily lives. Whether a woman had a scarce factory job or continued with her customary rural farm work, structural adjustment brought her hardship, hunger, and ill health, rather than improved livelihoods and a better life.

Education

Girls were more likely than boys to be kept home from formal schooling in many parts of Africa. They were needed to help with household chores, and families were much less comfortable sending daughters rather than sons to spend their days in that unfamiliar environment. Girls were subject to sexual harassment, and the problem of unwanted teenage pregnancies also forced many girls to cut their education short. Nonetheless, the number of girls attending school increased over time. Immediately after independence most new governments made improving access to school a high priority, and rates of attendance rose so that by 1970 continent-wide statistics indicated that 39 percent of primary students were girls; that percentage continued to rise to 45 percent in 1990. The number of girls in higher levels of education also rose, but remained a fraction of boys' enrollment. Secondary school rates for girls rose from 29 percent of all students in 1970 to 40 percent in 1990; tertiary enrollment rose from 16 percent female in 1970 to 31 percent in 1990.[15] Expanding and improving girls' educational opportunities remained a key issue for Africa.

In many African countries, girls had less access to western education, and a legacy of very low literacy rates persisted among women. In Mozambique fewer than 10 percent of women were literate in Portuguese, the official language; in

Fig. 7.2 Girls lined up for school, Bo, Sierra Leone, 1973. Photograph courtesy of Rebecca Busselle.

Mali, only 10 percent of women were literate in French. But such extremely low rates are not found for the entire continent, as statistics suggest that overall women's literacy rates continue to rise, from 40 percent in 1995 to 50 percent in 2000.

Women's Studies and Feminism

Beginning in the 1970s many African universities established women's studies programs and centers, a process which accelerated following the 1985 Nairobi Women's Meeting of the United Nations Decade for Women (see chapter 8 for more about the UN Decade for Women). By 2004 there were over thirty such centers in Africa, with four formal departments: the Department of Women and Gender Studies at Makerere University, Uganda, established in 1991; the Department of Women's Studies at Cameroon's University of Buea; the Gender Studies Department at the University of Zambia; and the African Gender Institute (AGI) at the University of Cape Town (UCT) in South Africa.

The African Gender Institute was established initially in 1993 in reaction to studies about the obstacles that faced women in universities. As their website states, "The newly formed AGI was given the mandate to provide a safe space where women in the academy could develop their intellectual and leadership

Table 7.1 Percentage of women over age 25 who were literate, 1990s, selected African countries

Benin	12	Kenya	46	Senegal	12
Botswana	60	Malawi	25	Seychelles	78
Burundi	18	Mali	9	Sudan	26
Cameroon	32	Mauritania	17	Swaziland	54
Cape Verde	37	Mauritius	69	Uganda	33
Central African Republic	13	Namibia	65	Zambia	47
Côte d'Ivoire	15	Niger	3	Zimbabwe	67
Djibouti	13	São Tomé e Príncipe	46		

Source: Kathleen Sheldon, *Historical Dictionary of Women in Sub-Saharan Africa.*

capacities; where African women writers, researchers, policy-makers and practitioners would be given new opportunities; where Africa-centric applied knowledges of gender, transformation, and democratic practice could be developed and propagated."[16] By 1999 the AGI became a formal unit within UCT and was granted a professorial chair in Gender Studies, eventually developing into a regular department committed to supporting projects devoted to women's issues, including publishing the online journal *Feminist Africa*.

Another important South African journal, *Agenda: A Journal about Women and Gender*, was started in 1987 by women at what was then called the University of Natal; eventually it moved beyond the university and was renamed as *Agenda: Empowering Women for Gender Equality*. A number of academic conferences were held and important books and journals were published on the continent. In 2002 the triennial "International Interdisciplinary Congress on Women" was held in Kampala. Some of the other important university centers included the Institute of Development Studies Women Studies Group at the University of Dar es Salaam, which was founded in 1980; the Women's Research Collective at the National University of Lesotho; and the Women's Research and Documentation Center (WORDOC) at the University of Ibadan, Nigeria. There were also a number of independent centers not based at universities, including the African Training and Research Center for Women, Women and Law in Southern Africa, and the Zimbabwe Women's Resource Center and Network.

Women scholars involved in women's studies centers often identified themselves as feminists. But the idea of feminism has been the subject of debate, both among African scholars and more widely. Feminism has been broadly defined as support for the complete equality of women with men, and has included action to bring about changes in laws and society that will permit such equality. Many feminists around the world have identified themselves in more specific terms, such as socialist feminist or ecological feminist; other variations include liberal feminist, radical feminist, and Marxist feminist. The overall concept of feminism has been critiqued for being western in its basis and biases.

African women in the 1990s embraced a feminism that developed out of their anticolonial struggles combined with an intrinsic appreciation of local customs and history. This approach was necessarily different from the elaboration of Western feminism, which was a reaction to the growth of industrial capitalism and individual rights.[17] African women have sometimes adopted new terms, such as *womanism* or *feminitude* to reflect their concern that Western-style feminism was too antagonistic to men and in other ways did not reflect African realities. Obioma Nnaemeka coined the term *nego-feminism* to emphasize the way that African feminists negotiate, collaborate, and compromise in their political work that aims to support women's needs.[18] African feminists also contributed to expanding the general definition of feminism to include broader struggles to end racism and imperialism.

Concerns about defining feminism have also addressed the issue of historical practices that would be considered feminist from a modern perspective, although the women of earlier eras might not have applied the term to their own beliefs and actions. It was common to refer to *feminisms* in the plural in order to acknowledge the differing approaches both in theory and in practice. It became a cliché to acknowledge that Western feminists listed equal pay and abortion rights among their top goals, while African feminists gave priority to improving educational opportunities and insuring clean accessible water as ways to improve women's lives. There was a continuing tension between the common goal of equality for women and the recognition of very real differences between women in different societies. Most feminists understood that such variations would necessarily draw on dissimilar theoretical approaches and practical activities, and recognized that men and patriarchy are not the sole source of women's oppression. Women organized as feminists in nongovernmental organizations that focused on research, such as the Association of African Women in Research and Development (AAWORD), the Feminist Studies Centre in Zimbabwe, the Tanzania Gender Networking Programme, and Women in Nigeria (WIN).

Land and Property

Conventional wisdom claimed that African women had little or no legal right to the land that they cultivated as the primary agricultural producers. While often true, that interpretation did not take into account the ways in which women were able to gain control over their land, although it was still common for women to lose access to land. Historically, in many areas land was not considered to be private property, but it was under the control of a clan or other group. Often male chiefs organized access to land for cultivation; in areas where women married into patrilineal systems, they farmed land that ostensibly "belonged" to their husbands, and they could lose that land if they were widowed or divorced.

Sometimes women were able to remain on their land if they had developed other connections with people in the village. In matrilineal areas the female kin group more often controlled access while the husbands moved in and women in those societies found it easier to retain control over their land.

When Western powers took over during the colonial era, ideas and practices about land being owned by an individual person became more prevalent, and in the colonial system it was usually a man whose name was set down in legal documents. Yet, even with the changes that were introduced, some women were able to maintain control and sometimes prove ownership of land through legal and social mechanisms.

A Patrilineal Society in Uganda

A study in rural Kabale district in Uganda found that women called on local concepts of fairness to insist that their agricultural labor brought them rights in the land they cultivated.[19] Historically, land was closely connected to marriage and considered to be owned communally. In the twentieth century, as the colonial government gained more power, land came to be associated with individual ownership, though most land in Kabale continued to be allocated in line with traditional practices. Women legally had access to land through marriage, and they also argued in courts of law for greater control by using the idea of social responsibility. Because of the centrality of their agricultural work to family and community survival, they claimed they should have greater access and control over land.

When a man who controlled land sought to sell off a parcel to raise money or for other reasons, he was supposed to allow household members the right of first refusal. Women rarely were able to intervene in order to retain access to land they were cultivating. Women whose husbands sold or transferred land without their permission responded by bringing those cases into court. As they began to take cases to local courts, however, they encountered various obstacles. Often men would characterize women's claims as "female misbehavior," situating the issue as a dispute between individuals rather than a systemic legal problem. Confronted with judges who sought to maintain social order, it was difficult to argue for justice. At the same time, women in Kabale experienced the courts as a place where they were not subordinate, but were able to argue their case before a magistrate on an equal footing to men in their family or clan.

Women's cases were bolstered by the obvious arduous nature of women's agricultural work. Most families used a dozen or more plots, sometimes widely separated and located in a steep terrain of mountains and valleys. They cultivated yams, sorghum, millet, maize, and other labor intensive crops. The history of women having some control was also important; women could pass access to plots of land to their own sons as well as to their daughters when there were no male offspring. Though descent was patrilineal, the connection of land to houses controlled by women was a custom that cut across male kin relations. And the understanding that there were "male" and "female" plots gave women additional claims to agricultural land. Those customary land practices gave women a de facto right to property ownership. However, the introduction of the colonial legal system and a cash crop economy based on coffee and tobacco undercut the strength of the earlier practices. In the 1950s and 1960s, cash cropping came to include vegetables and beans for sale in the growing urban centers, crops which were primarily cultivated by women and sold by men. Marriage had been cooperative, but many saw an exploitative relationship take precedence as men began to insist on their wives working in cash crop fields without proper compensation.

Women observed that men used the claim of their family responsibilities to maintain control of land access. They began to stake their own claims in the government courts, based on their agricultural labor and consequent contributions to family welfare. There were shifts in the courts' analysis of land throughout the twentieth century, but by the 1970s, courts more often considered the land that women received upon marriage to be a gift that the husband could not later reclaim or sell. As one magistrate claimed, "The land becomes hers and can only be inherited by her direct offspring."[20] Women's claims for keeping that land were based on the concept that their labor was how they fulfilled their social responsibility to the family, and as a result they should have access to land ownership. The legal view of women's land rights in Uganda continued to shift in the late twentieth century, but the evidence of a few court cases suggested how women have been able to gain rights despite patrilineal practices and customary assumptions about men having primary rights to land.

A Matrilineal Society in Mozambique

In Mozambique, all land was considered to belong to the state, and laws introduced in the 1990s were designed to protect the land rights of those peasants and women who could demonstrate a history of cultivating a plot of land even in the absence of proper documentation. A study in northern Mozambique found that land disputes rarely were taken to official courts, but they were most often resolved within the family or clan and that state laws had very little impact on how land was allocated.[21] Interviews with Makua women in rural and urban locations in Nampula province found that women had access to land for cultivation, and that the matrilineal descent system was one factor in women's ability to claim such rights. Historically, women in leadership positions within the community had been part of the discussions about land distribution, and in the late twentieth century their influence continued to affect women's land rights.

Although no one person could inherit land or buy or sell tracts, particular plots were recognized as being controlled by specific families and individuals. Among those interviewed, most had access to their land as a result of matrilineal kinship ties, and land use was distributed through the maternal side of the family. Many women enjoyed some independence from their husbands regarding the use of land belonging to their matrilineal kin. Women were also able to gain access to land through actively clearing new plots, a possibility because Nampula was sparsely settled and unclaimed land was still available. The most contentious time for women came with divorce, when men often claimed control over land at the expense of their wives, or with widowhood, especially for women who had married into the community and did not have the protection of local maternal kin.

Women's access to and use of land in northern Mozambique was seen to be collaborative, with the assumption that men and women would jointly discuss and determine how to use and distribute land for agriculture. Women were expected to provide crops to feed the family, while men were more likely to cultivate crops for sale in the market. But women were able to control their income and in most households they were in charge of the family economy, only coordinating with their husbands for major purchases. Men had greater access to being employed in waged labor as well as to growing and selling cash crops.

In modern urban communities, women have sometimes had problems because they have not had title to property. Urban housing was marked by substandard dwellings often on the periphery of burgeoning urban centers. Residents used whatever materials they could find to construct homes of cardboard and discarded wood. Most such neighborhoods lacked access to electricity and potable water. In some cities, only waged workers were allowed access to housing, so that men had an advantage beginning in the colonial era, and women had to prove either employment or marriage to get housing. Women found themselves in vulnerable conditions as renters, and they often had a history of frequent moves from lodging to lodging. They were usually not able to get credit that would help them improve their housing situation as a result of their lack of education and regular employment.[22]

Despite a perception that African women did not own their land, there were many counterexamples of women's ingenuity in gaining and retaining access. While stories emerged of husbands and other men taking control of land where their wives had labored, those experiences were not necessarily true across the continent. Changes in where women lived, in their knowledge of customary rules and modern legal rights, and shifts in family organization all contributed to women having the ability to control their own land and property.

Health

Health issues cover many topics, including physical and mental disease, disability, fertility and infertility, sexuality, nutrition, and importantly since the 1980s, HIV/AIDS. Women have a crucial role in all of these sectors as caretakers, educators, mothers, and as people who suffer from ill health. Women's work in the household puts them at the center of prevention because they usually are responsible for maintaining cleanliness and providing good food and fresh water. As in other world areas, women frequently train as nurses, a career which was considered one of the few appropriate jobs for women for many years.

Sexuality and Fertility

Sexuality is a central aspect of everyday life, and inextricably connected to health, marriage, fertility, infertility, and birth control, as well as to more contentious issues such as the spread of HIV/AIDS, the continuing practices of initiation rites, female genital cutting, and prostitution. Sexuality in African societies has been little studied in comparison to the research done in the West, though it has become more of a focus as a result of the devastation of HIV/AIDS since the 1980s. It is not possible to generalize for the whole continent, but it appears that in the past many African societies acknowledged female sexuality as a positive experience. In some communities sexual play was permitted between adolescents as long as it did not involve intercourse. For instance, among the Xhosa in South Africa, the practice of *ukumetsha* allowed a young couple who were promised in marriage to enjoy unconsummated intimacy, which relied on the girl keeping her leather apron-like garment between her legs. Girls learned about adult sexual behavior during rites of passage.

Marriage and motherhood were the common experience for the majority of women. Africa had one of the world's highest fertility rates, measured at 5.6 births per woman at the end of the twentieth century. Overall, the rate had fallen, though not as rapidly as in other world areas, from 6.6 children per woman in 1950 to 5.6 for sub-Saharan Africa in 2002, and then to 5.1 by 2010. The fertility rate was declining more rapidly in urban areas, with a 2002 rate of 4.8 children per woman in cities, compared with 6.6 in rural areas. The timing of the transition, based on longitudinal studies, appeared to have begun in the 1960s and 1970s in urban areas, followed by a decline a decade later in rural areas. Fertility rates also declined as women became more educated. Population growth was also marked by a decline in death rates, and experts considered that population stability would be achieved with a birth rate of 2.7.[23]

The central reason for the high rate was the hope for large families. There were several factors that led to African families to desire many children. One cause derived from the long-standing situation of an abundance of land and the need for labor to work the land. Many children symbolized wealth, as those children and their eventual spouses were directly involved in household labor, especially in rural communities. Families also had many children as insurance against the loss of family members to illness and death. As was discussed in chapter 1 and elsewhere, motherhood and fatherhood were the essential status that conferred adulthood. Those with few or no children were often pitied or viewed as less adult, and in some areas infertility was grounds for divorce.

With such deep-seated cultural expectations, African women have continued to express their longing to have many children. Though women in most of the world stated a goal of 2.5 to 4.5 children, African women's responses ranged as high as 8.5 children in Chad and Niger; at the lower end, Kenyan women communicated a goal of 4.1 children. The only exception to the stated desire for many children was South Africa where 3.3 children were seen as a model family size. Kenya, which once had one of the highest birth rates, embarked on an education campaign in the 1990s with a resultant drop in the fertility rate nationwide from 6.7 children per family in 1989 to 4.7 in 1998.[24] The education program emphasized the possibility of a better quality of life for the whole family when the number of children was restricted or reduced. In addition, women with higher levels of formal education had fewer children, so the expansion of education for girls was a major factor that resulted in smaller families.

Senegalese women continued to bear many children despite decades of family planning programs. In the early 1990s the fertility rate was 6.0, and it fell only to 5.3 by 2005.[25] The rate for urban women was 4.1, while rural women's was 6.4. Clearly there were other factors involved than simply access to birth control. Discussions with women found that the primary reason was a cultural expectation that all Senegalese women would marry and have children. While women did try to space their children's births, they generally followed a trajectory of marriage, birth of a first child within a year, and subsequent births every two years or so. The women expressed anxiety about contraception, from the belief that they would not take the pills properly, to concerns about their future ability to become pregnant following a period of taking the pill or getting a contraceptive shot (most commonly known by the brand name Depo-Provera). They regularly mentioned their own or a friend's negative experience with birth control as a reason for avoiding it. Because they also wanted to have many children, they were ready to believe the stories of difficulties that they heard from others.

Women also worried that if they did not have children frequently enough their husbands would seek a second wife; thus regular childbirth was an important factor in a happy marriage. The high value of wedding and birth celebrations meant that there was constant attention paid to a woman's fertility by her community. For many, the most important festivities were held for the naming ceremony of a first child, which ideally would be held early in a marriage. The party was an opportunity for the mother to exhibit her success at motherhood and to display her economic well-being through wearing a succession of new outfits and jewelry. The combination social expectations and cultural behaviors meant that few women actually used birth control of any kind other than relying on breast-feeding, withdrawal, and calculations about their menstrual cycles and

Fig. 7.3 Women and children attending a health clinic in Bagega, Zamfara state, northern Nigeria, 2013. Photograph by Akintunde Akinleye/Reuters.

periods of infertility. The advantage of these less reliable methods for Senegalese women was that they were easily reversed and did not have a lasting impact on a woman's ability to become pregnant. Similar findings applied to women in other African societies, as women continued to desire large families and distrusted modern birth control methods that might have long-term negative effects on their fertility. Social assumptions about adult women's primary role being a responsible mother meant that there was little incentive for most women to curtail their reproductive lives.

In many communities across the African continent, fertility problems were considered to be solely the responsibility of the woman, whether she never became pregnant or if she suffered repeated miscarriages or the early deaths of small children. Help in many cases was sought from religious leaders and local healers, who commonly suggested social reasons such as neighbors or kin casting a curse or blocking good outcomes. Treatment varied widely, but might include prayer, fasting, making sacrifices to deities, and other customary practices. Even into the late twentieth century many people avoided seeking help from modern medical practitioners due to high cost or low levels of trust.

In studies among the Hadendowa in eastern Sudan, women recognized a series of spirits who affected their lives including their ability to have children. Such spirits were experienced by women with both Muslim and Christian affiliations. The Hadendowa were a rural pastoral community, who increasingly settled into urban centers as the men found work on an oil pipeline project. They had long considered various spirits to be the cause of issues related to reproduction; in town, some of those anxieties and spirits were associated with the many foreigners living in close proximity.

Red spirits were particularly associated with colonialism and were known to "exhaust their hosts with their sudden visits and demands and cause great harm to women's and men's fertility at any point of their life cycle."[26] If a woman experienced infertility, it was usually assumed that a malevolent spirit was to blame, and she would visit her religious leader for advice. In a society that was profoundly patrilineal, women were marginalized if they failed to have children or only had daughters. The birth of a son was cause for public celebration and the mother was venerated. In the Hadendowa community, the women honored their ancestor Hadat, who gave birth to seven sons. Those sons grew to be the founders of seven Hadendowa lineages, while Hadat's seven daughters married outside the community and are not remembered. Women were valued for their fertility, and especially for giving birth to male heirs; any disruption of that process was cause for a spiritual and social crisis.[27] They brought their communally held ideas about fertility, disease, and solutions to health and reproductive problems from their homogenous rural village to the more ethnically complex urban community.

Contraceptive Struggles in Zimbabwe

Control over fertility was a key site of power conflicts in societies everywhere. Access to contraceptives and decisions about family planning were "conduits for that power."[28] In Zimbabwe in the 1970s, in the midst of their liberation war while a white minority controlled the government and the country was still called Rhodesia, people in rural communities engaged in a struggle over reproduction. The social and political consequences were far-reaching.

The white government introduced family planning as a result of their concerns with overpopulation in the African settlements. As in other areas of the continent where European settlers took African land, Africans were forced to live in restricted areas, a situation that exacerbated the perception that African women and men were choosing to have too many children. While the white government expressed concern about overcrowding on the land, there were also hidden fears about the shifting ratio of black and white residents. In 1960, the birth rate was 48.18 live births per year per 1,000 people. It began to decrease very gradually throughout the 1960s and 1970s, so that the 1980 rate was 46.69.[29] The rate for Africans was much higher than that of whites, contributing to an ever-increasing gap between the numbers of whites and blacks; in 1969, for example, there were 215,000 Africans born, and only 4,004 white babies.[30] The decreasing percentage of whites in the population was not only due to high African birth rates, but also reflected the increasing emigration of whites who left rather than continue to live in a conflict-ridden nation.

The new technologies of birth control pills and birth control injections (Depo-Provera) were introduced into Shona communities which held specific ideas about bodies and about women's self-determination. In contrast to the Western concepts of bodies having individual physical or biological limits, Shona beliefs centered on the interconnection of people in a society. Women did practice family planning, in particular child spacing, using local plants and other methods. They also relied on female elders to advise them when to resume sexual relations following childbirth, and it was common for families to observe a lengthy period of abstinence. Those methods were considered shared social knowledge, based on cooperation between older and younger people and between men and women. Young women were the necessary biological factor for children to be born, but men and older women, especially mothers-in-law, depended on a growing family for their social power. The new context, where an individual woman might make decisions about her own fertility without reference to the surrounding culture, challenged long-held social beliefs about the intersection of individual and social fertility and reproduction. The result was deep conflict about who had the right to make such decisions.

Women had a new possibility of limiting their family size. The technology of the pill and the injection allowed women to choose to use birth control without informing their husbands or other male kin. While pills were sometimes discovered by husbands, the Depo-Provera injection could be a woman's secret, as the procedure was done at a clinic and there was no material evidence to be found at home. Many women told of subterfuge, sometimes including support from staff to conceal clinic visits, in order to keep their husbands and mothers-in-law in the dark about their access to birth control.

Husbands and wives had long negotiated over such household issues as agricultural work, land access, and income. Now some families did discuss birth control decisions, and the new twist of discussing reproductive choice increased male anxiety. Men were already constrained by the legal and social restrictions of the racist colonial government. As they lost control over their reproductive options, they expressed that apprehension through a fear of "unleashed female sexuality" and their inability to "act as the interface between their wives and the world outside the domestic sphere."[31] Those changes, including the potential loss of male authority, were perceived by men as an assault on their own masculinity. Men believed female fertility should not be under women's power, but that fertility was an essential part of household well-being and was subject to male control. Family wealth depended on having children, and the only way men could get children was through a relationship with a woman. The conflict was not simply between men and women, but was also between elders and youth, as young people, especially men, moved away from rural communities and both young men and women sought to make their own way in a changing world.

In the 1970s, as the liberation struggle expanded throughout Zimbabwe, the issue of birth control became a strand of contention. Some freedom fighters viewed the introduction of the pill and the injection as a further indication of white culture intruding on African society, and in this particular case, into the most intimate realms of family and sexuality. The fact that pills and shots were physically put into women's bodies increased the sense of male impotence in a social as well as a sexual capacity. In general, women did not view birth control methods as a political danger, though they often were suspicious about their effects on their bodies. But the male combatants saw the new birth control techniques as a genocidal practice and as evidence of settler attacks on their patriarchal control in their own society. The political differences were not so simple, as some of those in the struggle spoke publically against birth control while using it in their private lives, and women fighting against colonial rule often viewed the new options as part of a larger politics of women's rights, which they believed were integral to a free Zimbabwe. The combination of changing ideas about families and the greater ease for women in obtaining birth control meant that by the year 2000 the birth rate had fallen from over 46 per 1000 to 30.30.

Though this example was focused on events in Zimbabwe during the mid-twentieth century, most parts of Africa witnessed similar patterns of change and conflict as a result of increased access to contraceptives and the entrance of reproductive issues and family planning into public discourse. Issues that had been the concern of families and local communities were subject to outside interests and interventions. As evident from this brief overview of the Shona experience in Zimbabwe, tensions could emerge along an assortment of fault lines. Profoundly private issues became public as health care and sexuality intersected with politics and national governmental interests. Many women were part of those changes as they worked to gain greater control over their reproductive lives even when that brought them into conflict with their husbands and families.

Polygyny

Most African societies accepted and even preferred a polygynous marital system in which men were permitted and sometimes expected to marry more than one wife. While statistics were not reliable and did not always account for second wives who were not legally married, in the late twentieth century polygyny rates in West Africa were as high as 40 percent of all marriages, ranged between 20 and 40 percent for much of central and southern Africa, and were under 20 percent in South Africa. Other sources suggested that from one-third to one-half of all African women were in polygynous marriages.

The historical record shows a few elite or royal men who had dozens or even hundreds of wives, usually married as a strategy to build political alliances. In one unusual modern example, King Mswati III of Swaziland came under international scrutiny in 2002 for abducting a teenage girl to be his tenth wife and marrying her in 2004. He was criticized for following the tradition of marriage by abduction as well as for marrying multiple women. His father had reportedly accumulated one hundred wives, but the practices of multiple wives and kidnapping girls had become less acceptable in the modern era. Swaziland's efforts to control the spread of HIV/AIDS, which had reached a 33 percent infection rate, included education about responsible sexual choices, a background that made Mswati III's actions particularly reprehensible.

More commonly, ordinary men would have two or three wives who were able to share the heavy workload of farming, cooking, and childcare. In some areas the second wife was chosen in agreement with the first wife, who could arrange for her younger sister or other kinswoman to join her household. In societies where women's daily labor was the basis of cultivating food, a household with more able-bodied women was more capable of survival. Although polygyny has been portrayed by Western feminists as inherently oppressive to women, the daily reality has been a wide range of experiences, from households where the co-wives were close, enjoyed sharing agricultural work and childcare responsibilities, and even were known to band together against the husband, to households where jealousy and acrimony were the prevalent sentiments.

Areas of Islamic influence appeared to have a greater number of polygynous relationships. Polygyny was one of the main practices that Christian missionaries struggled to bring to an end, and it has also been the focus of some governmental campaigns. In Mozambique in the early post-independence years, the government advocated for an end to practices that were considered oppressive to women, including polygyny and bridewealth. Although the practice was generally in decline as a result of urbanization, higher female educational levels, and increased costs of living, there was also a new adherence to the practice as some men and women saw polygyny as a particularly African form of marriage that should not be abandoned or eradicated. Men sometimes had an informal second wife, setting up two households which might or might not be aware of each other. In some cases the second wife was denied the legal protections and social status that the first wife had, while in other relationships it was the first wife who was abandoned in favor of a younger woman.

Female Genital Cutting

The practice of cutting or excising portions of girls' or women's genitals as part of initiation ceremonies was practiced in a number of African countries, and it was the center of an international campaign to end what was variously called "circumcision," "excision," "clitoridectomy," "infibulation," and "female genital mutilation" or FGM. It was generally assumed to be related to Islamic practice, though the Qur'an made no reference to excision. It was most common in West Africa and in Kenya, Sudan, and the Horn of Africa, and it was rare in southern Africa. According to United Nations estimates, 130 million women had already undergone the procedure, and every year as many as 2 million more were expected to go through the experience of genital cutting.

The actual cutting ranged from a minor nick just to draw blood, to the removal of the clitoris and the labia minora and majora, with the resulting wound sewn together and requiring re-cutting in order for intercourse to occur. It sometimes was done as part of a group coming-of-age process, and it was considered a requirement for a girl to be regarded as a proper adult woman who could marry and have children of her own. Frequently the cutting was done in extremely unsanitary conditions with dull implements and inadequate follow-up care. The history of the practice as well as earlier campaigns to end genital cutting in the Sudan and Kenya were discussed in chapter 4.

Despite that history of attempts to end genital cutting, the practice continued throughout the twentieth century and into the twenty-first. As described by Somali model Waris Dirie, her legs were tied together to prevent her from walking while the wound healed over the course of weeks, and she was given no medicines for pain or infection.[32] The rates of infection and death were not known, though clearly that was a reality given the conditions under which the cutting was performed. Likewise it was difficult to find reliable data on continuing health problems related to urination, menstruation, intercourse, and childbirth, and the sexual experience of women who have been cut has been little studied.

Western campaigns to end the procedure were not always well received by African women, who sometimes saw arrogance and attitudes of cultural superiority rather than concern about women's lives. Beginning with the efforts of Christian missionaries in Kenya in the 1930s, through feminists concerned about the well-being of women in the 1980s and 1990s, the impact of non-Africans on ending the practice has been complicated. Prominent in initially bringing the custom to international attention in the 1980s were the British campaigner Fran Hosken who initiated the Women's International Network (WIN) News and Efua Dorkenoo from Ghana, who established the Foundation for Women's Health, Research and Development (FORWARD). Senegalese activist Awa Thiam founded another early group, Commission pour l'Abolition des Mutilations Sexuelles (CAMS, Commission for the Abolition of Sexual Mutilation). African women began working to transform the rites in order to sanitize the cutting and to introduce non-surgical practices in the 1990s. Local groups and projects included Tostan (an American organization based in Senegal), PATH (Program for Appropriate Technology in Health) in Kenya and elsewhere, REACH in Uganda, and Water for Life in Somalia. Womankind Kenya was a grassroots organization based in northeastern Kenya. They recruited local women who initiated discussions with the individual women who performed the cutting, convincing them one at a time that the procedure should be stopped. Though it was a slow process, it was combined with development activities that emphasized girls' education, income-generating projects, and other health improvements such as better access to clean water.

In 2003 a prominent element in the Protocol on the Rights of Women in Africa prohibited excision (discussed further in chapter 9). Prior to that, the only countries that had passed national legislation specifically calling for an end to the practice were Senegal and Tanzania, though other nations were pursuing education and some were expanding existing laws such as those concerning assault to include the practice of genital cutting.

HIV/AIDS

The epidemic of HIV/AIDS (human immunodeficiency virus/acquired immunodeficiency syndrome) has had a devastating impact on Africa since it was recognized in the early 1980s. Figures from 2003 estimated that thirty million Africans were infected, amounting to 70 percent of the world total. The United Nations projected that sixty million Africans were affected, as they were either living with HIV, had died of AIDS, or were AIDS orphans. In 2002, women made up 58 percent of infected Africans, making it a significant health issue for women.

In the wake of the increasing death rate, there were studies of sexuality designed to discover whether African sexual practices might have influenced the spread of the disease. Though later proven false, some researchers implicated African women as pivotal in the spread of the disease. In trying to understand why some countries had particularly high rates of infection, it was suggested that girls' initiation rites that included female genital cutting might have been a factor, as well as polygyny, prostitution, and widespread illiteracy. Research in Uganda in the 1990s showed that the high rates of infection might be related to the practice of having concurrent (rather than sequential) long-term sexual relationships, not only involving men in polygynous marriages, but women who engaged in liaisons with two or more long-term simultaneous partners. Thus educational programs that warned people about prostitutes did not address the more prevalent web of HIV/AIDS infection that resulted from people believing that their friends and long-term partners were safe sexual companions.[33] Women were also at risk due to their vulnerability to domestic violence and rape.

The subordinate position of women in male-female relationships was described as a component in the spread of the disease. It appeared that African men refused to use condoms, the easiest barrier to the virus, and women faced difficulties in asking or requiring that their male partners wear them. Investigators have shown that poverty was a major element, while particular African sexual practices were not the main factors. The rate of infection was much lower in West Africa, a fact that was usually ascribed to Islamic practices that limited women's sexual freedom. Recent research into regional variations found that societies that commonly circumcised men, including Islamic West Africa, had lower rates, and that male circumcision might reduce the risk of acquiring HIV/AIDS by up to 70 percent.

For women there were some specific concerns. One was the rising number of children whose parents had died from AIDS. As women most often had responsibility for childcare, they found themselves caring for ever-increasing numbers of orphans as relatives and friends succumbed to the disease. That reality was a factor in the work of the Ugandan Women's Effort to Save Orphans. In 2002 there were 14 million AIDS orphans, and although that number was expected to rise, the use of antiviral drugs and other preventive measures helped control the spread of the disease. South Africa and other southern and eastern African nations held the greatest numbers of AIDS orphans, and regional and national differences figured into African women's experiences.

A second phenomenon was the increase in older men, sometimes called "sugar daddies," who entered into relationships with teenage girls. While the men chose relatively young women because they believed those women were free of HIV, it was frequently the case that the women contracted AIDS through relations with the man, who sometimes supported them generously with money for school, clothes, and food. Girls in Africa between 15 and 19 years of age had HIV infection rates as much as six times higher than boys of the same age group.

Women were instrumental in HIV/AIDS organizing, founding the Society for Women and AIDS in Africa (SWAA) to facilitate a specifically African female response to the crisis. African first ladies formed the Organisation of African First Ladies Against HIV/AIDS (discussed further in chapter 8). Women also played a leading role in local community groups that developed HIV/AIDS programs, such as the Hlomelikusasa Othandweni Women's Group in South Africa, the Lesotho Women's Institute, and Maendeleo ya Wanawake in Kenya. International organizations such as the United Nations Development Fund for Women (now called UN Women) and the Africa Women's Forum also made HIV/AIDS work a priority.

Arts and Leisure

Women have made many contributions to the arts in Africa, and in recent years they have become prominent in other fields including sports. In this section some of the important artistic work in literature, music, and film, will be surveyed. In all areas, women's artistic output has tended to reflect a particular female point of view that was often lacking in art by men. Women athletes have made an impression with their skill and strength.

Literature

Although many women wrote and published fiction, including short stories, novels, and poetry, there continued to be constraints on female authors. Women were less likely to have the time to pursue a writing career, and they faced opposition from male family members who went as far as burning manuscripts to prevent women from publishing. It was also suggested that women were more modest, and therefore hesitated to submit their manuscripts for publication. In Zimbabwe by 1987, as one example, 179 men had been published compared to only 31 women. Women writers found strength in working together in associations such as the Zimbabwe Women Writers group and by organizing the Women Writers Conference affiliated with the Zimbabwe International Book Fair in 1999. African women writers have also won important awards, including the Commonwealth Writers' Prize (Africa region), which has been won by Tsitsi Dangarembga, Nadime Gordimer, Margaret Ogola, and Yvonne Vera.

Flora Nwapa was one of Nigeria's foremost novelists. Born in 1931, she was educated at the University of Ibadan and earned a diploma in education from the University of Edinburgh in Scotland in 1958. When she returned to Nigeria she worked as a "woman education officer," and even after gaining fame as a writer she served as the assistant registrar at the University of Lagos (1962–1976), as minister of health and social welfare for East Central State (1970–1971), and as minister of lands, survey, and urban development (1971–1974). Her first novel, *Efuru* (1966), portrayed the life of a rural woman whose husbands left her and whose daughter died. It was one of the first English-language novels published by an African woman.[34] In addition to four more novels, she published collections of short stories (*This is Lagos, Wives at War,* and *Women are Different*) and poems, as well as several books for children. In response to poor treatment by her publisher, she established her own publishing house in Nigeria, first Tana Press in 1974, and later Flora Nwapa Books in 1977, through which she put out her own publications as well as those of other Nigerian writers. All of her writing sought to present a more realistic portrayal of Nigerian women as strong independent individuals, to improve women's ideas of their own possibilities, and to better the condition of African women.

Grace Ogot was a Kenyan writer of novels and short stories who also served in the Kenyan government. She was born in Kenya in 1930, and trained as a nurse in Uganda and England. Her first short story appeared in 1962, and her novel *The Promised Land* was printed in 1966 (the same year as Flora Nwapa's *Efuru*).[35] She published two other novels, *The Graduate* and *The Strange Bride*, and three short story collections, *The Other Woman, The Island of Tears,* and *Land without Thunder*. A prominent theme of her stories was the struggle between men and women, often centering on male brutality toward women. Even though she raised such issues as rape and domestic violence in her stories, she only rarely spoke out on these issues in Kenya. She also used her fiction to discuss missions, hospitals, and modern medicine, often shown in conflict with African witchcraft, which she presented as part of African reality without condemning it. Ogot was a founding member of the Writers' Association of Kenya. Although many of her works were available in English, she also wrote novels in the Luo language, Dholuo.

Grace Ogot's political work included positions in community development, business, and public relations. She was employed as a journalist with the *East African Standard* and for local radio, as well as owning a Nairobi boutique that carried items for girls and babies. Ogot was a member of parliament from 1983 to 1992, first entering as an appointee of President arap Moi. She served as the assistant minister of culture and social services from 1985 to 1993, and also was Kenya's representative to the United Nations and the United Nations Educational, Scientific and Cultural Organization (UNESCO).

Buchi Emecheta began publishing in the 1970s, with novels that told the story of Nigerian women struggling to gain control over their lives. The most widely read is *The Joys of Motherhood*, which tells about the troubles of a young woman in Nigeria during the years of British colonial rule.[36] Though the life trajectory of that fictional character, Nnu-Ego, included one tragedy after another, the story encompassed marriage and polygyny, motherhood, fertility and child mortality, market work and colonial employment, and the impact on families of the demands of colonialism. Nnu-Ego married twice, and did not find long-term happiness in either marriage. She eventually had four children, but endured conflict with co-wives, ethnic differences with in-laws, and neglect by her children, two of whom traveled overseas for their education. The "joys" of motherhood were not to be hers, as the character died alone and lonely, though her children celebrated her life with an elaborate funeral. The social expectation that women would be revered for bearing and raising children was directly countered by Emecheta's story of hardship, poverty, and ungrateful offspring. Her writings clearly placed the female characters in a real world of abusive men and a changing political landscape.

African women continued to write and publish, often focusing on women's lives. Because their work frequently centered on domestic activities and family, they were not accorded recognition as important national authors, in contrast to male authors such as Chinua Achebe and Ngugi wa Thiong'o, whose writings more explicitly addressed issues of national politics. Nonetheless, women's work and family life were changing in profound ways as a result of colonialism, nationalism, and independence, and old and new fiction by women reflected the "domestic" aspect of politics.[37] South Africa's Nobel-prize winning author, Nadine Gordimer, was straightforward in her writing on politics, beginning with her first publications in the 1950s. But other African women only later began to write more directly about politics and history.

Women's views of polygyny were put forward in important fiction by Mariama Bâ (*Une si longue lettre*, translated as *So Long a Letter*) and Ama Ata Aidoo (*Changes: A Love Story*). Bâ's short novel, written as a letter to a friend, presented the view of an older Senegalese woman whose husband married a young girl as a second wife.[38] He did not seek permission from his first wife, and compounded the insult by marrying a friend of their daughter's. The book was often used to demonstrate the problems of polygyny. In contrast, Aidoo's novel centered on a modern woman in Accra, Ghana, and her love affair with a man who was already married.[39] She was already married herself, but was in constant conflict with her husband over his desire for more children and her wish to have no more than the one child they already had. She decided to divorce her husband and marry the new man as his second wife, despite the opposition of their family and friends. For her, the situation allowed her the security of marriage and the independence of keeping aspects of her own work, though the second marriage also broke down within a few years. Both books addressed the persistence of polygyny in modern urban settings, and in their contrasting outcomes, suggested the variety of experiences and possibilities for women.

Tsitsi Dangarembga's novel, *Nervous Conditions*, presented the story of two female cousins who encountered obstacles as well as support for their education in 1960s Zimbabwe, which was still under white-minority control.[40] Their respective families suggested some of the gaps in lifestyle and gender expectations between rural and urban families, and expanded options that were opening for girls during that era. It represented the beginning of a shift to greater political content while focusing on the personal lives of girls and women.

By the early twenty-first century there was a proliferation of published writing by women. One aspect was a growth in genre fiction, with African women writing romance novels that were entertaining while having less literary merit. At the same time, Chimamanda Ngozi Adichie won praise for *Half of a Yellow Sun*, her novel of Nigerian sisters and those close to them, navigating the treacherous times of the Biafran war in 1960s Nigeria. Published in 2006, her work was described as being "about the end of colonialism, about ethnic allegiances, about class and race," clearly recognizing the larger political context of the personal stories of love and kinship.[41]

While the first modern novels written by African women were neglected and considered politically unimportant, the increasing authority of women's writing over the decades has brought forward fiction that presents women's lives as integrated into the development of the nation and of the modern world. When they described women's lives in earlier decades, their stories helped illuminate historical settings. The early novels were also about politics, though in a muted and sometimes obscured way. They paved the road for the fiction of the twenty-first century, when the stories are both more overtly political and the audience recognized the politics of seemingly domestic narratives.

Music

Women have been renowned as singers and performers both individually and as part of choral groups, though they have been less often recognized as composers. Songs have recalled historic events and praised rulers, and they were composed and sung for festive occasions, including as a part of initiation rites, weddings, and funerals. Singing while performing collective work was also a common practice; for example, as women pounded grain with the mortar and pestle they would often sing in rhythm with the work. In many areas women played only designated instruments, thus they were not expected to play stringed instruments or drums in public, though they may have had the ability and knowledge. Performances were frequently a group experience, with women singing in a chorus while other members of the community drummed and played instruments. Dance and song were commonly part of the same performance, whether part of a private ritual or on a stage before an audience.

Griottes were women in West Africa who participated in society as bards, praise-singers, storytellers, historians, or genealogists. They sang songs that included family lineage information, accounts of historic events, morality tales, and laudatory lyrics about rulers and other prominent people. Their role was much broader in some communities, where they acted as counselors, diplomats, interpreters, teachers, and ritual leaders and participants. Women singers were especially involved in weddings and baptisms, but they were not as likely to sing the epics commonly associated with male *griots*. Though they were often accompanied by male musicians playing stringed instruments and beating on drums, women also played an instrument made from a gourd with attached cowrie shells that rattled rhythmically as it was tossed and shaken during the performance. Recordings of *griottes'* compositions and renditions were very popular in West African cities. Women from Mali, drawing on their experience as *griottes*, had many followers who prized their songs for their beauty and spirituality. Some of the best known performers were Fanta Damba, Sira Mori Diabaté, and Oumou Sangaré.

In the late twentieth century, more women singers and musicians became known through recordings and radio play. Internationally famous singers from West Africa include Cesaria Evora and Angelique Kidjo, while singers from eastern and southern Africa who gained wide recognition included Brenda Fassie, Miriam Makeba, Dorothy Masuka, and Siti Binti Saad.

Miriam Makeba was a singer from South Africa who attained international recognition for her interpretation of songs and music from southern Africa. Born in Johannesburg in 1932, she began singing in school choirs, was asked to join the Manhattan Brothers in 1952, and initially released one of her best known songs, "Pata Pata," in 1956. She played herself in the 1959 semi-documentary film "Come Back Africa." In 1960, after she began to be active in anti-apartheid politics, she left South Africa and then was not allowed to return until 1990. While in exile, Makeba became active in the anti-apartheid movement and spoke about the injustice of the apartheid system before the United Nations General Assembly. She was briefly married to renowned South African trumpet player, Hugh Masekela, and later to the African-American civil rights and black power activist, Stokely Carmichael. Because his politics made it impossible for them to live in the United States, and she could not return to South Africa, they lived in Guinea and she took Guinean citizenship. She continued recording and performing her unique style of popular African music, releasing nearly three dozen albums and compact discs over the years, until her death while on tour in Italy in 2008.

Malian singer Oumou Sangaré was born in Bamako, but she learned the musical traditions of her family's home region in southwestern Mali. She left school in the eighth grade to pursue a singing career, and she toured Europe in 1986 with the Bamba group Joliba Percussion. Her 1989 recording *Moussolou* (*Women*) reportedly sold over two hundred thousand copies throughout West Africa, and it was followed by the compilation recording of Sangaré and other Malian women in *The Wassoulou Sound: Women of Mali* (1994). The themes of her songs included such female concerns as arranged marriage and polygyny.

One of the best known African performers is Angelique Kidjo, who became an international star in the late twentieth century. Born in Benin in 1960, Kidjo moved to Europe and was later based in Paris and New York. Her first recording was released in 1989, with a dozen releases by 2014. She was particularly noted for mixing West African and Brazilian tempos and musicians into a vibrant mode of modern popular music. In her album, *Eve*, a tribute to African women, she recorded local women's choirs in Benin and elsewhere as part of the mix. In her words, "*Eve* is an album of remembrance of African women I grew up with and a testament to the pride and strength that hide behind the smile that masks everyday troubles."[42] She has also used her fame and wealth to support African girls' education, and to travel as a goodwill ambassador for UNICEF.

Film

Although little known, there were African women making films, often dealing with issues central to women's lives. More often interesting films have been made by men and non-Africans that addressed central issues of women's condition; among the most important of those are *Finzan* by Cheikh Oumar Sissoko that dealt with initiation rites, and many of Sembene Ousmane's films, including

Xala, which focused on women and politics in Senegal, and *Moolaade*, which was about female genital cutting.

One of the earliest films by a woman was a thirty-minute documentary by Thérèse Sita-Bella, *Tam Tam à Paris* (1963) about the Paris performances of the National Dance Company of Cameroon. Women also made films for television as well as a number of documentaries. Mozambican director Fatima Alburquerque made *No meu pais existe uma guerra* (*In my country there is a war*, 1989) about the war of the 1980s. Safi Faye of Senegal made ethnographic films, recorded Serer religious rites, and documented economic issues. Anne-Laure Folly of Togo made *Femmes aux yeux ouverts* (*Women with Open Eyes*, 1994) about West African women organizing around marital rights, reproductive health, and other issues. Other notable female filmmakers include Mariama Hima, who filmed artisans in Niger, and Lola Fani-Kayode who produced documentaries for Nigerian television (the best known was *Mirror in the Sun* about modern urban life, 1984). Flora M'mbugu-Schelling filmed a documentary in 1992 about Mozambican women refugees working in a rock quarry in Tanzania (*These Hands*), while Anne Mungai made several documentaries about Kenyan women. Female filmmakers have been less successful in finding support for feature films, though such films have been made by Tsitsi Dangarembga and Sarah Maldoror, among others. Many women regarded as African filmmakers lived and worked in Europe, though they concentrated on African topics. In recognition of the increasing numbers of African women making films, the African Women's Film Festival was held in Johannesburg, South Africa, in 2004, with the theme "film from a woman's perspective."

Artists

A number of women have made important contributions as artists in genres, including painting, ceramics, and textiles. In a few cases, female artists using various media have gained international acclaim.

Magdalene Odundo is an innovative Kenyan ceramicist and sculptor whose designs have been exhibited around the world. Born in 1950, she was trained in graphic arts in England in the 1970s, when she studied at the precursor of the Surrey Institute of Art and Design and in the master's program at the Royal College of Art, finishing her degree in 1982. She also studied pottery techniques with Pueblo Indian and Mexican artists. Her vessels were noted for their elegant and sinuous lines, often executed in glossy burnished shades of ochre and ebony. Odundo has had one-person shows in Hamburg, Germany, in a traveling show in the United States, and elsewhere. Her ceramic art is in the collections of the Smithsonian, the British Museum, the Victoria and Albert Museum, and many other noted institutions. In 2002, she was named a professor at the Surrey

Institute. Her contributions to art were recognized when she was appointed an Officer of the Order of the British Empire (OBE) in 2008.

Nike Davies is an internationally known batik artist who sold her striking garments in venues throughout the world.[43] Born in 1952 to a rural Yoruba family in Nigeria, she fled as a teenager in order to avoid an unwanted arranged marriage. As she became interested in art, she began working for a male artist and eventually married him as one of numerous co-wives. While she lived with him between 1970 and 1986 the compound had a reputation for harmony, and while married Nike learned techniques of batik art, which she further developed as an independent artist. Behind the compound walls, however, household relations were marked by maltreatment, and Nike and most of the wives divorced their common husband. Nike was best known for original indigo batik designs on cotton cloth, known as *adire* (see chapter 4 for the historical background to adire). She later established the Nike Center for Arts and Culture, which expanded to five centers throughout Nigeria, where women and men obtained training in the production and marketing of a range of artistic techniques.

Bertina Lopes, a painter and sculptor admired internationally, was born in Lourenço Marques (now Maputo), Mozambique, in 1924 to a Portuguese father and an African mother. Her early schooling was in Mozambique, and her later training was in Portugal where she earned a degree in painting and sculpture. In 1953, she returned to Mozambique and taught in a technical school until 1962. She was influenced by Noémia de Sousa's poetry, and she incorporated social themes into her art. She traveled to Portugal to study ceramics with a Gulbenkian Foundation fellowship, and because of the increasing intransigence of Portuguese colonialism in the 1960s, she remained in exile, moving to Rome where she resided until her death in 2012.

The international success of African female artists was a result of their skill and innovation. They have used traditional methods and sometimes styles, yet they have brought new sensibilities and techniques to their work. In some cases their work has been displayed and sold in galleries in Europe and elsewhere, admired for its beauty and recognized for its contributions to world culture.

Sports

Although African women were introduced to sports programs in their schools by the early twentieth century, few became well-known as athletes. They were hampered by the lack of resources, sponsorship, and training facilities that affected all Africans, and also by continued gender segregation in sport in general. Nonetheless, there is a developing history of African women's involvement with athletic activities. Some of the earliest sports clubs appear to have been formed in

South Africa in the 1880s, when African women who had graduated from missionary schools formed croquet and tennis associations. White women in South Africa were also involved in cricket and other sports from the late nineteenth and early twentieth centuries. In Tanzania there were interschool athletic meets in the Lake Victoria region as early as the 1930s that included girls' track competitions and gymnastics. Nigerian women were encouraged by the British colonial government, which introduced tennis and athletics. The first all-woman athletic meeting was held in Lagos in 1951; that year also marked the founding of the Women's Amateur Athletic Association of Nigeria. By 1955 regional meets were held with female athletes from Ghana.

Track and field, which has seen a number of women become world champions, was one area where women were able to progress. The first black African woman to win an Olympic gold medal was the Ethiopian runner Derartu Tulu. Track included women marathon runners such as Tegla Loroupe of Kenya, who won the New York City Marathon in 1994 and 1995. Another prominent female athlete is Maria de Lurdes Mutola, an Olympic gold-medalist from Mozambique who won the 800-meter race in Sydney in 2000.

In the 1990s, more women began playing soccer, netball, volleyball, cricket, and other team sports. Across the continent women organized their own clubs, such as the Soweto Ladies soccer team in South Africa. In 1995 the newly-formed Women's South African Football Association competed in the All Africa Women's Football Competition. South Africa was also the site of Women and Sport in South Africa, which worked to increase girls' and women's participation in athletic activities.

Athletic endeavors were another route for women to be active in their communities, including international competitions, and to find satisfaction in their achievements.

Conclusion

The initial post-independence decades did not immediately bring improvements for most women, as they continued their rural farm work. Efforts at development by both African governments and international agencies often neglected women and introduced policies that had a negative impact on them. At the same time, some women's lives changed in noticeable ways, as they gained access to more education, moved to urban areas where they found more employment opportunities, and discovered increased options in their personal lives. Some of the new opportunities for women were evident in the production of literature, art, films, and music, much of which directly discussed women's condition in diverse African societies. The late twentieth century saw some women improve their lives even while others remained in oppressive situations.

Notes

1. Kevane, *Women and Development in Africa*, 159–160.
2. Wooten, *The Art of Livelihood*, 52–56.
3. Ibid., 100–102.
4. Gerrard, "Clans, Gender and Kilns."
5. Ibid., 237.
6. Hanlon, et al., *Just Give Money to the Poor.*
7. Sheldon, "Markets and Gardens," 378.
8. United Nations, *Women's Indicators and Statistics Database* (2000), http://unstats.un.org /unsd/demographic/gender/wistat/, later statistics found at http://www.un.org/womenwatch/.
9. Sheldon, "Sewing Clothes and Sorting Cashew Nuts."
10. Baylies and Wright, "Female Labour in the Textile and Clothing Industry of Lesotho," 582.
11. There is an extensive literature on structural adjustment and women in Africa. See the contributions to these edited collections: Gladwin, ed., *Structural Adjustment and African Women Farmers*, and Thomas-Emeagwali, ed. *Women Pay the Price.*
12. Sheldon, *Pounders of Grain*, 247–250; Penvenne, *Women, Migration and the Cashew Economy.*
13. Elabor-Idemudia, "Nigeria: Agricultural Exports and Compensatory Schemes."
14. Ibid., 154.
15. Sheldon, *Historical Dictionary of Women in Sub-Saharan Africa.*
16. Africa Gender Institute, History: (accessed February 3, 2016) http://agi.ac.za/about.
17. Mikell, Introduction to *African Feminism.*
18. Nnaemeka, "Nego-Feminism."
19. Khadiagala, "Justice and Power in the Adjudication of Women's Property Rights."
20. Ibid., 116.
21. Bonate, "Women's Land Rights in Mozambique."
22. Sithole-Fundire, et al., *Gender Research on Urbanization, Planning, Housing and Everyday Life.*
23. Drawn from online United Nations statistical sources; see World Fertility Survey for various years.
24. Opiyo, "Fertility Levels, Trends, and Differentials."
25. Foley, "Overlaps and Disconnects in Reproductive Health Care."
26. Fadlalla, *Embodying Honor*, 69.
27. Ibid., 110.
28. Kaler, *Running After Pills.*
29. http://www.indexmundi.com/facts/zimbabwe/birth-rate, accessed March 20, 2014.
30. Cited in Kaler, *Running after Pills*, 35.
31. Ibid., 22.
32. Dirie, *Desert Flower.*
33. Obbo, "HIV Transmission."
34. Nwapa, *Efuru.*
35. Ogot, *The Promised Land.*
36. Emecheta, *The Joys of Motherhood.*
37. Andrade, *The Nation Writ Small.*
38. Bâ, *So Long a Letter.*
39. Aidoo, *Changes.*

40. Dangarembga, *Nervous Conditions*.

41. Book jacket description of Adichie, *Half of a Yellow Sun*.

42. Interview with *Billboard*, October 23, 2013, accessed November 21, 2016, http://www.billboard.com/articles/news/5763237/angelique-kidjo-to-release-eve-album-in-january-exclusive-song-premiere.

43. Vaz, *The Woman with the Artistic Brush*.

8 Women and Politics after Independence

As AFRICAN NATIONS became independent, women began to involve themselves in new organizations. Although some were directly associated with politics, legal issues, and women's status, others were related to community concerns and women's troubled economic situation. Another important area of women's political activism was in peace-building, as women in several nations sought to end traumatic conflicts during the 1990s and after. All of these efforts contributed to women finding their place in modern independent African nations. This chapter will present the ways in which women were involved in democratization, internal conflicts, and international struggles during the late twentieth century.

Women have been active in political organizations throughout history. In earlier times African women held political power as queen mothers and as spiritual leaders. In the late nineteenth century and into the twentieth century, women were noted for their contributions to nationalist causes. In the post-independence era, though women continued to face many obstacles to equality in government, and were particularly noted for their absence from the centers of power, they also pushed forward in their efforts to change the inequality they experienced.

United Nations Decade for Women

The United Nations sponsored a series of international meetings on women's issues which had important implications for African women. The first three meetings were part of the designated "Decade for Women," and they were held in Mexico City in 1975, in Copenhagen in 1980, and in Nairobi in 1985. The fourth, held in Beijing in 1995, was added as a way to sum up and bring closure to the official decade. At each of the international gatherings, African women participated as representatives of their governments and of nongovernmental organizations, and they were able to introduce issues that were important to them which were not always on the agenda of women from other world areas. In addition, individual African women rose to international prominence as a result of their work on the UN meetings.

During the first part of the UN project, Annie Jiagge from Ghana helped write the Convention on the Elimination of All Forms of Discrimination against

Women (CEDAW). UN members had been working on early versions of this document, which was introduced at the Mexico City meeting and adopted by the United Nations General Assembly in 1979. Born in Lomé, Togo, in 1919, Jiagge moved to Ghana and was the first female lawyer there, where she was admitted to the bar in 1950. She was later appointed as a justice on Ghana's Supreme Court. After Kwame Nkrumah was ousted as Ghana's president in 1966, she led the Jiagge Commission, which investigated corruption in his government. In 1968, she was elected to chair the 21st session of the United Nations Commission on the Status of Women, where she was the first African woman to hold that post. She remained active in other international organizations, including as president of the World Council of Churches from 1975 to 1983. She passed away in 1996.

CEDAW consisted of a preamble and thirty articles, and was considered an international bill of rights for women, as it outlined a specific program for individual nations to implement in order to end discrimination against women. The Convention defined discrimination against women as "any distinction, exclusion or restriction made on the basis of sex which has the effect or purpose of impairing or nullifying the recognition, enjoyment or exercise by women, irrespective of their marital status, on a basis of equality of men and women, of human rights and fundamental freedoms in the political, economic, social, cultural, civil or any other field."[1] Any nation that adopted CEDAW committed itself to incorporating the principle of equality of men and women in their legal system, to abolish all discriminatory laws, and to adopt appropriate new laws prohibiting discrimination against women. All African governments except Somalia and Sudan passed the Convention, and although further compliance has only been completed by a few, it has proved to be a support for citizens to push their governments for continuing legal improvements for women.

Esther Ocloo was a Ghanaian who was strongly influenced at the initial UN meeting in Mexico City. Ocloo was a market woman who was born in 1919 as the daughter of poor farmers. She attended high school in Accra on a scholarship from the Cadbury chocolate company. After she finished high school in the 1940s, her aunt offered her financing of less than one dollar, which Ocloo used to purchase the materials to make twelve jars of marmalade. With her earnings from selling those jars she eventually expanded into making juice, won a contract with the military to supply orange juice, and increased her manufacturing to include other canned foods. She used her income to finance her own further education in food technology in Britain, and she invested in projects designed to improve women's economic opportunities. In 1975 at the UN meeting in Mexico City, she learned about micro-loan programs, in which poor women come together in support groups to gain access to very small loans; those loans have demonstrated a high rate of repayment due to the women meeting regularly and gaining solidarity. In 1979, Ocloo and several other women, including Annie

Fig. 8.1 Maasai women at the nongovernmental sessions at the UN Decade for Women meeting, Nairobi, Kenya, July 1985. Photograph by Janet Goldner.

Jiagge pioneered micro-loans in Africa when they established Women's World Banking as a vehicle to make such loans, and Ocloo was named chairwoman. She passed away in 2002.

The Nairobi Women's Meeting in 1985

The third meeting of the United Nations Decade for Women, designed to review and appraise the achievements of the Decade, was held in Nairobi, Kenya, in July 1985. Kenyan politician Margaret Kenyatta presided over the meeting, which was marked by a massive attendance of sixteen thousand women, with a notable presence of African women. The primary official document issued from the meeting was the "Forward-looking Strategies for the Advancement of Women" that provided a blueprint that individual governments could implement to improve women's rights and status.

Concurrent with the official meeting was a nongovernmental assembly that was the site of many lively workshops and discussions, and was for many attendees the most important part of the gathering. African women at the nongovernmental meeting formulated The Nairobi Manifesto, in which they raised a number of issues of primary importance to African women, including the persistence of the apartheid government in South Africa, exploitative structural adjustment policies imposed on African countries by international agencies, the crisis in agriculture, widespread forced migrations, and the spread of religious fundamentalism. They called for the implementation of alternate programs that addressed the specificity of the African condition.[2]

African women, motivated by their experiences and contacts made at the meeting, returned home and formed activist organizations, including Action for Development (ACFODE) in Uganda and the Tanzania Media Women's Association. The Nairobi women's meeting had a major positive impact on the ability of African women to network across the continent. Women who were working to improve women's conditions in many African nations were able to use the platform of the "forward-looking strategies" to introduce new legislation among other efforts.

Gertrude Mongella and the Beijing Women's Meeting in 1995

The Nairobi meeting was followed in 1995 by a Fourth World Conference on Women in Beijing, which was chaired by Gertrude Mongella. Mongella was an internationally known Tanzanian politician who was committed to women's issues and had participated in numerous international meetings concerning women's rights, peace, and development. Born in 1945, she was the daughter of farmers, and she went on to earn a degree in education from the University of Dar es Salaam. As an activist in the ruling party, Chama cha Mapinduzi (CCM, Party of the Revolution), she served in the Tanzanian parliament from 1980 to 1993, and was a member of the CCM central committee from 1977 to 1992. In 1982 she was the only female member of the CCM central committee, and that year she was also appointed as minister of state in the prime minister's office, a position she held until 1988. As leader of the Tanzanian delegation to the Nairobi Women's Meeting in 1985, she was named as one of the vice-chairs of that meeting. Mongella was minister of lands, natural resources and tourism from 1986 to 1987, and after losing her position in the CCM central committee, she was minister without portfolio in the president's office from 1987 to 1990. She was then named minister of state for women's affairs and served as Tanzanian High Commissioner to India from 1992, until she was named as secretary-general of the UN meeting in Beijing. In 1996, Mongella was one of the founding members of the nongovernmental organization Advocacy for Women in Africa, and she served on the boards of numerous international organizations in subsequent years.

The Beijing meeting resulted in the Platform for Action with a set of provisions designed to promote equality for women and girls. The participants agreed that the goals set forth in the earlier United Nations meetings had not been met, and that women continued to encounter severe obstacles due to conflict, poverty, and ongoing discrimination against women. Specific areas of concern were enumerated as education, health, violence against women, and persistent inequality between men and women in all sectors of society from the family to the highest levels of government. The Platform for Action outlined specific measures that governments were called upon to enact in order to bring women into equal standing in their societies.

Many governments and development agencies adopted a "gender-mainstreaming" approach in part as a result of the UN meetings. Though seemingly a positive step that would bring women into all sectors of society, in many places the outcome was disappointing as women continued to be marginalized and treated unfairly. In assessments made fifteen years after the Beijing meeting, feminist scholars found that the approach had brought about a new group of bureaucrats, both men and women, who were recognized as gender experts and who were ensconced in comfortable positions in government and development agencies, but who only rarely reflected the concerns of community-based feminist organizations.

Women activists in Ghana experienced the adoption of gender mainstreaming as having a negative impact on their organizing. Gender mainstreaming led to the introduction of gender specialists in several different ministries; those specialists then spent their time and budgets on holding training within in the ministry, writing reports, and ensuring that women and gender were included in all other ministry publications. As the gender bureaucracy grew, resources for women's rights work was redirected, and work on women was depoliticized and delinked from community activism on women's issues.[3] Women who had been long advocating for women found that they had to interact with civil servants who held gender positions in government departments. Those civil servants often were not connected to the ongoing work of community organizations, but were doing very limited work to bring women into government projects.

Related to the establishment of those new positions within various ministries was a shift in how donor funding was allocated. Women observed that money that had previously gone directly to support women's organizations was being used for "structural changes and policy development in state institutions."[4] Rather than going to women who were working with community organizations, the funding went to support the new positions for gender specialists and reports that sat on ministry shelves. Not only was less money going to community organizers, it had little impact on improving gender-related work in the government. Women activists were involved in work concerning women in the communities, while civil servants focused on policy that was far removed from the daily needs of women. Similar complaints were heard in other African countries.

Despite the limitations found in the long-term implementation of international development goals, the international meetings brought African women in contact with women from around the world who introduced them to new ideas and projects and who benefited from learning about African priorities. The United Nations also was a site where African women exercised leadership on a global stage, beginning in the years after World War II.

Democratization

In the 1990s the issue of democratization came to prominence in many African nations, often guided by Western aid donors' demand for more Western-style democracies particularly marked by contested multiparty elections. The advent of new political parties as well as other political lobby groups appeared to offer an opportunity for women to become more involved in electoral and legislative politics, in a shift from earlier emphases on development and income-generation.[5] In reality most new parties were still male-dominated. Women did move into many more positions of power and authority, however, as some nations introduced systems that reserved a percentage of legislative seats for women and more women were named to ministerial positions.

With the international pressure for democratization in the 1990s, women were able to find more opportunities for participating, though the obstacles they faced continued to be daunting. Few women have been heads of state or heads of government for an African nation, but they have made progress in being appointed to cabinet positions, and in nineteen countries they are guaranteed a percentage of seats in the national legislature through either a party or electoral quota system. There have also been advances at the level of local government; for example, following elections in Uganda in 1998 there were more than ten thousand women holding office in local councils and other lower-level positions.[6]

The situation of women in national parliaments is well documented. In 1960, when African nations were just beginning the era of independence, women were only 0.94 percent of legislative bodies. After thirty years, women were still only 7.78 percent in African legislatures. Increased levels of democratic activism and greater involvement by women in political organizations and elections helped bring the average to about 15 percent female legislators for sub-Saharan Africa in 2003, nearly matching the international average of 15.1 percent. By 2007, female legislators counted as 17.4 percent, with many nations substantially higher.[7]

Many countries introduced specific policies designed to boost the numbers of women in legislative bodies. Tanzania amended its Constitution to reserve 15 percent of the seats in the parliament and 25 percent of local council seats for women. Benin named four women to cabinet positions in 1998, but with no clear policy to bring women into government, there were still only six women in parliament out of eighty-two total members. Rwanda's Constitution was amended in 2003 to require that women make up at least 30 percent representation in all decision-making levels of the state. With that support, following elections in 2003, Rwanda leaped to the number one spot in the world, with 48.8 percent women in the national legislature, and the ratio continued to rise to 64 percent in 2013 (the 1994 genocide in Rwanda is discussed later in this chapter). In the early years of the twenty-first century, Eritrea, Mozambique, Namibia,

Fig. 8.2 Participants at the 17th Meeting of the Network of Women Parliamentarians of Central Africa (RFPAC), on the topic of Fighting Violence Against Women, N'Djamena, Chad, May 2014. Photograph courtesy of AWEPA (Association of European Parliamentarians with Africa).

Seychelles, South Africa, Tanzania, and Uganda had between 20 and 30 percent female representatives, among the highest rates in the world. For comparison, in 2014, the United States counted only 18.5 percent women holding seats in the House of Representatives, and 20 percent in the Senate. In other African countries, especially some of the Francophone nations, women accounted for fewer than 10 percent of legislators. Senegal was an exception with nearly 20 percent female parliamentarians, but Niger was among the lowest in the world with only 1.2 percent women members in the legislature.[8]

Women parliamentarians have worked together across national boundaries, as seen with the Network of Women Parliamentarians of Central Africa (Réseau de Femmes Parlementaires d'Afrique Centrale, RFPAC), which includes representatives from Angola, Burundi, Cameroon, Gabon, Equatorial Guinea, Central African Republic, Democratic Republic of Congo, Republic of Congo, Rwanda, and Chad. They have met regularly since 2002 in order to discuss key issues and strategize about their legislative struggles. Once women gain seats, they have used their positions to support legislation in such areas as marriage and inheritance and to work for family laws and citizenship provisions that can benefit women. While having a group of female law-makers is important, it is also crucial to have at least one or two women who will strongly push for such new legislation. In 2012, women legislators in Rwanda introduced a law that was passed that legalized abortion in cases of rape, incest, and to protect the mother's health. Women also have influenced the inclusion of women's rights provisions in new constitutions, lobbied against corruption and patronage in politics, and were often visible in movements for inclusion across potential divisions of ethnicity, race, and religion.

Political Party Organizations

In many African countries the only sanctioned women's organization was one that was affiliated with, and often established by, the ruling party. Although there were variations, in most cases the nation's first lady played a leadership role, and the primary work of the organization was to support the ruling party rather than to focus on women's needs. At the same time the presence of these groups allowed women to raise women's issues in the public arena at the national level, and often to have their concerns taken seriously. As democratization spread in the 1990s there was an opening for the party-affiliated organizations to operate independently and there were greater opportunities for many new issue-focused groups to emerge.

A new development in the 1990s was the appearance of political parties initiated by women, in response to their continuing marginalization in traditional parties and the limited scope of women's auxiliaries. Zambia's National Party was founded in 1991 by Inonge Mbidusita-Lewanika, and the Kopanang Basotho party in Lesotho was founded by Limakatso Ntakatsane in 1992. Margaret Dongo started the Zimbabwe Union of Democrats in 1999. Women also headed parties in the Central African Republic and Angola, while Charity Ngilu and Wangari Maathai each headed parties in Kenya. Although none of these parties was particularly successful, they helped women engage at the center of their nation's politics and suggested new routes for women to gain power.

Case Studies of Democratization

The impact of movements for greater democracy on women and politics and women's contributions to democratization can be seen by looking at case studies from Ghana, South Africa, and Kenya.

DEMOCRATIZATION IN GHANA

After gaining its independence in 1957, Ghana experienced a series of autocratic rulers and military coups, culminating in 1981 when Flight Lieutenant Jerry Rawlings took power on December 31. Rawlings ruled unilaterally for the next decade, suspending the Constitution and banning political parties. His wife, First Lady Nana Konadu Agyeman Rawlings, sponsored the 31st December Women's Movement, which was established in Ghana in 1982. She served as president of the organization beginning in 1984. It operated as the women's wing of the Provisional National Defense Council (PNDC), that is, as a typical women's auxiliary of a political party organization. An attempt in the early 1980s to merge with the Federation of Ghanaian Women ended in failure and the demise of the federation. In 1984 the All Women's Association of Ghana tried to establish itself as an alternative organization, but it was not able to extend its reach beyond market women in Accra.

Ghana suffered an economic decline during the 1980s, and eventually a new constitution was passed in 1992 and multiparty elections were held. After the 1990s the 31st December Movement registered as a nongovernmental organization (NGO), though it was also allied with the National Democratic Congress, another political party. The focus of the group's activities was on self-help projects and rural development, including initiating income-generating actions and encouraging women to become more involved in the public life of their communities. One of its major efforts was running childcare centers that were established to support market women and later expanded to serve a broader clientele. At the same time, women were notably absent from official government structures, with only two women serving briefly in cabinet ministries; by 1990, there were no women cabinet ministers. Women participated in community organizations, as they acted to improve their own living conditions. That activity was complicated by the role of the 31st December Women's Movement, which as an NGO had privileged access to donor funding and was able to dominate many other organizations by controlling the distribution of that money.

By the end of the 1990s, however, the political scene was shifting. Under the new constitution, Rawlings won the presidency in 1992 and again in 1996. Prohibited from running for a third term, Rawlings' vice president, John Atta Mills entered the race in 2000, only to lose a close race to John Agyekum Kufuor. Some analysts argued that the key to Kufuor's success in 2000 was due at least in part to women's work to get women involved in the campaign. Groups including the United Women's Front, Women in Law and Development in Africa (WiLDAF), and the local branch of the international women's lawyers' group known as FIDA-Ghana (Federación Internacional de Abogadas) held a series of workshops to inform women about their electoral rights, traveling around Ghana to reach women in diverse communities.[9]

A key factor may have been a tragic series of murders. Accra, the capital city, had been plagued by as many as thirty murders of women beginning in 1997, and it appeared that the police were doing little to solve the killings. As women feared for their safety in the city, several women's groups came together in a coalition called Sisters' Keepers, which pressured the police and organized demonstrations. The women had gained organizing experience and knowledge about each others' groups during the previous decade of increasing democratization, and were able to coalesce in important ways at the end of the 1990s in response to the crisis.

When the initial election in December 2000 was too close to determine a final winner, the women became more outspoken in the runoff, calling on the government to take action. Women members of parliament spoke out about police inaction on solving the murders, and Sisters' Keepers sponsored a demonstration in Accra, where women wore mourning and sang dirges to call attention to the violent deaths. The women's complaints were ignored by Rawlings' party, but Kufuor's campaign sponsored an advertisement that emphasized the importance of public safety and called for action in the unsolved murders. With that positive response from the Kufuor campaign, women stepped up their individual and organizational efforts on his behalf in the run-off election.

Kufuor narrowly won the run-off election, and many viewed the women's intervention as a significant reason for his success. After becoming president, Kufuor added to the resources that police could use in their investigations, and within four months a suspect was arrested and the serial killings ended. Kufuor also established a Ministry of Women and Children's Affairs and initiated a special fund to support women in business.[10] The women's groups worked with the new ministry and other government structures to introduce a bill against domestic violence; after a contentious public debate that focused on one section in the bill related to sexual violence within marriage (termed "marital rape"), an altered version of the bill, omitting any reference to marriage, was passed in 2007.[11]

The pattern in Ghana was similar to that seen in other democratizing African nations. With the introduction of free elections, multiparty political systems, and new constitutions, women seized the increased opportunities for political activism. Historically, women had been involved in public life, and in Ghana they had experience in the market women's organizations that controlled women's primary economic concerns, and with strong women in government who had ruled as queen mothers. At the end of the twentieth century they were able to use new conditions to increase their visibility and activity in national politics.

DEMOCRATIZATION IN SOUTH AFRICA

South African women were involved in many ways as the political system there shifted dramatically. Apartheid was ended and the first open multiparty elections were held in 1994. The level of political activity was high, as a new constitution was written that codified a nonracial political system and included strong legal supports for women. Women's organizations formed in the context of the new openness, and they pressed for women's issues to be considered and included at all levels of political life.

Historically, the most active women's organizations in South Africa had been part of the African National Congress. In the 1980s new groups began to form within a wider expansion of workers' organizations and increased local and civic activism. Many organizations were connected to the United Democratic Front (UDF), a coalition of anti-apartheid organizations that was founded in 1983. Women's groups based in Transvaal, Natal, and other regions, played an important role in the UDF, working to bring women's voices to the larger struggle and simultaneously providing a space for women to gain organizing practice and political knowledge.[12]

One example among the many groups that formed to deal with local problems was seen in Hambanati, an African community in Natal province. In the highly racially divided system of the 1980s, families did not have access to land for burials, and they were forced to either cremate deceased kin (a practice considered abhorrent to many Zulu who lived in Natal), or to travel long distances to an approved segregated cemetery. As a result, women faced obstacles in organizing the burial of family members. They came together to organize the Hambanati Women's Action Group specifically to deal with this issue, and they took their complaints to the Port Natal Administration Board. They went on to address other problems faced by the community, and as they met with success in their campaigns, the administration board recognized them as representing local people's concerns. They joined with other women's groups in the Natal Organisation of Women (NOW).

Women workers in the 1980s also increased their involvement in trade union activities. They experienced barriers from their male co-workers as well as from husbands and other male family members, who did not want them to contest the conventional expectations of women's domestic tasks. Women trade unionists expanded workplace issues to include demands for maternity leave and recognition of the problem of sexual harassment, both issues that many male union organizers would have preferred to ignore.

The assortment of activities was extensive, and they cannot be properly covered here; but the women's activism of the 1980s laid a strong foundation for women in the 1990s to press for inclusion in the new constitution and to increase women's presence in electoral politics and leadership positions. In a situation where activist women wanted to simultaneously recognize class and race differences, and yet make nonracialism a basis for their organizing, they found a shared experience as mothers.[13] The idea of women focusing on the shared personal histories of motherhood has been observed in many world areas; in South Africa it formed an important basis for women from long separated communities to come together. Though some feminists resisted viewing women solely as mothers, it served as common ground for many individual women.

While women were navigating new ways of organizing, the larger political landscape was shifting dramatically. In 1990, Nelson Mandela was released from prison after twenty-seven years of incarceration. That same year, the white-minority ruling National Party lifted long-standing bans on political organizations, allowing the African National Congress including the Women's League to end decades of activists' exile and enable them to return to political work inside South Africa. While there were issues related to autonomy for the Women's League, the ANC women were also in a position to push for the greater inclusion of women in ANC efforts. Yet the years of exile added another division, that between women who had lived overseas and had a particular kind of international experience, and women who had been involved in local organizing inside South Africa and had much deeper understanding and experience in grassroots politics.

The first democratic multiparty elections were held in 1994. Women were able to play a central role in developing the new participatory documents and practices, in contrast to many other nations where women were marginalized even where they had played central roles in the national liberation movements. In the early 1990s, preparations for South Africa's first multiparty elections included work on a new constitution and on a women's charter that would encompass many of the rights desired by women. After numerous contentious discussions, women's organizations approved a document that included the recognition of equality as the basis for all other components of the charter, and dealt with equality in the law, the economy, education, development and the environment, family law, social services, religion, health, the media, and included a clause about violence against women.[14]

One aspect of the debate concerning what the new political process should look like focused on the goal of increasing the numbers of women through a system of quotas. Most people could agree that getting more women into government would aid in bringing attention and possibly change to issues that particularly affected women. However, there was tension between that goal and ideas of what was framed as "true" democracy, in which each person's vote would be influential without setting up special conditions for underrepresented groups. In South Africa the liberal parties tended to argue that special supports were not needed and that in a free and democratic society a good candidate would be elected whether that person was male or female.

The gender equality clause in South Africa's constitution paved the way for introducing proportional representation, which allowed party leaders to ensure that women were included on lists of candidates. The ANC adopted this process, with the stated goal of having no less than one-third women candidates on any list. As the ANC was also the winning party with by far the most seats in parliament in the early years following the end of apartheid, women legislators were predominantly ANC members. While the South African parliament counted around 30 percent women from 1994 to 2004, that presence did not always translate into women-centered laws.

Female politicians had some success in passing legislation guaranteeing access to abortion, adding protections against domestic abuse, improving mothers' access to financial support from former partners for maintenance of their shared children, and recognizing women in customary marriages as equal and thereby ending their previous problematic legal status. But women political activists faced stronger opposition from traditional leaders when they tried to ensure gender equality in land tenure. Intense debates ensued about who should be considered part of a community which controlled land ownership and access. Those advocating for gender equality found themselves arguing against those who supported the continued power of local leaders who were mainly male. In the end the issue was not completely resolved.[15]

The South African example demonstrated both notable advances for women in government and the continuing restrictions and obstacles that faced those working to improve conditions for women in modern society. Democratization opened up many opportunities, including new activism from issue-specific groups in local communities, the expansion of national organizations and coalitions, and improved involvement for women in political parties and in government structures. But even with striking progress seen in the numbers of women holding office and in the passage of new laws, it continued to be difficult for women to play a central role, or for women's equality to truly occur.

Democratization in Kenya

After the struggle of Mau Mau in the 1950s, at independence in 1963 the Kenya African National Union (KANU) had come to power with Jomo Kenyatta as president. He served for fifteen years, until his death in 1978, and was then followed by his vice president, Daniel arap Moi, who served until 2002. Although for some of those decades multiparty elections were legal, in fact Kenya was a one-party state, and the ruling party introduced a series of laws that increasingly centralized power in the office of the president. In 1982, in response to the efforts of an opposition party to register and participate in elections, the Constitution was amended to formally make Kenya a one-party state. That amendment was rescinded in 1992 in reaction to growing protests and a strong campaign to bring about multiparty democratic structures, but Kenyan authorities continued to obstruct and limit opposition political reform efforts. Even though opposition parties were legal, the 1990s were marked by attacks on democracy activists and by elections that were manipulated to keep Moi in power.

The important role of women in Kenyan politics throughout the twentieth century has been discussed in earlier chapters. Women were involved in an array of nationalist activities, and continued to bring their perspective to the national scene in the face of violent repression.[16] Despite their historic role and continuing contributions, they were largely excluded from national political office, with the first female minister being appointed only in 1995, to coincide with the UN Beijing Conference on Women. In the 1990s and the first decade of the twenty-first century, women worked to expand their involvement in politics by pushing for women-centered policies, organizing new political parties, and running for office, including as presidential candidates.

One of the most dynamic women was the well-known activist Wangari Maathai. Maathai was an internationally renowned environmental leader. Born in a rural community in 1940, she was trained in veterinary anatomy, and she was the first Kenyan woman to earn a PhD (and according to some sources, the first African woman to do so), which she received in 1971 from the University of Nairobi where she later taught. She was instrumental in organizing the Green Belt Movement in 1977, with a goal to combine environmental conservation, women's empowerment, and income generation. Under the auspices of the National Council of Women of Kenya, which she chaired from 1981 to 1987, Maathai introduced a project that recruited women to plant trees in a belt around the capital city of Nairobi with a focus on maintaining natural resources. Later they expanded the tree-planting to rural areas as well. By 1992, over ten million trees had been planted and survived, while eighty thousand women were working in the tree nurseries. Maathai's important work was brought to international attention when she received the Nobel Peace Prize in 2004, recognizing her contributions to building a peaceful world through environmental activism.

Maathai was involved with political movements for grassroots empowerment and increased democracy in Kenya, and she incurred the enmity of then-President Moi. Maathai and the Green Belt Movement successfully organized to stop the construction of a sixty-story building on the outskirts of Nairobi, keeping that area as part of the Green Belt.[17] She participated in a hunger strike for democracy in 1992, based at a peaceful camp set up in Nairobi's Uhuru Park (*uhuru* means freedom in Kiswahili). The camp was attacked by the police; Maathai was hospitalized as a result and spent part of 1993 in hiding from government forces. She helped organize the Forum for the Restoration of Democracy (FORD), and ran unsuccessfully for president in 1997 as the Liberal Party candidate. In 2002, Maathai was elected to the Kenyan parliament and named as deputy minister of environment, natural resources and wildlife under the government of President Mwai Kibaki in January 2003. She published a memoir, called *Unbowed*, before she passed away in 2011.[18]

Charity Ngilu was another influential Kenyan politician who was best known for her presidential candidacy in 1997, when she was the first woman to run for that office. Born in 1952, she was educated at the Alliance Girls High School in Kenya, trained as a secretary and worked at the Central Bank of Kenya in the 1970s. She continued her education and worked briefly for the Chase Manhattan Overseas Corporation before opening a bakery and restaurant. Ngilu expanded her business interests into new fields, including a plastics factory that produced PVC water pipes.

Her political career emerged on the national scene when she ran for parliament as an opposition candidate in 1992 with the Democratic Party (DP) of Kenya, defeating a former cabinet member who was supported by President Moi and KANU. She had numerous confrontations with the police, as the authorities repeatedly tried to shut down civic education forums and other events that she organized. When she was in parliament there were only 6 women out of 188 members, though even that number represented an increase over previous years. She joined the Social Democratic Party (SDP) and had support from the National Commission on the Status of Women when she ran for president representing the SDP. She came in fifth, garnering 7.9 percent of the votes. She quit the SDP when she had differences with it, and she helped form the National Alliance for Change that later became the National Party of Kenya (NPK). During the election in 2002 Ngilu was the NPK prime minister designate, and she was minister of health from 2003 to 2007 under President Mwai Kibaki. She continued to serve in parliament until 2013.

Women in Kenya pushed for an expansion of democratic reforms, and they were able to take advantage of some of the changes as they formed political parties and ran for high office. The most prominent female politician, Wangari Maathai, built a base from her work with women, and she became known for her environmental innovations, as well as her formidable political labors.

War and Peace

In the post-independence era, many African nations suffered from internal conflicts. An early devastating war was in the late 1960s in Nigeria, when the region of Biafra fought for its own independence. During the 1990s local combat and civil wars brought misery to Liberia, Sierra Leone, Rwanda, and other nations. Conflicts persisted in Sudan, the Democratic Republic of the Congo, northern Uganda, and Somalia into the 21st century, and women's experience of famine, rape, and displacement were prominent features in reports from those regions. The roots of such violence were deep and complicated, making it difficult to see a common thread or motivation between even neighboring nations.

Women were most often portrayed as victims of war. The documented evidence of women afflicted by rape, abduction, forced migration as refugees, and other forms of violence as the result of war is overwhelming. They have seen their husbands and children killed, faced injury from landmines in their fields, and lost access to their agricultural and market livelihoods.

One area that gained attention internationally was in Sudan, which endured decades of conflict, primarily between the north and south. Often characterized as a war between Islamic Arabs in the north and African followers of Christianity and local religions in the south, the situation became more complicated with increased violence against people in the western Darfur region from 2003 to 2010. Eventually, international pressure mitigated some of the worst violence, and in 2011 a referendum led to the Sudan splitting into a northern country called Sudan and a separate nation, South Sudan. Women were again severely impacted in the extended conflict, forced to flee their homes and live in refugee camps, where they watched their children starve and die from disease, and they unable to support themselves.

The incidence of rape has been documented particularly during war, for instance, in Mozambique in the 1980s and in Rwanda and the Democratic Republic of the Congo (DRC) in the 1990s. Women were humiliated by being raped with their children or neighbors as witnesses, and they were often subjected to additional torture and mutilation. Women victims were at a much increased risk for HIV/AIDS or sexually transmitted diseases; as reported by a physician in the DRC, 30 percent of the raped women treated at a hospital in Bukavu had the HIV virus. Although women who were subjected to such brutality often faced problems in reintegrating into their communities, women activists began to change attitudes and official practice in dealing with rape victims.

Judge Navanethem Pillay and her fellow judges set legal precedent in 1998 on the International Criminal Tribunal for Rwanda when they included rape as a war crime when committed during conflict. Following an uprising in the Central African Republic in 2002, the Organisation des femmes centrafricaines (Organization of Central African Republic Women) made a public appeal for humanitarian aid for women subjected to sexual attacks during the conflict. In a forward-looking and exceptional case, the post-conflict Truth and Reconciliation Commission in Sierra Leone scheduled a special two-day session devoted to hearing women's testimony about their experiences of sexual violence during the civil war that wracked Sierra Leone in the 1990s. In 2004 the United Nations court in Sierra Leone agreed to prosecute "forced marriage" as a crime against humanity.

There have been millions of Africans driven into exile as refugees as a result of violence and war in their home countries. Women generally made up about half of such refugees, but their situation was not the same as male refugees. Often women were responsible for their children, while men were more likely to seek asylum as individuals. In Rwanda families deliberately split up in order to increase their chances for safe emigration. Women frequently suffered rape and other sexual violence in the refugee camps, and found it difficult to speak about their suffering to gatekeepers and officials, who were often men. They also were more vulnerable to exploitation in the camps or other new settings where they no longer had protectors. In studies of Mozambican refugees in camps in Malawi in the 1980s it was found that training programs favored male refugees in the kinds of skills that were taught. Women developed their own livelihoods outside of official projects, basing their efforts on prior experience with pottery or other crafts. Women had difficulty being taken seriously as individuals because many programs for training and for repatriation assumed that they would be affiliated with a family unit headed by a male head of household. Sometimes women were denied access to legal supports if they did not have a husband or other male family member to vouch for them. In addition, women faced fresh problems when trying to resettle since they could not adequately prove their legal rights to land access or ownership in either their home area or in a new residence.[19]

In the 1990s, women were instrumental in developing new initiatives for an end to conflict and to actively bring peace to Africa. They were involved in negotiations for peace and organized continent-wide groups that worked to end conflict. The Kampala Action Plan on Women and Peace in 1993 was one of the first declarations from women that specifically focused on peace issues. Several associations were established, including African Women's Anti-War Coalition, African Women's Committee for Peace and Development, the Federation of African Women for Peace, and Femmes Africa Solidarité.

Local peace groups also formed. Ruth Sando Perry and others formed a lobbying group, Women as Partners for Peace in Africa (WOPPA), focused on the intransigent conflict in the Democratic Republic of the Congo. WOPPA promoted a negotiated peace settlement among the warring groups and simultaneously argued that women's voices should be included in that process. After the devastation of the 1994 genocide, women in Rwanda formed Pro-Femmes Twese Hamwe. In Sudan, women desiring an end to the long conflict there formed the Sudan Women's Voice for Peace; similarly, the Sierra Leone Women's Movement for Peace, founded prior to 1995, worked to end the conflict in that country. Women in Sierra Leone intervened directly by sitting outside the rooms where men were holding peace talks; they were allowed to enter and participate.

Women's efforts had an important source of support in the United Nations' Security Council Resolution 1325 on Women, Peace and Security. The resolution was submitted by Namibia in 2000 at the instigation of Netumbo Nandi-Ndaitwah, Namibia's minister of women's affairs, and it was passed unanimously by the council. The focus of the new measure was to encourage the protection of women from rape and other gendered violence in conflict, to include women in all peace-making efforts, and to reaffirm the centrality of women's contributions to all peace and security activities, with a number of specific directives that would drive the implementation of the more general tenets. A task force was established, and by 2004 they had published a checklist to enable member states and UN bodies to begin the improvement of women's inclusion in peace processes and ongoing security practices.[20]

In the next section, the Biafran secession attempt, the related civil wars in Liberia and Sierra Leone, the 1994 genocide in Rwanda, and the ongoing war in the Democratic Republic of the Congo will be examined from a gendered perspective, as women were centrally involved in all of these conflicts, often as victims. The advent of peace and rebuilding allowed for women's participation in new ways, including increased and improved political authority for women in the peaceful aftermath of war.

The Biafran War in Nigeria

Nigeria entered the postcolonial years as a very large and diverse independent nation in 1960, with strong divisions along ethnic and religious lines between the primarily Muslim Hausa and Fulani people in the north and between southern sectors of Yoruba people in the west and Igbo in the east. Disputes about who controlled the government and the economy escalated until a 1966 coup led by Igbo military men resulted in the death of important leaders from the north. Northern soldiers retaliated with a coup in 1967 that targeted Igbo, and it facilitated the murder of as many as thirty thousand Igbo who were living in the north. Later that year the Igbo declared the independence of the southeastern region as Biafra, setting off three years of war which resulted in widespread famine and death. Biafra, as the site of much of Nigeria's oil wealth, was not going to be allowed to separate itself from the rest of Nigeria, and the national government attacked with great power.

The role of women in the civil war has not been closely examined. The few scholarly studies suggest how Igbo women went to great effort to find food when confronted with the starvation of their families, including using guava leaves and small snails that had previously been shunned, cooking cattle hide to use as meat, and even garnishing local soups with the unfamiliar cheese dropped by plane from European humanitarian agencies. They helped establish orphanages for the many children whose parents were killed or lost in the confusion of war. Those women close to the border between Biafra and Nigeria engaged in clandestine trading, as the blockaded frontier forced women to use their usual marketing skills in a new context. Women contributed as messengers and spies, though only rarely as soldiers, in common with other women in wars of independence.[21] One source of information has been fiction, including Flora Nwapa's early stories and a later novel by Chimamanda Ngozi Adichie.[22] Buchi Emecheta's novel, *Destination Biafra*, suggested that the male-dominated political sphere of Nigeria was a factor in the fomenting of the war, and that the failure of Biafra to win its independence was a result of women's marginalization from power and politics.[23]

Conflict in Sierra Leone and Liberia

SIERRA LEONE

Women in Sierra Leone had a history as active market women and political leaders. Yet their prominence in earlier centuries was reduced under British colonialism. The women who had been successful traders in the eighteenth and nineteenth centuries in Freetown, Sierra Leone, were not able to maintain their trade into the twentieth century. Several changes had a negative impact on their marketing endeavors. As formal colonialism increased its control over Africa, the British in West Africa began to reorient their trade to improve their own situation. Complex international forces brought new settlers from Lebanon, who gained primacy in the local trade networks when the British colonialists gave them preference in banking and credit operations. The Lebanese were able to rely on their family and kin to develop trading corporations, in part because their patrilineal family organization allowed them to pass management of the family businesses from father to son. The Lebanese traders even became dominant in the kola trade, which Krio (Creole) women had built up and controlled for decades. While women in Sierra Leone continued to have some economic autonomy and trained their daughters to follow them into market trading, their share of the local market declined during the twentieth century.[24]

While women's position was weakened, other changes in Sierra Leone after independence compounded the difficulties they faced. Sierra Leone had wealth from alluvial diamonds (found in rivers rather than mines) and a history of military coups and autocratic government under Siaka Stevens, who ruled as prime minister from 1967 to 1971 and subsequently as president until 1985. Stevens organized a series of patronage chiefs who controlled diamond collection at the local level, and his legacy was of economic disaster and widespread corruption. Though he died in 1988, his policies set the stage for the war that began in 1991 when the Revolutionary United Front (RUF) attempted to stage a coup with the help of Liberia's war-mongering leader, Charles Taylor. The RUF was comprised primarily of young men who were motivated to join by high levels of poverty and joblessness, despite the lack of a clear political agenda. The militia beckoned by offering activity and a purpose, however spurious. They began funding their undertakings by controlling the diamond collection in Sierra Leone, gems which were called "blood diamonds" or "conflict diamonds," as their sale directly supported the civil war. After a few years the RUF became known for atrocities, and new members were more often forcibly recruited by kidnapping.

The civil war that resulted lasted for eleven years and brought extensive disruption and death to the country. Throughout the 1990s, there were a series of cease-fire and peace agreements, which repeatedly failed as one party or the other proved unable or unwilling to enact their part in the accord. President Ahmad Tejan Kabbah won an election in 1996 but was unable to end the conflict, as Charles Taylor continued to support the rebels in the RUF. Not until 2002, when the British intervened in support of United Nations forces, was Kabbah able to take control as the leader and finally end the war.

As with other civil wars, women were victimized by the disruption of their lives and by widespread sexual assaults. Yet information from Sierra Leone also indicated that women were involved as soldiers and supporters of the RUF, participating as cooks, medics, spiritual leaders, and combatants as well as the often-reported sex slaves and wives in forced marriages with male rebels and soldiers.[25] Many male members of the official army joined the rebel forces, emphasizing the high level of militarization of the society and of social confusion. While women were marginalized, they also found joining the conflict as one of very few options for survival.

Although overt sexual assaults gained the most attention, women also suffered when their family members were abducted and killed. Their work was disrupted by violence in their communities and the rupture of markets and supply routes. Their health suffered not only from war-related wounds and assaults, but from the closure of health posts and clinics, leading to death from illness and pregnancy. So many men were killed or absent, that women faced the burden of maintaining their households without any male support. Confronted with a bad and worsening situation, many women were involved in efforts to bring peace and democracy to Sierra Leone.[26] Women were deeply involved in associations such as the Women's Forum, a coalition of over fifty women's groups that lobbied strongly for an end to conflict, a return to constitutional rule, and an increase in women's representation in government. They organized demonstrations for peace and mobilized a mass movement that was influential in eventually ending the war.

LIBERIA

Liberia suffered a devastating civil war from 1998 to 2003. The links with Sierra Leone go beyond their shared border, as one of the rebel and then official leaders was Charles Taylor, who also fomented a return to conflict in Sierra Leone while leading the war in Liberia. Liberia's history differed from most of Africa because of the presence of an influential community of Americo-Liberians, Africans who had been enslaved in the United States and who returned to settle in Liberia in the nineteenth century. Liberia was established an independent nation in 1847 and was never colonized, though the descendents of those early Christian, educated settlers constituted a wealthier group than most indigenous communities, and they ruled Liberia even though they were a minority. The continuing rift between the American settlers and local people, even after generations, was a factor in the conflict.

Liberia, like Sierra Leone, was home to Sande societies, women's secret initiation groups which provided a space for women to develop leadership and from which they exerted authority in their society (see chapter 2). But by the end of the twentieth century, Sande had lost much of its earlier power. Divisions based on ethnicity, religion, and class all played a role in the developing conflict. In 1980, Samuel Doe overthrew the elected president, ending the rule of Americo-Liberians.

Though he staged the coup to end a repressive regime, he became more autocratic himself as years passed. In 1985 he held elections, which he narrowly won and which were condemned as fraudulent by international observers. People began to organize against Doe's rule, and in 1989 Charles Taylor, a former follower of Doe who had been exiled, raised a military force and invaded northern Liberia. As civil war spread, Prince Johnson, one of Taylor's followers, broke away from him and formed his own ethnically-based force. The Liberian army under Doe retaliated with violence against villages they believed were supporting Taylor. In 1990 Doe was captured, tortured, and killed by Johnson, all of the gruesome proceedings videotaped and the recording widely circulated in Liberia and beyond.

Throughout the 1990s there were ongoing and sporadic negotiations involving other West African nations, the United Nations, and the various government and rebel forces. None of the treaties were successful. After an abortive reconciliation in 1995, negotiations established the Council of State the following year, with Ruth Sando Perry named as chairperson. Born in 1939, she was trained as a teacher, and eventually became involved in her nation's troubled politics, serving as a senator. She was also a supervisor of the Chase Manhattan Bank in Liberia, and worked for child welfare organizations. When she was appointed by the Economic Community of West African States (ECOWAS) as Chairperson of the Council of State in Liberia, she made history as the first female head of state of Liberia, and as one of the first women to lead any African government. Perry presided over the transitional government for less than one year, serving from September 3, 1996, until August 2, 1997. She often referenced women's role as mothers in her rule, saying that the children, referring to the warlords, must obey their mother. The image of a strong mother in most African contexts is a positive one, in which women protect their families, provide economic support, and offer guidance to family members, especially younger kin.[27] In that capacity, she was responsible for disarming the warring factions as a prelude to democratic government. She went on to establish the Perry Center for Peace, Stability and Development in Africa, and to support others working on peace-building efforts across the continent, including her work with Women as Partners for Peace in Africa.

Elections were held in tense and troubled circumstances in 1997, and Charles Taylor was elected president. He then ruled over a severely damaged nation, in which two hundred thousand people had been killed (one out of seventeen people in the country) and as many as one million were forced into exile or as internal refugees. Most Liberians had witnessed or experienced horrible atrocities. The accord and election result did not last because people rose against Taylor in 1999, bringing about further conflict that lasted until 2003.

Many girls and young women grew up in the conflict, sometimes beginning as kidnapped children performing domestic chores in the rebel camps and later being forced into sexual relationships with soldiers and rebels. Women testified after the war ended, telling horrific stories of daily beatings, rapes, and mutilations. They continued to suffer when their home communities viewed them as collaborators who willingly joined the rebels, or as morally damaged as a result of their forced marriages and often subsequent pregnancies and children who resulted from sexual assault. But as with young women in Sierra Leone, not all females who were involved with the rebel fighters were victims; some deliberately chose to join and participate as a way of surviving during a time of dislocation and disorder. Having a male patron, however disreputable, meant that the girl or young woman and her family would have access to food and supplies (though most likely looted), while enjoying some protection that saved them from being attacked and looted themselves.[28]

While acknowledging the reality of such extensive losses, it was also possible to recognize that women could make some gains in the postwar society. Liberia was particularly noted for the post-conflict election of longtime political activist Ellen Johnson Sirleaf as president. She was born in Monrovia in 1939 of mixed Americo-Liberian and Gola parentage. She was trained as an economist and earned a master's degree in public administration from Harvard University. She served both in the public and private sectors, as assistant minister of finance in Liberia and as a senior loan officer in the World Bank. She returned to Liberia in 1979 when she was named minister of finance under the elected President Tubman, who was later overthrown by Doe. She was also the president of the Liberian Bank for Development and Investment.[29]

Johnson Sirleaf helped found the Liberia Action Party and as a result was jailed by Doe for sedition in 1985, though she served only a few months of her ten-year sentence. In 1986, she led five hundred women in a protest against the imprisonment of opposition political leaders by the Samuel Doe government, which led to her arrest again for treason. She escaped and lived in exile in the United States, where she was on the executive board of Equator Bank (1986–1992) and director of the United Nations Development Programme, Regional Bureau for Africa (1992–1997). In 1997 she returned to Liberia to represent the Unity Party in the election. She came in second with only 10 percent of the vote, while Charles Taylor won with 75 percent. She was once again charged with treason and went into exile. She returned in 2003 after the Special Court for Sierra Leone, an entity that was investigating the conflict, charged Taylor with war crimes and forced him out of office.

In early 2004 Johnson Sirleaf was appointed to head Liberia's anti-corruption committee, the Commission on Good Governance, and she announced plans to run for president in elections scheduled for 2005. When she won with 59 percent of the vote in the run-off she became the first woman elected to the presidency of any modern African nation. Johnson Sirleaf ran for re-election as president

Fig. 8.3 Liberian women demonstrate at the American Embassy in Monrovia at the height of the civil war in July 2003. Photograph courtesy of Pewee Flomoku.

in 2011, and though she was forced into a run-off again, in that run-off election she garnered 90.7 percent of the vote. She was one of three women peace activists honored with the Nobel Peace Prize in 2011, along with Tawakkul Karman of Yemen, and fellow Liberian Leymah Gbowee. She was elected as chair of ECOWAS in 2016, again as the first woman to hold that position.

Liberian women were instrumental in forming the African Women and Peace Support Group in 1997, an international organization that documented African women's involvement in peace activities.[30] Liberia was notable for the activism of women working for peace, as they marched in the streets of Monrovia, gathered for prayer meetings, and wore white in order to draw the attention of the male politicians who passed by the growing masses of women on the route to the peace negotiations. Women also chose delegates who arrived at meetings without official sanction, and they eventually won the right to contribute to negotiations. The Mano River Women Peace Network of Liberia was one of six organizations that were awarded the United Nations Human Rights Prize in 2003 for their efforts.

The peace activities brought Muslim and Christian women together, joined rural and urban women, and united other groups not always in agreement, with the single goal of ending the war and violence and bringing peace to Liberia. One newsworthy aspect of their years-long efforts was a call for women to refuse to have sex with their husbands and partners until peace was established. Although Leymah Gbowee commented that it was not very practical and lasted only a few months, the idea of such an action helped bring attention to women's efforts to bring peace, and was effective for that reason.[31] What it does demonstrate is the innovation and persistence that Liberian women brought to the eventual success of the peace efforts.

Women continued their activism after the war, working to improve women's lives and increase their presence in political office. Ellen Johnson Sirleaf would not have won the presidency without women's support, and she has named women to a number of important offices, including as minister of justice.

Conflict in Rwanda

Rwanda's history from the nineteenth century has involved tensions between the two primary ethnic groups, the Tutsi and the Hutu. When German colonialism gained control at the end of the nineteenth century, the area included what became the small neighboring country of Burundi, and both modern nations at that earlier time were home to farmers who were mainly Hutu and cattle herders who were mainly Tutsi. A smaller group, the Twa, lived in the forests and survived as hunters and gatherers. The Tutsi at some point in the past formed a militarized and centralized kingdom as a way to control what were ongoing conflicts over access to land between the different populations. While the communities were mainly patriarchal, women had authority as spirit mediums, and the queen mother had substantial influence on issues of succession and acted to counter-balance the power of the king. The herders imposed a labor tax that the farmers had to pay in order to gain access to land for cultivation. Despite some differences between the two groups, they also shared many characteristics including language (they all spoke Kinyarwanda) and many cultural attributes. The few elements that distinguished one group from the other were used by the colonialists to emphasize minor ethnic distinctions.

The arrival of German colonialists marked an increased rigidity in social formations, a systematic refusal to recognize women's authority, and a reliance on ethnic difference that contributed to a series of internecine clashes throughout the twentieth century. German colonial rule was replaced by the Belgians after World War I. While there had been two parallel systems of land-holding, one under the king and the other with land held by clans and lineages, the Belgians worked with the royal administration to bring all land under a central kingdom. Violence between Hutu and Tutsi populations escalated in 1959, and the Hutu majority (comprising about 85 percent of the total population) began attacking Tutsi and forced the Tutsi king to go into exile. Further political maneuvering in both Rwanda and Burundi continued until they become independent as two separate countries in 1962.

After a Hutu politician won the presidency in Rwanda, changes were introduced that included new forms of access to land. The king's herds no longer had their own extensive grazing lands, and the labor tax was abolished. While some of the tension was along ethnic lines, geographic differences also played a part, with northern Hutu acting to restrict southern Hutu from access to land. The postcolonial government was widely seen as corrupt, and in 1973 there was a coup that ended the reign of a (southern) Hutu president and ushered in the rule of northern Hutu and pro-Tutsi President Juvénal Habyarimana. Women had faced social and legal restrictions that left them under the control of their husbands or other male kin since independence, and the coup did nothing to change their subordinate position.[32]

As the decades passed, Rwandans continued to experience poverty and unemployment, lack of access to land while some leaders amassed large holdings for themselves, and escalating ethnic animosity. Women reacted to the mounting difficulties by initiating a series of civic programs and organizations, especially concerning economic issues. For instance, women were involved in developing cooperatives, a women's credit association called Duterembere, a legal aid group, and a nationwide network of women's development efforts called Reseau des Femmes. Encouraged by these ventures women began taking leadership in democratization efforts, and Monique Mujawamariya spearheaded the organization of the Rwandan Association for Human Rights and Civil Liberties.

By 1990, tensions had risen even further, and the arrival of the long-exiled Rwandan Patriotic Front (RPF), mainly Tutsi who had been based in neighboring Uganda, brought civil war to Rwanda. Their presence reinforced the divisive attitude of extremist Hutu who felt directly threatened by the RPF, and led to an increase in anti-Tutsi propaganda and the development of Hutu militia who began attacking Tutsi and also moderate Hutu people who did not support the extreme ethnic politics espoused by some Hutu. Those Hutu extremists who wished to remove Tutsi from Rwanda acted in April 1994, assassinating President Habyarimana, along with Burundi's president Cyprien Ntaryamira and other officials, by shooting down their plane as it arrived at the airport near the Rwandan capital, Kigali. The presidents were returning from discussions about future political directions when their labors to avert greater conflict were destroyed.

Prime Minister Agathe Uwilingiyimana was assassinated the day after the plane crash. She was born in 1953 in a rural area and trained as a teacher. She taught high school science for ten years, earning a master's degree in chemistry and working in industry before entering politics. She was a Hutu who was considered a moderate because she worked to diminish ethnic tension in her country. She joined the opposition party, Mouvement Démocratique Républicain (MDR,

Democratic Republican Movement), and in 1992 she was named minister of education as part of a power-sharing agenda. While serving as minister she tried to end the system of favoritism that governed admissions to secondary schools, introducing measures to control the printing of exams so that no one could get advance copies, and enhancing transparency by publicly posting the examination results. She was assaulted in a probable intimidation effort, though it was made to look like a robbery rather than a politically motivated attack. Women demonstrated in her support, calling for an end to war.

Uwilingiyimana was appointed prime minister in July 1993 as a compromise candidate among five contending parties. The MDR was involved in a power-sharing arrangement with the other major opposition parties, confronting the former single-party government of the Mouvement Républicain National pour la Démocratie et le Développement (MRND, National Republican Movement for Democracy and Development). It was expected that she would step down after a transition period ended in 1994.

She was overtaken by events when the Hutu presidents of Rwanda and Burundi were killed. Immediately, Hutus initiated a genocidal attack on Tutsis as well as on Hutus who were perceived as being too moderate. Uwilingiyimana was not on the doomed plane, but she was planning to broadcast a plea for calm and was at her home under limited protection from Ghanaian and Belgian troops, when the guards were disarmed and she was assassinated along with her husband.

The murders of the leaders were the opening to the terrible genocide of 1994. Though no accurate records were kept, various authorities estimate that between five hundred thousand and one million Rwandans (in a total population of around 10 million) were killed by other Rwandans, mostly in horrific attacks using machetes and other hand-held weapons. The United Nations considers the total to be eight hundred thousand people killed, mostly in just three months. The attacks were nearly all by Hutus against Tutsis, though as the initial assaults on Hutu leaders demonstrates, Hutus who were seen as too conciliatory were also attacked. While the rest of the world seemed stunned into inaction, or was simply oblivious to the horrors, Rwanda suffered one of the worst periods of violence in world history. The level of gruesome brutality included maiming and other atrocities, and a shocking number of sexual assaults and rapes.

Women were present as perpetrators of violent acts, but they were particularly noted as victims. Some have argued that women were attacked in response to their increasing public activism in the preceding decade. Human rights leader Monique Mujawamariya was able to escape, but many other women were deliberately targeted, including the early murder of the prime minister. Most leaders of the newly formed women's organizations were killed.

One incident highlighted women's survival and made an interesting link to the past. As reported by survivor Hassan Habiyakane, a woman healer called

Sula Karuhimbi saved seventeen people in her shrine to well-known spiritual presence, Nyabingi (see chapter 5). When the men carrying out the genocide arrived she told them that "if they entered her shrine they would incur the wrath of Nyabingi. They were frightened so our lives were saved for another day."[33]

The high incidence of rape and other sexual violence was considered a deliberate attempt to humiliate women and their families. The attacks were often public, and in acts of public ethnic erasure, women were forced to become pregnant from encounters with men of a different ethnic group. Nearly half of all Rwandan women reported being raped, including Hutu women assaulted by Tutsi men, and Tutsi women who were victimized after fleeing Rwanda for refuge in eastern Congo, where Tutsi soldiers raped women and forced them into sham marriages. Rape has always been a part of war and aggression, with women the victims who carry the marks of the assaults on their bodies and in their families if pregnancy results.[34]

The worst period of conflict ended with the victory of the RPF forces over Rwanda's regular army. As many as two million Rwandans, mainly Hutu, fled into exile, fearing further reprisals from the now ruling minority power. The war then became intertwined with conflict already present in eastern Congo.

Women were central to the post-genocide efforts to rebuild Rwandan society and to democratize Rwandan politics. Despite the loss of personnel, women's groups wielded authority and lobbied for an improved role for women in government. Women worked to encourage income-generating efforts, provide civic training, offer health care including counseling, and support for survivors, especially widows. A new organization, Pro-Femmes, developed out of a Tutsi widow's group and included the Reseau des Femmes in a new national coalition of women's associations that actively worked for women's rights. Many individual women were able to move from activism and leadership in the civil society groups to political positions. At the same time the RPF, now the ruling party under Paul Kagame, was committed to increasing the number of women in parliament and ministries. Before official quotas for women in government were enacted, there were many women in the legislature, and women made up 27 percent of the elected judges in the system of reconciliation tribunals called *gacaca*.[35]

In a new constitution approved in 2003, 30 percent of the seats in the lower house of parliament were reserved for women; women also won a number of seats that were not reserved along gender lines, so that the election results of that year found that women held 48.8 percent of the seats. With that election, Rwanda became the country with the highest percentage of female legislators in the world. In the decade following that election, the percentage continued to increase, while at the same time the government grew more authoritarian.

Conflict in the Democratic Republic of Congo

The conflict in Rwanda was resolved, but continued in an altered form in neighboring Democratic Republic of the Congo, known previously as Zaire. Many thousands of Rwandans had fled across the border, and continued to live in refugee camps around the town of Goma and other areas close to the border. Mobutu Sese Seko, a despot who robbed the country for his own personal wealth, had ruled Zaire for decades, until he was deposed in 1996 by Laurent Kabila, a military leader from eastern Congo. Laurent Kabila was assassinated in 2001 after seven years in office and was succeeded by his son, Joseph Kabila. A huge geographic area in central Africa, Congo had been the site of ongoing conflict since independence, at least in part due to the mineral riches found in Katanga and other eastern regions. The eastern province of Kivu had been a site of turmoil since at least 1993, so the Rwandan refugees found themselves in the middle of an ongoing crisis. They were subject to assault by local Congolese warlords as well as by continuing murderous efforts by other Rwandans who also fled across the border when they determined that they would be subject to punishment for their role in the genocide.[36] Further, northern Congolese provinces were closely connected to Uganda, and Ugandan soldiers were present for much of the 1990s, as were members of the Rwandan army in eastern Congo. The west and south were under the control of the Kabila government based in Kinshasa. In 1998, Laurent Kabila sent all of the foreign armies away and took measures to regain control of the country. Violence continued with women active both as combatants in the Congolese army (perhaps as many as 15 percent of soldiers were female), as victims of war-related assaults, and as activists for peace.

Women were particularly victimized in the fluid and unstable conditions, with the scope of rape of both Rwandan refugees and Congolese women perhaps in the hundreds of thousands. The conditions that preceded the situation found in the early twenty-first century were complicated. One key factor was the presence of desirable minerals such as copper, and more recently tantalum, tin, cobalt, and tungsten, all used in cell phones and laptop computers and therefore in high demand on the international market. The initial phase of violence in 1996–1997 was instigated by the Rwandan genocide, and the continuing conflict, sexual violence, and murder of Hutus in the Congo should be considered a genocidal situation as well.[37] A second phase of the conflict appeared more like a civil war, with rebels fighting a central government. Lasting from 1998 to 2002, the devastated economy meant that women seeking firewood, food, and other necessities had to travel to markets, fields, and other sites where they were vulnerable to attack and rape. The government led by Joseph Kabila signed a peace treaty in 2002 that brought some male rebel fighters into the government, and brought peace to some regions of the nation. Though restricted geographically, a third phase of conflict continued after 2003, despite a peace accord that was negotiated in 2006. Mass rapes were recorded in August 2010 and on New Year's Day 2011 in South Kivu. Repeated accounts of terrible assaults led to the designation of the Congo as the "rape capital of the world" by Margot Wallström, the UN Special Representative of the Secretary General on Sexual Violence in Conflict.[38]

In reaction to the horrors experienced by so many Congolese women, the government passed important legislation in 2010 that potentially could remove some of the legal obstacles facing women who wished to press charges against their violators. Among the provisions were a new more exact definition of "rape," and the inclusion of an amendment that covered "any act of a sexual nature performed under coercive circumstances."[39] Though not a perfect law, it allowed women and their lawyers to seek justice in the Congolese court system. Other observers suggested that women's increased independence that resulted from the disruption of war sometimes had positive results, as they were no longer forced to turn over their market earnings to their husbands. Estimates that 60 to 80 percent of women were single heads of households may have indicated a high level of poverty, but for some women it also signaled freedom from male control in the household.[40]

Many women's organizations were revived or newly formed to facilitate networking and activism for peace. With the support of the United Nations, the numbers of women delegates involved in peace negotiations was increased. As mentioned in the section on Liberia, Ruth Sando Perry visited Congo and supported the establishment of Women as Partners for Peace in Africa (WOPPA), which collaborated with the transnational organization Femmes Africa Solidarité (FAS) to advance the peace process through the integration of women and women's concerns into discussions. In 2002, more than forty Congolese women met in Kenya and issued the Nairobi Declaration, calling for women to be involved at the top levels of the peace process, for the implementation of the Convention on the Elimination of All Forms of Discrimination against Women (CEDAW), which had been ratified by the Congolese government, and for support from international organizations in reaching those goals.[41]

Conflict: Conclusion

The spread of what is sometimes termed "low-level" conflict has taken a terrible toll on African women. Beyond the events profiled here, serious clashes occurred in other areas that attracted international attention. Somalia suffered from years of autocratic rule until the state collapsed in 1991 leading to a lengthy period of war among various clan leaders that involved US and UN military forces. Eventually dividing into Somaliland in the north and Somalia in the south, the situation only began to be resolved after more than twenty years of violence. The costs were enormous with one million Somalis fleeing into exile and hundreds of thousands killed. With attention on the fundamentalist Islamists, the military leaders who were called warlords, and other male authorities, the impact on women was ignored. More recent attention to women has found that they suffered from assaults that were directed specifically at women, such as rape, and that their ability to support themselves and their families was undermined by the lack of official infrastructure. Without denying that reality, the disruption of conflict as in other places allowed some women the opportunity to become more independent economically and politically. Women contributed to social stability when they initiated organizations, worked in the markets, and established a human rights center and an orphanage. Dr. Hawa Abdi gained international recognition for founding a women's hospital that brought needed services to a destitute population. Women contributed to peace efforts, attending numerous peace conferences, holding demonstrations, and calling for peace as they recited poetry.[42]

In northern Uganda, people endured decades of disruption and violence, beginning with the emergence of Alice Auma Lakwena, who played a central role in the conflict in the 1980s. Lakwena was an Acholi woman who became a prophet. Born in 1956, her father, Severino Lukoya, was active in the Church of Uganda and she was an adherent of the Anglican faith when she was young. She married twice but never had children, and because of that her husbands divorced her. After a spiritual crisis in 1985, she claimed that she was possessed by a powerful Christian spirit called Lakwena, which remained her primary identity though she alleged possession by a number of other spirits as well. She founded and led the Holy Spirit Movement (HSM, sometimes called the Holy Spirit Mobile Forces) in a war against the Ugandan central government from 1986 until she was defeated in 1987, after which she went into exile in Kenya. In the early years of HSM activities, Lakwena and her followers espoused egalitarianism between men and women and advocated an intense purity of spirit and body, including abstinence from alcohol, tobacco, sex, and thievery. She quickly rose to prominence, drawing on the disenfranchised sensibility of many poor Ugandans, and she used magical invocations and concoctions to promise special powers for her followers.

The army Lakwena raised posed a serious threat to the government of Ugandan President Yoweri Museveni, as they marched across Uganda and came within two hundred miles of the capital, Kampala, before being decisively defeated by government forces. The total number of casualties attributed to attacks by and on the HSM cannot be ascertained, but was likely in the thousands. Some of her followers continued to fight from northern bases into the 1990s. In 2004 she appealed to the United Nations High Commissioner for Refugees in Kenya, saying she wished to return to Uganda, but she died in a Kenyan refugee camp in 2007.[43] Violent attacks continued in the twenty-first century in Uganda under the leadership of Joseph Kony, who became the focus of an international campaign to stop the kidnapping of children by the Lord's Resistance Army, a splinter group that had evolved out of the HSM.

Women have been able to expand their political participation in some post-conflict societies, especially after the 1990s.[44] That result is due to a combination of events and influences, including the disruption of gender norms as a result of the conflict, the important support of international agencies for women's issues, and the development of women's organizations that allow women space to develop leadership and strategies.

Women in Leadership

Women have made important contributions to national politics as elected and appointed officials and by taking advantage of their prominence as first ladies. While not all women in leadership have focused on issues relevant to women, many have used the platform they attained to form women's organizations, to advocate for policy change, and to provide support to women in difficult situations.

Presidents

While more women were being appointed as heads of their governments, being elected as a head of state remained an elusive goal for African women. There were royal women who ruled in Ethiopia (Empresses Zauditu and Menetewab) and Madagascar (Ranavalona I, II, and III) in earlier historic periods. But in the modern era, there were few examples of national female rulers. As discussed earlier, Ruth Sando Perry served as chair of an interim governing council in Liberia in 1996–1997, a position that was head of state, but was appointed rather than elected. In the 1990s, however, the numbers of women announcing themselves as candidates in presidential races increased and drew renewed attention. The election of Ellen Johnson Sirleaf in Liberia in 2005, discussed in this chapter, was noted as the first time that a woman was elected to the office of president in Africa. While other women ran for the office, no others had won a presidential election as of 2015. The presidential race in Nigeria in 1992 was marked by the entry of three women into the race. Alda Bandeira ran in São Tomé e Príncipe in 1996, and in 1997 Charity Ngilu ran in Kenya and Ellen Johnson Sirleaf ran in Liberia, though she did not win until a later election. Other notable women who attempted to gain their nation's presidency included Antonieta Rosa Gomes in Guinea-Bissau in 1994 and 1999, and Vera Chirwa in Malawi in 2004.

Joyce Banda became president of Malawi in 2012 following the death of President Bingu wa Mutharika, whom she served as vice president. She was born in Malawi in 1950, and she was a successful businesswoman prior to entering politics in 1999, when she ran for and won a seat in the national legislature. She was appointed as minister of gender and community services where she developed a national plan of action on orphans and abused children, and worked unsuccessfully to pass a law concerning domestic violence. Reelected to parliament in 2004, she was named foreign minister in 2006, becoming one of the few women in the world to hold that office.

In 2009, Banda ran as the vice-presidential candidate on the Democratic Progressive Party (DPP) ticket, and she won. Controversy ensued when President Mutharika tried to remove her from office in favor of his own wife, a move that was blocked by the Malawian courts. She was cut off from the DPP, however, and as a result formed her own political party, the People's Party. Despite Mutharika's effort to marginalize the office of vice president, and his attempt to name his brother Peter as his successor, she kept her position in the government because of the legal authority of the Constitution. When Mutharika passed away, there was some opposition to her taking office as president, as his supporters claimed she forfeited the right to succeed when she formed an opposition party. However, the high court supported the law, which maintained her as vice president and which recognized the sitting vice president as the proper successor when a president died while in office. When she took office as president, her first actions focused on repairing damaged foreign relations, devaluing the national currency in order to regain access to international loans, and announcing that she would work to overturn Malawi's ban on homosexuality. She also took a personal pay cut and sold the presidential fleet of luxury cars and jet to set an example for governmental control over expenditures.[45] She was not able to continue her reform projects, however, as she lost the subsequent election in 2014, which saw Peter Mutharika winning the presidency.

In early 2014, the Central African Republic was endangered by violence between Muslim and Christian groups engaged in street fighting. The sitting president, whose seizure of power some months before had fomented the violence, was forced to resign. Ten days later the legislature voted on an interim president, electing Catherine Samba-Panza to the post. Previously, her success in business had resulted in her being named as mayor of Bangui, the capital city. Her election as president, though designed to last only until elections could be organized, was greeted with joy and excitement by women in the assembly chamber, and she held that office for two years, until new elections were held in February 2016.

Prime Ministers

Beginning in the 1990s a growing number of women sought to lead their countries, and a few served as prime ministers, or heads of government, though most served abbreviated terms.

Elisabeth Domitien was the first woman to head a modern African government, in the Central African Republic (CAR) from 1975 to 1976, though under less than auspicious circumstances since she served with a notorious dictator, Jean-Bedel Bokassa. She was born in 1926, and as a young woman she got involved in local politics. In 1972, she moved into the vice-presidency of the Mouvement pour l'évolution sociale de l'Afrique noire (MESAN, Movement for the Social Evolution of Black Africa), the only legal political party in CAR. She was instrumental in organizing women in support of Bokassa. She was vice president of CAR when Bokassa, who had been raised in her father's house and was a close family friend, named her to the newly-created position of premier in January 1975. Domitien was fired in April 1976 when she criticized Bokassa's plans to make himself monarch of the re-named Central African Empire. She remained active in politics, however, and was jailed in 1980 when Bokassa was overthrown. She was later a successful businesswoman until her death in 2005.

One of the briefest terms was served by Carmen Pereira, who was acting head of government in Guinea-Bissau for two days in 1984. Agathe Uwilingiyimana's tragic brief tenure as Rwanda's prime minister in 1994 was discussed earlier in this chapter. Other women prime ministers included Sylvie Kinigi in Burundi in 1993–1994, Mame Madior Boye in Senegal in 2001, and Maria das Neves Ceita Batista de Sousa in São Tomé e Príncipe in 2002 to 2003.

Breaking the mold of women only holding the high office of prime minister for very brief periods of time was Luisa Diogo, who was prime minister of Mozambique from 2004 to 2010. She was born in 1958 in the western province of Tete and educated in Mozambique, earning her undergraduate degree at Universidade Eduardo Mondlane in 1983 before earning her master's degree in finance economics from the University of London in 1992. She began working in the Mozambican finance ministry in 1980, became a department head in 1986 and was national budget director from 1989 to 1992. She worked briefly for the World Bank in Mozambique (1993–1994), but she returned to government as deputy finance minister after elections in 1994. She was named minister of finance in 1999 and continued to hold that position while serving as prime minister. Since leaving office, she has continued to work with other women leaders in international endeavors to improve conditions for women and girls.

First Ladies

In the years before women were able to exercise political authority at the national level, a number of women took advantage of their position as first ladies to initiate programs and to work to advance women.

One of the best known first ladies was Graça Machel, who was a significant political leader in Mozambique and internationally, and she also held the distinction of being the only woman to serve as first lady of two countries, Mozambique and South Africa. She was born in Mozambique in 1945 and educated in modern languages at University of Lisbon in Portugal. She joined FRELIMO (Frente de Libertação de Moçambique, Mozambique Liberation Front) in 1972, and she went to Tanzania, where she received military training. She married Samora Machel shortly after he became Mozambique's first post-independence president. Graça Machel was appointed minister of education in 1975 and served until 1990; she was the only female government minister in Mozambique during those years. She was also active in the Organização da Mulher Moçambicana (OMM, the Organization of Mozambican Women), and in the FRELIMO Central Committee. Samora Machel was killed in 1986 in a plane crash that many believe was engineered by the apartheid regime in South Africa. In 1998 Graça Machel married Nelson Mandela while he was president of South Africa.

Graça Machel was active in the United Nations, focusing on the problem of child soldiers around the world and drawing from her observations of war in Mozambique in the 1980s. She initiated and led a nongovernmental organization, the Fundação para o Desenvolvimento da Comunidade (Foundation for Community Development), which supported child-oriented programs. She has continued to work with international organizations involved in women's and children's causes.

Projects developed by first ladies have sometimes been criticized for focusing on ventures that benefited elite women. In Nigeria, the Better Life Programme for the Rural Woman (BLP) was established in 1987 by Maryam Babangida, who was the first lady from 1985 to 1993. Funded by the government, it was designed to improve women's lives through organizing income-producing projects in agriculture, trade, and small-scale production. Initially the program was promising, sponsoring over nine thousand new cooperatives, nearly one thousand cottage industries, and shops, markets, farms, and women's centers. As time passed, it became a forum for elite women with little service to the poor rural farmers who were supposed to benefit, and it was eventually integrated into the National Commission for Women. A similar pattern was seen with Ghana's 31st December Women's Movement, discussed in this chapter.

Other first ladies have been involved with organizations that had a wider appeal, including Ruth Khama of Botswana who headed the Botswana Red Cross and worked with the Girl Guides and the Botswana Council of Women. Janet Museveni sponsored Uganda Women's Effort to Save Orphans (UWESO), which was founded in 1986 to care for children orphaned as the result of war and conflict, shifting in 1990 to working with the estimated one to two million HIV/AIDS orphans in Uganda. Transforming itself to serve women in need, UWESO, with a United Nations partner organization, offered AIDS prevention workshops, and it provided low-interest loans to women to help them generate an income and

Fig. 8.4 African first ladies meet in 2015 in Johannesburg, South Africa, to discuss their work with young women concerning HIV/AIDS. Photograph courtesy of the Organisation of African First Ladies (OAFLA).

support themselves, The program taught loan recipients about business management and enjoyed a repayment rate of 90 percent.

First ladies have also gathered across national lines to work on particular projects. The Organisation of African First Ladies against HIV/AIDS (OAFLA) was founded in 2002, with a mission to focus on women and AIDS. They have since broadened their scope and shortened their name (to Organisation of African First Ladies). They have met regularly to coordinate work on HIV/AIDS, maternal and child health, the situation of adolescent girls and young women, and related issues, while also investigating poverty and advocating for empowering women. Such efforts can galvanize policy makers and improve conditions for all young women.

Women's Organizations and Political Activism

Women's political work in the postindependence era included many women-centered projects. A few of these will be discussed in this section to provide some idea of the variety of activities, from working to change a discriminatory citizenship law in Botswana, to protesting the environmental and economic degradation of the oil-drilling companies in Nigeria. These examples suggest the continuing role that women play across the political landscape of Africa.

Citizenship in Botswana

Citizenship has sometimes been a contentious legal issue in African countries, where leaders have become concerned with national identity and the enduring legacy of colonialism. In Botswana in 1982, a law was passed that restricted citizenship to those who could claim descent through their father's line, not simply those who were born in the country. Thus women who were married to foreigners were legally denied the right to pass their own Botswana citizenship to their children, even when those children were born in Botswana. This provision reflected traditional patrilineal ideas about the father's family having a claim on children's allegiance. The new restrictions were especially difficult for women married to men living in Botswana as exiles from apartheid South Africa; as those men were essentially stateless, denying Botswana citizenship to their children made them stateless as well.

Women formed the Emang Basadi Women's Association in 1986 in order to confront the government about the new law. The name Emang Basadi, meaning "Stand Up Women" in Setswana, was considered a comment on the national anthem that exhorted men to "rise up," and women to "rise up" and "stand behind your men." The women who formed the organization were concerned with promoting the legal, social, cultural, and economic status of women. Members actively networked with other women's organizations both inside Botswana and internationally. Emang Basadi focused in particular on women and politics, doing educational and organizational work to improve the situation of women in governance. The group trained female candidates, held workshops for voters, and worked with the women's sections of political parties. It also published a series of informational pamphlets, including a report on their ongoing Political Education Project.[46] Until 1993, Emang Basadi was run by volunteers; after that date it was able to set up an office and recruit paid staff to perform the work of the organization.

In the 1980s, Emang Basadi supported Unity Dow, a lawyer who took on the citizenship law when she sued the government for sex discrimination. The case went through the courts to the High Court of Botswana, which in 1992 ruled in favor of Dow's claim that the citizenship law was in conflict with women's rights as guaranteed under the Constitution. A new law was passed by parliament in 1996.

Born in rural Botswana in 1959, Dow's parents encouraged education for all of their children. She eventually earned law degrees at the University of Botswana and Swaziland and at Edinburgh, Scotland. She worked in the Botswana attorney general's office before opening a private law office with a woman partner. Dow was a cofounder of Women and Law in Southern Africa, and she also founded the

Metlhaetsile Women's Center in Botswana in 1990. She was appointed a judge on the High Court in 1998, the first woman to hold that position in Botswana, and she returned to private practice in 2009. She has also written a series of novels that address social issues concerning women in Botswana. Her lawsuit focused attention on the discriminatory citizenship law, while Emang Basadi's ongoing effort to raise issues of gender equality were a key factor that resulted in the successful introduction of the new law.

Tanzania Media Women's Association

The Tanzania Media Women's Association (TAMWA) began when a group of women journalists met in 1979 to discuss their work and the role of women in the media. Initially, TAMWA produced radio programs, beginning with a series on schoolgirl pregnancies that was broadcast in Kiswahili and English. Despite the popularity of the show, the second series they produced on domestic violence was blocked by male authorities. After several years of no activity, the women met again in 1986 following the Nairobi Women's Meeting and decided to work together and form an official organization. It was an early example of organizing among African urban professional women; such organizations proliferated in the 1990s. TAMWA began publishing an internal newsletter, *Titbits*, in 1987, which later became the magazine, *Sauti ya Siti* (*Voice of Siti*, named for famed singer Siti binti Saad, discussed in chapter 5). It also established a reference library on women, with an electronic database to facilitate retrieval of sources. The members continued to produce radio programs, and they published monographs that documented the condition of women in Tanzania. In the early 1990s, TAMWA returned to the issue of domestic violence, publishing a special issue of *Sauti ya Siti* on the topic and producing radio programs, posters, and other materials to raise public awareness of the problem. It also expanded to provide training for community activists in legal issues, counseling for women victims, and to pursue court cases related to domestic violence.

Trade Unions

Women were a distinct minority among unionized workers across the continent; however, when they found employment in factories and other sites of worker's unions, they joined and agitated for issues important to them. It was usually perceived that women were less likely than men to join trade unions, explained by their heavy load of domestic responsibilities that did not allow them the time and energy needed to be involved in work-related organizations. Often women joined a gender-identified affiliate, such as the Women's Wing of the National Union of Plantation and Agricultural Workers in Uganda, the Nigeria Labour Congress Women's Wing or the Comité das Mulheres Trabalhadoras (COMUTRA, Working Women's Committee) in Mozambique. The international organization, Union Network International-Africa, which was formed in 2000 from a merger of several large unions and which represented as many as 655,485 trade unionists in Africa, had a women's section headed by Madeleine Ouedraogo.

Such affiliates have acted to focus women's organizing, but they also have segregated women's issues from the main work of trade unions, to the detriment of their overall objectives of improving working conditions for women. Issues such as pregnancy leave were relegated to women alone, with no recognition that men and families in general also had a stake in improving women's working conditions. There were also cases of employers preferring to hire women because they believed women would be less apt to be involved in unions or to otherwise contest poor wages and working conditions, as was documented at a garment factory in Nigeria. South Africa had one of the strongest records of women's involvement in trade union organizing and included individual activists such as Frances Baard, Emma Mashinini, and Lilian Ngoyi.[47]

Rotating Savings and Credit Associations

Rotating savings and credit associations, sometimes called ROSCAS or SACCOS (Savings and Credit Co-operatives), were generally local informal groups that assisted people in pooling income and saving for large expenses. Women have found this method of budgeting to be helpful because they can avoid banks (which have excluded women at times) and interest payments, as well as keep their own income out of the reach of husbands and other male kin. Rotating credit and savings organizations are often formed among kin, neighbors, and friends. The typical method calls for each member to put a set amount of money into a common pot on a regular basis (usually daily or weekly), and for the members to then take turns in rotation withdrawing a lump sum that can be used to capitalize a small business or pay for medical or funeral costs. Such groups were an important component in the economy of the informal sector, and they also became a cornerstone of many development projects. The associations sometimes had a specific name, such as *stokvel* in South Africa, *tontine* in Cameroon and Senegal, or *upato* in Tanzania, where historically they involved sharing clothing or food rather than money.

Pentecostal Churches

From the first introduction of Christian beliefs, Africans added their own understanding of spiritual activities to official church practices. While there were some independent churches from early in the twentieth century (see chapter 4), the 1970s marked the beginning of a huge expansion in adherents to Pentecostal or Charismatic Christian churches. Women were sometimes leaders of these organizations, although most were headed by men despite the fact that the majority of members were female and women were recognized as the mainstays.[48] Pentecostal practice begins with an emphasis on the occurrence of being "born again," when the adherent experiences a conversion in their devotion to Christ. By the 1990s, Pentecostal churches were the fastest growing churches in Africa, with numerous new independent churches established across the continent.

Such churches were attractive to women because of such factors as women's history as spiritual leaders in African communities, a role that was not found in mainline Christian churches. Women also found the Pentecostal independent churches welcoming because they included new opportunities for women to lead and guide church adherents, and female members were able to advocate for women's liberation from oppression, with particular attention to such detrimental practices as witchcraft and polygyny. Often, independent churches, especially those initiated by women, would set up specific ministries to deal with problems with fertility or marriage, thus drawing in more female members. Alice Lenshina was an example of a female founder of a church (see chapter 6), as is Mai Chaza, who founded the Guta la Jehova (City of God) in Zimbabwe in the 1950s with a mission to serve barren and disabled women.

Those earlier churches were not themselves always Pentecostal, but they set a precedent for the later development of Charismatic churches with women at the forefront. One reason for women's prominence was the churches' recognition of people with specific gifts as prophets and visionaries, without regard for gender. Such influential women then provided care for women and advocated for women's leadership and equality. The church organizations often included theological institutes, where women gained an education that also contributed to their status within and outside the church. The importance of healing to the mission of the Pentecostal churches offered a central role for women through spiritual and medical healing practices.

Another aspect of the Pentecostal churches was their energetic outreach and evangelical activities. Drawing from the historic model of biblewomen in southern Africa, women were pastors and preachers, and increasingly used media such as religious tracts, radio, and the internet to gain followers. All of those practices allowed women who were active in the church to recruit other women, so the churches grew with a strong female presence. Despite the continued existence of patriarchal practices and restrictive behavior by church members, many women find solace and community in the independent church movement.

Ethnic Politics in Kenya

Wambui Otieno, a Gikuyu woman who had been active in the Mau Mau rebellion in Kenya, came to wider prominence in 1986 when her husband, renowned lawyer Silvano Melea Otieno (always called S. M. Otieno), died without leaving a written will. The events that followed brought modern concerns about ethnicity, gender, inheritance, widowhood, and power to the forefront of public debate in

Kenya and elsewhere.[49] After independence Wambui settled in Nairobi where she continued to be active in politics, and she met S. M., a Luo. Their marriage embodied the interethnic ideals of the era when the new leadership promulgated the idea of being Kenyan rather than identifying with a particular ethnicity. When S. M. died, Wambui planned to bury him on land they owned together in Nairobi, where he had requested to be buried. His Luo clan insisted on burying him in his homeland, so Wambui took them to court to protect her rights as his wife. In the court case, Wambui's lawyers argued that S. M. had turned away from his Luo roots by marrying a Gikuyu woman, living in Nairobi, and converting to Christianity. His clan claimed that S. M.'s birth and childhood as a Luo had primacy, and the courts sided with them. Many observers felt the decision, which resulted in a triumphant "homecoming" burial in the Luo home district, undercut legal gains made by women and also encouraged ethnic dissension.

Conclusion

The decades following independence were a period of increased political activity for women in Africa. They entered into formal politics, eventually gaining leadership at the national level in many countries. Two divergent developments were of primary importance, and both influenced the rise of both numbers and influence of women. One was the experience of internal conflict in several countries. Though women suffered enormously from wars in their nations, they also demonstrated resilience and in some cases were able to rebound and gain public support. The simultaneous spread of the ideas and practices of democratization opened new space for women to gain seats in national legislatures, to take on leadership roles, and to use those spaces to advocate for laws and policies that would support women and end some of the most oppressive customs. These advances signified real success for women's rights, despite the continuation of obstacles to women's interests in family life, politics, and community activities.

Notes

1. The text of CEDAW is available at this link: http://www.un.org/womenwatch/daw/cedaw/cedaw.htm.
2. "The Nairobi Manifesto."
3. Madsen, "Mainstreaming from Beijing to Ghana."
4. Ibid., 578.
5. Tripp, "The New Political Activism in Africa."
6. Ahikire, "Gender Equity and Local Democracy in Contemporary Uganda," 213.
7. Fallon, *Democracy and the Rise of Women's Movements*, 3.
8. Current statistics regarding the numbers of women in parliaments around the world can be found at the website of the Inter-Parliamentary Union, www.ipu.org.

9. Fallon, *Democracy and the Rise of Women's Movements*, 75–76.
10. Ibid., 1–2.
11. Ibid., 100–110.
12. Hassim, *Women's Organizations and Democracy in South Africa*.
13. Ibid., 75–76.
14. Ibid.,, 269–277, for the text of the 1994 second draft of the charter.
15. For a useful overview of the land debate, see Hassim, *Women's Organizations and Democracy in South Africa*, 202–208.
16. Nzomo, "Kenya: The Women's Movement."
17. Their informative website is at http://www.greenbeltmovement.org/.
18. Maathai, *Unbowed*.
19. Apeadu, "An Ignored Population."
20. See the United Nations, Office of the Special Adviser on Gender Issues and Advancement of Women for more detailed information, (accessed January 17, 2014) http://www.un.org/womenwatch/osagi/wps/.
21. Achebe, "Igbo Women in the Nigerian-Biafran War," and Uchendu, *Women and Conflict in the Nigerian Civil War*.
22. Nwapa, *Wives at War* and Adichie, *Half of a Yellow Sun*.
23. Emecheta, *Destination Biafra*, and Adams, "It's a Woman's War."
24. White, *Sierra Leone's Settler Women Traders*.
25. Coulter, *Bush Wives and Girl Soldiers*.
26. Steady, *Women and Collective Action*.
27. Moran, "Our Mothers Have Spoken."
28. Utas, "Agency of Victims."
29. Johnson Sirleaf, *This Child Will Be Great*.
30. African Women and Peace Support Group, *Liberian Women Peacemakers*.
31. Gbowee and Mithers, *Mighty Be Our Powers*, 147.
32. Longman, "Rwanda: Achieving Equality or Serving an Authoritarian State?"
33. Display at the Kigali Genocide Memorial Center in Rwanda, November 2013.
34. Burnet, "Situating Sexual Violence in Rwanda."
35. Longman, "Rwanda: Achieving Equality or Serving an Authoritarian State?"
36. Brittain, "Calvary of the Women."
37. Zongwe, "The New Sexual Violence Legislation in the Congo."
38. Ibid., 40.
39. Ibid.,
40. Puechguirbal, "Women and War in the Democratic Republic of the Congo."
41. Ibid., 1276.
42. Ingiriis and Hoehne, "The Impact of Civil War and State Collapse on the Roles of Somali Women."
43. Behrend, *Alice Lakwena and the Holy Spirits*.
44. Tripp, *Women and Power in Postconflict Africa*.
45. Gerson, "A New Leader for Africa."
46. Molokomme, "Emang Basadi."
47. Berger, *Threads of Solidarity*.
48. Mwaura, "Gender and Power in African Christianity."
49. Otieno, *Mau Mau's Daughter*.

9 Women at the Beginning of the Twenty-First Century

IT SOMETIMES SEEMS as though women are stagnating in African societies, continuing as the family members who are primarily responsible for agricultural labor and facing ongoing hindrances to gaining education and employment equal to African men. Illiteracy levels remain high across the continent despite increased schooling for girls. Women still have serious problems in the areas of polygyny, divorce, inheritance, and widowhood, as stories emerge about the families of deceased husbands arriving to claim the household goods as their own rather than belonging to the widow and her children. Since the 1980s, the scourge of HIV/AIDS has inflicted untold hardships on women either through acquiring the disease itself or through the added burdens of caring for ill or orphaned kin and others. And recent decades have been marked by terrible "low-intensity" wars in over a dozen countries, with women frequently the victims of war-related violence, sexual assault, dislocation, disease, and other traumas.

At the same time, there is evidence that more African women are taking a central role in international politics. Nobel Peace Prize winners have included the Kenyan environmental activist Wangari Maathai in 2004 and Liberians Ellen Johnson Sirleaf and Leymah Gbowee in 2011 (see chapter 8). In 2003, women activists celebrated a victory when the African Union adopted a landmark Protocol on the Rights of Women that encouraged African nations to enact an impressive catalog of woman-friendly legislation. One of the most acclaimed authors in the new century was Nigerian-born Chimamanda Ngozi Adichie, who not only wrote important novels and short stories, but was noted for her public talks on feminism and finding peoples' stories. Mexican-born Kenyan actress Lupita Nyong'o won the Academy Award for Best Supporting Actress in 2014 for her role in the film *12 Years a Slave*.

African women's varied experiences means that there is no single assessment of their current situation. However, some key topics that have gained prominence since 2000 can be addressed, including legal issues related to shari'a law, kidnapping of girls by Islamist extremists in Nigeria, continuing female resistance to political and economic oppression, and newly prominent concerns about sexuality, land grabbing, and women's rights as human rights. The opportunities and restrictions faced by African women are constantly shifting, though the general trend was for women to seize more choices for personal independence, and to fight to extend those options to other women and future generations.

Law

In recent decades, African women lawyers have used their expertise to advance legal issues concerning women, such as domestic violence. Female lawyers played a leading role in fighting infringements of women's rights under Shari'a law in Islamic northern Nigeria. In other legal actions, women actively lobbied for the passage of family laws that would provide greater protection for women's rights. Two important groups that lobbied on women's issues were the regional Women and Law in Southern Africa (WLSA) and Women in Law and Development in Africa (WiLDAF), which coordinated efforts to improve women's legal situation.

Some prominent African women lawyers included Aduke Alakija, who served as president of the International Federation of Female Lawyers, and Pendukeni Iivula-Ithana, the first female attorney general in Namibia. Fatoumata Dembélé Diarra from Mali and Navanethem Pillay from South Africa both served on international courts and were named to the initial group of judges on the International Criminal Court in 2003.

Human Rights

Human rights arose as a concept following World War II, and by the 1980s and 1990s the issue of human rights for African women had become a hotly debated topic among international legal authorities and human rights activists. It was part of a larger debate about incorporating specific concerns pertaining to women, such as female genital cutting and domestic violence, into the broader interests of human rights. One difficulty was determining how to address the universal nature of human rights while trying to respect the particularity of different cultures. Historically, human rights advocates focused on state abuses of rights, especially political and civil rights, and relegated abuse of women to the private sphere or considered problems to be individual rather than social in nature. Many African countries continue to operate under a dual system of customary law and a legal system derived from Western law, a duality that can act as an obstacle to enacting women's rights. Marriage laws in particular were prone to being relegated to the customary sphere, which is rarely favorable to women's rights.

Beginning in the 1980s, human rights promoters argued that women's rights should not be divided off as a special case, but deserved attention at the center of human rights campaigns. Gender-based violence, whether in the home or an aspect of war, was analyzed as part of the broader culture, not more narrowly as a woman's problem. Some writers argued that polygyny and the exchange of bridewealth also infringed on women's human rights, in part because those customs were intrinsically not equal between men and women and placed women at a disadvantage in their communities. Some of the discussions about gender aspects of human rights incorporated larger philosophical dilemmas about the nature of the individual in society.

Two of the legal and human rights issues that have a particular impact on women have been the focus of feature-length films. *Sisters in Law: Stories from a Cameroon Court* was a documentary made in 2005 by Florence Ayisi and Kim Longinotto. Set in a small Muslim town, the film followed four specific cases dealing with marital violence, kidnapping, child abuse, and rape. Women were supported, and their cases were pursued by two lawyers, State Prosecutor Vera Ngassa and Court President Beatrice Ntuba, as they struggled to find justice for women who were victims of domestic violence. Ngassa and Ntuba were determined and clever, using strategic approaches to help the women and to get a positive result of stiff sentences for the perpetrators. That outcome was a complete change in direction in that town, where no one had been convicted of domestic violence for years. Though the stories might have portrayed women as victims, the images of women in the film were also positive, exhibiting persistence and strength as they went to court, worked to escape violent relationships, and advanced the legal situation of women under Cameroonian law. A second film, *Difret (Courage*, 2014), about forced marriage in Ethiopia, also highlighted the role of women lawyers in fighting for women's rights. *Difret* is a feature film, directed by Zeresenay Berhane Mehari and executive produced by Angelina Jolie, that told the true story of Meaza Ashenafi, a lawyer who founded the Ethiopian Women Lawyers Association, a women's legal aid clinic. Ashenafi and other lawyers in the association took on the case of Hirut, a fourteen-year-old girl who was on her way home from school when she was kidnapped and raped by a man who wanted to marry her. Hirut seized an opportunity to escape, but when that man tried to prevent her from leaving, she killed him. She was then taken into custody to be tried for the murder. Ashenafi tried the case as self-defense, arguing that the real crime was the kidnapping and rape. The film showed both the path of the legal case through the courts, and it also enacted the debate in the local community, which accepted marriage by abduction as a common practice but discussed other options in Hirut's case. Ashenafi risked her own career, and she and her colleagues took the case to Ethiopia's high court, where she won the case and set a precedent for the illegality of forced child marriage.

As illustrated in the films, African women lawyers have been in the forefront of efforts to apply human rights values to women's lives in Africa. Their work has defended women who were suffering from oppressive practices, both those that were experienced in all cultures, such as rape and domestic violence, and some that are more specific to some African societies, such as marriage by abduction and unwanted polygamous marriage. New legal precedents and new laws will not immediately end all such incidents, but they set a framework for women to continue to struggle for better lives for themselves and their daughters, as well as for the men in their lives.

Protocol on the Rights of Women in Africa

In 2003, the African Union held a summit meeting in Maputo, Mozambique, where the members passed a new protocol on women's rights as a supplement to the African Charter on Human and Peoples' Rights. Often called the Maputo Protocol, it is usually referred to as the Protocol on the Rights of Women in Africa. Fifteen member nations had to ratify it in order for it to come into effect; by 2016, thirty-one nations had signed and ratified the protocol, another fifteen had signed but not ratified it, and six had neither signed nor ratified the document. Despite weaknesses, especially regarding enforcement, the protocol was widely recognized as providing a groundbreaking framework for improving women's lives. Two major provisions set precedent in international law regarding abortion and female genital cutting. Abortion was established as a right of women who have been raped, subject to incest, or when the mother's life or health is in danger. The document also explicitly called on member states to prohibit the practice of female genital cutting. Further sections addressed the issues of domestic violence and supported affirmative action in politics and employment.

The protocol set forth detailed provisions that could substantially improve African women's legal position in many key issues, from ensuring equal access to land to introducing funding to reduce maternal mortality rates. An important element was the proactive role taken by a number of women's organizations to ensure that the protocol would pass; some of those involved were the Africa Gender Institute at the University of Cape Town, African Women's Development and Communication Network (FEMNET), Femmes Africa Solidarité (FAS), and Women and Law in Southern Africa.[1]

There were serious obstacles to implementing the protocol, including a lack of political will in the various governments, the continuing strength of patriarchal traditions, the complicated situation of multiple and parallel systems of law, the weakness of both the women's movements and the key institutions that should be advocating for women's legal rights, and inadequate financial and human resources. Most countries did not include provisions in their budgets, money that was required to implement the new policies, and they lacked personnel with the proper training. Thus, while the protocol was welcomed in part for simply being a potential instrument for women's rights, the much-extolled provisions mostly languished.

At the March 2004 inaugural meeting of the Pan-African Parliament of the African Union, Gertrude Mongella was elected to serve a five-year term as president of the parliament by an overwhelming majority (166 out of 202 sitting legislators). This action was considered an important commitment to women's rights, following on the July 2003 approval of the Protocol on the Rights of Women in Africa.

Shari'a Law in Northern Nigeria

Following the implementation of a new Constitution in Nigeria in 1999, Muslim-dominated states in northern Nigeria introduced strict laws in 2000 following shari'a Islamic precepts. Several elements of shari'a law specifically discriminated against women. One was the provision that allowed husbands to physically chastise their wives as long as they did not cause "grievous bodily harm," which was broadly interpreted to permit husbands to beat their wives nearly to the point of death. Another law enforced seclusion by restricting women from appearing in public without a male escort, a severe limitation that kept women from participating in community business and activities. Women were only allowed to be in the presence of male relatives; all other men were off-limits, including physicians and other professionals, and in some areas Muslim women were required to cover their hair and bodies with modest clothing. The implementation of these laws varied from state to state, but there was some popular male interest in extending the laws that controlled women.

Attempts to apply the laws drew international outrage, including condemnation of a judgment in 2001 against Safiya Hussaini Tungar Tudu. She was raped and became pregnant as a result, but she was found guilty of adultery, with the pregnancy being the main evidence of her supposed transgression. She was defended by prominent feminist and human rights lawyer Hauwa Ibrahim. In 2002, her case was dismissed on technicalities related to the timing of her alleged adultery, which, it was argued, occurred prior to the implementation of shari'a law.[2] A similar case was Amina Lawal's prosecution for adultery in 2002; she was found guilty and sentenced to death by stoning under shari'a law. Her adultery was also discovered because she became pregnant, and her sentence was postponed until her infant daughter was weaned. Feminist Muslim lawyers publicized the case, raising a worldwide outcry. Her case went forward under appeals until 2003, when the Katsina State Shari'a Court of Appeals revoked the sentence, citing irregularities in the prosecution of her case. Another case concerned Bariya Ibrahima Magazu, a young teenager who received one hundred lashes for being pregnant and unmarried. She told the court that she had been raped by three married men, but because the attack was not witnessed, she was unable to produce the required four "upstanding" men to vouch for her story. Although the national Nigerian government has not openly opposed the laws, Nigerian women's organizations have been active in their resistance.

BOKO HARAM

Boko Haram, founded in 2002, is the Nigerian form of Islamist organizations related to Al-Qaeda. While shari'a law was legally in force in northern Nigeria, members of Boko Haram did not accept that government as being Islamic enough, and they fought for the imposition of an extremely strict version of shari'a law and the creation of an Islamic state. They opposed social practices they viewed as Western and even other Muslims who they deemed insufficiently committed to conservative Islam. Their name has been most often translated as "Western education is forbidden." The ideology they espoused was detrimental to many aspects of society, including education, freedom of religion, and democratic government. They became increasingly violent, and they were held responsible for a series of deadly attacks on markets, churches, and schools with thousands of victims.

One of the most widely publicized attacks occurred in April 2014, when they kidnapped 276 Christian teenage girls from their boarding school in Chibok in Borno State. They announced their intention to force the girls to convert to Islam and marry Boko Haram militants or be sold into slavery. As many as 50 of the girls escaped, but the Nigerian government was very slow to react, and for months no serious attempt was made to find and recover the kidnapped students. The families staged a series of protests, trying to force the government to act. The mothers and other women carried signs saying, "#Bring Back Our Girls," a phrase and hashtag that spread around the world. Despite the attention of the international community, nearly two years later most of the girls had not been returned home.

The dramatic story of Chibok was only part of the history of Boko Haram's assault on women in northern Nigeria and in neighboring Cameroon and Chad. They had abducted as many as 500 women and girls beginning in 2009. A 2014 report found that women held by Boko Haram were subjected to violence and torture, including forced marriage and rape.[3] They were held in remote camps where they cooked, cleaned, and carried goods for the militants. Women who were able to return to their home communities were often unwilling to report their treatment, and were not given counseling or other support. Many families lived in anxiety and fear for their female kin. The high level of vulnerability led some women to move away from their homes to areas regarded as safer, disrupting family life and leaving both individuals and families in uncertainty and despair.

While this section has focused on northern Nigeria, other areas of Africa have also been subjected to fundamentalist jihadist movements, most notably northern Mali, which saw a violent insurgency in 2012. Eastern Africa also suffered from the spread of Al-Shabaab in Somalia, which attacked the Westgate

Fig. 9.1 Parents of the girls who were kidnapped by Boko Haram hold a "Bring Back Our Girls" banner during their meeting with Nigeria's President Muhammadu Buhari at the presidential villa in Abuja, Nigeria, January 14, 2016. Photograph by Afolabi Sotunde/Reuters.

shopping mall in Nairobi, Kenya, in 2013, and from Al-Qaeda itself, which was responsible for destructive and deadly bombings in Dar es Salaam, Tanzania, and Nairobi, Kenya, in 1998.

Land Grabbing

Land was increasingly owned or controlled by international interests in the twenty-first century, and women appeared to be losing access to land they required for agriculture as well as for foraging and collecting firewood. Often that land had been held communally rather than controlled by individuals, and women seldom held clear title to the land they farmed. In a process that was hard to track, cross-border and international companies gained access to large parcels of land, with no input from the farmers who lived and worked there. While women in some communities were able to gain or retain access to land they used for their farming, they faced an unprecedented struggle when confronted with large enterprises that grabbed immense swaths of agricultural fields and introduced industrialized cultivation of export crops. Their struggle was exacerbated by African governments that explicitly supported the companies, or silently ignored what was happening. Deforestation was also a major concern as Chinese and other international traders bought up forest lands and clear-cut the exotic hardwood timber.

Governments and international agencies claimed that only large farms could produce enough to feed growing populations, although there was increasing evidence that small farmers were more efficient. Small farmers were also more likely to contribute to community food needs because they grew food for their own families and for regional markets, not for export. Despite recognition that women were the primary local farmers, there was little analysis of the gender dimensions of the changing landscape of rural land ownership. Women farmers had deep experience and knowledge about the advantages of interplanting different crops and of maintaining trees. Trees were desirable for their fruits and other products, and for their environmental benefits of shade and erosion control. Women farmers also increased productivity by paying close attention to microclimates; their farming featured a series of smaller dispersed plots, each with its own special use for a certain crop or set of crops best suited to the soil and weather of a niche area. Companies often arrived, with government acquiescence, and introduced single-crop cultivation over a wide area, hiring local farmers as paid laborers while disrupting the pre-existing agricultural practices. One of the most discouraging aspects of this process was that similar schemes had been introduced over many years and had often failed, but the lessons of those experiences were not acknowledged.

Analysis of the new land grabbing proposals suggested that women's lost access to land arose from the intersection of several factors. Women often did not have legal title to the land, they faced increased problems in obtaining recognition for their work maintaining the health and well-being of their families and themselves, and the local knowledge held by small farmers was not valued. Local studies of land grabbing uncovered larger issues such as the negative impact on social cohesion and the increased experience of conflict.[4] Environmental activists such as Wangari Maathai recognized the wider influence of changing patterns of land and agricultural production, but even though her work gained international renown, land alienation continued and rural African women lost land and livelihoods.

ACCESS TO LAND IN CAMEROON

In a situation that demonstrates the role of local African governments, women farmers in Cameroon lost access to land despite decades of negotiation and protest. Cameroon was the site of the colonial-era protest known as Anlu, discussed in chapter 5. Women continued to form organizations when they saw their access to land in peril. In rural northwest Cameroon, the conflict between farmers, who were mainly Aghem women, and cattle herders, who were mainly Fulani men, had a history that began in the 1930s.[5] Local rulers negotiated the allocation of land to new cattle herders in 1937, and the British colonial administrator then followed through by allotting some land for cattle in 1948. However, the herders did not begin to arrive until 1957, and at that time they did not restrict their cattle to the designated areas. The conflict simmered, with cattle encroaching on farmers' plots of land, until 1968, when women tried to negotiate a solution. They were repeatedly rebuffed by the authorities, so in 1972 they turned to a traditional shaming action seen in many African societies, and they removed their clothing and marched naked in Wum, the division capital. Despite that dramatic gesture, the issues remained unsettled the following year, when the women's organizations gathered more than one thousand women who marched eighty kilometers from Wum to seek an audience with the governor in Bamenda.

The grazers continued to ignore their allocated land and to trespass on farmers' fields. In 1981, there was a major demonstration known as the "Wum affray," which ended in violence when government soldiers fired on a crowd of protesters. Both men and women were present, and nine men were killed and several women severely injured in the fighting. The bloodshed made the women determined to continue without the men because the issue, access to land for farming, was a woman's issue. The women reactivated a traditional Aghem group known as *ndofoumbgui*, and they reached out to women to join local affiliates and be ready to protest again.

In 2003, the local government acquiesced to cattle herders' demands, taking communal land used by six hundred women farmers and allowing two herders to use that land for their cattle. Cattle overran women's farms and destroyed their crops. The women called together the *ndofoumbgui*, and eight thousand women staged sit-ins at seven different sites of local traditional leaders. Those rulers were held hostage for forty-eight days, while the women held their ground despite difficult weather, illness, and other obstacles. The women also boycotted their usual domestic duties and conjugal relations. Neighboring women supported those in the rulers' courtyards by bringing food and drink.

The local leaders were reluctant to make a final decision because they saw both sides as crucial to the local economy. The cattle herders paid taxes and were the main source of beef, while the women's crops were essential to local well-being. Officials claimed that rural chiefs sold land to the herders because they needed the cash, while neglecting to tell the women or the herders that the farming land was being re-allocated without the permission of the farmers. Some sectors of the government viewed the rowdy rural women as acting inappropriately, but those women were using traditional protest methods in their efforts to save their livelihood. The local authorities refused to accept a meeting with the women's organization because it was not a registered group. In a modern bureaucratic response, many commissions were established to study the problem, but since the commission members were predominantly urban men, they failed to come to any solution. The intersection of vibrant rural groups of women with restrictive governmental regulations left the situation in a stalemate. Despite the lack of a resolution, the continuing land conflict and decades of protest by rural women indicated their resolve and innovation in their intense efforts to protect their land and their community.

Sexuality and Lesbianism

Although "sexuality" is obviously not an issue that suddenly arose in the twenty-first century, it has recently emerged into public debate in Africa in new ways. With the spread of HIV/AIDS in the late twentieth century, it became more accepted to discuss sexual behavior in public forums, including addressing ideas about responsible behavior (see chapter 7). And while there were certainly homosexual individuals in the past, the overt persecution of lesbians and gay men only became a prominent issue in the early twenty-first century.

Attacks on gay men and women were noted in Uganda and South Africa in particular. One factor was their greater visibility, which was countered by the increased role of Christian evangelical preachers, many arriving from the United States. In Uganda, those clergy played a public role as they encouraged antigay opinion and called for drastic measures, including death sentences for those known or even suspected of being gay. In the 2014 law that was eventually passed in Uganda, the death sentence was not included, but the "Uganda Anti-Homosexuality Act, 2014" broadened the criminalization of same-sex relationships with the penalty of life in prison. Thirty-eight African nations have made homosexuality illegal, based in part on ideas that such practices are not "African" and that they present a threat to the African family. The Ugandan law gained international attention due to the role of non-Ugandan religious activists and the extreme punishments. A prominent gay activist, David Kato, was murdered in 2011, following an antigay campaign that publicized his sexuality, his politics, and his home address.

South Africa and Namibia were the only African nations that legalized homosexuality, though that legal status was not enough to end assaults on gays, lesbians, and others considered to be outside of sexual norms. South African lesbians were attacked and raped in violent attempts to "convert" them to heterosexuality. Zanele Muholi, an internationally recognized photographer who documented black lesbian lives in South Africa, was the subject of controversy in 2009 when Minister of Culture Lulu Xingwana walked out of an exhibit of her photographs and denounced them as "immoral." Muholi was targeted in 2012, when thieves broke into her apartment and stole her computer hard drives, resulting in the loss of her digital archive of thousands of photographs that she had taken over five years.

A related clamor occurred in 2009 when South African runner Caster Semenya was publicly questioned about her sex following her improved performance at international competitions in her signature 800-meter race. The International Association of Athletics Federations (IAAF) stated that they were obliged to check for drug use following that improvement, and they also asked her to undergo gender testing. That news leaked just prior to the World Championship final, though she was allowed to compete, and she won the gold medal. After that victory, the press raised doubts about her genetic makeup, with some claiming she was not female. The IAAF did not release the results of her test until 2010, causing her to miss several meets; the test results then cleared her to participate in international competitions. The consensus was that the entire incident was badly handled by the IAAF and others, who failed to protect the privacy of her medical records, and who were accused of racism and sexism in their assumptions about her biological sexual identity. In the end, despite international speculation that she was intersex, the results of the test were not released. She was selected as the flag-bearer for South Africa at the 2012 Olympic Games, where she also won the silver medal in the 800-meter race. In 2014, she announced her planned marriage to her partner and fellow athlete, Violet Raseboya.

Health

One health crisis that emerged in 2014, Ebola, had a severe impact on women in West Africa. It is a highly contagious and deadly virus that was quickly spread through interpersonal contact in Sierra Leone, Liberia, and Guinea. Though the epidemic was contained within a few months, many thousands of people died. Statistics suggested that more than half of those who fell ill with the disease were adult women, and that women accounted for as many as 75 percent of the deceased. Women were particularly vulnerable due to their responsibilities for caring for the ill. People often chose to remain in their homes when they were sick, and they relied on female kin to care for them. As the disease spread through contact with bodily fluids, including blood and vomit, those women caregivers were unable to avoid the risk of Ebola. In many communities, women were placed directly in contact with those carrying the disease due to their centrality to the tasks related to organizing funerals, including washing and preparing the bodies for burial and women's position as spiritual leaders and healers. One widely-reported case centered on a female healer who passed away; dozens of her followers subsequently contracted Ebola as a result of preparing the body of their leader for her funeral. Women were present in the labor force as nurses and caregivers, where they were also in constant contact with the disease, though they were more likely to have protective clothing and protocols than those in private homes.

Women also suffered as quarantines and border controls were set in place. Estimates of women involved in cross-border trade found that 70 percent of the traders were women, and their work was halted by the border closures that were designed to limit the spread of the disease. Women in both rural and urban areas also faced constraints to their work in agriculture, and their ability to sell produce in local markets was impacted when markets were shut down.

With international support and focused efforts by local health workers, the outbreak was contained by 2015, but the experience underlined the importance of understanding the gendered aspects of health and disease, as women performed their expected roles as caregivers.

Women and Resistance

Women in the twenty-first century continued to encounter threats to their livelihoods that demanded public responses. In many cases, the women drew on earlier experiences to inform their grievances and their method of protesting. They staged shaming performances where they protested discrimination by presenting their nude bodies to officials, and they also pursued modern political protests such as sit-ins to make their concerns known to a wider audience.

Elections in Côte d'Ivoire in 2010–2011

In the aftermath of contested elections in Côte d'Ivoire in 2010, women were in the forefront of demonstrations that were attacked by the military. After ten years of no elections, the voting in 2010 resulted in a very close outcome that included the ballots of seven northern regions being invalidated. The sitting president, Laurent Gbagbo, was declared the winner, but the opposition candidate, Alassane Ouattara, his followers and members of his liberal party, the Rassemblement des Républicains (RDR, Assembly of the Republicans), and international observers claimed that he had won, leading to months of negotiation. Ouattara's followers eventually began a military attack and gained control of much of the country outside of Abidjan, Côte d'Ivoire's major city (the capital city is Yamoussoukro).

A massive demonstration on March 3, 2011, brought fifteen thousand women into the streets of Abidjan in a peaceful protest. Many of them wore black, though some evoked traditional protests by wearing leaves or marching naked, directing their criticism to Laurent Gbagbo for refusing to step down. Organized by Ouattara supporters including Sirah Drane, the executive secretary of the women's wing of the RDR, the women believed that the military would not fire on unarmed women. When Gbagbo's security forces opened fire on the marchers, seven women were killed and more than one hundred injured. Another women's leader, Elizabeth Jouhair, evoked history when she commented that, "Before independence, it was the women marched to Bassam to free our leaders from jail. Now it's our turn to free our president once more"[6] (see chapter 6). There were further women killed and injured in protests that followed in reaction to the attack on the women demonstrators, including a march on International Women's Day, March 8. The crisis ended when Gbagbo was taken prisoner by the Ouattara forces. Ouattara was sworn in as the new president (and re-elected in 2015) and Gbagbo was taken before the International Criminal Court on charges of human rights violations, where hearings on his case continued into late 2016.

Oil Protests in Nigeria

Women in Nigeria have been involved in a series of resistance activities directed at the international oil producing companies that extracted oil along the Nigerian coastline. Unlike the protest in Cameroon, discussed earlier in this chapter, which got little attention in the press beyond the local area, the Nigerian women's actions were discussed in the international media, reflecting both widespread interest in the oil companies and the boldness of the protests. Nigeria depended on oil exports, which accounted for over 90 percent of its foreign exchange income. Beginning in 1986, women demonstrated to protest their loss of access to land in Ekpan and the burden of increased taxes in Ughelli. They formed the pressure group Niger Delta Women for Justice.

In 2002, women gained international interest when they took over the Escravos export terminal and held hundreds of Chevron workers hostage as they demanded that more local people be employed on the project. They threatened to remove their clothing in a traditional shaming practice unless their demands were met, and Chevron responded with a promise to hire twenty-five workers from the local community. Although women had been involved in many earlier protests, it was believed that the Escravos takeover was the first action entirely by women in the delta. One leader, Anunu Uwawah, commented that "We will no longer take this nonsense, this is the beginning of the trouble they have been looking for."[7] In each of the instances women won some or all of their demands, including the increased employment of local people in the oil industry. Ultimately, protestors wanted the oil revenue to be divided fifty-fifty between the local and national government to rectify the existing division that gave 87 percent to the national coffers while only 13 percent went to the state governments in the oil region. In a major legal victory, in early 2013 a Dutch court ruled that Shell Oil was responsible for the pollution of farmlands in Ikot Ada Udo, Akwa Ibom State, in the Niger Delta region of Nigeria, though farmland degradation in neighboring regions was not found to be the fault of Shell Oil.

Conclusion

At the beginning of the twenty-first century, African women were national leaders, artists and authors, researchers and scholars, market women and entrepreneurs, scientists and athletes, working in old occupations and new careers across the continent. Although the majority of women were still primarily cultivating food for their families, the presence of even a few women on the international stage was making an impact. They brought a specific history and set of knowledge to their work to improve the future prospects for their daughters and their sons, and for people everywhere. Their options and their impact, built on centuries of experience in work and family life, have expanded in many unexpected but not insignificant directions.

Women have built on their long history as political activists based on complementary male and female structures that allowed women to control their own spheres of occupation. Whether through kin relations, especially their experience as mothers, or from their ongoing role as spiritual leaders and healers, women have continued to find ways to influence the direction of their communities in order to improve women's lives. That is not to suggest that women do not suffer from oppression and limitations, as many obstacles make life difficult. But African women do not see those obstacles as defining their political or social conditions.

African women have persisted in the face of the massive problems of patriarchy, war, hunger, corporate globalization, and HIV/AIDS. They can look back and see measurable progress in recent decades and know that the advances are the result of their own efforts and initiative.

Notes

1. Musa, Mohammed, and Manji, eds., *Breathing Life into the African Union Protocol on Women's Rights in Africa*, and Mukasa, *The African Women's Protocol*. The text can be read in full at the website of the African Commission on Human and Peoples' Rights: http://www.achpr.org/instruments/women-protocol/.

2. Tudu and Masto, *I, Safiya*.

3. Human Rights Watch/Africa, '*Those Terrible Weeks in Their Camp.*'

4. Kachingwe, *From Under Their Feet*, and Hobbes, "The Untouchables," http://foreignpolicy.com/2016/04/11/the-untouchables-zimbabwe-green-fuel-multinational-corporations/.

5. Fonchingong, et al., "Traditions of Women's Social Protest Movements."

6. "Soldiers Open Fire on Women Protest in Ivory Coast," *The Telegraph*, March 4, 2011 (accessed September 26, 2014), http://www.telegraph.co.uk/news/worldnews/africaandindianocean/cotedivoire/8360781/Soldiers-open-fire-on-women-protest-in-Ivory-Coast.html.

7. "Nigeria: Women's Stand-off with Chevron-Texaco in Day Four," *Irin News*, July 11, 2002, accessed July 16, 2002. See also Ikelegbe, "Engendering Civil Society."

Bibliography

This bibliography is a small selection from the huge literature now available on African women's history. The sources listed here are those that were quoted or specifically used in this textbook. Many other publications have valuable insights and have informed my understanding of African history and women's place in it; unfortunately, it is impossible to list everything that is worth reading. For further advice on what to read, see the bibliography in my *Historical Dictionary of Women in Sub-Saharan Africa* (second edition, 2016), and the online *Oxford Bibliographies in African Studies*, which includes several entries on women (http://www.oxfordbibliographies.com/obo/page/african-studies).

Abubakr, Sa'ad. "Queen Amina of Zaria." In *Nigerian Women in Historical Perspective*, edited by Bolanle Awe, 11–23. Lagos: Sankore, 1992.

Achebe, Christie. "Igbo Women in the Nigerian-Biafran War 1967–1970: An Interplay of Control." *Journal of Black Studies* 40, 5 (May 2010): 785–811.

Achebe, Nwando. *The Female King of Colonial Nigeria: Ahebi Ugbabe*. Bloomington: Indiana University Press, 2011.

Adams, Ann Marie. "It's a Woman's War: Engendering Conflict in Buchi Emecheta's 'Destination Biafra.'" *Callaloo* 24, 1 (Winter 2001): 287–300.

Adichie, Chimamanda Ngozi. *Half of a Yellow Sun*. New York: Alfred A. Knopf, 2006.

Afigbo, A. E. "Revolution and Reaction in Eastern Nigeria: 1900–1929 (The Background to the Women's Riot of 1929)." *Journal of the Historical Society of Nigeria* 3, 3 (1966): 539–557.

African Women and Peace Support Group. *Liberian Women Peacemakers: Fighting for the Right to Be Seen, Heard, and Counted*. Trenton, NJ: Africa World Press, 2004.

Ahikire, Josephine. "Gender Equity and Local Democracy in Contemporary Uganda: Addressing the Challenge of Women's Political Effectiveness in Local Government." In *No Shortcuts to Power: African Women in Politics and Policy Making*, edited by Anne Marie Goetz and Shireen Hassim, 213–239. London: Zed Books, 2003.

Aidoo, Agnes Akosua. "Asante Queen Mothers in Government and Politics in the Nineteenth Century." In *The Black Woman Cross-Culturally*, edited by Filomina Chioma Steady, 65–77. Cambridge, MA: Schenkman, 1981.

Aidoo, Ama Ata. *Changes: A Love Story*. New York: Feminist Press, 1991.

Akyeampong, Emmanuel. "Sexuality and Prostitution among the Akan of the Gold Coast c. 1650–1950." *Past and Present*, no. 156 (August 1997): 144–173.

Allman, Jean. "The Disappearing of Hannah Kudjoe: Nationalism, Feminism, and the Tyrannies of History." *Journal of Women's History* 21, 3 (2009): 13–35.

———. "Making Mothers: Missionaries, Medical Officers and Women's Work in Colonial Asante, 1924–1945." *History Workshop Journal* 38 (1994): 23–47.

Allman, Jean, and Victoria Tashjian. *"I Will Not Eat Stone": A Women's History of Colonial Asante*. Portsmouth, NH: Heinemann, 2000.

Allman, Jean, Susan Geiger, and Nakanyike Musisi, eds. *Women in African Colonial Histories*. Bloomington: Indiana University Press, 2002.

Alpers, Edward A. "The Story of Swema: Female Vulnerability in Nineteenth-Century East Africa." In Robertson and Klein, *Women and Slavery in Africa*, 185–219.

Andrade, Susan Z. *The Nation Writ Small: African Fictions and Feminisms, 1958–1988*. Durham, NC: Duke University Press, 2011.

Apeadu, Nana. "An Ignored Population: Female-Headed Households among Refugees in Africa." In *Where Did All the Men Go: Female-Headed/Female-Supported Households in Cross-Cultural Perspective*, edited by Joan P. Mencher and Anne Okongwu, 171–191. Boulder, Col.: Westview, 1993.

Aubrey, Lisa. *The Politics of Development Cooperation: NGOs, Gender and Partnership in Kenya*. New York: Routledge, 1997.

Awe, Bolanle. "The Iyalode in the Traditional Yoruba Political System." In *Sexual Stratification: A Cross-Cultural View*, edited by Alice Schlegel, 144–160. New York: Columbia University Press, 1977.

Bâ, Mariama. *So Long a Letter*. Trans. Modupé Bodé-Thomas. London: Heinemann, 1981.

Baard, Francis, and Barbie Schreiner. *My Spirit is Not Banned*. Harare: Zimbabwe Publishing House, 1986.

Bastian, Misty. "Dancing Women and Colonial Men: The Nwaobiala of 1925." In *"Wicked" Women and the Reconfiguration of Gender in Africa*, edited by Dorothy L. Hodgson and Sheryl A. McCurdy, 109–129. Portsmouth, NH: Heinemann, 2001.

Bastian, Misty L. "'Vultures of the Marketplace': Southeastern Nigerian Women and Discourses of the Ogu Umunwaanyi (Women's War) of 1929." In Allman, Geiger, and Musisi, *Women in African Colonial Histories*, 260–281.

Bay, Edna G. *Wives of the Leopard: Gender, Politics, and Culture in the Kingdom of Dahomey*. Charlottesville: University of Virginia Press, 1998.

Baylies, Carolyn, and Caroline Wright. "Female Labour in the Textile and Clothing Industry of Lesotho." *African Affairs* 92 (1993): 577–591.

Beach, D. N. "An Innocent Woman, Unjustly Accused? Charwe, Medium of the Nehanda Mhondoro Spirit, and the 1896–97 Central Shona Rising in Zimbabwe." *History in Africa* 25 (1998): 27–54.

Beach, David. "Cognitive Archaeology and Imaginary History at Great Zimbabwe." *Current Anthropology* 39, 1 (1998): 47–72.

Beck, Linda J. "Democratization and the Hidden Public: The Impact of Patronage Networks on Senegalese Women." *Comparative Politics* 35, 2 (January 2003): 147–69.

Behrend, Heike. *Alice Lakwena and the Holy Spirits: War in Northern Uganda, 1985–97*. London: James Currey, 1999.

Belcher, Wendy Laura. "Sisters Debating the Jesuits: The Role of African Women in Defeating Portuguese Proto-Colonialism in Seventeenth-Century Abyssinia." *Northeast African Studies*, 13, no. 1 (2013): 121–166.

Belcher, Wendy Laura, and Michael Kleiner. *The Life and Struggles of Our Mother Walatta Petros: A Seventeenth-Century African Biography of an Ethiopian Woman, Written by Galawdewos*. Princeton, NJ: Princeton University Press, 2015.

Berger, Iris. "Fertility as Power: Spirit Mediums, Priestesses and the Precolonial State in Interlacustrine East Africa." In *Revealing Prophets: Prophecy in East African History*, edited by David M. Anderson and Douglas H. Johnson, 65–82. London: James Currey, 1995.

———. *Threads of Solidarity: Women in South African Industry, 1900–1980.* Bloomington: Indiana University Press, 1990.

Berns, Marla C. "Art, History, and Gender: Women and Clay in West Africa." *African Archeological Review* 11 (1993): 129–148.

Bessell, M. J. "Nyabingi." *Uganda Journal* 6, 2 (October 1938): 73–86.

Biersteker, Ann. "Language, Poetry, and Power: A Reconsideration of 'Utendi wa Mwana Kupona'." In *Faces of Islam in African Literature*, edited by Kenneth W. Harrow, 59–77. Portsmouth, NH: Heinemann, 1991.

Biobaku, Saburi. "Madame Tinubu." In *Eminent Nigerians of the Nineteenth Century*, edited by Nigerian Broadcasting Corporation, 33–41. Cambridge: Cambridge University Press, 1960.

Bivins, Mary Wren. *Telling Stories, Making Histories: Women, Words, and Islam in Nineteenth-Century Hausaland and the Sokoto Caliphate.* Portsmouth, NH: Heinemann, 2007.

Boahen, A. Adu. *Yaa Asantewaa and the Asante-British War of 1900–1.* Oxford: James Currey 2003.

Boddy, Janice. *Wombs and Alien Spirits: Women, Men, and the Zar Cult in Northern Sudan.* Madison: University of Wisconsin Press, 1989.

———. *Civilizing Women: British Crusades in Colonial Sudan.* Princeton: Princeton University Press, 2007.

Bonate, Liazzat. "Women's Land Rights in Mozambique: Cultural, Legal and Social Contexts." In *Women and Land in Africa: Culture, Religion and Realizing Women's Rights*, edited by L. Muthoni Wanyeki, 96–132. London: Zed Books, 2003.

Boserup, Ester. *Woman's Role in Economic Development.* New York: St. Martin's Press, 1970.

Bradford, Helen. "Women, Gender and Colonialism: Rethinking the History of the British Cape Colony and Its Frontier Zones, c. 1806–70." *Journal of African History* 37 (1996): 351–370.

Brantley, Cynthia. "Mekatalili and the Role of Women in Giriama Resistance." In *Banditry, Rebellion and Social Protest in Africa*, edited by Donald Crummey, 333–350. Portsmouth, NH: Heinemann, 1986.

Brittain, Victoria. "Calvary of the Women of Eastern Democratic Republic of Congo (DRC)." *Review of African Political Economy* 29, no. 93/94 (September/December 2002): 595–601.

Broadhead, Susan Herlin. "Slave Wives, Free Sisters: Bakongo Women and Slavery c. 1700–1850." In Robertson and Klein, *Women and Slavery in Africa*, 161–181.

Brooks, George E. *Eurafricans in Western Africa: Commerce, Social Status, Gender, and Religious Observance from the Sixteenth to the Eighteenth Century.* Athens: Ohio University Press, 2003.

———. "The *Signares* of Saint-Louis and Gorée: Women Entrepreneurs in Eighteenth-Century Senegal." In Hafkin and Bay, *Women in Africa*, 19–44.

Burnet, Jennie E. "Situating Sexual Violence in Rwanda (1990–2001): Sexual Agency, Sexual Consent, and the Political Economy of War." *African Studies Review* 55, 2 (September 2012): 97–118.

Byfield, Judith A. *The Bluest Hands: A Social and Economic History of Women Dyers in Abeokuta (Nigeria), 1890–1940*. Portsmouth, NH: Heinemann, 2002.

———. "Taxation, Women, and the Colonial State: Egba Women's Tax Revolt." *Meridians: Feminism, Race, Transnationalism* 3, 2 (2003): 250–277.

Callaway, Barbara, and Lucy Creevey. *The Heritage of Islam: Women, Religion, and Politics in West Africa*. Boulder, Col.: Lynne Rienner, 1994.

Candido, Mariana P. "Concubinage and Slavery in Benguela, c. 1750–1850." In *Slavery in Africa and the Caribbean: A History of Enslavement and Identity Since the 18th Century*, edited by Olatunji Ojo and Nadine Hunt, 65–84. New York: I.B. Tauris, 2012.

———. *An African Slaving Port and the Atlantic World: Benguela and its Hinterland*. Cambridge: Cambridge University Press, 2013.

Chuku, Gloria. "Tinubu, Efinroye." In *Dictionary of African Biography*, vol. 6, edited by Emmanuel K. Akeyampong and Henry Louis Gates Jr., 28–30. Oxford: Oxford University Press, 2011.

Clarke, Marieke Faber, and Pathisa Nyathi. *Lozikeyi Dlodlo: Queen of the Ndebele*. Bulawayo: Amagugu Publishers, 2010.

Conrad, David C. "Mooning Armies and Mothering Heroes: Female Power in the Mande Epic Tradition." In *In Search of Sunjata: The Mande Oral Epic as History, Literature, and Performance*, edited by Ralph A. Austen, 189–229. Bloomington: Indiana University Press, 1999.

Constantinides, Pamela. "The History of *Zar* in the Sudan: Theories of Origin, Recorded Observation and Oral Tradition." In *Women's Medicine: The Zar-Bori Cult in Africa and Beyond*, edited by I.M. Lewis, Ahmed Al-Safi, and Sayyid Hurreiz, 83–99. Edinburgh: Edinburgh University Press, 1991.

Coulter, Chris. *Bush Wives and Girl Soldiers: Women's Lives through War and Peace in Sierra Leone*. Ithaca: Cornell University Press, 2009.

Crais, Clifton, and Pamela Scully. *Sara Baartman and the Hottentot Venus: A Ghost Story and a Biography*. Princeton, NJ: Princeton University Press, 2009.

Cummings-John, Constance Agatha. *Memoirs of a Krio Leader*. Edited by LaRay Denzer. Ibadan: Sam Bookman for Humanities Research Centre, 1995.

Dangarembga, Tsitsi. *Nervous Conditions*. Seattle: The Seal Press, 1988.

Dapper, Olfert. *Olfert Dapper's Description of Benin (1668)*. Edited by Adam Jones. Madison: African Studies Program, University of Wisconsin, 1998.

Day, Lynda. *Gender and Power in Sierra Leone: Women Chiefs of the Last Two Centuries*. London: Palgrave, 2012.

Daymond, M. J., Dorothy Driver, and Sheila Meintjes, eds. *Women Writing Africa: The Southern Region*. New York: Feminist Press, 2003.

de Castilho, Augusto. "O Pilão Africano." *O Occidente*, 4, no. 101 (October 11, 1881), 228.

de Sousa, Noémia. "Magaiça," "Black Blood," and "If You Want to Know Me." In *When Bullets Begin to Flower*, edited and translated by Margaret Dickinson. Nairobi: East African Publishing House, 1972.

Denzer, LaRay. "Towards a Study of the History of West African Women's Participation in Nationalist Politics: The Early Phase, 1935–1950." *Africana Research Bulletin* 6, 4 (July 1976): 65–85.

———. "Women in Freetown Politics, 1914–61: A Preliminary Study." *Africa* 57, 4 (1987): 439–455.

Diabate, Henriette. *La marche des femmes sur Grand-Bassam*. Dakar: Nouvelles Editions Africaines, 1975.

Dirie, Waris. *Desert Flower: The Extraordinary Journey of a Desert Nomad*. New York: William Morrow, 1998.

Edgar, Robert R., and Hilary Sapire. *African Apocalypse: The Story of Nontetha Nkwenkwe, A Twentieth-Century South African Prophet*. Athens: Ohio University Center for International Studies, 2000.

Ehret, Christopher. *The Civilizations of Africa: A History to 1800*. Charlottesville: University Press of Virginia, 2002.

———. "Matrilineal Descent and the Gendering of Authority: What Does African History Have to Tell Us?" Unpublished paper, 2012.

Ekejiuba, Felicia Ifeoma. "Omu Okwei of Osomari." In *Nigerian Women in Historical Perspective*, edited by Bolanle Awe, 89–104. Lagos: Sankore, 1992.

Elabor-Idemudia, Patience. "Nigeria: Agricultural Exports and Compensatory Schemes - Rural Women's Production Resources and Quality of Life." In *Mortgaging Women's Lives: Feminist Critiques of Structural Adjustment*, edited by Pamela Sparr, 134–164. London: Zed, 1994.

Elkins, Caroline. *Imperial Reckoning: The Untold Story of Britain's Gulag in Kenya*. New York: Henry Holt, 2005.

Emecheta, Buchi. *Destination Biafra*. New York: Allison & Busby, 1982.

———. *The Joys of Motherhood*. New York: George Braziller, 1979.

Evans-Pritchard, E. E. "An Alternate Term for Brideprice." *Man* 31, 42 (1931): 36–39.

Fadlalla, Amal Hassan. *Embodying Honor: Fertility, Foreignness, and Regeneration in Eastern Sudan*. Madison: University of Wisconsin Press, 2007.

Fair, Laura. "The Music of Siti binti Saad: Creating Community, Crafting Identity, and Negotiation Power through Taarab." In Laura Fair, *Pastimes and Politics: Culture, Community, and Identity in Post-Abolition Urban Zanzibar, 1890–1945*, Chapter 6. Athens: Ohio University Press, 2001.

Fallon, Kathleen M. *Democracy and the Rise of Women's Movements in Sub-Saharan Africa*. Baltimore: Johns Hopkins University, 2008.

Falola, Toyin, and Adam Paddock. *The Women's War of 1929: A History of Anti-Colonial Resistance in Eastern Nigeria*. Durham, NC: Carolina Academic Press, 2011.

Foley, Ellen E. "Overlaps and Disconnects in Reproductive Health Care: Global Policies, National Programs, and the Micropolitics of Fertility and Contraceptive Use in Northern Senegal." *Medical Anthropology* 26, 4 (2007): 323–354.

Fonchingong, Charles C., Emmanuel Yenshu Vubo, and Maurice Ufon Beseng. "Traditions of Women's Social Protest Movements and Collective Mobilisation: Lessons from Aghem and Kedjom Women." In *Civil Society and the Search for Development Alternatives in Cameroon*, edited by Emmanuel Yenshu Vubo, 125–141. Dakar: Codesria, 2008.

Freedman, Jim. *Nyabingi: The Social History of an African Divinity*. Tervuren, Belgium: Musée Royal de l'Afrique Centrale, 1984.

Gaitskell, Deborah. "Hot Meetings and Hard Kraals: African Biblewomen in Transvaal Methodism, 1924–60." *Journal of Religion in Africa* 30, 3 (2000): 277–309.

——. "'Wailing for Purity': Prayer Unions, African Mothers and Adolescent Daughters, 1912–1940." In *Industrialisation and Social Change in South Africa: African Class Formation, Culture, and Consciousness, 1870–1930*, edited by Shula Marks and Richard Rathbone, 338–357. London: Longman, 1982.

Gbowee, Leymah, and Carol Mithers. *Mighty Be Our Powers: How Sisterhood, Prayer, and Sex Changed a Nation at War*. New York: Beast Books, 2011.

Geiger, Susan. *TANU Women: Gender and Culture in the Making of Tanganyikan Nationalism, 1955–1965*. Portsmouth, NH: Heinemann, 1997.

Gerrard, Siri. "Clans, Gender and Kilns: Examples from a Fisheries Development Project in Sota Village, Tanzania." In *Gender and Change in Developing Countries*, edited by Kristi Anne Stølen and Mariken Vaa, 223–246. Oslo: Norwegian University Press, 1991.

Gerson, Elliott. "A New Leader for Africa." *HuffPost Impact*, January 19, 2013. http://www.huffingtonpost.com/elliot-gerson/a-new-leader-for-africa_b_2511815.html.

Gladwin, Christina H., ed. *Structural Adjustment and African Women Farmers*. Gainesville: University of Florida Press, 1991.

Gordon, David M. *Nachituti's Gift: Economy, Society, and Environment in Central Africa*. Madison: University of Wisconsin Press, 2006.

Green, M. M. *Ibo Village Affairs*. New York: Frederick A. Praeger, 1964. Originally published in 1947.

Grier, Beverly. "Pawns, Porters, and Petty Traders: Women in the Transition to Cash Crop Agriculture in Colonial Ghana." *Signs* 17, 2 (1992): 304–328.

Hackett, Rosalind I. J. "Women in African Religions." In *Religion and Women*, edited by Arvind Sharma, 61–92. Albany: State University of New York Press, 1994.

Hafkin, Nancy J., and Edna G. Bay, eds. *Women in Africa: Studies in Social and Economic Change*. Stanford: Stanford University Press, 1976.

Hanlon, Joseph, Armando Barrientos, and David Hulme. *Just Give Money to the Poor: The Development Revolution from the Global South*. West Hartford, Conn.: Kumarian Press, 2010.

Hanretta, Sean. "Women, Marginality and the Zulu State: Women's Institutions and Power in the Early Nineteenth Century." *Journal of African History* 39, 3 (1998): 309–415.

Hanson, Holly. *Landed Obligation: The Practice of Power in Buganda*. Portsmouth, NH: Heinemann, 2003.

Harms, Robert. "Sustaining the System: Trading Towns along the Middle Zaire." In Robertson and Klein, *Women and Slavery in Africa*, 95–110.

Hassim, Shireen. *Women's Organizations and Democracy in South Africa: Contesting Authority*. Madison: University of Wisconsin Press, 2006.

Havik, Philip J. *Silences and Soundbytes: The Gendered Dynamics of Trade and Brokerage in the Pre-Colonial Guinea Bissau Region*. Munich: LIT, 2004.

Healy-Clancy, Meghan. "Women and the Problem of Family in Early African Nationalist History and Historiography." *South African Historical Journal* 64, 3 (2012): 450–471.

Herbert, Eugenia W. *Iron, Gender, and Power: Rituals of Transformation in African Societies*. Bloomington: Indiana University Press, 1993.

Hewlett, Bonnie L. *Listen, Here Is a Story: Ethnographic Life Narratives from Aka and Ngandu Women of the Congo Basin*. New York: Oxford University Press, 2013.

Hinfelaar, Hugo F. *Bemba-Speaking Women of Zambia in a Century of Religious Change (1892–1992)*. Leiden: Brill, 1994.

Hobbs, Michael, "The Untouchables: Why It's Getting Harder to Stop Multinational Corporations," *Foreign Policy* (April 11, 2016) (accessed April 12, 2016) http://foreignpolicy.com/2016/04/11/the-untouchables-zimbabwe-green-fuel-multinational-corporations/.

Hodgson, Dorothy L. "Pastoralism, Patriarchy and History: Changing Gender Relations among Maasai in Tanganyika, 1890–1940." *Journal of African History* 40, 1 (1999): 41–65.

Hoehler-Fatton, Cynthia. *Women of Fire and Spirit: History, Faith, and Gender in Roho Religion in Western Kenya*. New York: Oxford University Press, 1996.

Hoffer, Carol P. "Madam Yoko: Ruler of the Kpa Mende Confederacy." In *Woman, Culture, and Society*, edited by Michelle Zimbalist Rosaldo and Louise Lamphere, 173–187. Stanford: Stanford University Press, 1974.

Hopkins, Elizabeth. "The Nyabingi Cult of Southwestern Uganda." In *Rebellion in Black Africa*, edited by Robert I. Rotberg, 60–132. New York: Oxford University Press, 1971.

Huffman, Thomas N. "Where You Are the Girls Gather to Play: The Great Enclosure at Great Zimbabwe." In *Frontiers: Southern African Archaeology Today*, edited by M. Hall, G. Avery, D. M. Avery, M. L. Wilson, and A. J. B Humphreys, 252–265. Cambridge Monographs in African Archaeology 10; BAR International Series 207. Cambridge: British Archaeological Reports, 1984.

Hughes, Heather. "'A Lighthouse for African Womanhood': Inanda Seminary, 1869–1945." In *Women and Gender in Southern Africa to 1945*, edited by Cherryl Walker, 197–220. London: James Currey, 1990.

Human Rights Watch/Africa. *'Those Terrible Weeks in Their Camp': Boko Haram Violence against Women and Girls in Northeast Nigeria*. New York: Human Rights Watch, 2014.

Hunt, Nancy Rose. *A Colonial Lexicon: Of Birth Ritual, Medicalization, and Mobility in the Congo*. Durham, NC: Duke University Press, 1999.

Ifeka-Moller, Caroline. "Female Militancy and Colonial Revolt: The Women's War of 1929, Eastern Nigeria." In *Perceiving Women*, edited by Shirley Ardener, 127–157. New York: John Wiley, 1975.

Ikelegbe, Augustine. "Engendering Civil Society: Oil, Women Groups and Resource Conflicts in the Niger Delta Region of Nigeria." *Journal of Modern African Studies* 43, 2 (June 2005): 241–270.

Ingiriis, Mohamed H., and Markus V. Hoehne. "The Impact of Civil War and State Collapse on the Roles of Somali Women: A Blessing in Disguise." *Journal of Eastern African Studies* 7, 2 (2013): 314–333.

Ipsen, Pernille. *Daughters of the Trade: Atlantic Slavers and Interracial Marriage on the Gold Coast*. Philadelphia: University of Pennsylvania Press, 2015.

Jackson, Lynette. "Sex and the Politics of Space in Colonial Zimbabwe: The Story of Chibheura (Open Your Legs) Exams." In *Contested Terrains and Constructed*

Categories: Contemporary Africa in Focus, edited by George Clement Bond and Nigel C. Gibson, 299–320. Boulder, Col.: Westview, 2002.

James, Stanlie M., and Claire C. Robertson, eds. *Genital Cutting and Transnational Sisterhood: Disputing US Polemics*. Urbana: University of Illinois Press, 2002.

Jell-Bahlsen, Sabine. *The Water Goddess in Igbo Cosmology: Ogbuide of Oguta Lake*. Trenton, NJ: Africa World Press, 2008.

Johnson Sirleaf, Ellen. *This Child Will Be Great: Memoir of a Remarkable Life by Africa's First Woman President*. New York: HarperCollins, 2009.

Johnson-Odim, Cheryl and Nina Emma Mba. *For Women and the Nation: Funmilayo Ransome-Kuti of Nigeria*. Urbana: University of Illinois Press, 1997.

Joseph, Helen. *If This Be Treason*. London: A. Deutsch, 1963.

———. *Side by Side: A Personal Account of One South African Woman's Struggle against Apartheid*. New York: William Morrow, 1986.

Kachingwe, Nancy. *From Under Their Feet: A Think Piece on the Gender Dimensions of Land Grabs in Africa*. Johannesburg: ActionAid International, 2012.

Kaler, Amy. *Running After Pills: Politics, Gender, and Contraception in Colonial Zimbabwe*. Portsmouth, NH: Heinemann, 2003.

Kanduza, Ackson. "'You Are Tearing My Skirt': Labotsibeni Gwamile LaMdluli." In *Agency and Action in Colonial Africa: Essays for John E. Flint*, edited by Chris Youé and Tim Stapleton, 83–99. New York: Palgrave, 2001.

Kanogo, Tabitha. "Kikuyu Women and the Politics of Protest: Mau Mau." In *Images of Women in Peace and War: Cross-Cultural and Historical Perspectives*, edited by Sharon Macdonald, Pat Holden, and Shirley Ardener, 78–99. Madison: University of Wisconsin Press, 1988.

Keim, Curtis A. "Women in Slavery among the Mangbetu c. 1800–1910." In Robertson and Klein, *Women and Slavery in Africa*, 145–159.

Kéita, Aoua. *Femme d'Afrique: La vie d'Aoua Kéita racontée par elle-même*. Paris: Présence Africaine, 1975.

Kent, Susan, ed. *Gender in African Prehistory*. Walnut Creek, Calif.: AltaMira, 1998.

Kenyatta, Jomo. *Facing Mount Kenya: The Tribal Life of the Gikuyu*. New York: Vintage Books, 1965. Originally published in 1938.

Kevane, Michael. *Women and Development in Africa: How Gender Works*. Boulder, Col.: Lynne Rienner, 2004.

Khadiagala, Lynn S. "Justice and Power in the Adjudication of Women's Property Rights in Uganda." *Africa Today* 49, 2 (Summer 2002): 101–121.

Kodesh, Neil. *Beyond the Royal Gaze: Clanship and Public Healing in Buganda*. Charlottesville: University of Virginia Press, 2010.

Krige, Eileen J., and J. D. Krige. *The Realm of the Rain-Queen: A Study of the Pattern of Lovedu Society*. London: Oxford University Press, 1943.

Landau, Paul S. *Popular Politics in the History of South Africa, 1400–1948*. Cambridge: Cambridge University Press, 2010.

Larsson, Birgitta, *Conversion to Greater Freedom?: Women, Church and Social Change in North-Western Tanzania under Colonial Rule*. PhD diss., Uppsala University, 1991.

Lawrance, Benjamin N. "La Révolte des Femmes: Economic Upheaval and the Gender of Political Authority in Lomé, Togo, 1931–33." *African Studies Review* 46, 1 (2003): 43–67.

Leach, Fiona. "African Girls, Nineteenth-Century Mission Education and the Patriarchal Imperative." *Gender and Education* 20, 4 (2008): 335–347.

Lihamba, Amandina, Fulata L. Moyo, M. M. Mulokozi, Naomi L. Shitemi, and Saïda Yahya-Othman, eds. *Women Writing Africa: The Eastern Region*. New York: Feminist Press, 2007.

Longman, Timothy. "Rwanda: Achieving Equality or Serving an Authoritarian State?" In *Women in African Parliaments*, edited by Gretchen Bauer and Hannah E. Britton, 133–150. Boulder, Col.: Lynne Rienner, 2006.

Lye, William F. "The Difaqane: The Mfecane in the Southern Sotho Area, 1822–1824." *Journal of African History* 8, 1 (1967): 107–131.

Maathai, Wangari. *Unbowed: A Memoir*. New York: Alfred A. Knopf, 2006.

Mack, Beverly B., and Jean Boyd. *One Woman's Jihad: Nana Asma'u, Scholar and Scribe*. Bloomington: Indiana University Press, 2000.

Madsen, Diana Højlund. "Mainstreaming from Beijing to Ghana—the Role of the Women's Movement in Ghana." *Gender and Development* 20, 3 (November 2012): 573–584.

Mann, Kristin. *Marrying Well: Marriage, Status and Social Change among the Educated Elite in Colonial Lagos*. Cambridge: Cambridge University Press, 1985.

Martin, Phyllis M. *Catholic Women of Congo-Brazzaville: Mothers and Sisters in Troubled Times*. Bloomington: Indiana University Press, 2009.

Matera, Marc, Misty L. Bastian, and Susan Kingsley Kent. *The Women's War of 1929: Gender and Violence in Colonial Nigeria*. London: Palgrave, 2012.

Mba, Nina E. "Heroines of the Women's War." In *Nigerian Women in Historical Perspective*, edited by Bolanle Awe, 73–88. Lagos: Sankore, 1992.

———. *Nigerian Women Mobilized: Women's Political Activity in Southern Nigeria, 1900–1965*. Berkeley: University of California Institute for International Studies, 1982.

McCord, Margaret. *The Calling of Katie Makanya*. New York: John Wiley and Sons, 1995.

Mikell, Gwendolyn, ed. *African Feminism: The Politics of Survival in Sub-Saharan Africa*. Philadelphia: University of Pennsylvania Press, 1997.

Miller, Joseph C. "Introduction: Women as Slaves and Owners of Slaves." In *Africa, the Indian Ocean World, and the Medieval North Atlantic, Women and Slavery, Vol. 1*, edited by Gwyn Campbell, Suzanne Miers, and Joseph C. Miller, 1–40. Athens: Ohio University Press, 2007.

Molokomme, Athaliah. "Emang Basadi (Botswana)." *Signs* 16, 4 (Summer 1991): 848–851.

Monson, Jamie. "Relocating Maji Maji: The Politics of Alliance and Authority in the Southern Highlands of Tanzania, 1870–1918." *Journal of African History* 39, 1 (1998): 95–120.

Moran, Mary. "Our Mothers Have Spoken: Synthesizing Old and New Forms of Women's Political Authority in Liberia." *Journal of International Women's Studies* 13, 4 (September 2012): 51–66.

Mukasa, Rosemary Semafumu. *The African Women's Protocol: Harnessing a Potential Force for Positive Change*. South Africa: Fanele, 2008.

Musa, Roselynn, Faiza Jama Mohammed, and Firoze Manji, eds. *Breathing Life into the African Union Protocol on Women's Rights in Africa*. Oxford: Solidarity for African Women's Rights, 2006.

Musisi, Nakanyike B. "Women, 'Elite Polygyny,' and Buganda State Formation." *Signs* 16, 4 (Summer 1991): 757–786.

Mwana Kupona binti Msham. "From *A Mother's Advice and Prayer: An Epic Poem*," edited by Naomi L. Shitemi, and selections translated by Ann Biersteker and Naomi L. Shitemi. In *Women Writing Africa: The Eastern Region*, edited by Lihamba, Moyo, Mulokozi, Shitemi, and Yahya-Othman, 72–80. New York: Feminist Press, 2007.

Mwaura, Philomena Njeri. "Gender and Power in African Christianity: African Instituted Churches and Pentecostal Churches." In *African Christianity: An African Story*, edited by Ogbu U. Kalu, 410–445. Pretoria: University of Pretoria, 2005.

"The Nairobi Manifesto." *Issue: A Journal of Opinion* 17, 2 (Summer 1989): 44–46.

Nasimiyu, Ruth. "Changing Women's Rights over Property in Western Kenya." In *African Families and the Crisis of Social Change*, edited by Thomas S. Weisner, Candice Bradley, and Philip L. Kilbride, 283–298. Westport, Conn.: Greenwood, 1997.

Nast, Heidi. *Concubines and Power: Five Hundred Years in a Northern Nigerian Palace*. Minneapolis: University of Minnesota Press, 2005.

Nauright, John. "'I Am With You as Never Before': Women in Urban Protest Movements, Alexandra Township, South Africa." In *Courtyards, Markets, City Streets: Urban Women in Africa*, edited by Kathleen Sheldon, 259–83. Boulder, Col.: Westview, 1996.

Nhongo-Simbanegavi, Josephine. *For Better or Worse? Women and ZANLA in Zimbabwe's Liberation Struggle*. Harare: Weaver Press, 2000.

Nnaemeka, Obioma. "Nego-Feminism: Theorizing, Practicing, and Pruning Africa's Way." *Signs* 29, 2 (Winter 2004): 357–385.

Nwapa, Flora. *Efuru*. London: Heinemann Educational Books, 1966.

———. *Wives at War and Other Stories*. Enugu, Nigeria: Tana Press, 1980.

Nzomo, Maria. "Kenya: The Women's Movement and Democratic Change." In *The African State at a Critical Juncture: Between Disintegration and Reconfiguration*, edited by Leonardo A. Villalón and Phillip A. Huxtable, 167–184. Boulder, Col.: Lynne Rienner, 1998.

Obbo, Christine. "HIV Transmission: Men Are the Solution." In *Theorizing Black Feminisms: The Visionary Pragmatism of Black Women*, edited by Stanlie M. James and Abena P. A. Busia, 160–181. London: Routledge, 1993.

Ogot, Grace. *The Promised Land*. Nairobi: East African Publishing House, 1966.

Okonjo, Kamene. "The Dual-Sex Political System in Operation: Igbo Women and Community Politics in Midwestern Nigeria." In Hafkin and Bay, *Women in Africa*, 45–58.

Opiyo, Collins. "Fertility Levels, Trends, and Differentials." In *Kenya Demographic and Health Survey 2003*, 51–62. Nairobi: Bureau of Statistics, 2004.

Opoku-Agyemang, Naana Jane. "Recovering Lost Voices: The Short Stories of Mabel Dove-Danquah." In *Writing African Women: Gender, Popular Culture and Literature in West Africa*, edited by Stephanie Newell, 67–80. London: Zed, 1997.

Otieno, Wambui Waiyaki, and Cora Ann Presley. *Mau Mau's Daughter: A Life History*. Boulder, Col.: Lynne Rienner, 1998.

Ouzman, Sven. "Between Margin and Centre: The Archaeology of Southern African Bored Stones." In *Our Gendered Past: Archaeological Studies of Gender in Southern Africa*, edited by Lyn Wadley, 71–106. Witwatersrand University Press, 1997.

Owen, Hilary. *Mother Africa, Father Marx: Women's Writing of Mozambique, 1948–2002*. Lewisburg, Penn.: Bucknell University Press, 2007.

Pantoja, Selma. "Nzinga a Mbandi." In *Dictionary of African Biography*, vol. 4, edited by Emmanuel K. Akyeampong and Henry Louis Gates, Jr., 527–528. New York: Oxford University Press, 2012.

Parkington, John. "Men, Women, and Eland: Hunting and Gender among the San of Southern Africa." In *In Pursuit of Gender: Worldwide Archaeological Approaches*, edited by Sarah Milledge Nelson and Myriam Rosen-Ayalon, 93–117. Walnut Creek, Calif.: Altamira Press, 2002.

Parpart, Jane L. "Class and Gender on the Copperbelt: Women in Northern Rhodesian Copper Mining Communities, 1926–1964." In *Women and Class in Africa*, edited by Claire Robertson and Iris Berger, 141–160. New York: Holmes & Meier/Africana Publishing, 1986.

Peires, J. B. *The Dead Will Arise: Nongqawuse and the Great Xhosa Cattle-Killing Movement of 1856–1857*. Bloomington: Indiana University Press, 1989.

Pemberton, Carrie. *Circle Thinking: African Women Theologians in Dialogue with the West*. Leiden: Brill, 2003.

Penvenne, Jeanne Marie. *Women, Migration and the Cashew Economy in Southern Mozambique, 1945–1975*. London: James Currey, 2015.

Poewe, Karla O. *Matrilineal Ideology: Male-Female Dynamics in Luapula, Zambia* (New York: Academic Press, 1981).

Presley, Cora Ann. *Kikuyu Women, the Mau Mau Rebellion, and Social Change in Kenya*. Boulder, Col.: Westview Press, 1992.

Puechguirbal, Nadine. "Women and War in the Democratic Republic of the Congo." *Signs* 28, 4 (Summer 2003): 1271–1281.

Pybus, Cassandra. "'One Militant Saint': The Much Traveled Life of Mary Perth." *Journal of Colonialism and Colonial History* 9, 3 (Winter 2008).

Ranchod-Nilsson, Sita. "'This, Too, is a Way of Fighting': Rural Women's Participation in Zimbabwe's Liberation War." In *Women and Revolution in Africa, Asia, and the New World*, edited by Mary Ann Tétreault, 62–88. Columbia: University of South Carolina Press, 1994.

Roberts, Mary Nooter. "The King is a Woman: Shaping Power in Luba Royal Arts." *African Arts* 46, 3 (Autumn 2013): 68–81.

Roberts, Richard. "Women's Work and Women's Property: Household Social Relations in the Maraka Textile Industry of the Nineteenth Century." *Comparative Studies in Society and History* 26, 2 (1984): 229–250.

Rosander, Eva Evers. "Mam Diarra Bousso: La bonne mere de Porokhane, Senegal." *Africa* (Rome) 58, 3–4 (2003): 296–317.

Ruete, Emily. *Memoirs of an Arabian Princess from Zanzibar*. 2nd ed. Edited by Patricia Romero. Princeton, NJ: Markus Wiener, 1989. Originally published in 1888.

Sacks, Karen. *Sisters and Wives: The Past and Future of Sexual Equality*. Urbana: University of Illinois Press, 1979.

Saidi, Christine. *Women's Authority and Society in Early East-Central Africa*. Rochester, NY: University of Rochester Press, 2010.

Santoru, Marina E. "The Colonial Idea of Women and Direct Intervention: The Mau Mau Case." *African Affairs*, 95 (1996): 253–267.

Sargent, R. A. "Found in the Fog of the Male Myth: Analysing Female Political Roles in Pre-Colonial Africa." *Canadian Oral History Association Journal* 11 (1991): 39–44.

Scarnecchia, Timothy. "Poor Women and Nationalist Politics: Alliances and Fissures in the Formation of a Nationalist Political Movement in Salisbury, Rhodesia, 1950–6." *Journal of African History* 37 (1996): 283–310.

Schoenbrun, David Lee. *A Green Place, A Good Place: Agrarian Change, Gender, and Social Identity in the Great Lakes Region to the 15th Century*. Portsmouth, NH: Heinemann, 1998.

Semley, Lorelle D. *Mother is Gold, Father is Glass: Gender and Colonialism in a Yoruba Town*. Bloomington: Indiana University Press, 2011.

Sereke-Brhan, Heran. "'Like Adding Water to Milk': Marriage and Politics in Nineteenth-Century Ethiopia." *International Journal of African Historical Studies* 38, 1 (2005): 49–77.

Shanklin, Eugenia. "*Anlu* Remembered: The Kom Women's Rebellion of 1958–1961." *Dialectical Anthropology* 15, 2/3 (1990): 159–181.

Sheldon, Kathleen. *Historical Dictionary of Women in Sub-Saharan Africa*. 2nd ed. Lanham, Md.: Rowman and Littlefield, 2016.

———. "Markets and Gardens: Placing Women in the History of Urban Mozambique." *Canadian Journal of African Studies* 37, 2 and 3 (2003): 358–395.

———. *Pounders of Grain: A History of Women, Work, and Politics in Mozambique*. Portsmouth, NH: Heinemann, 2002.

———. "Sewing Clothes and Sorting Cashew Nuts: Factories, Families, and Women in Beira, Mozambique." *Women's Studies International Forum* 14, 1/2 (1991): 27–35.

Shumway, Rebecca. "Castle Slaves of the Eighteenth-Century Gold Coast (Ghana)." *Slavery and Abolition* 35, 1 (January 2014): 84–98.

Sithole-Fundire, Sylvia, Agnes Zhou, Anita Larsson, and Ann Schlyter, eds. *Gender Research on Urbanization, Planning, Housing and Everyday Life: GRUPHEL, Phase One*. Harare: Zimbabwe Women's Resource Centre and Network, 1995.

Smedley, Audrey. *Women Creating Patriliny: Gender and Environment in West Africa*. Walnut Creek, Calif.: AltaMira Press, 2004.

Smith, Andrew B., and Lita Webley. "Women and Men of the Khoekhoen of Southern Africa." In *Rethinking Pastoralism in Africa: Gender, Culture and the Myth of the Patriarchal Pastoralist*, edited by Dorothy L. Hodgson, 72–96. Oxford: James Currey, 2000.

Spear, Thomas, ed., *Oxford Bibliographies in African Studies*, http://www .oxfordbibliographies.com/obo/page/african-studies.

Spink, Kathryn. *Black Sash: The Beginning of a Bridge in South Africa*. London: Methuen, 1991.

Steady, Filomina Chioma. *Women and Collective Action in Africa: Development, Democratization, and Empowerment, with Special Focus on Sierra Leone*. New York: Palgrave Macmillan, 2005.

Stephens, Rhiannon. *A History of African Motherhood: The Case of Uganda, 700–1900.* Cambridge: Cambridge University Press, 2013.

Summers, Carol. "Intimate Colonialism: The Imperial Production of Reproduction in Uganda, 1907–1925." *Signs* 16, 4 (Summer 1991): 787–807.

Sunseri, Thaddeus. "Famine and Wild Pigs: Gender Struggles and the Outbreak of the Majimaji War in Uzaramo (Tanzania)." *Journal of African History* 38, 2 (1997): 235–259.

Sutherland-Addy, Esi, and Aminata Diaw, eds. *Women Writing Africa: West Africa and the Sahel.* New York: Feminist Press, 2005.

Terretta, Meredith. "A Miscarriage of Revolution: Cameroonian Women and Nationalism." *Vienna Journal of African Studies* 12 (2007): 61–90.

Thomas, Lynn M. *Politics of the Womb: Women, Reproduction, and the State in Kenya.* Berkeley: University of California Press, 2003.

Thomas-Emeagwali, Gloria, ed. *Women Pay the Price: Structural Adjustment in Africa and the Caribbean.* Trenton, NJ: Africa World Press, 1995.

Thornton, John K. "Elite Women in the Kingdom of Kongo: Historical Perspectives on Women's Political Power." *Journal of African History* 47, 3 (2006): 437–460.

———. *The Kongolese Saint Anthony: Dona Beatriz Kimpa Vita and the Antonian Movement, 1684–1706.* Cambridge: Cambridge University Press, 1998.

Thuku, Harry, with Kenneth King. *Harry Thuku: An Autobiography.* Nairobi: Oxford University Press, 1970.

Toliver-Diallo, Wilmetta J. "'The Woman Who Was More Than a Man': Making Aline Sitoe Diatta into a National Heroine." *Canadian Journal of African Studies* 39, 2 (2005): 338–60.

Tripp, Aili Mari. "The New Political Activism in Africa: Women and Democracy." *Journal of Democracy* 12, 3 (July 2001): 141–55.

———. *Women and Power in Postconflict Africa.* Cambridge: Cambridge University Press, 2015.

Tuck, Michael W. "Women's Experiences of Enslavement and Slavery in Late Nineteenth- and Early Twentieth-Century Uganda." In *Slavery in the Great Lakes Region of East Africa*, edited by Henri Médard and Shane Doyle, 174–188. Athens: Ohio University Press, 2007.

Tudu, Safiya Hussaini Tungar, and Raffaele Masto. *I, Safiya.* Sydney: Pan Macmillan, 2004.

Turrittin, Jane. "Aoua Kéita and the Nascent Women's Movement in the French Soudan." *African Studies Review* 36, 1 (April 1993): 59–89.

———. "Colonial Midwives and Modernizing Childbirth in French West Africa." In Allman, Geiger, and Musisi, *Women in African Colonial Histories*, 71–91.

Uchendu, Egodi. *Women and Conflict in the Nigerian Civil War.* Trenton, NJ: Africa World Press, 2007.

Utas, Mats. "Agency of Victims: Young Women in the Liberian Civil War." In *Makers and Breakers: Children and Youth in Postcolonial Africa*, edited by Alcinda Honwana and Filip De Boeck, 53–80. Trenton, NJ: Africa World Press, 2005.

Van Allen, Judith. "'Sitting on a Man': Colonialism and the Lost Political Institutions of Igbo Women." *Canadian Journal of African Studies* 6, 2 (1972): 165–181.

————. "'Aba Riots' or Igbo 'Women's War?' Ideology, Stratification, and the Invisibility of Women." In Hafkin and Bay, *Women in Africa*, 59–85.

Vaz, Kim Marie. *The Woman with the Artistic Brush: A Life History of Yoruba Batik Artist Nike Davies*. Armonk, NY: M.E. Sharpe, 1995.

Vera, Yvonne. *Nehanda*. Harare: Baobab Books, 1993.

Wadley, Lyn, ed. *Our Gendered Past: Archaeological Studies of Gender in Southern Africa*. Johannesburg: Witwatersrand University Press, 1997.

Wanyoike, Mary W. *Wangu wa Makeri*. "Makers of Kenya's History" No. 12. Nairobi: East African Educational Publishers, 2002.

Weir, Jennifer. "'I Shall Need to Use Her to Rule': The Power of Royal Zulu Women in Pre-Colonial Zululand." *South African Historical Journal* 43 (November 2000): 3–23.

Wells, Julia C. "Eva's Men: Gender and Power in the Establishment of the Cape of Good Hope, 1652–74." *Journal of African History* 39, 3 (1998): 417–437.

————. "Passes and Bypasses: Freedom of Movement for African Women under the Urban Areas Act of South Africa." In *African Women and the Law: Historical Perspectives*, edited by Margaret Jean Hay and Marcia Wright, 126–150. Papers on Africa VII. Boston: Boston University African Studies Center, 1982.

————. "Why Women Rebel: A Comparative Study of South African Women's Resistance in Bloemfontein (1913) and Johannesburg (1958)." *Journal of Southern African Studies* 10, 1 (October 1983): 55–70.

Werner, Alice, William Hichens, and Mwana Kupona. *The Advice of Mwana Kupona upon the Wifely Duty from the Swahili Texts*. Medstead: Azania Press, 1934.

White, E. Frances. 1987. *Sierra Leone's Settler Women Traders: Women on the Afro-European Frontier*. Ann Arbor: University of Michigan Press.

White, Luise. *The Comforts of Home: Prostitution in Colonial Nairobi*. Chicago: University of Chicago Press, 1990.

Wipper, Audrey. "Kikuyu Women and the Harry Thuku Disturbances: Some Uniformities of Female Militancy." *Africa* 59, 3 (1989): 300–337.

Wooten, Stephen. *The Art of Livelihood: Creating Expressive Agri-Culture in Rural Mali*. Durham, NC: Carolina Academic Press, 2009.

Worley, Barbara A. "Property and Gender Relations among Twareg Nomads." *Nomadic Peoples* 23 (1987): 31–36.

Wright, Marcia. *Strategies of Slaves and Women: Life-Stories from East/Central Africa*. New York: Lilian Barber Press, 1993.

Zeleza, Paul. "Gender Biases in African Historiography." In *Engendering African Social Sciences*, edited by Ayesha M. Imam, Amina Mama, and Fatou Sow, 81–115. Dakar: Codesria, 1997.

Zimba, Benigna. *Mulheres Invisíveis: O Género e as Políticas Comerciais no Sul de Moçambique, 1720–1830*. Maputo: Promedia, 2003.

Zimbabwe Women Writers. *Women of Resilience: The Voices of Women Ex-Combatants*. Harare: Zimbabwe Women Writers, 2000.

Zongwe, Dunia Prince. "The New Sexual Violence Legislation in the Congo: Dressing Indelible Scars on Human Dignity." *African Studies Review* 55, 2 (September 2012): 37–57.

Index

Gbagbo, Laurent, 298-299
Gbanye, 157
Gbowee, Leymah, 268-269, 287. *See also* peace-building
gender mainstreaming, 250
Germany, 68-70, 195, 241; as colonial power, 92-93, 136-139, 176, 183; in Rwanda, 269
Ghana, 115-116, 128-129, 165, 170, 233, 246-247; cocoa cultivation, 97-100, *101*; early history, 12, 22; 18th century, 49-50; gender mainstreaming, 250; in literature, 238; politics, 253-255, 279; nationalism, 173; queen mothers, 154-156; sports, 243
Ghanaian Women's League, 173
Gikuyu, 54, 108, 134-35, 284-285; anticolonial activities, 140-142, 185-188; female genital cutting, 125-127; land allocation, 96-97; religious beliefs, 20-21. *See also* Mau Mau
Giriama, 137-138
Girl Guides, 279
Goa, 195
goddesses, 21-22, 52; water deities, 62-63. *See also* religion
Gola, 267
gold, 12, 105, 146, 155, 195-196; jewelry, 46, 51. *See also* mining
Gold Coast. *See* Ghana
Goma, 273
Gomes, Antonieta Rosa, 276. *See also* presidential candidates
Gordimer, Nadine, 236, 237. *See also* literature
Gordon, General Charles George, 122-123
government, 276-280; judges, 247, 261, 272, 282, 288;. *See also* cabinet ministers; democratization; elected to legislature; mayors; presidents; prime ministers; quotas
Grand Bassam, 171-172, *171*, 298. *See also* anticolonial protests
Great Britain, as colonial power, 96-97, 104, 117, 170, 237, 295; Cameroon, 176-178; Ghana, 155-156; Kenya, 125-127, 140-142, 185-193; Nigeria, 157-158, 159-163, 174, 243; Sierra Leone, 76, 156; South Africa, 144-145; Sudan, 122-125; Swaziland, 143-144; Tanzania, 139-140, 183-185; Uganda, 128, 136-137; Zimbabwe, 143, 145-149, 199-203. *See also* slavery, abolition
Great Lakes region (Central Africa), 15-16, 31-32, 56-57. *See also* Buganda; Uganda
Great Zimbabwe, 11
Green Belt Movement, 259. *See also* environment; Maathai, Wangari

Griffith, Seeiso, Paramount Chief, 179
griottes, 239
Griqua, 81
Guinea, 29, 240, 297-298
Guinea-Bissau, 37-39; 103, 194, 276
Guta la Jehova, 284. *See also* African independent churches

Habiyakane, Hassan, 271-272
Habyarimana, Juvénal, 270
Hadendowa, 228-229. *See also* pastoral societies
Haggard, Rider, 89
Hagos, Ileni, 133
Haili Selassie, 133
Half of a Yellow Sun (Adichie), 238, 263. *See also* Biafran War; literature
Hambanati Women's Action Group, 256
Harare, 200-201
Harvard University, 267
Hatch, John, 183
Hausa, 13, 65-67, 71, 102, 263; slavery in Hausa city-states, 30-31. *See also* Islam
Haya, 110-111
health, 108, 111, 112-113, 219, 225-231; colonial concerns, 122-130; Ebola, 297-298; women's hospitals and maternity centers, 275. *See also* influenza pandemic; HIV/AIDS; fertility
Hehe, 138
Hima, Mariama, 241
historical linguistic evidence, 1-3, 7, 14, 19, 24-25
HIV/AIDS, 226, 232, 234-235, 261, 279-280, 287, 296; orphans, 279
Hlomelikusasa Othandweni Women's Group, 235
Hodgson, Francis, 156
Holy Spirit Movement, 275-276. *See also* Lord's Resistance Army
homosexuality, laws concerning, 277
Hosken, Fran, 233
Hottentot Venus. *See* Baartman, Sara
housing, 200-201, 225
human rights, 288-290
hunting and gathering, 3-6, 269
Hutu, 269-273

Ibrahim, Hauwa, 291. *See also* lawyers
Igbo, 52, 104, 107, 157; Aba Women's War, 159-163; Biafran war, 263; religious beliefs, 62-63
Iivula-Ithana, Pendukeni, 288. *See also* lawyers
Inanda Seminary, 74-76. *See also* education
incarceration, 38, 137, 171-172, 187, 278, 296, 299; Cameroon, 176-177; Kenya, 115, 138, 141, 187,

KATHLEEN SHELDON is an independent scholar who has a research affiliation with the Center for the Study of Women at the University of California, Los Angeles. She is the author of *Pounders of Grain: A History of Women, Work, and Politics in Mozambique* and the *Historical Dictionary of Women in Sub-Saharan Africa*.

Lightning Source UK Ltd.
Milton Keynes UK
UKHW021524241120
373816UK00022B/751